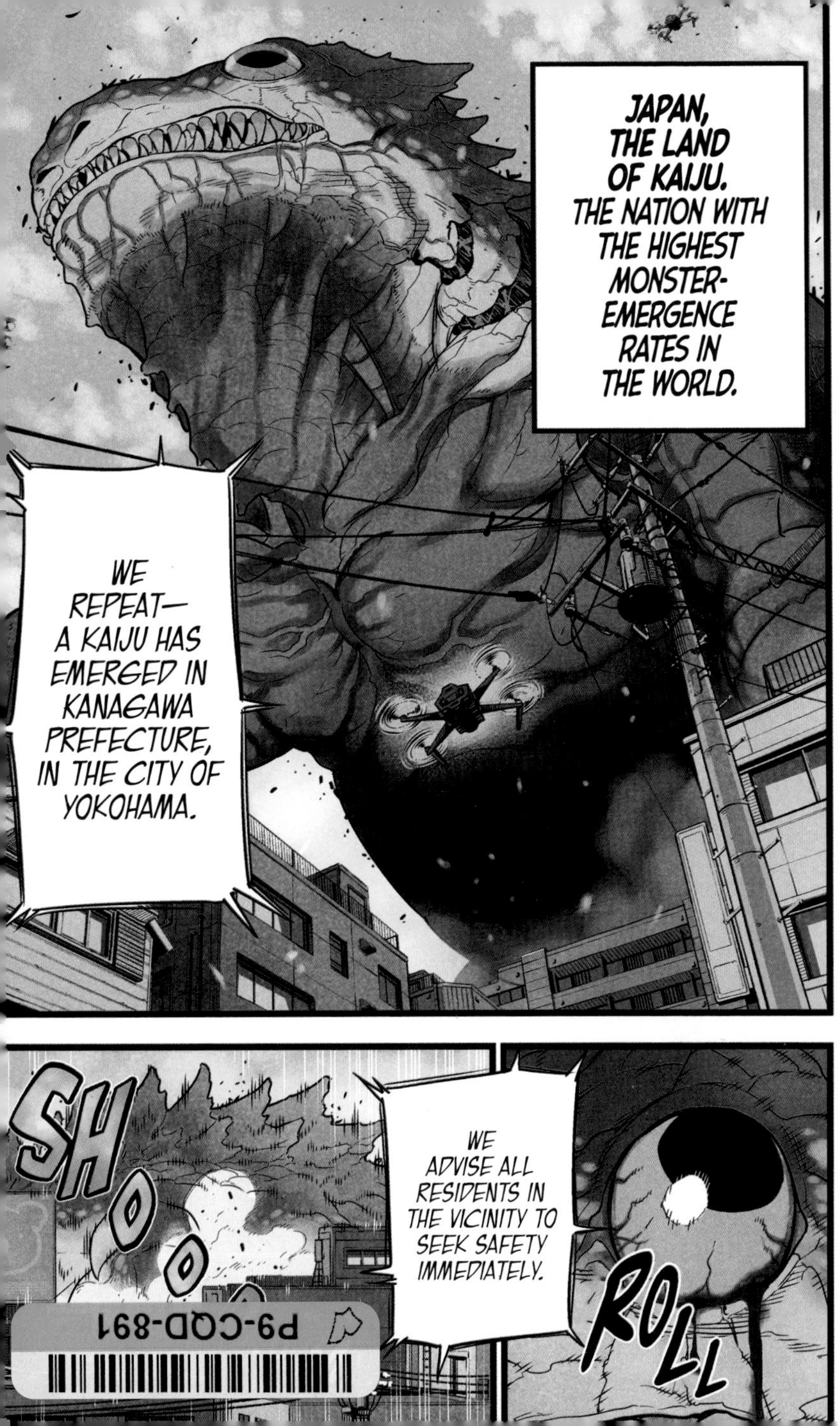
JAPAN, THE LAND OF KAIJU. THE NATION WITH THE HIGHEST MONSTER-EMERGENCE RATES IN THE WORLD.
WE REPEAT—A KAIJU HAS EMERGED IN KANAGAWA PREFECTURE, IN THE CITY OF YOKOHAMA.
ROLL
WE ADVISE ALL RESIDENTS IN THE VICINITY TO SEEK SAFETY IMMEDIATELY.
SHOOO

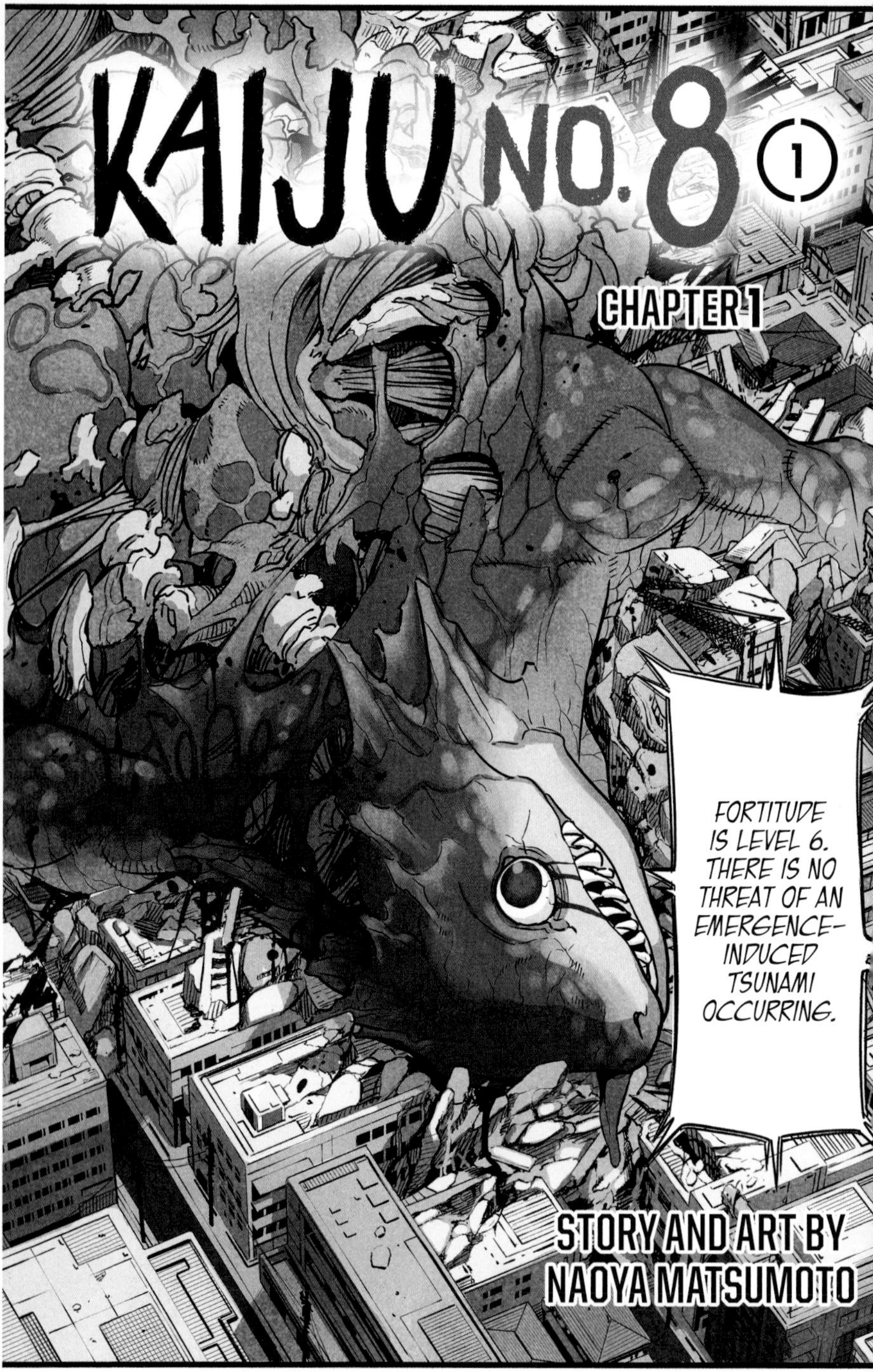
KAIJU NO. 8 1
CHAPTER 1
FORTITUDE IS LEVEL 6. THERE IS NO THREAT OF AN EMERGENCE-INDUCED TSUNAMI OCCURRING.
STORY AND ART BY NAOYA MATSUMOTO

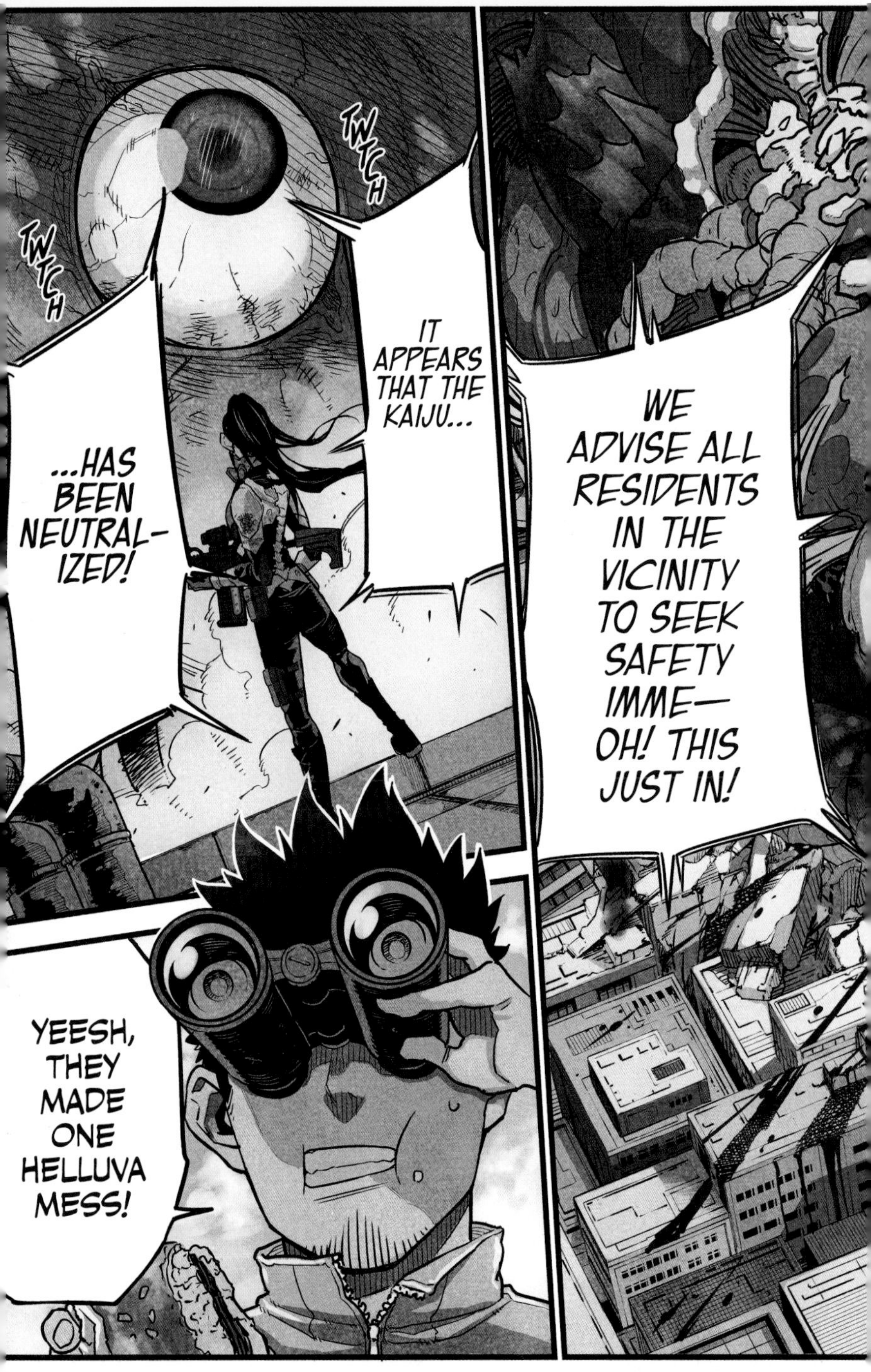
WE ADVISE ALL RESIDENTS IN THE VICINITY TO SEEK SAFETY IMME— OH! THIS JUST IN!
TWITCH
TWITCH
IT APPEARS THAT THE KAIJU...
...HAS BEEN NEUTRAL-IZED!
YEESH, THEY MADE ONE HELLUVA MESS!

CONTENTS

# KAIJU NO. 8

1



CONTENTS

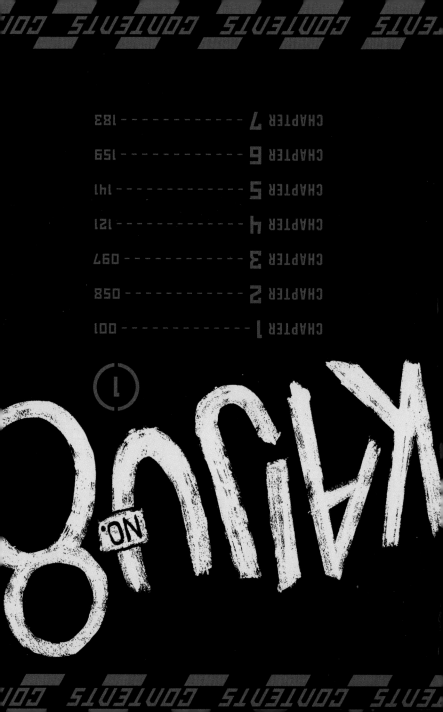

ALERT! EMERGENCY ALERT! EMER

# YOU'RE READING THE WRONG WAY!

4
3
2
1
2
1
8
7
6
5
4
3
9
5
142

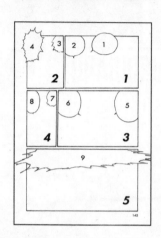

For your own protection, the last page of the book has been sealed off to prevent the ending from being spoiled. To safely consume the contents of *Kaiju No. 8* in their intended order, please flip the book over and start again.

*Kaiju No. 8* reads from right to left, starting in the upper-right corner, to preserve the original Japanese orientation of the work. That means that the action, sound effects, and word-balloons are completely reversed from English order.

ENTER! DO NOT ENTER! DO NOT

# EXPERIENCE THE INTRODUCTORY ARC OF THE INTERNATIONAL SMASH HIT SERIES *RWBY* IN A WHOLE NEW WAY—MANGA!

# RWBY THE OFFICIAL MANGA

Story and Art by BUNTA KINAMI
Based on the Rooster Teeth series created by MONTY OUM

**M**onsters known as the Grimm are wreaking havoc on the world of Remnant. Ruby Rose seeks to become a Huntress, someone who eliminates the Grimm and protects the land. She enrolls at Beacon Academy and quickly makes friends she'll stand side-by-side with in the battles to come!

VIZ

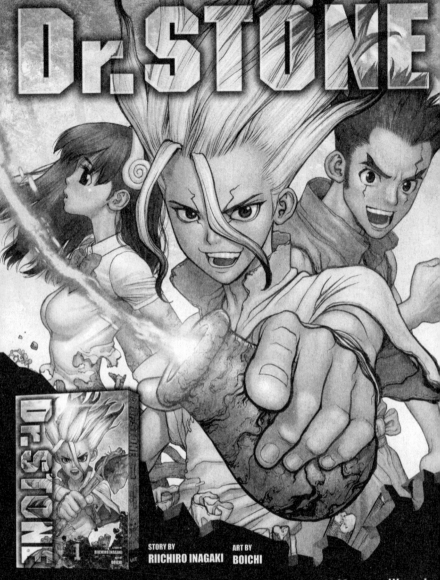

# Dr. STONE

STORY BY
**RIICHIRO INAGAKI**

ART BY
**BOICHI**

One fateful day, all of humanity turned to stone. Many millennia later, Taiju frees himself from petrification and finds himself surrounded by statues. The situation looks grim—until he runs into his science-loving friend Senku! Together they plan to restart civilization with the power of science!

DR. STONE © 2017 by Riichiro Inagaki, Boichi/SHUEISHA Inc.

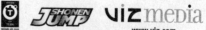

# CAN MUSCLES CRUSH MAGIC?!

# MASHLE

## MAGIC AND MUSCLES

STORY AND ART BY
## HAJIME KOMOTO

In the magic realm, magic is everything—everyone can use it, and one's skill determines their social status. Deep in the forest, oblivious to the ways of the world, lives Mash. Thanks to his daily training, he's become a fitness god. When Mash is discovered, he has no choice but to enroll in magic school where he must beat the competition without revealing his secret—he can't use magic!

# KAIJU NO. 8 ①

## SHONEN JUMP EDITION

## STORY AND ART BY
## NAOYA MATSUMOTO

TRANSLATION
**DAVID EVELYN**

TOUCH-UP ART & LETTERING
**BRANDON BOVIA**

DESIGN
**JIMMY PRESLER**

EDITOR
**KARLA CLARK**

KAIJYU 8 GO © 2020 by Naoya Matsumoto
All rights reserved.
First published in Japan in 2020 by SHUEISHA Inc., Tokyo.
English translation rights arranged by SHUEISHA Inc.

Printed in Italy

Published by VIZ Media, LLC
P.O. Box 77010
San Francisco, CA 94107

10 9 8 7 6 5 4 3 2
First printing, December 2021
Second printing, August 2021

**PARENTAL ADVISORY**
KAIJU NO. 8 is rated T for Teen and is recommended
for ages 13 and up. This volume contains crude humor
and depictions of violence.

viz.com

# NAOYA MATSUMOTO

My first work in five years. My plan is to really hit you with everything I've got! I hope you enjoyed *Kaiju No. 8* volume 1!

---

Naoya Matsumoto published his first serialized series, *Neko Wappa!*, in *Weekly Shonen Jump* in 2009. His next series, *Pochi Kuro*, began serialization in *Shonen Jump+* in 2014. *Kaiju No. 8* is his follow-up series.

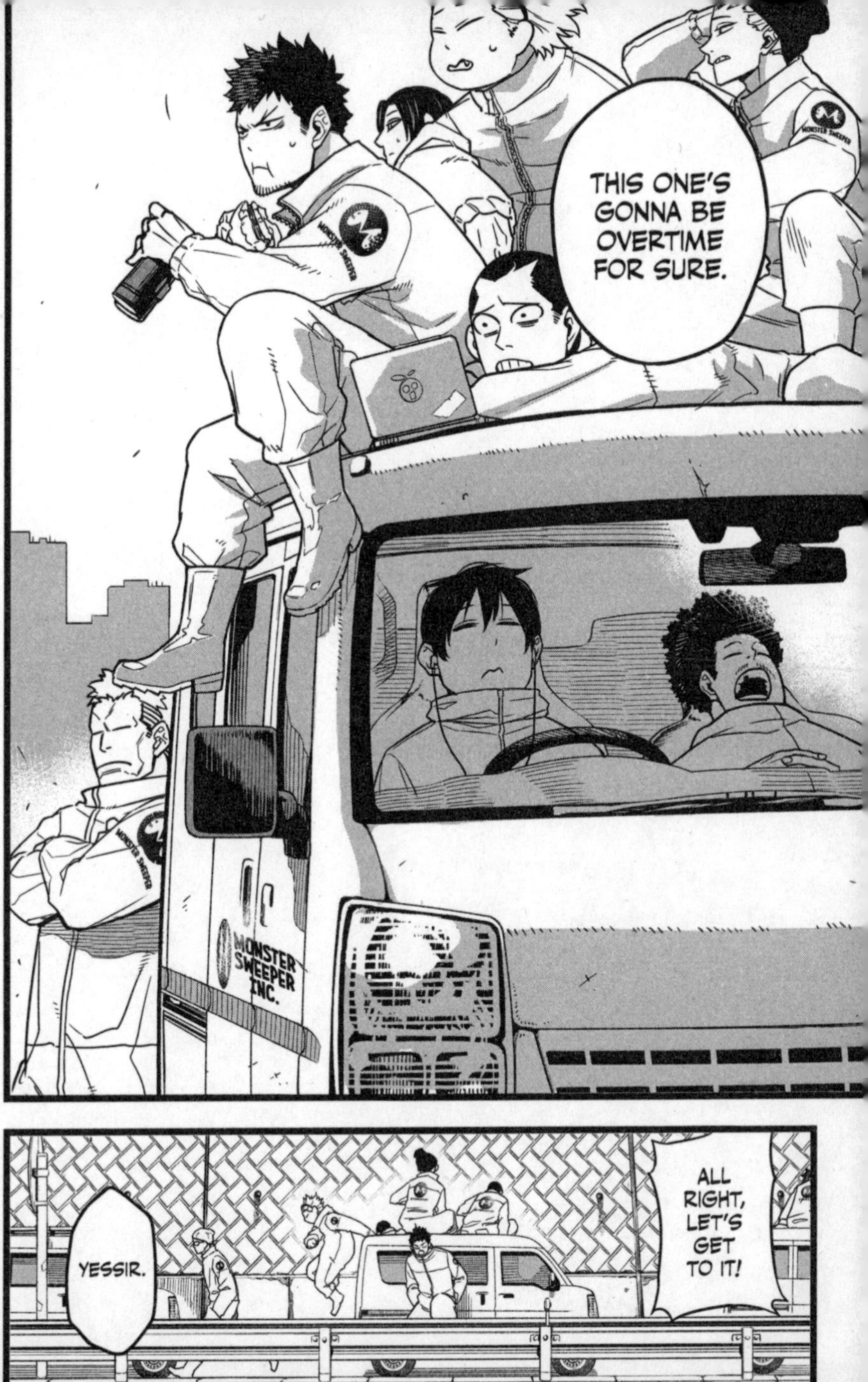
THIS ONE'S GONNA BE OVERTIME FOR SURE.
MONSTER SWEEPER INC.
ALL RIGHT, LET'S GET TO IT!
YESSIR.

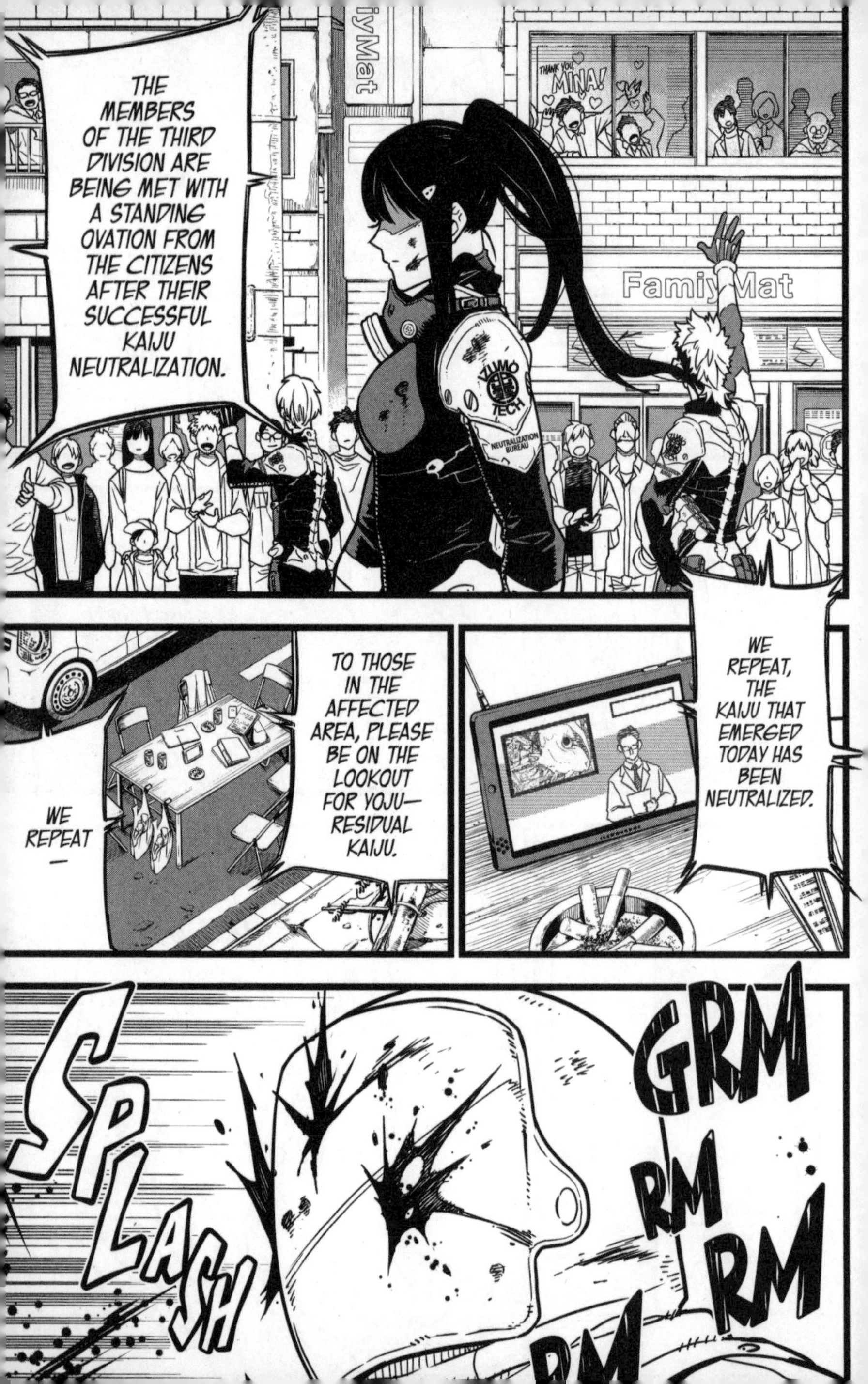
THE MEMBERS OF THE THIRD DIVISION ARE BEING MET WITH A STANDING OVATION FROM THE CITIZENS AFTER THEIR SUCCESSFUL KAIJU NEUTRALIZATION.
iyMat
THANK YOU, MINA!
Famiy Mat
IZUMO TECH
NEUTRALIZATION BUREAU
WE REPEAT, THE KAIJU THAT EMERGED TODAY HAS BEEN NEUTRALIZED.
TO THOSE IN THE AFFECTED AREA, PLEASE BE ON THE LOOKOUT FOR YOJU—RESIDUAL KAIJU.
WE REPEAT —
GRM
RM
RM
SPLASH

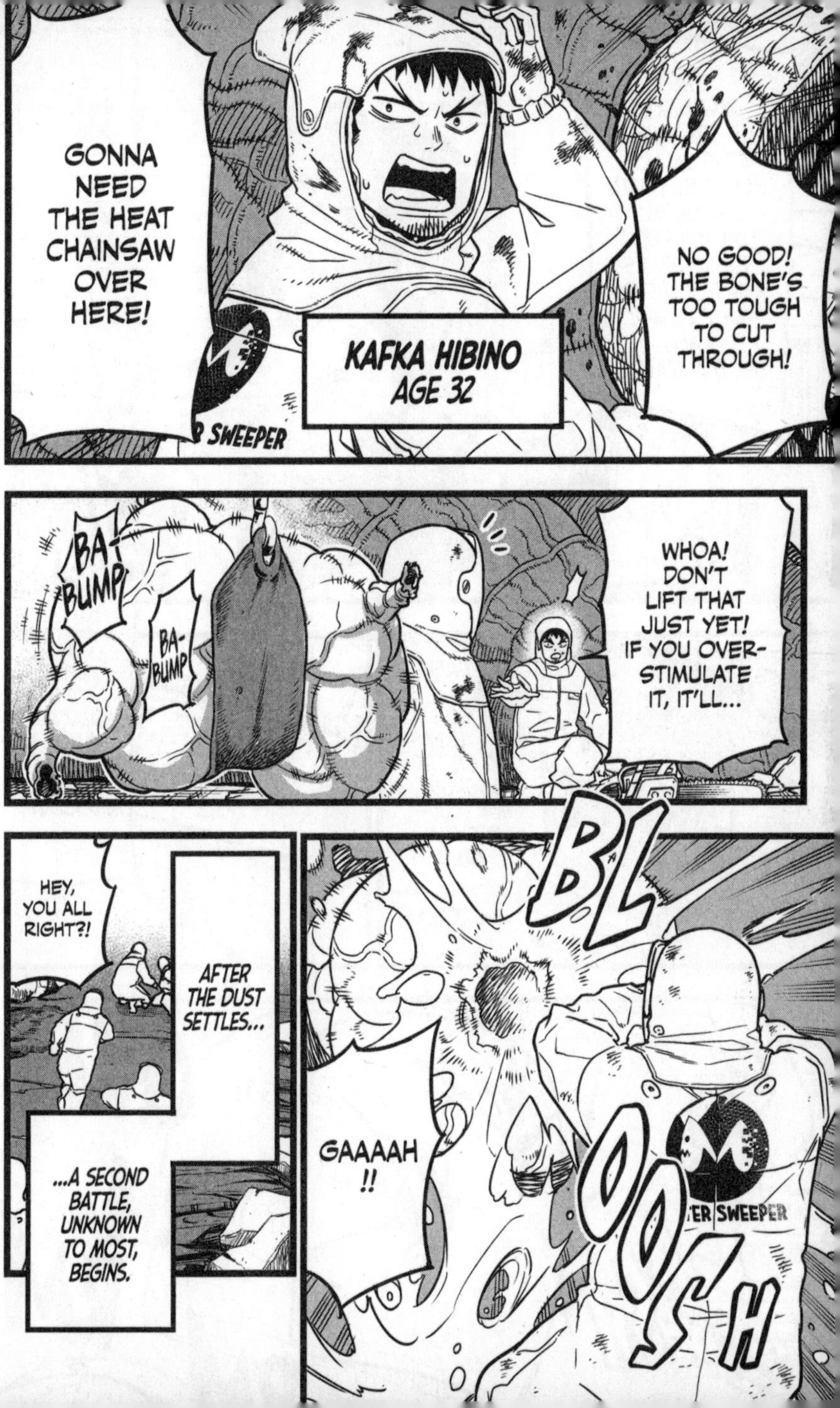
NO GOOD! THE BONE'S TOO TOUGH TO CUT THROUGH!
KAFKA HIBINO AGE 32
GONNA NEED THE HEAT CHAINSAW OVER HERE!
WHOA! DON'T LIFT THAT JUST YET! IF YOU OVER-STIMULATE IT, IT'LL...
BA-BUMP
BA-BUMP
BLOOOSH
GAAAAH !!
HEY, YOU ALL RIGHT?!
AFTER THE DUST SETTLES...
...A SECOND BATTLE, UNKNOWN TO MOST, BEGINS.

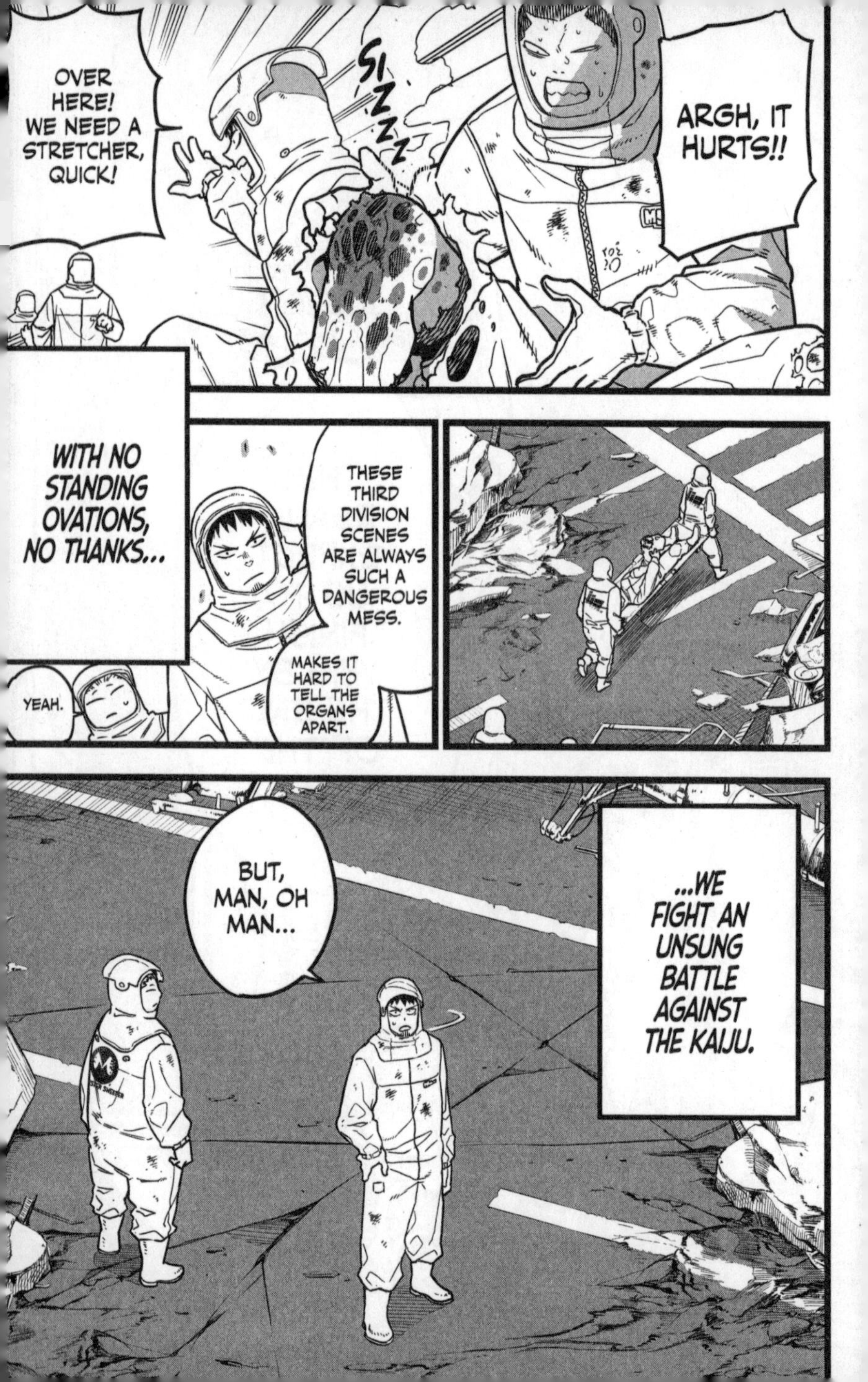
ARGH, IT HURTS!!
SIZZZ
OVER HERE! WE NEED A STRETCHER, QUICK!
THESE THIRD DIVISION SCENES ARE ALWAYS SUCH A DANGEROUS MESS.
MAKES IT HARD TO TELL THE ORGANS APART.
YEAH.
WITH NO STANDING OVATIONS, NO THANKS...
...WE FIGHT AN UNSUNG BATTLE AGAINST THE KAIJU.
BUT, MAN, OH MAN...

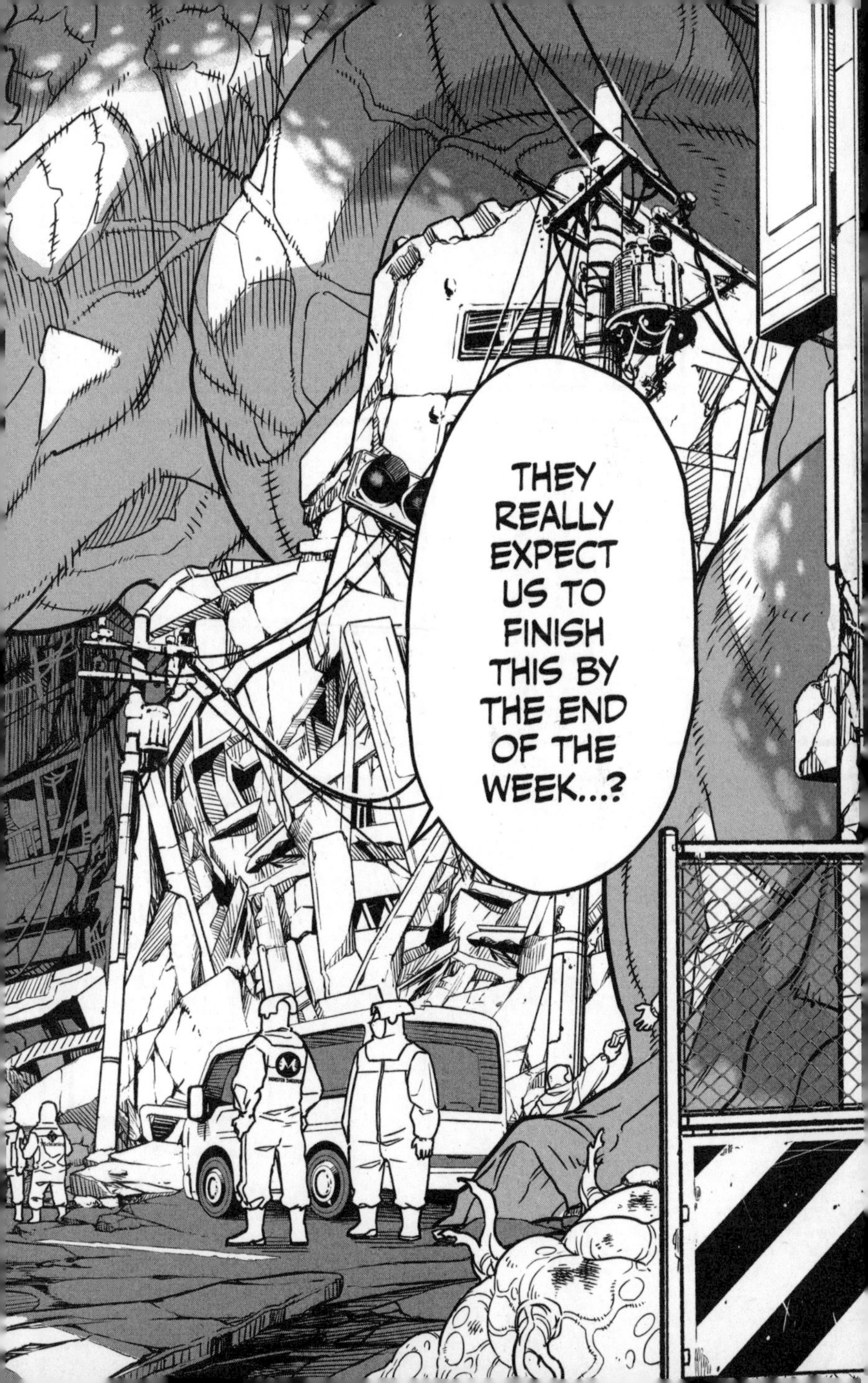
THEY REALLY EXPECT US TO FINISH THIS BY THE END OF THE WEEK...?

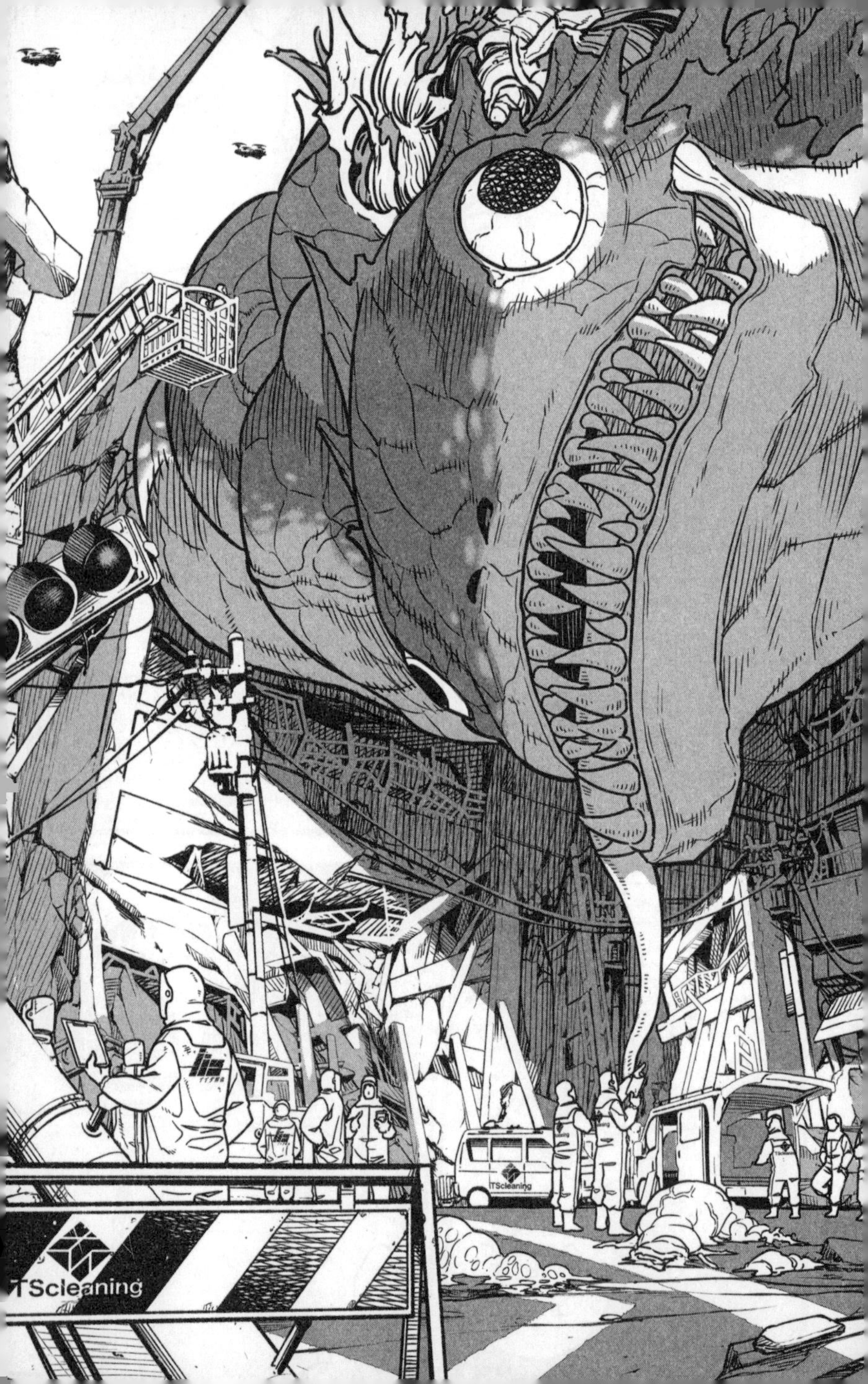
TScleaning
TScleaning

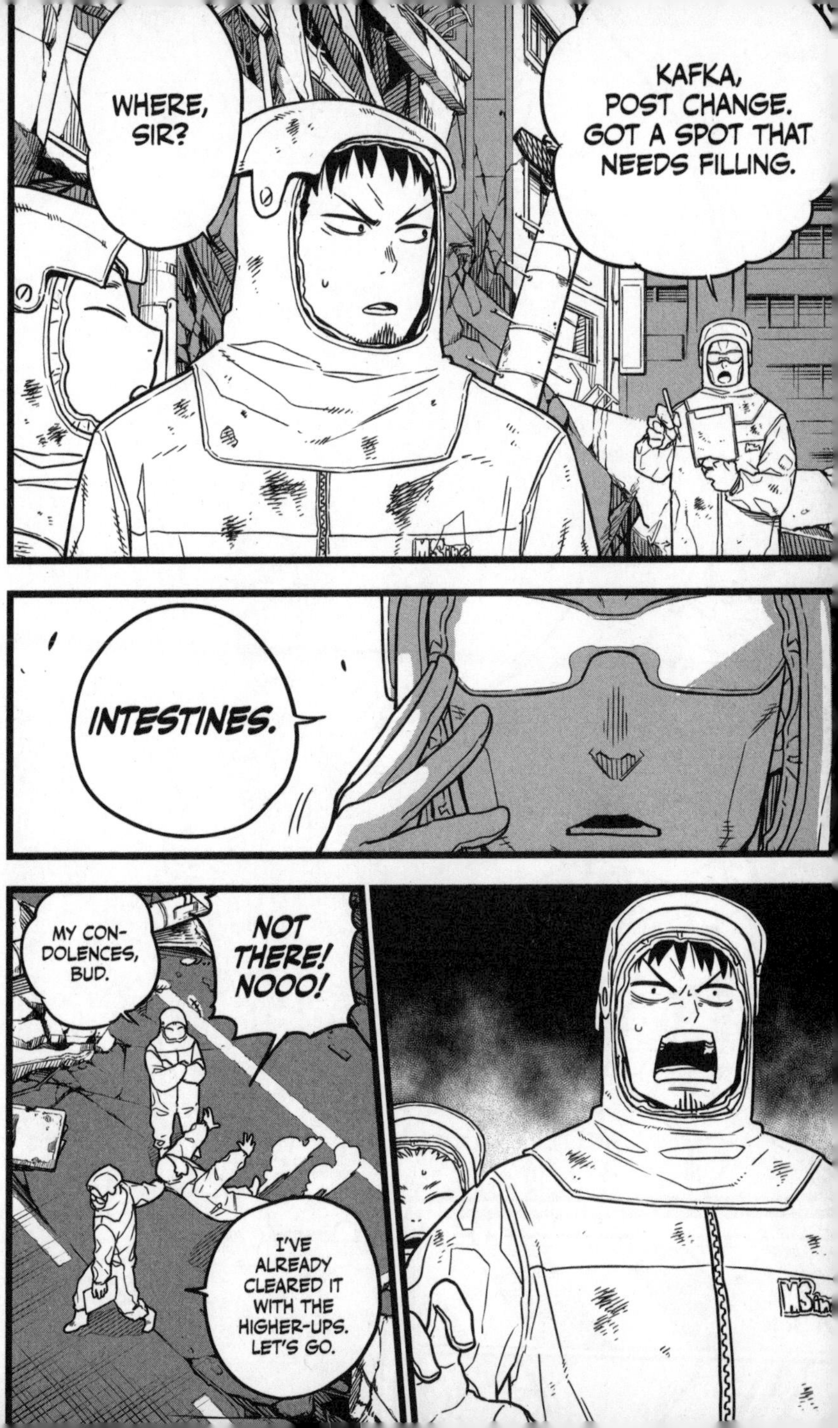

KAFKA, POST CHANGE. GOT A SPOT THAT NEEDS FILLING.
WHERE, SIR?
INTESTINES.
NOT THERE! NOOO!
MY CON-DOLENCES, BUD.
I'VE ALREADY CLEARED IT WITH THE HIGHER-UPS. LET'S GO.

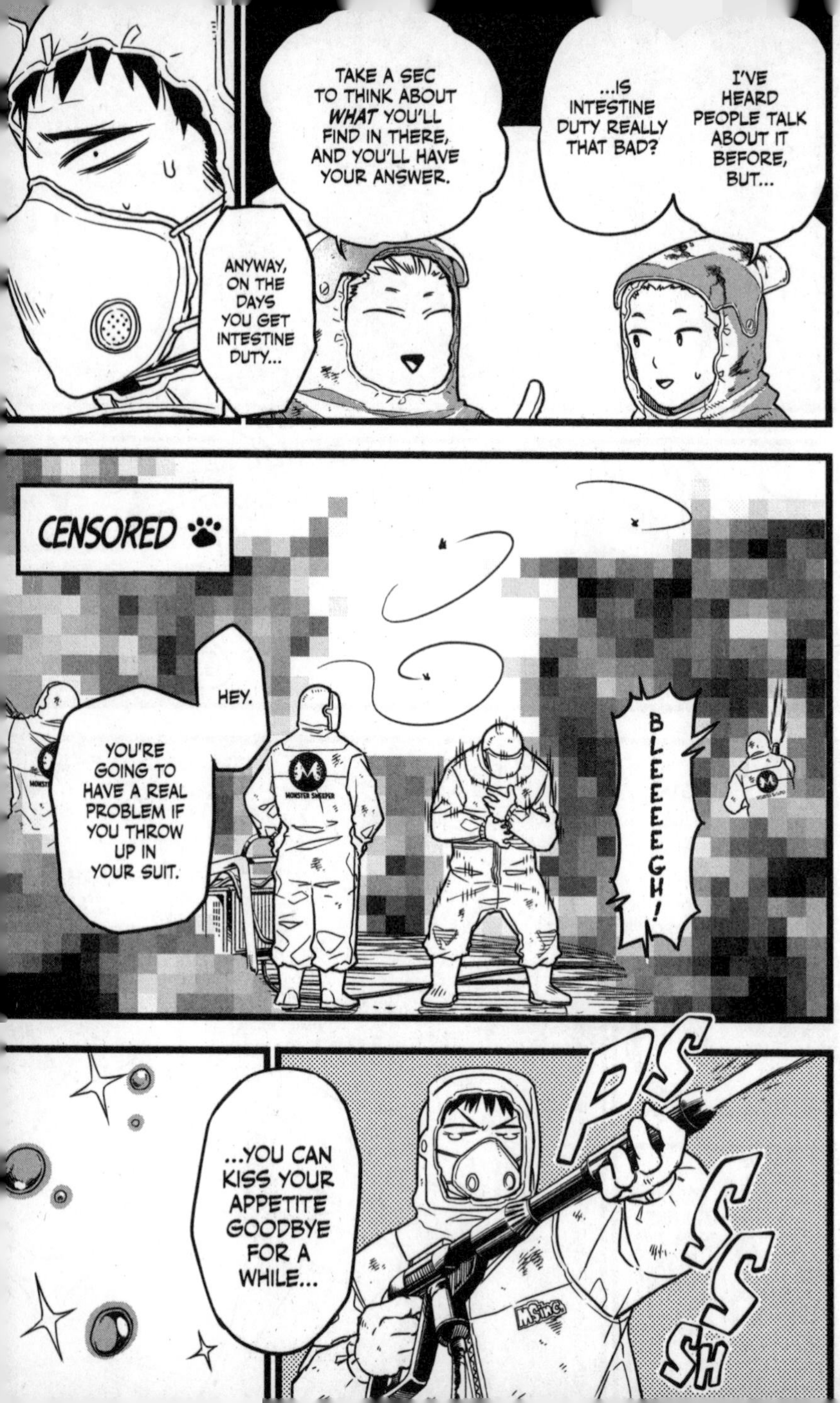
I'VE HEARD PEOPLE TALK ABOUT IT BEFORE, BUT...
...IS INTESTINE DUTY REALLY THAT BAD?
TAKE A SEC TO THINK ABOUT *WHAT* YOU'LL FIND IN THERE, AND YOU'LL HAVE YOUR ANSWER.
ANYWAY, ON THE DAYS YOU GET INTESTINE DUTY...
CENSORED
BLEEEEEGH!
MONSTER SWEEPER
HEY.
YOU'RE GOING TO HAVE A REAL PROBLEM IF YOU THROW UP IN YOUR SUIT.
PSSSSH
...YOU CAN KISS YOUR APPETITE GOODBYE FOR A WHILE...
MS inc.

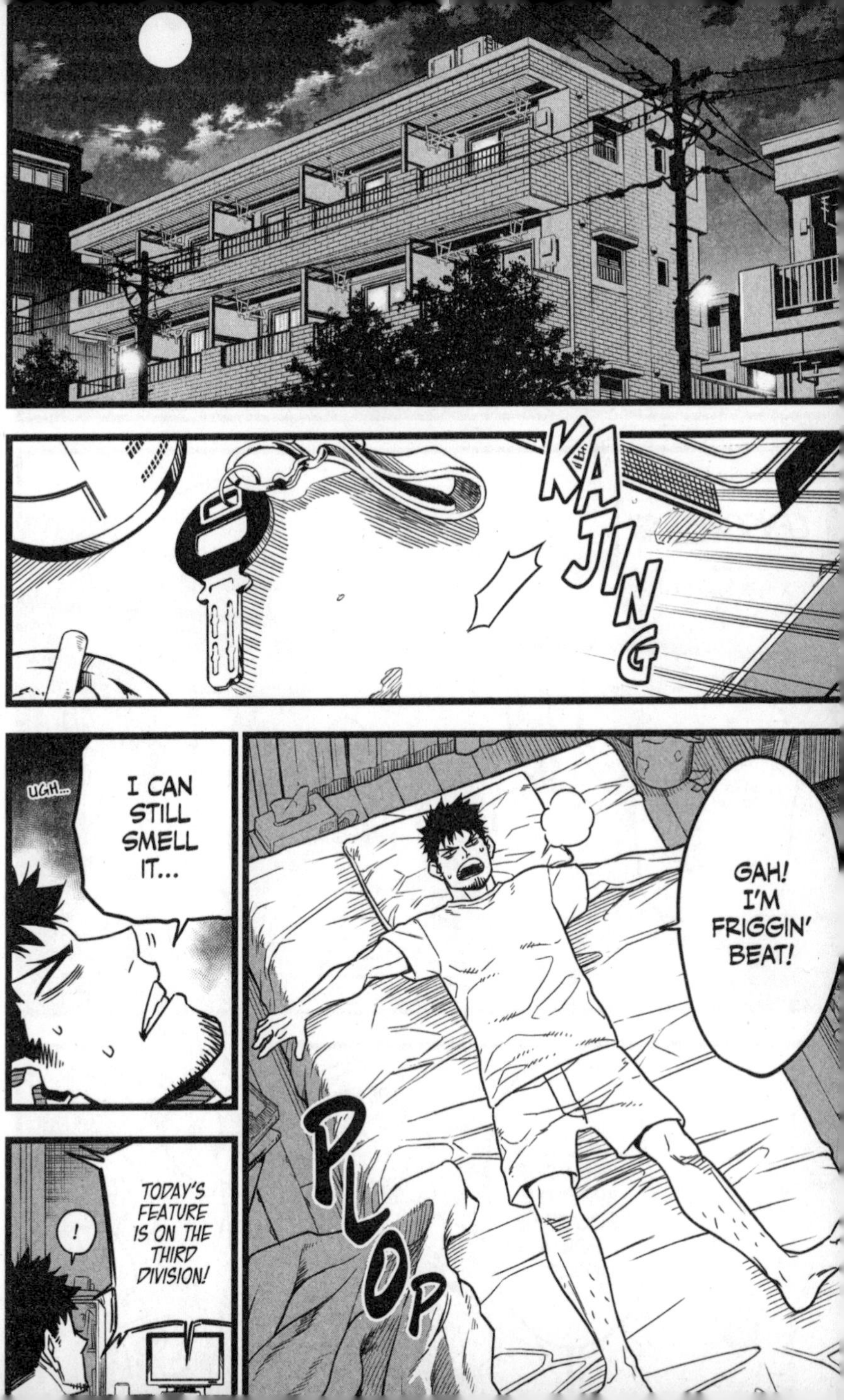
KAJING
GAH! I'M FRIGGIN' BEAT!
PLOP
UGH...
I CAN STILL SMELL IT...
TODAY'S FEATURE IS ON THE THIRD DIVISION!
!

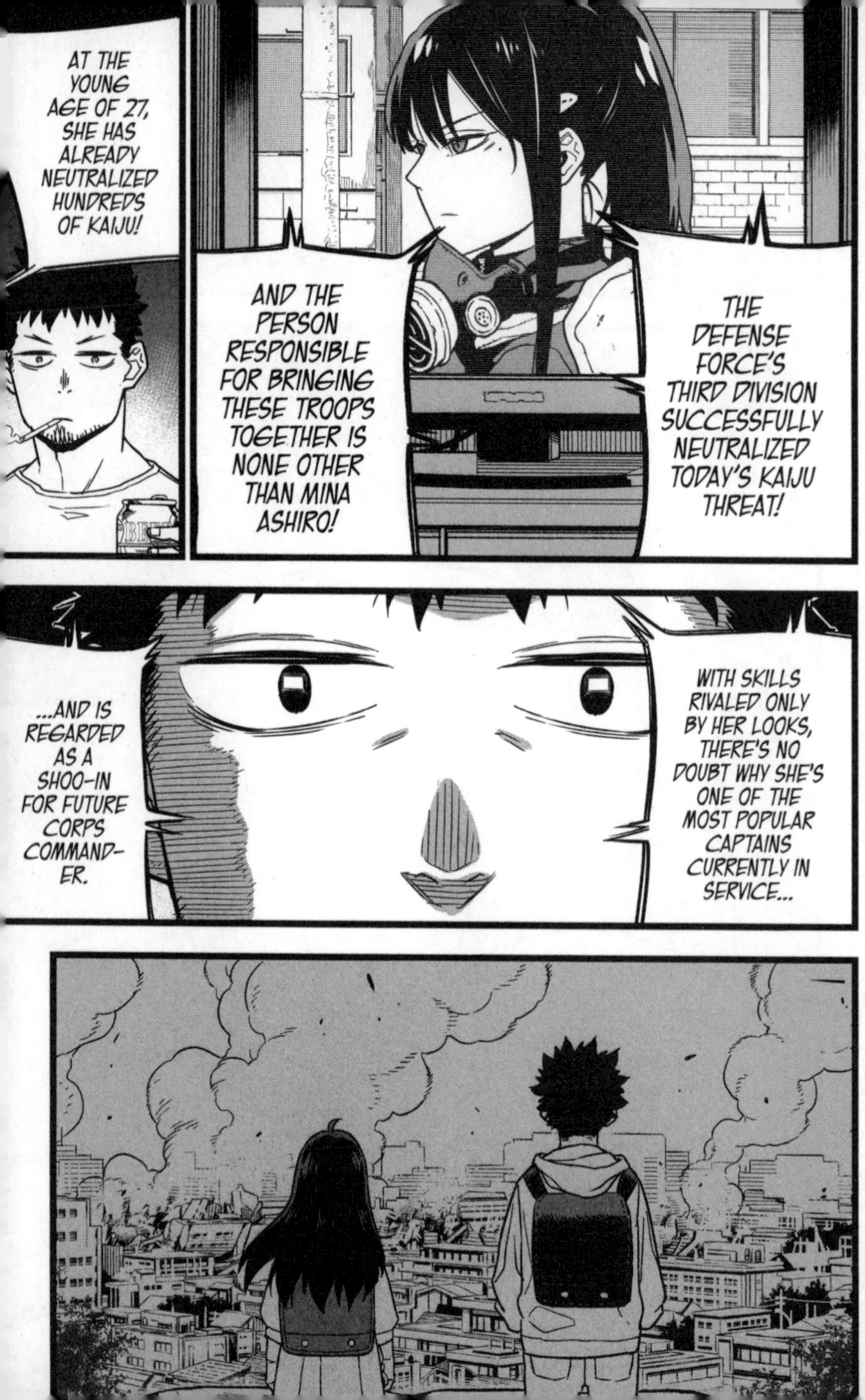
THE DEFENSE FORCE'S THIRD DIVISION SUCCESSFULLY NEUTRALIZED TODAY'S KAIJU THREAT!
AND THE PERSON RESPONSIBLE FOR BRINGING THESE TROOPS TOGETHER IS NONE OTHER THAN MINA ASHIRO!
AT THE YOUNG AGE OF 27, SHE HAS ALREADY NEUTRALIZED HUNDREDS OF KAIJU!
WITH SKILLS RIVALED ONLY BY HER LOOKS, THERE'S NO DOUBT WHY SHE'S ONE OF THE MOST POPULAR CAPTAINS CURRENTLY IN SERVICE...
...AND IS REGARDED AS A SHOO-IN FOR FUTURE CORPS COMMANDER.

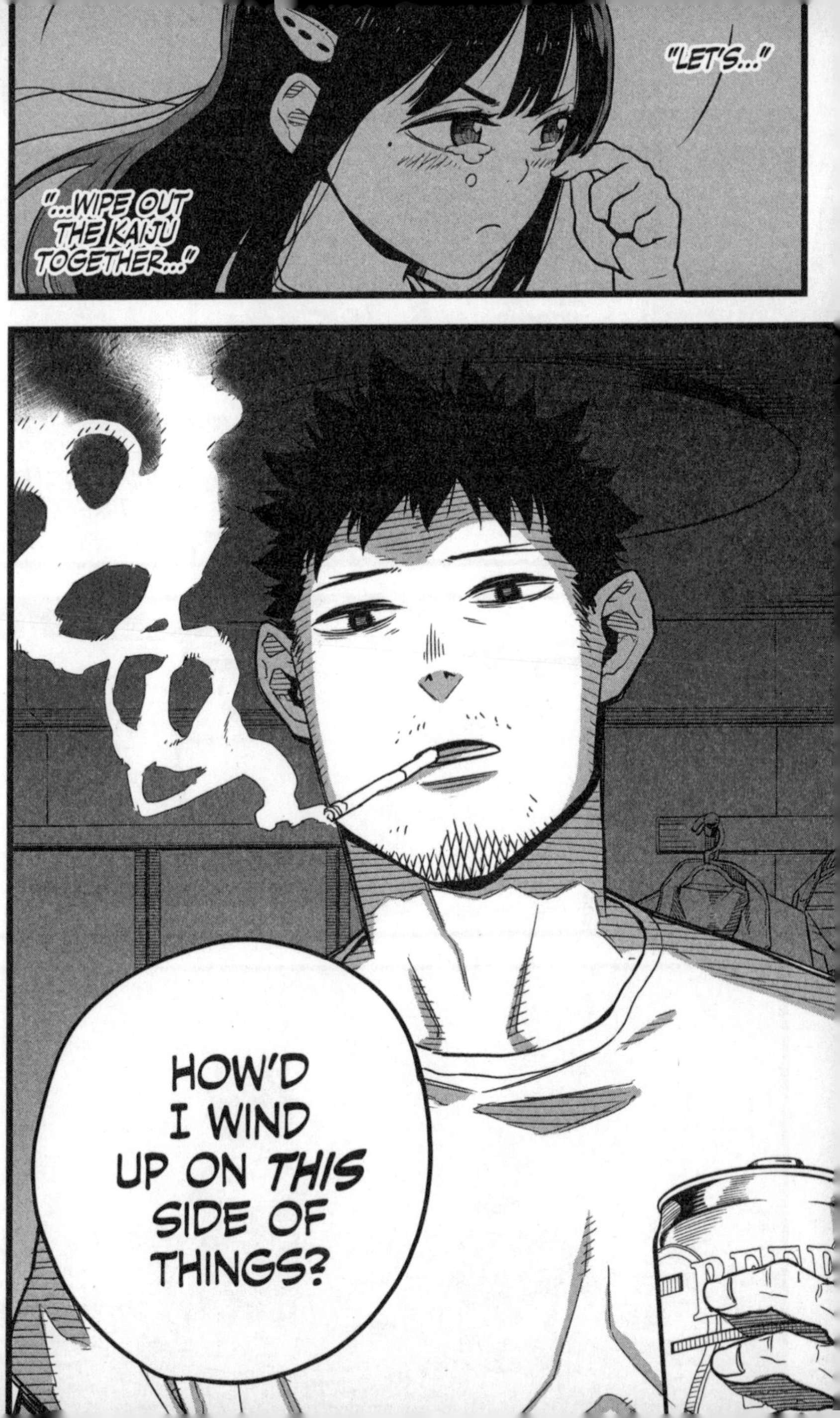
"LET'S..."
"...WIPE OUT THE KAIJU TOGETHER..."
HOW'D I WIND UP ON *THIS* SIDE OF THINGS?

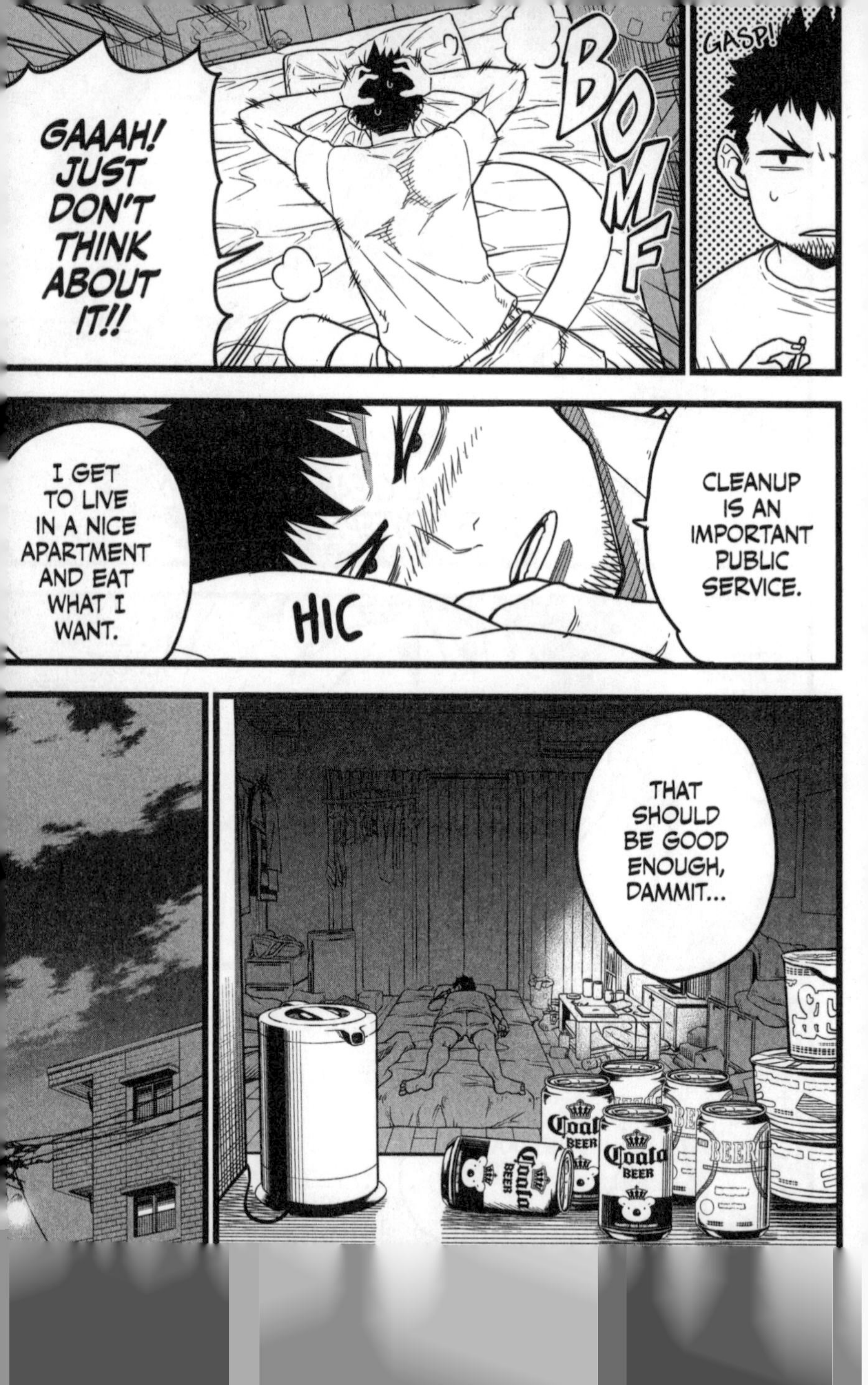
GASP!
BOMF
GAAAH! JUST DON'T THINK ABOUT IT!!
CLEANUP IS AN IMPORTANT PUBLIC SERVICE.
I GET TO LIVE IN A NICE APARTMENT AND EAT WHAT I WANT.
HIC
THAT SHOULD BE GOOD ENOUGH, DAMMIT...

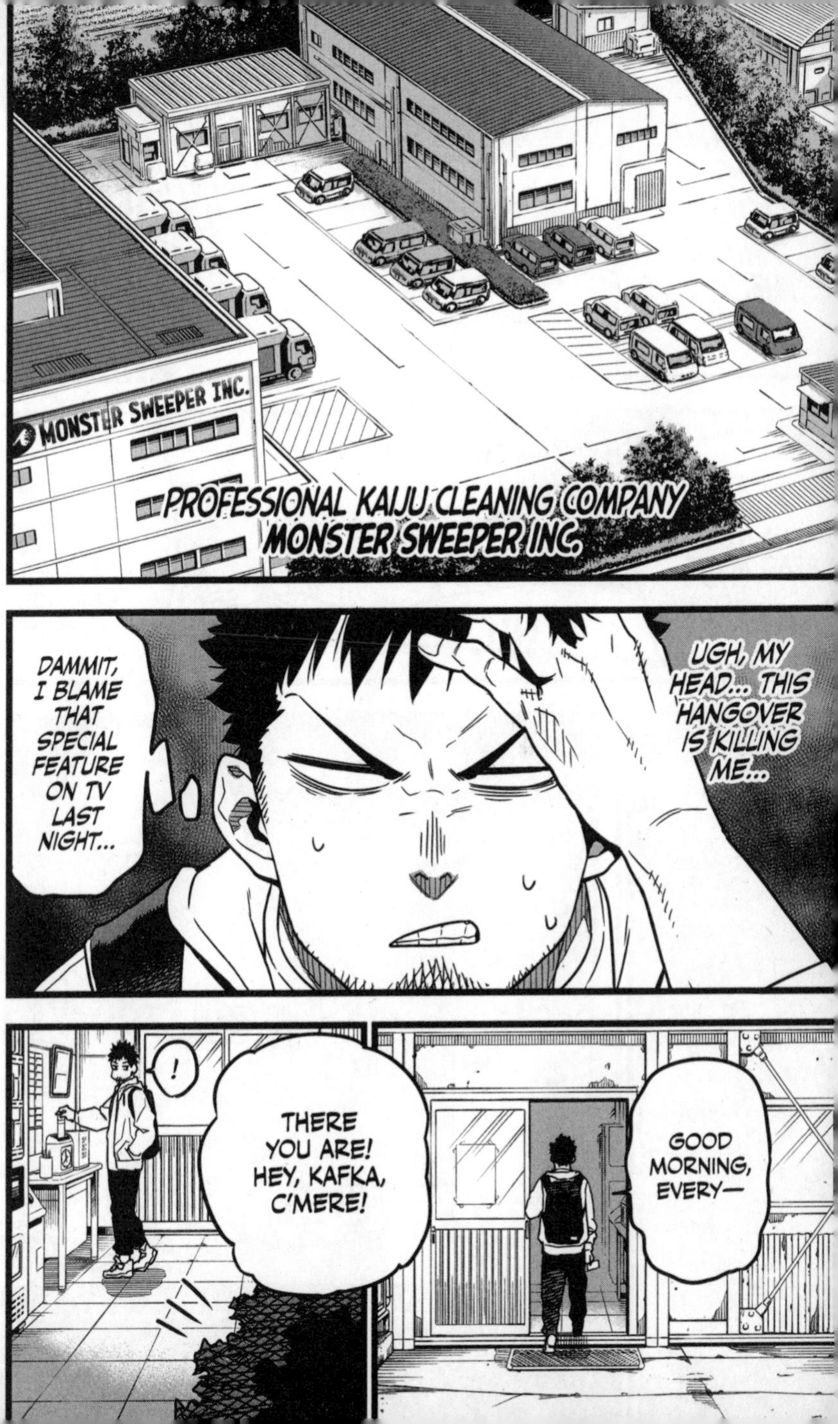
MONSTER SWEEPER INC.
PROFESSIONAL KAIJU CLEANING COMPANY MONSTER SWEEPER INC.
UGH, MY HEAD... THIS HANGOVER IS KILLING ME...
DAMMIT, I BLAME THAT SPECIAL FEATURE ON TV LAST NIGHT...
GOOD MORNING, EVERY—
THERE YOU ARE! HEY, KAFKA, C'MERE!
!

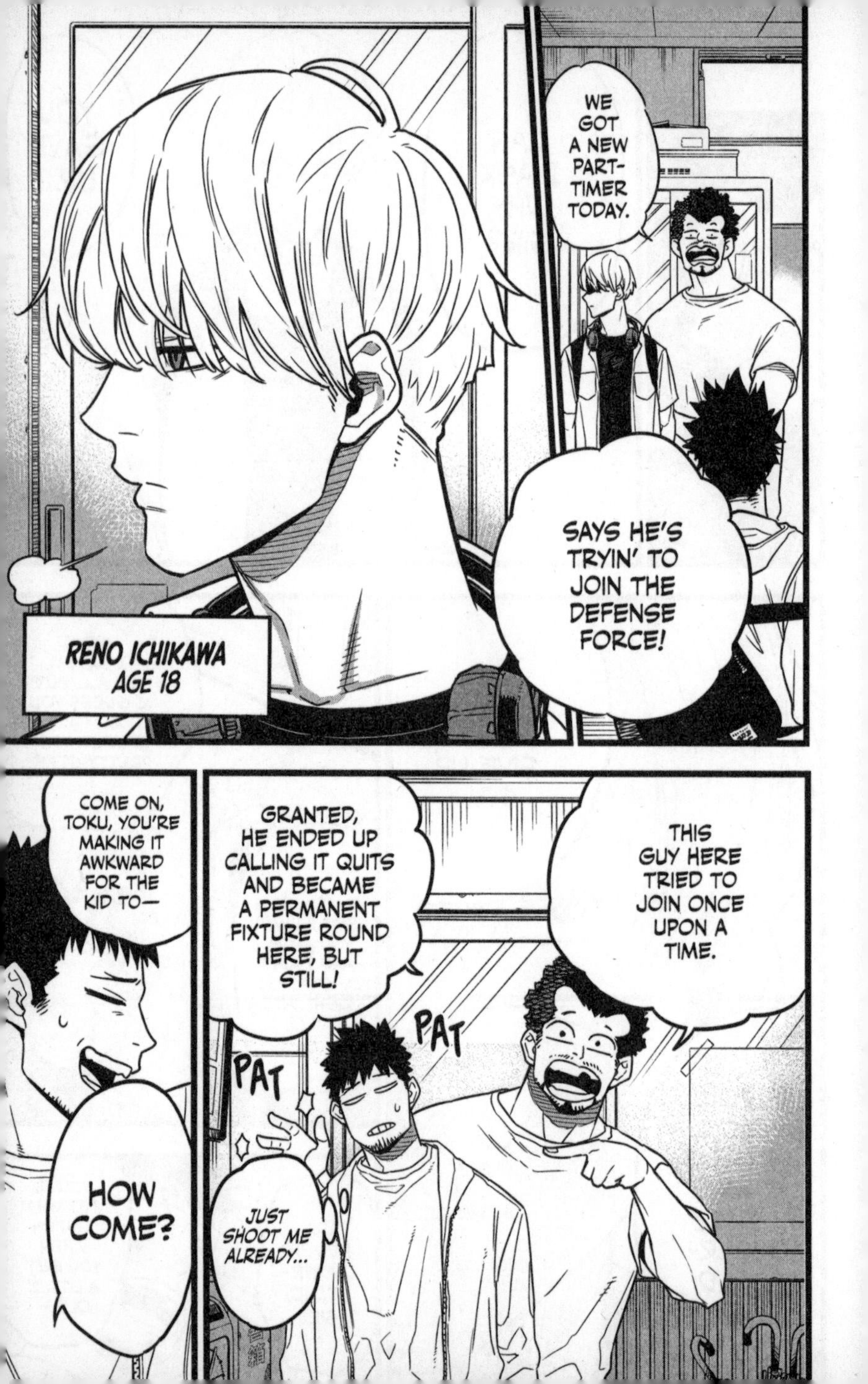
WE GOT A NEW PART-TIMER TODAY.
SAYS HE'S TRYIN' TO JOIN THE DEFENSE FORCE!
RENO ICHIKAWA AGE 18
THIS GUY HERE TRIED TO JOIN ONCE UPON A TIME.
PAT
GRANTED, HE ENDED UP CALLING IT QUITS AND BECAME A PERMANENT FIXTURE ROUND HERE, BUT STILL!
PAT
JUST SHOOT ME ALREADY...
COME ON, TOKU, YOU'RE MAKING IT AWKWARD FOR THE KID TO—
HOW COME?

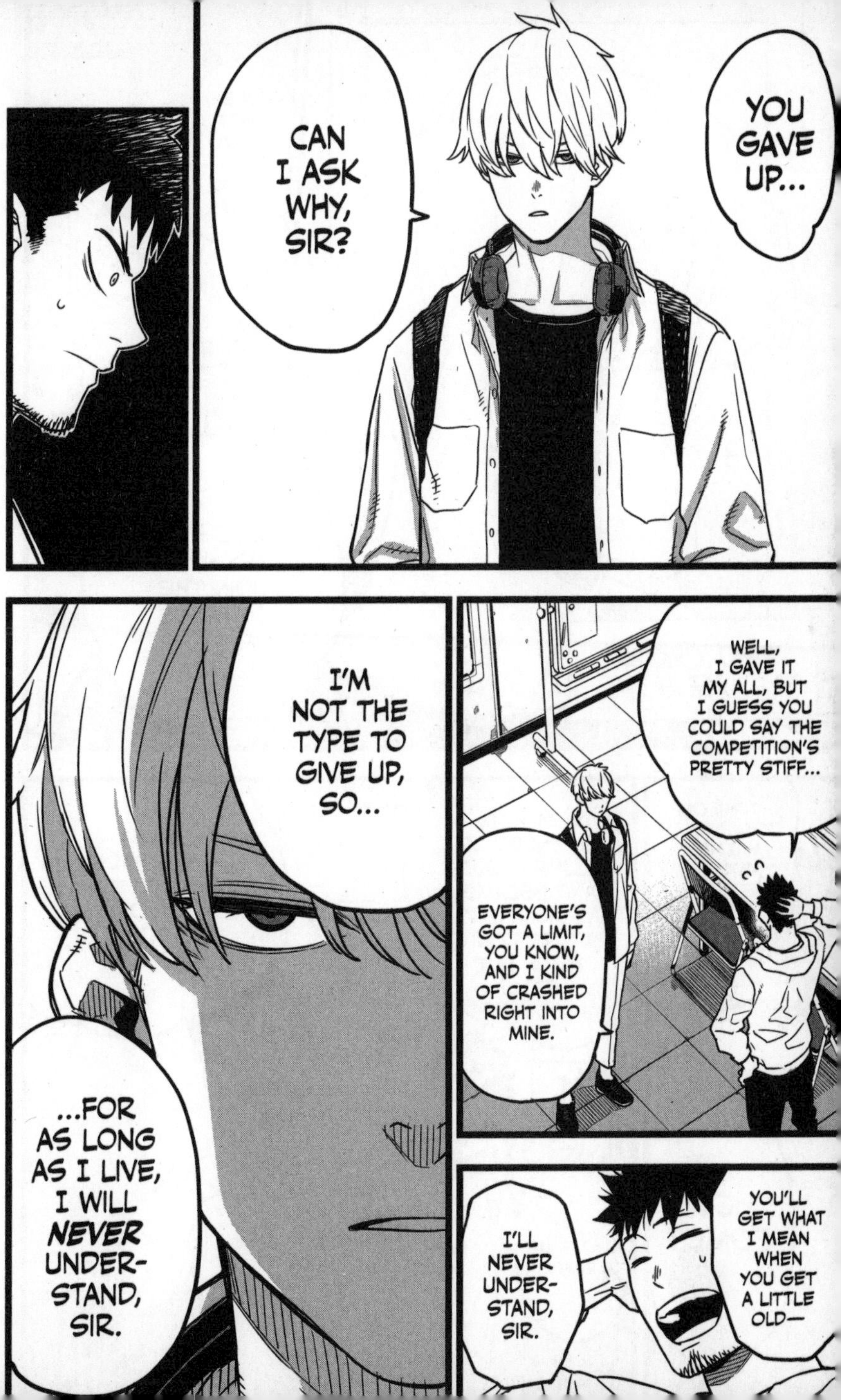
YOU GAVE UP...
CAN I ASK WHY, SIR?
WELL, I GAVE IT MY ALL, BUT I GUESS YOU COULD SAY THE COMPETITION'S PRETTY STIFF...
EVERYONE'S GOT A LIMIT, YOU KNOW, AND I KIND OF CRASHED RIGHT INTO MINE.
YOU'LL GET WHAT I MEAN WHEN YOU GET A LITTLE OLD—
I'LL NEVER UNDERSTAND, SIR.
I'M NOT THE TYPE TO GIVE UP, SO...
...FOR AS LONG AS I LIVE, I WILL *NEVER* UNDERSTAND, SIR.

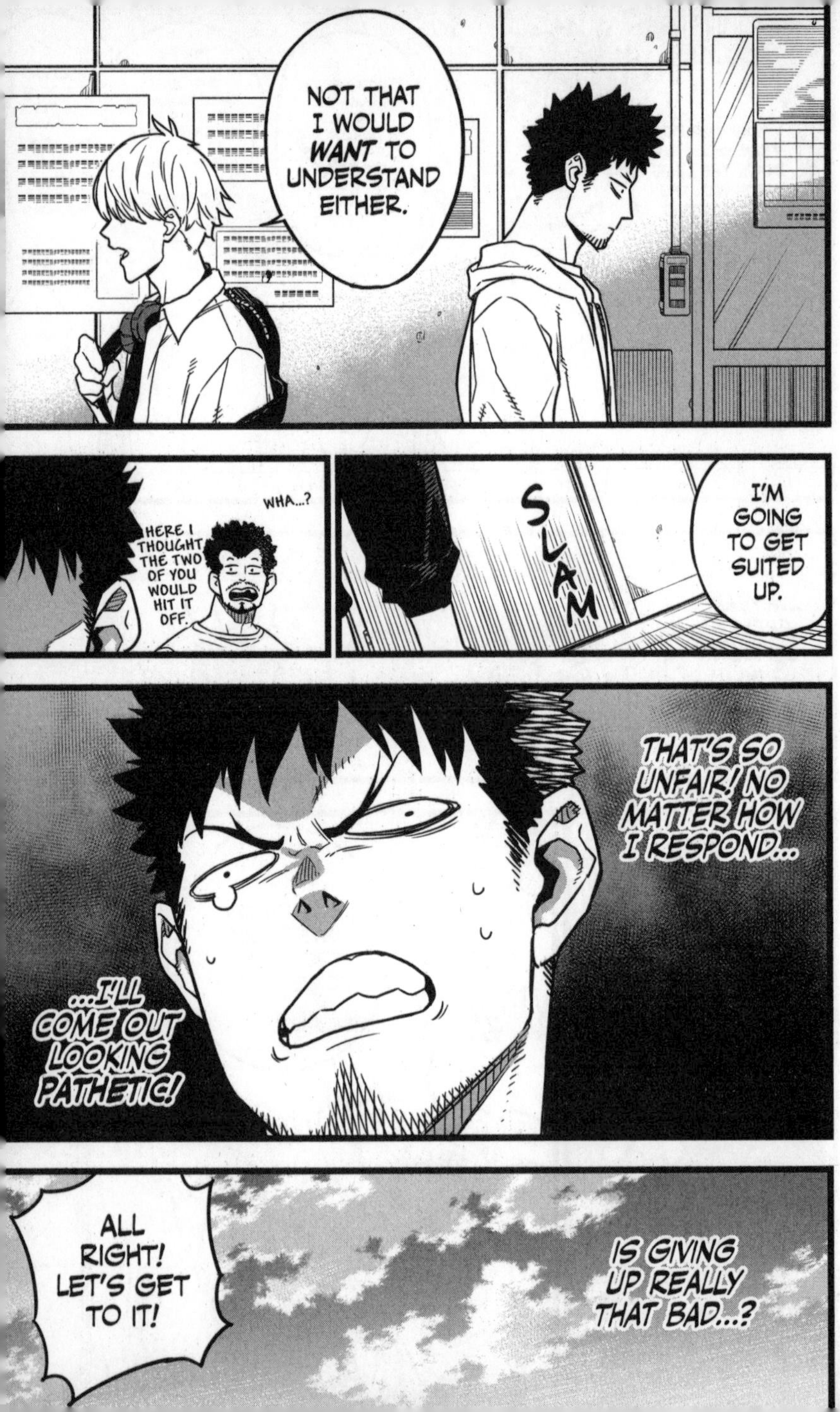
NOT THAT I WOULD *WANT* TO UNDERSTAND EITHER.
I'M GOING TO GET SUITED UP.
SLAM
WHA...?
HERE I THOUGHT THE TWO OF YOU WOULD HIT IT OFF.
THAT'S SO UNFAIR! NO MATTER HOW I RESPOND...
...I'LL COME OUT LOOKING PATHETIC!
IS GIVING UP REALLY THAT BAD...?
ALL RIGHT! LET'S GET TO IT!

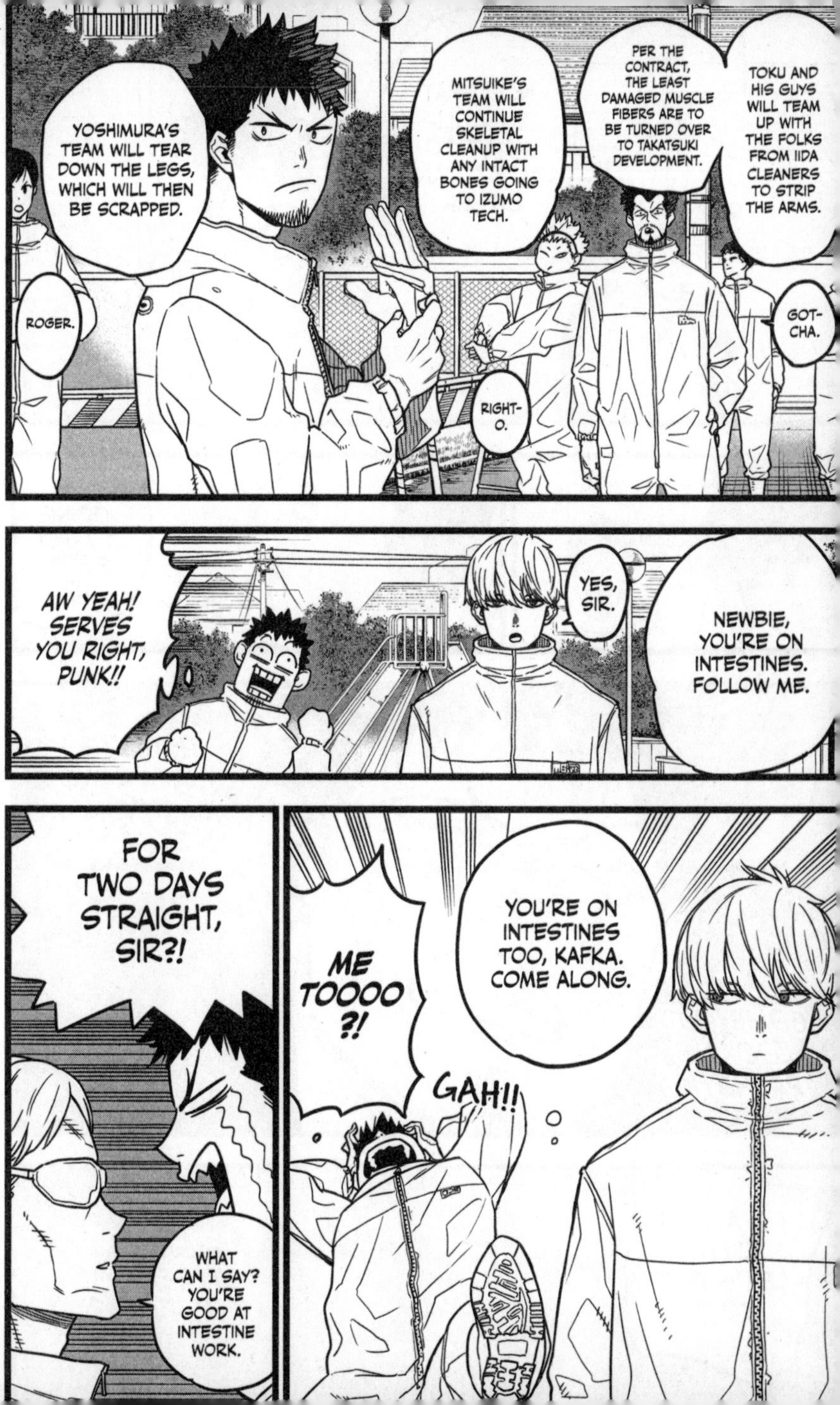
TOKU AND HIS GUYS WILL TEAM UP WITH THE FOLKS FROM IIDA CLEANERS TO STRIP THE ARMS.
PER THE CONTRACT, THE LEAST DAMAGED MUSCLE FIBERS ARE TO BE TURNED OVER TO TAKATSUKI DEVELOPMENT.
MITSUIKE'S TEAM WILL CONTINUE SKELETAL CLEANUP WITH ANY INTACT BONES GOING TO IZUMO TECH.
YOSHIMURA'S TEAM WILL TEAR DOWN THE LEGS, WHICH WILL THEN BE SCRAPPED.
GOT-CHA.
RIGHT-O.
ROGER.
NEWBIE, YOU'RE ON INTESTINES. FOLLOW ME.
YES, SIR.
AW YEAH! SERVES YOU RIGHT, PUNK!!
YOU'RE ON INTESTINES TOO, KAFKA. COME ALONG.
ME TOOOO?!
GAH!!
FOR TWO DAYS STRAIGHT, SIR?!
WHAT CAN I SAY? YOU'RE GOOD AT INTESTINE WORK.

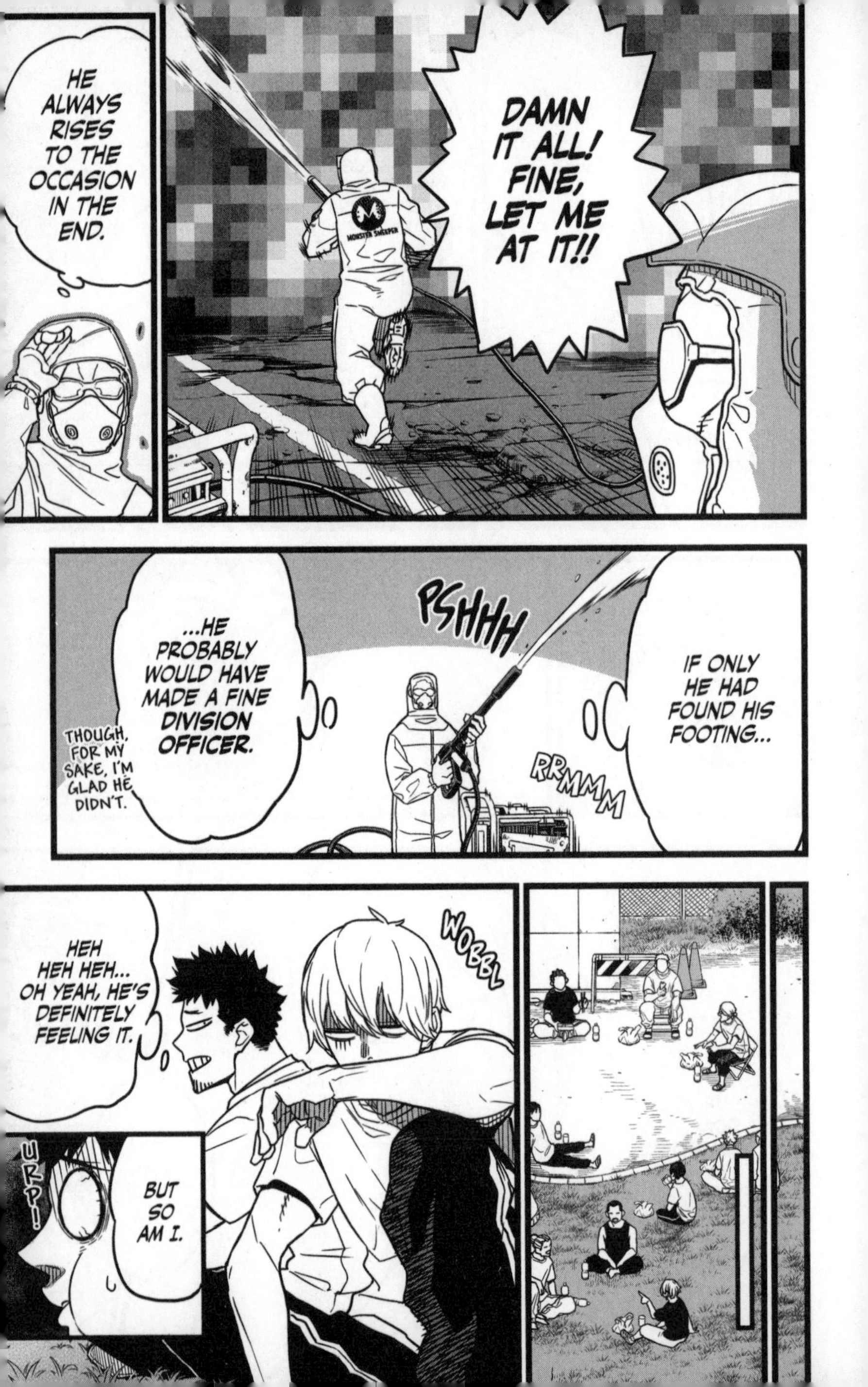
DAMN IT ALL! FINE, LET ME AT IT!!
HE ALWAYS RISES TO THE OCCASION IN THE END.
IF ONLY HE HAD FOUND HIS FOOTING...
PSHHH
RRMMMM
...HE PROBABLY WOULD HAVE MADE A FINE DIVISION OFFICER.
THOUGH, FOR MY SAKE, I'M GLAD HE DIDN'T.
WOBBL
HEH HEH HEH... OH YEAH, HE'S DEFINITELY FEELING IT.
URP!
BUT SO AM I.

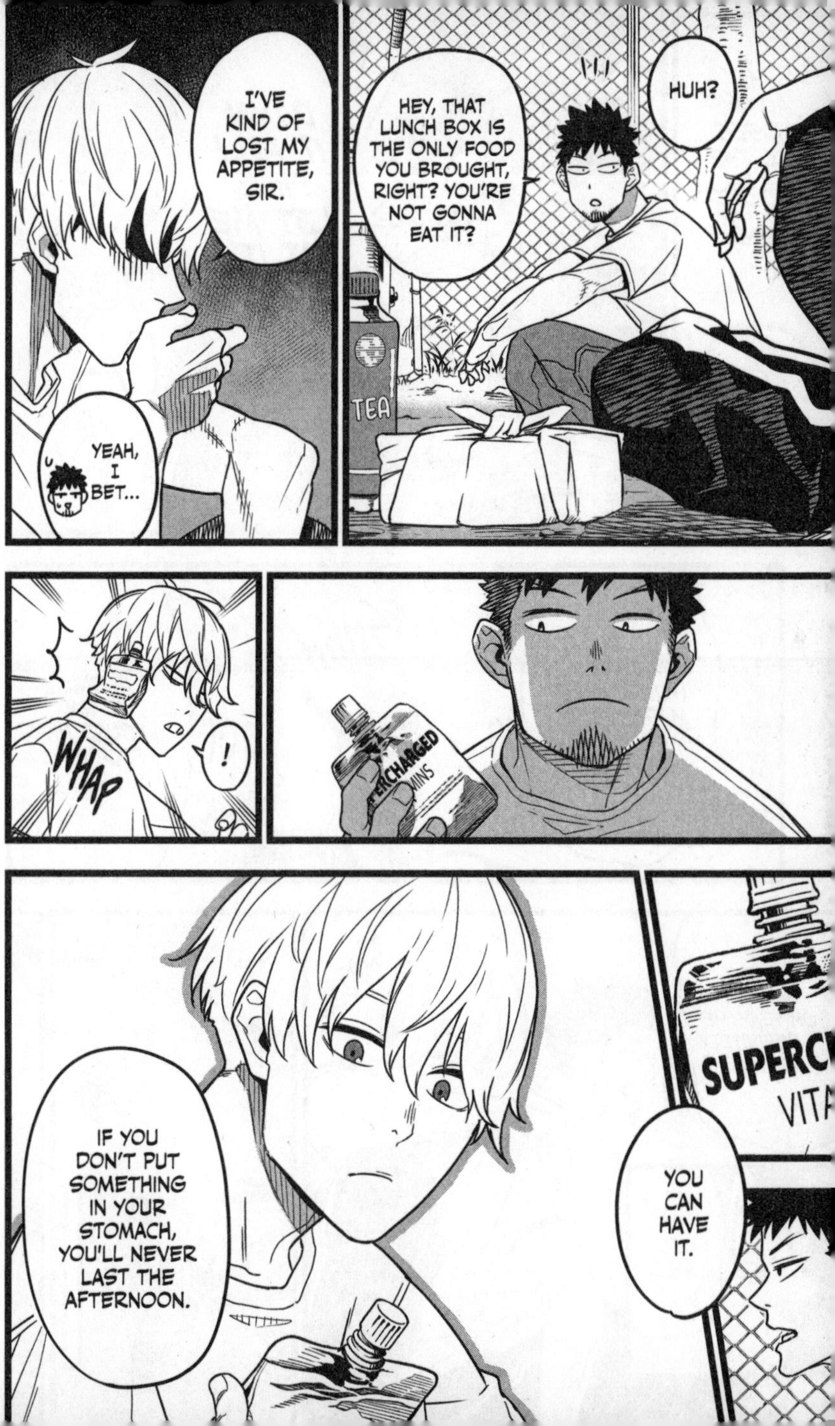
HUH?
HEY, THAT LUNCH BOX IS THE ONLY FOOD YOU BROUGHT, RIGHT? YOU'RE NOT GONNA EAT IT?
TEA
I'VE KIND OF LOST MY APPETITE, SIR.
YEAH, I BET...
WHAP
!
YOU CAN HAVE IT.
IF YOU DON'T PUT SOMETHING IN YOUR STOMACH, YOU'LL NEVER LAST THE AFTERNOON.

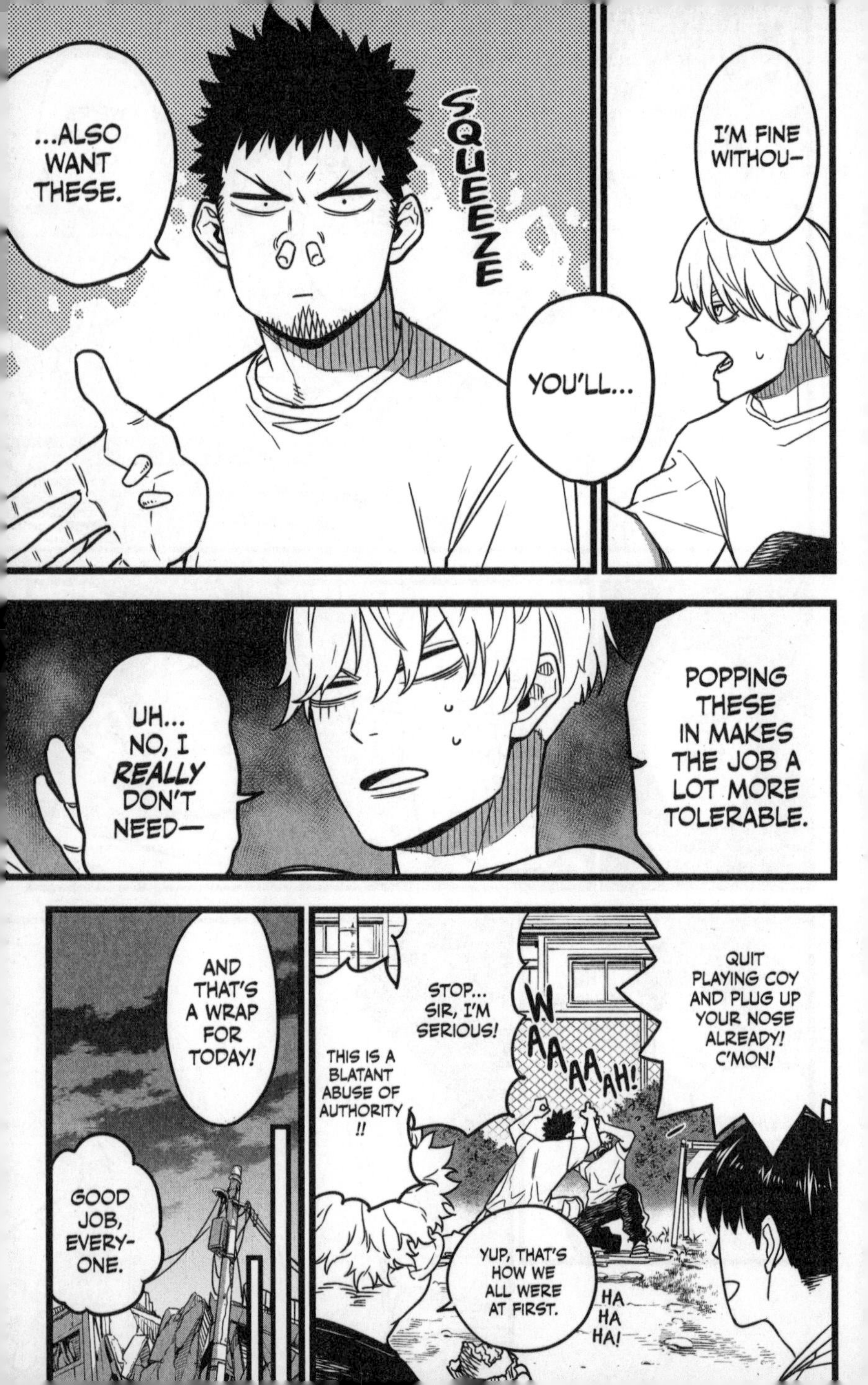
I'M FINE WITHOU—
YOU'LL...
...ALSO WANT THESE.
SQUEEZE
POPPING THESE IN MAKES THE JOB A LOT MORE TOLERABLE.
UH... NO, I *REALLY* DON'T NEED—
QUIT PLAYING COY AND PLUG UP YOUR NOSE ALREADY! C'MON!
WAAAAAH!
STOP... SIR, I'M SERIOUS!
THIS IS A BLATANT ABUSE OF AUTHORITY!!
YUP, THAT'S HOW WE ALL WERE AT FIRST.
HA HA HA!
AND THAT'S A WRAP FOR TODAY!
GOOD JOB, EVERYONE.

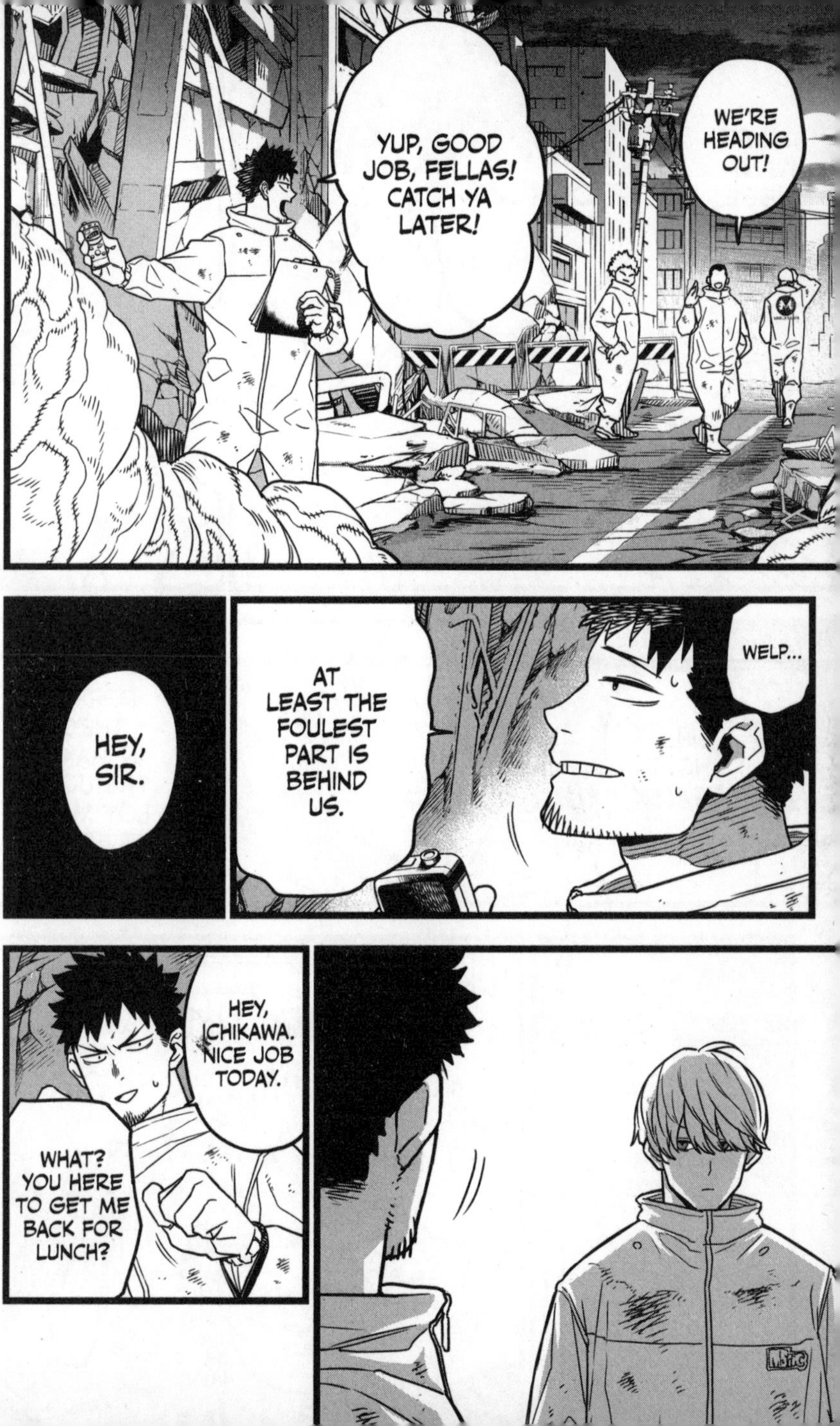
WE'RE HEADING OUT!
YUP, GOOD JOB, FELLAS! CATCH YA LATER!
WELP...
AT LEAST THE FOULEST PART IS BEHIND US.
HEY, SIR.
HEY, ICHIKAWA. NICE JOB TODAY.
WHAT? YOU HERE TO GET ME BACK FOR LUNCH?

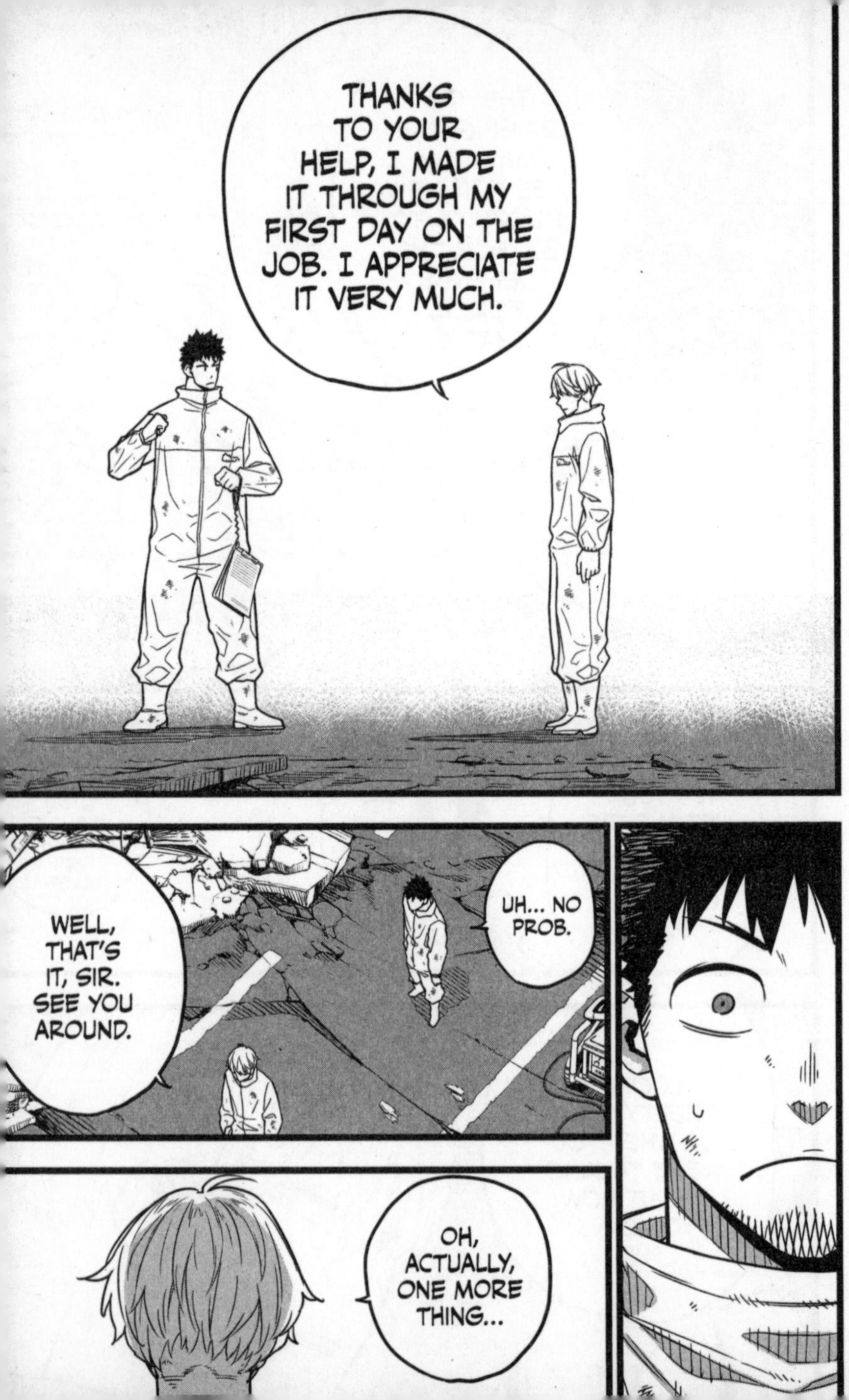
THANKS TO YOUR HELP, I MADE IT THROUGH MY FIRST DAY ON THE JOB. I APPRECIATE IT VERY MUCH.
UH... NO PROB.
WELL, THAT'S IT, SIR. SEE YOU AROUND.
OH, ACTUALLY, ONE MORE THING...

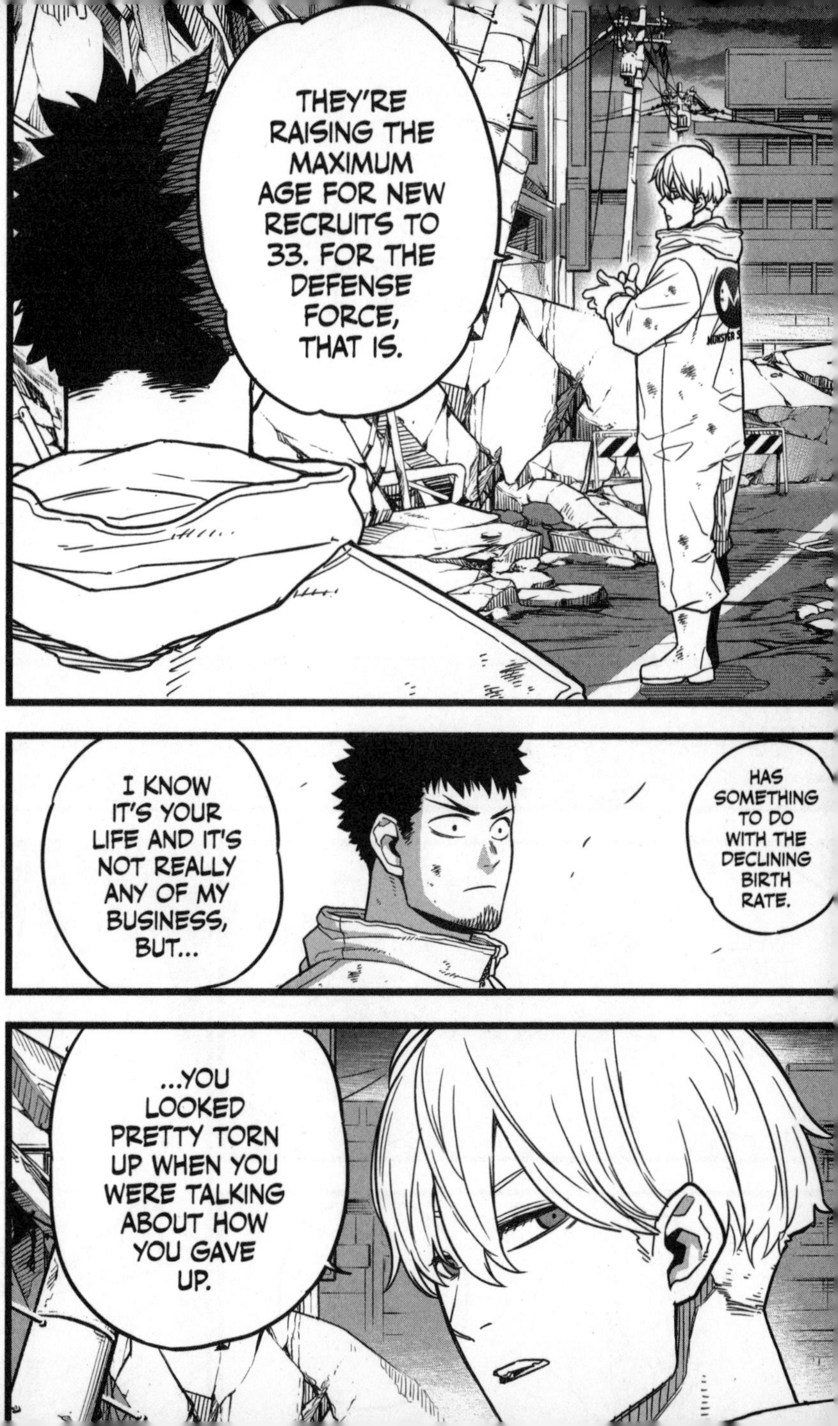
THEY'RE RAISING THE MAXIMUM AGE FOR NEW RECRUITS TO 33. FOR THE DEFENSE FORCE, THAT IS.
HAS SOMETHING TO DO WITH THE DECLINING BIRTH RATE.
I KNOW IT'S YOUR LIFE AND IT'S NOT REALLY ANY OF MY BUSINESS, BUT...
...YOU LOOKED PRETTY TORN UP WHEN YOU WERE TALKING ABOUT HOW YOU GAVE UP.

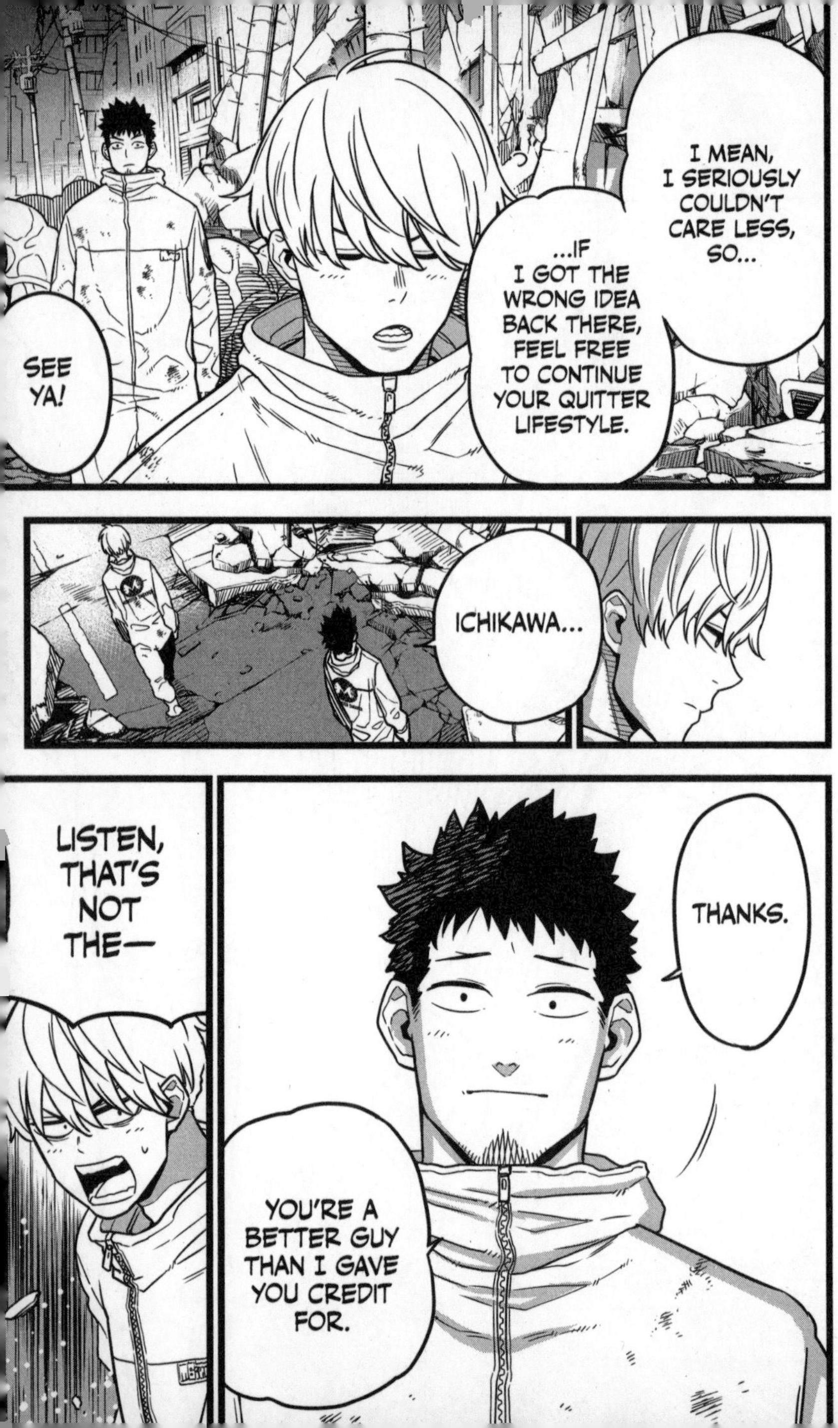
I MEAN, I SERIOUSLY COULDN'T CARE LESS, SO...
...IF I GOT THE WRONG IDEA BACK THERE, FEEL FREE TO CONTINUE YOUR QUITTER LIFESTYLE.
SEE YA!
ICHIKAWA...
THANKS.
YOU'RE A BETTER GUY THAN I GAVE YOU CREDIT FOR.
LISTEN, THAT'S NOT THE—

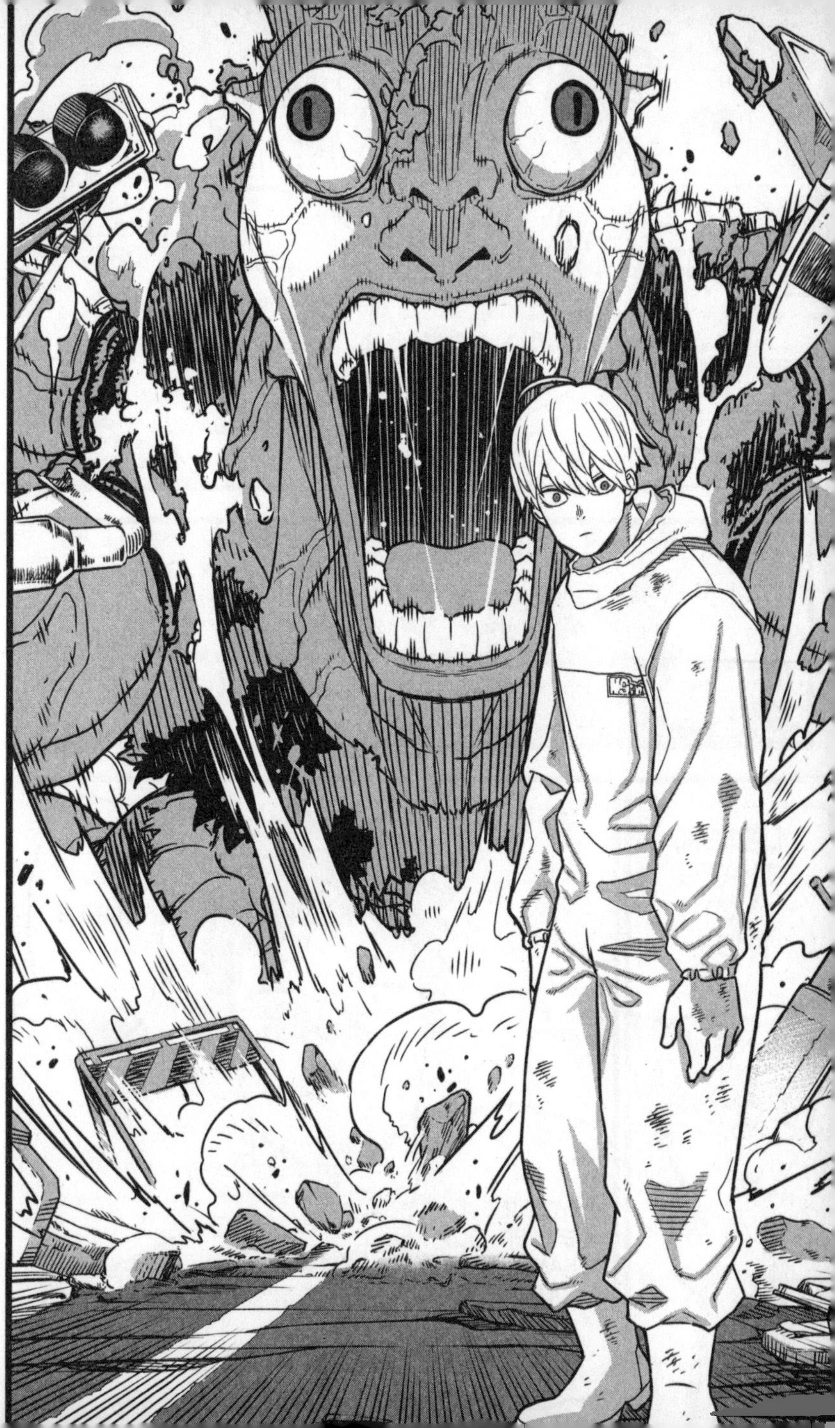

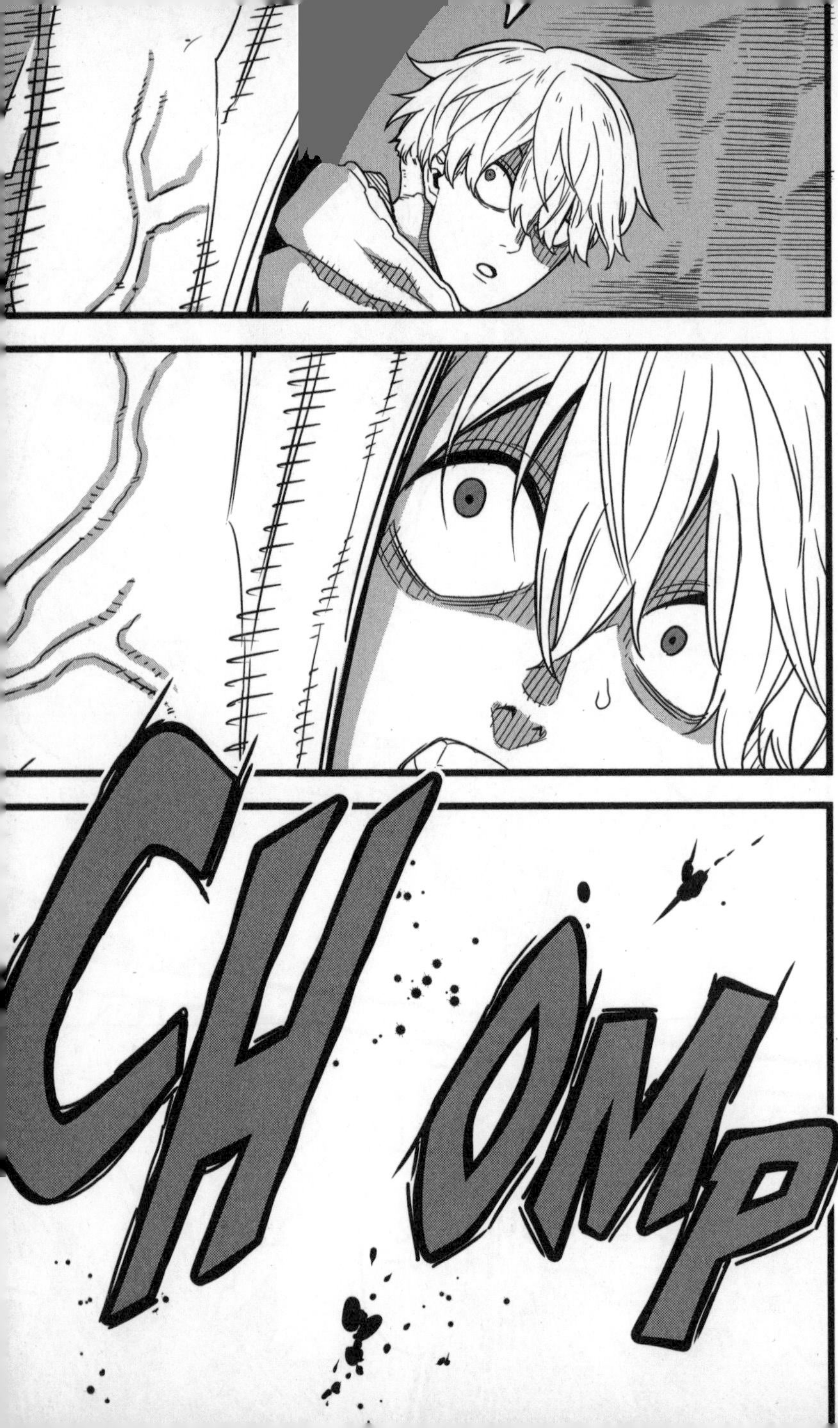
CHOMP

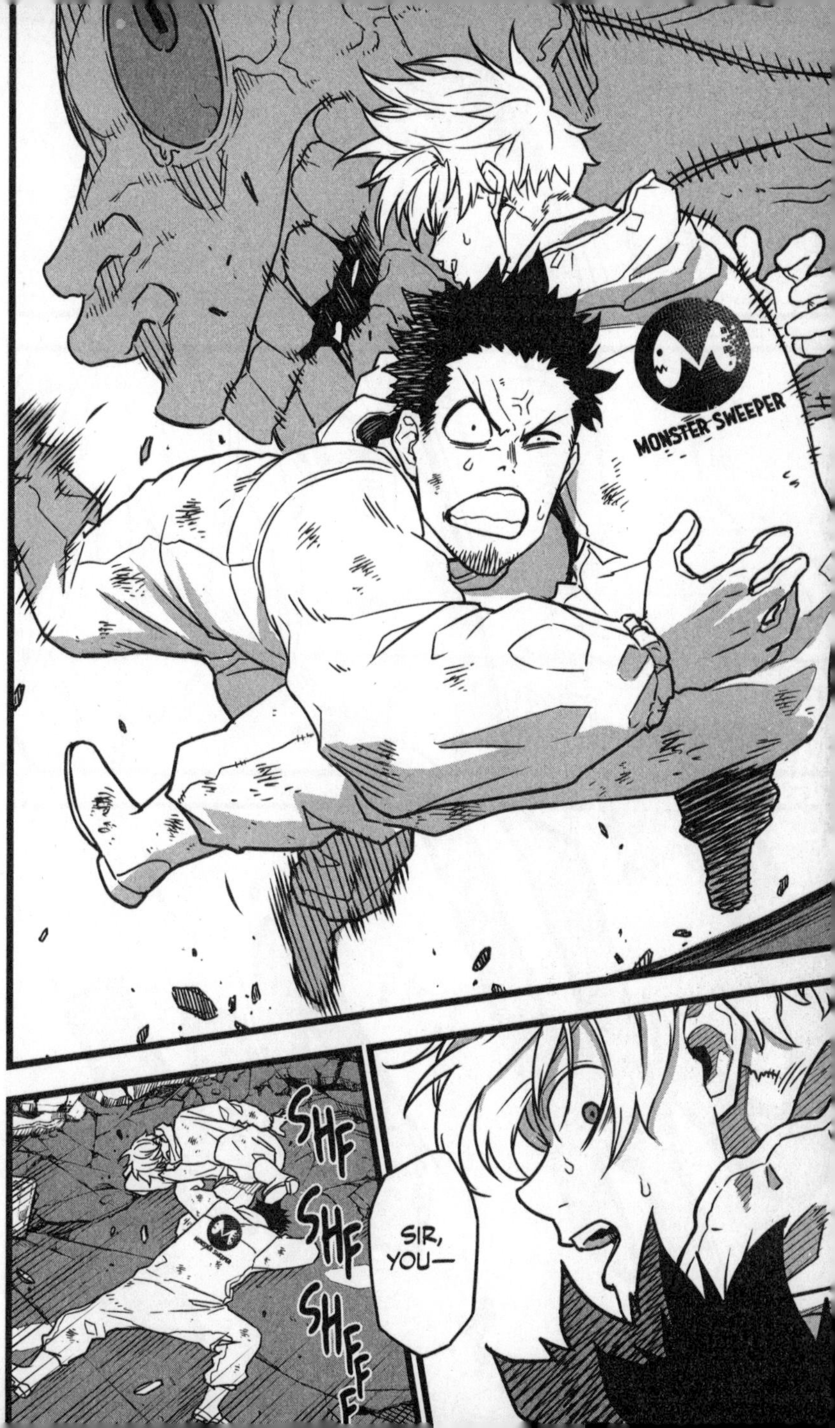
MONSTER SWEEPER
SIR, YOU—
SHF SHF SHFFF
MONSTER SWEEPER

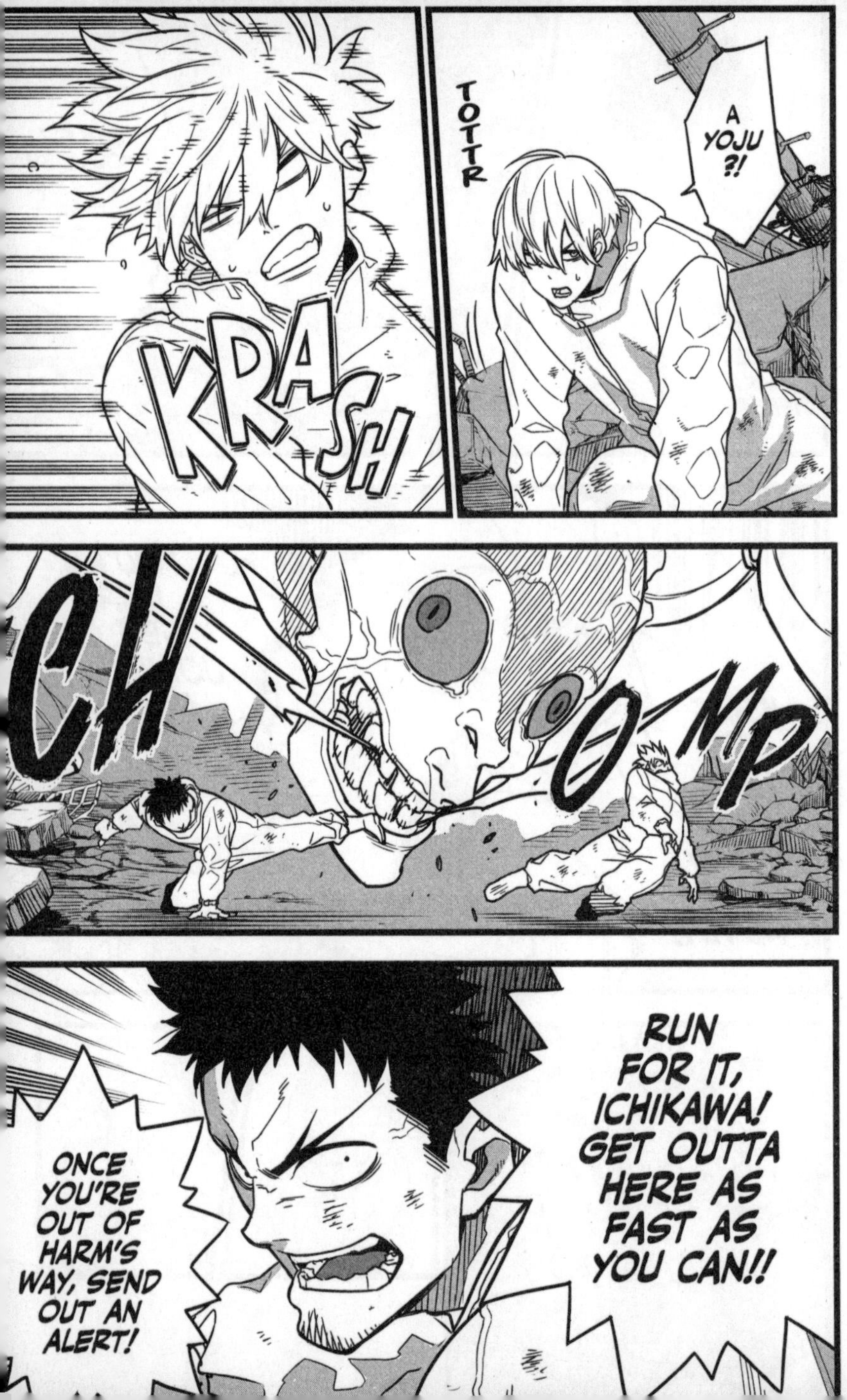
A YOJU ?!
TOTTR
KRASH
CHOMP
RUN FOR IT, ICHIKAWA! GET OUTTA HERE AS FAST AS YOU CAN!!
ONCE YOU'RE OUT OF HARM'S WAY, SEND OUT AN ALERT!

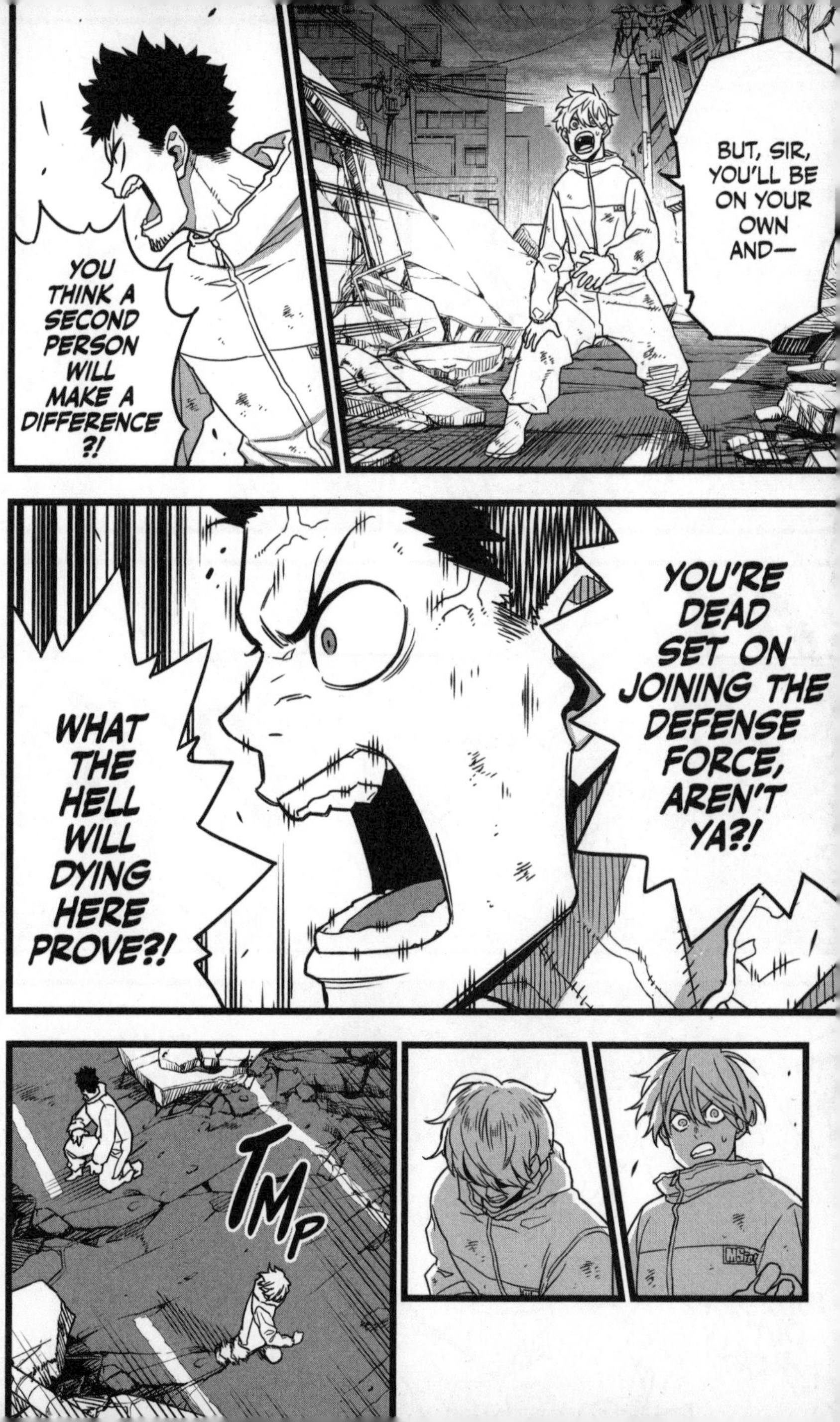
BUT, SIR, YOU'LL BE ON YOUR OWN AND—
YOU THINK A SECOND PERSON WILL MAKE A DIFFERENCE ?!
YOU'RE DEAD SET ON JOINING THE DEFENSE FORCE, AREN'T YA?!
WHAT THE HELL WILL DYING HERE PROVE?!
TMP

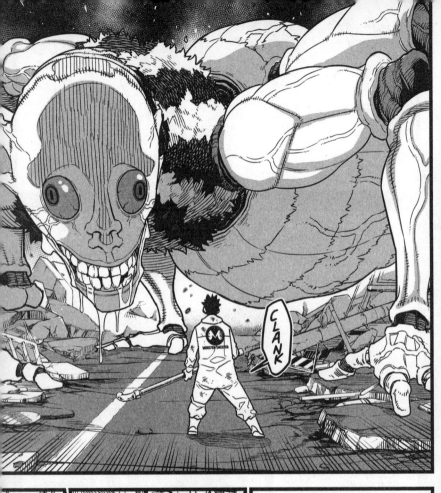

CLANK

GONK

YEAH... I'M COMPLETELY SCREWED...

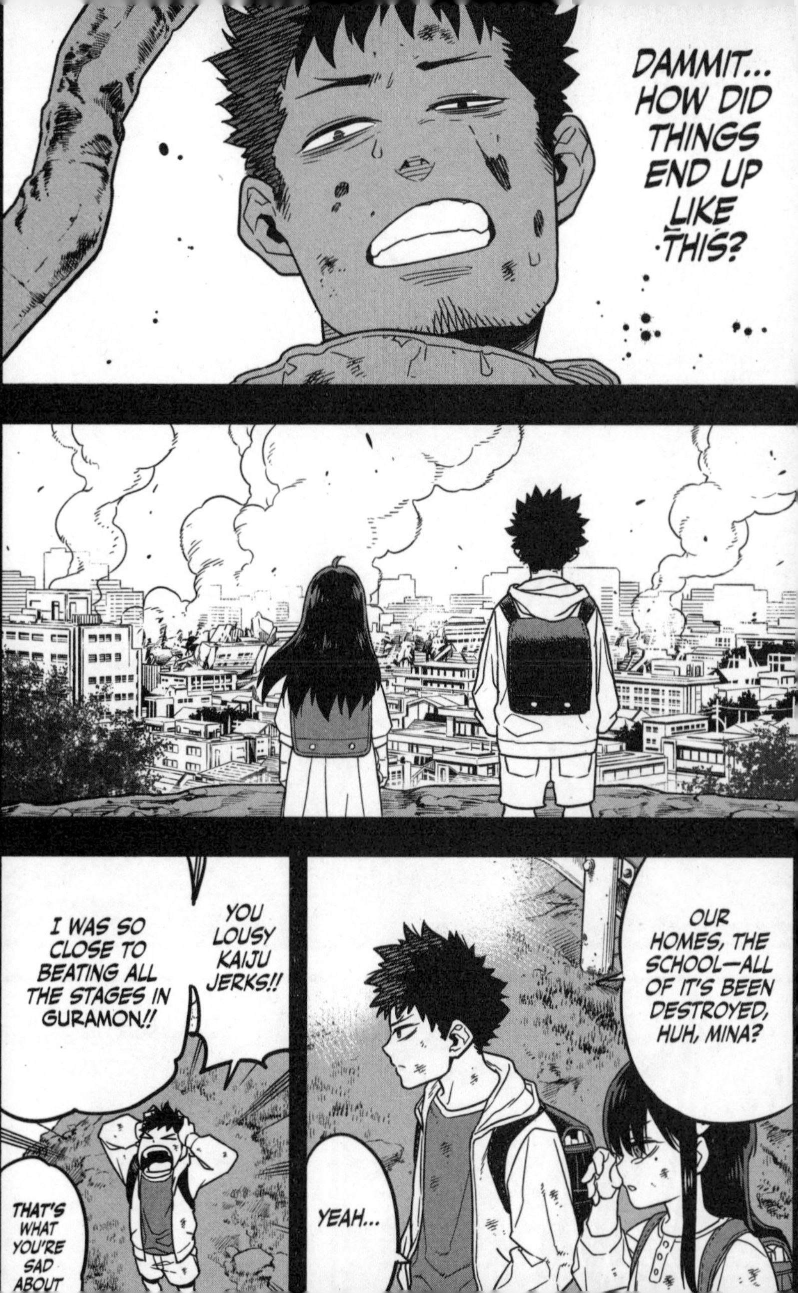
DAMMIT... HOW DID THINGS END UP LIKE THIS?
OUR HOMES, THE SCHOOL—ALL OF IT'S BEEN DESTROYED, HUH, MINA?
YEAH...
YOU LOUSY KAIJU JERKS!!
I WAS SO CLOSE TO BEATING ALL THE STAGES IN GURAMON!!
THAT'S WHAT YOU'RE SAD ABOUT

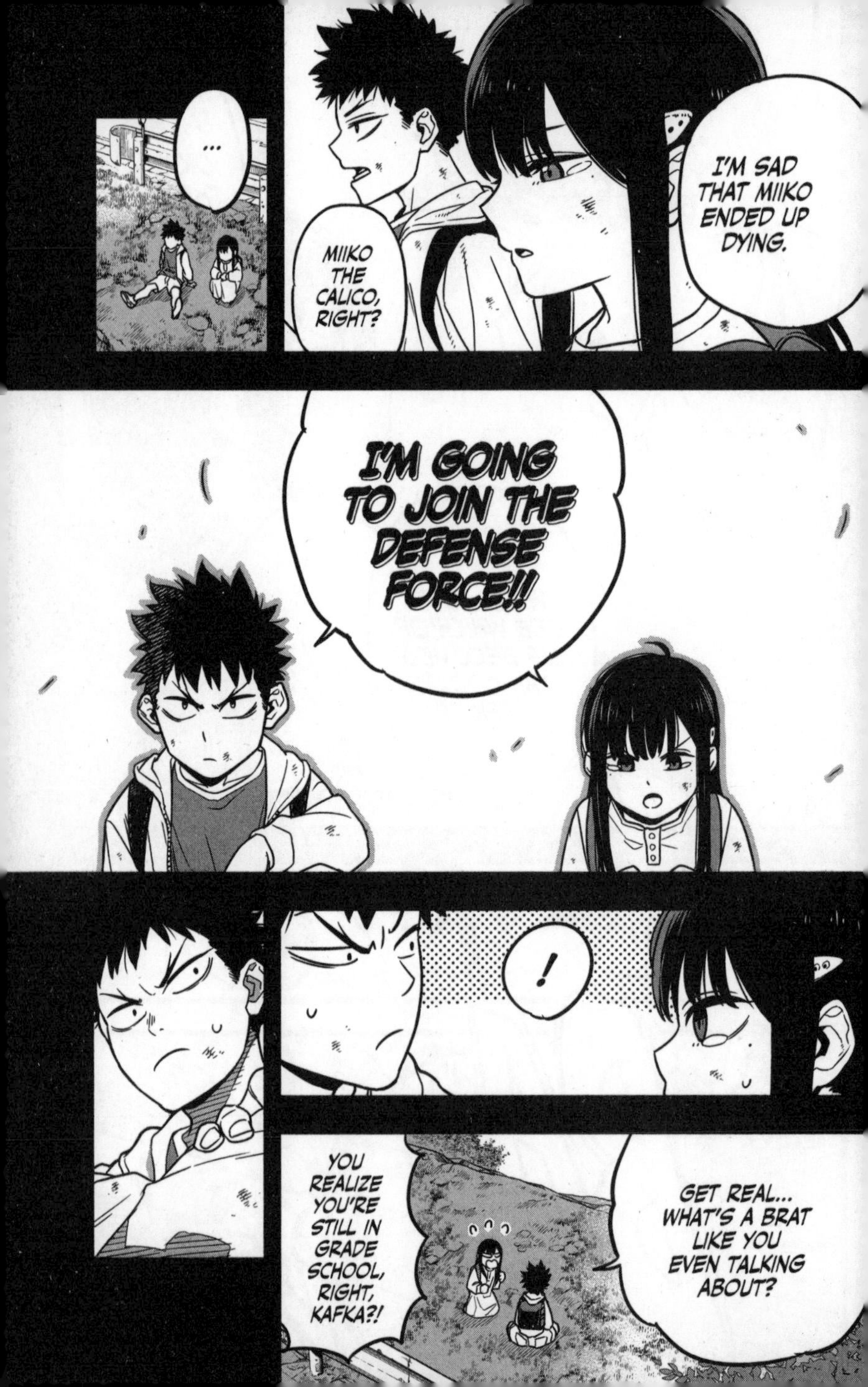
I'M SAD THAT MIIKO ENDED UP DYING.
MIIKO THE CALICO, RIGHT?
...
I'M GOING TO JOIN THE DEFENSE FORCE!!
!
GET REAL... WHAT'S A BRAT LIKE YOU EVEN TALKING ABOUT?
YOU REALIZE YOU'RE STILL IN GRADE SCHOOL, RIGHT, KAFKA?!

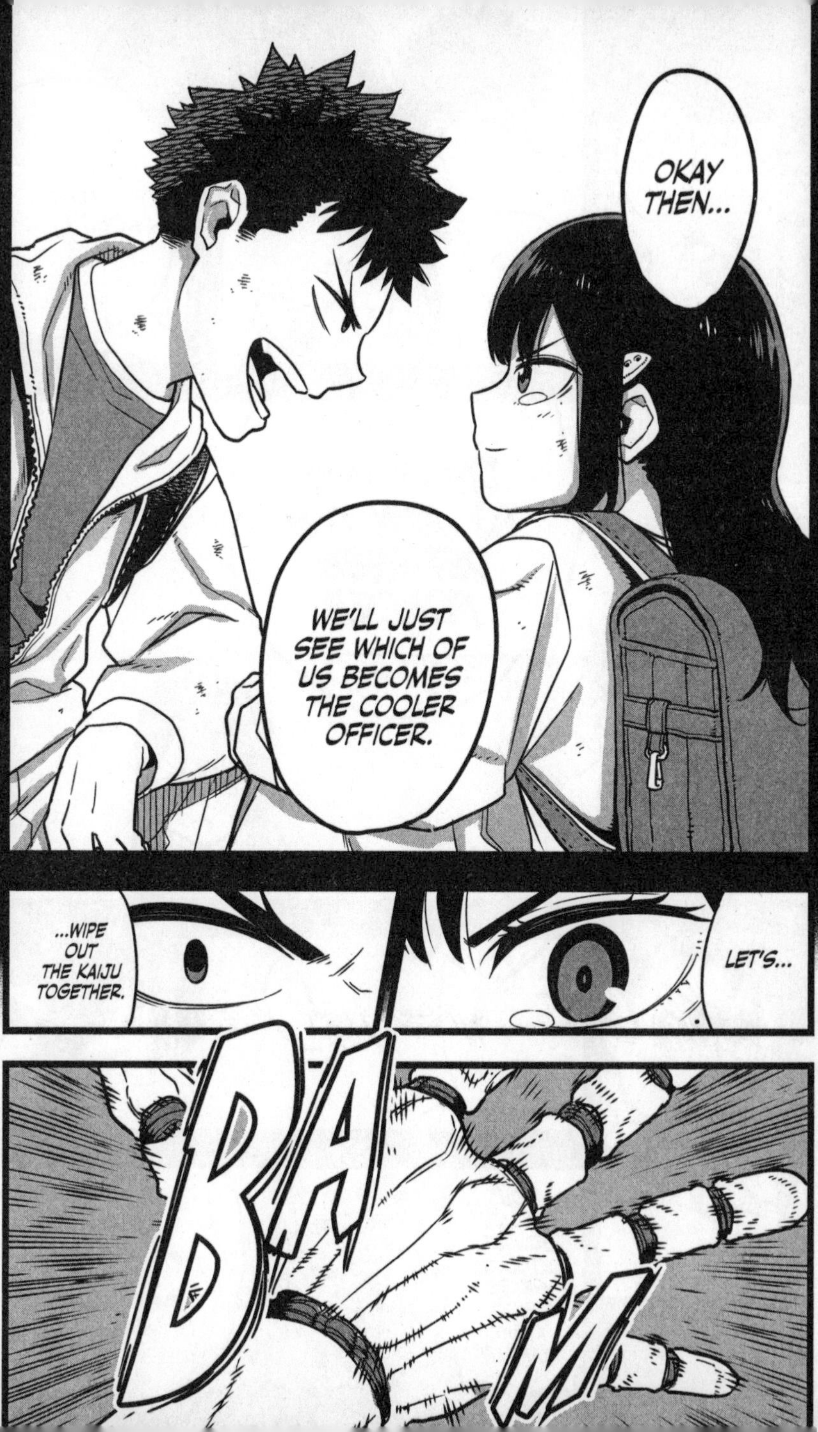
OKAY THEN...
WE'LL JUST SEE WHICH OF US BECOMES THE COOLER OFFICER.
LET'S...
...WIPE OUT THE KAIJU TOGETHER.
BAM

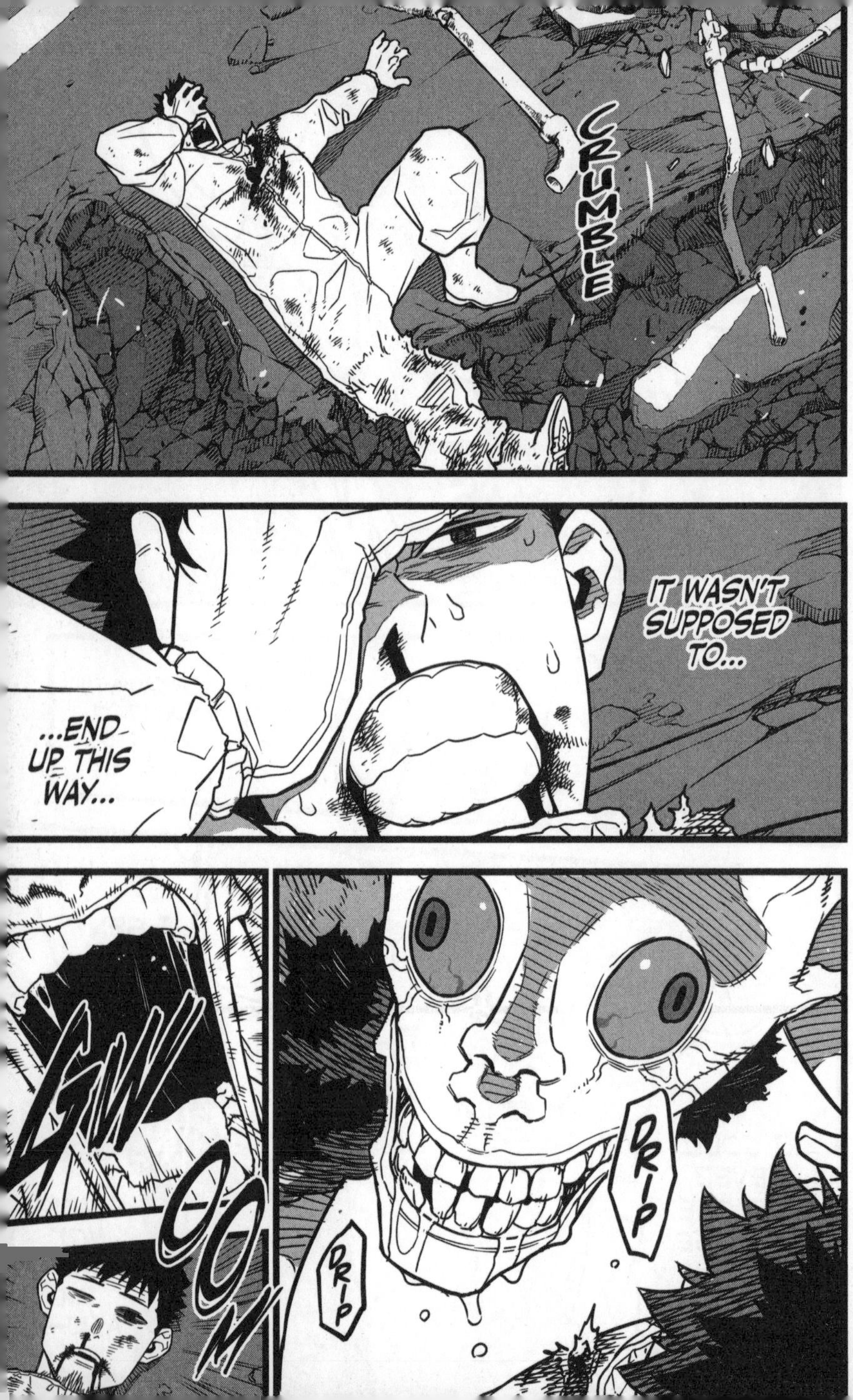
CRUMBLE
IT WASN'T SUPPOSED TO...
...END UP THIS WAY...
DRIP
DRIP
GWOOOM

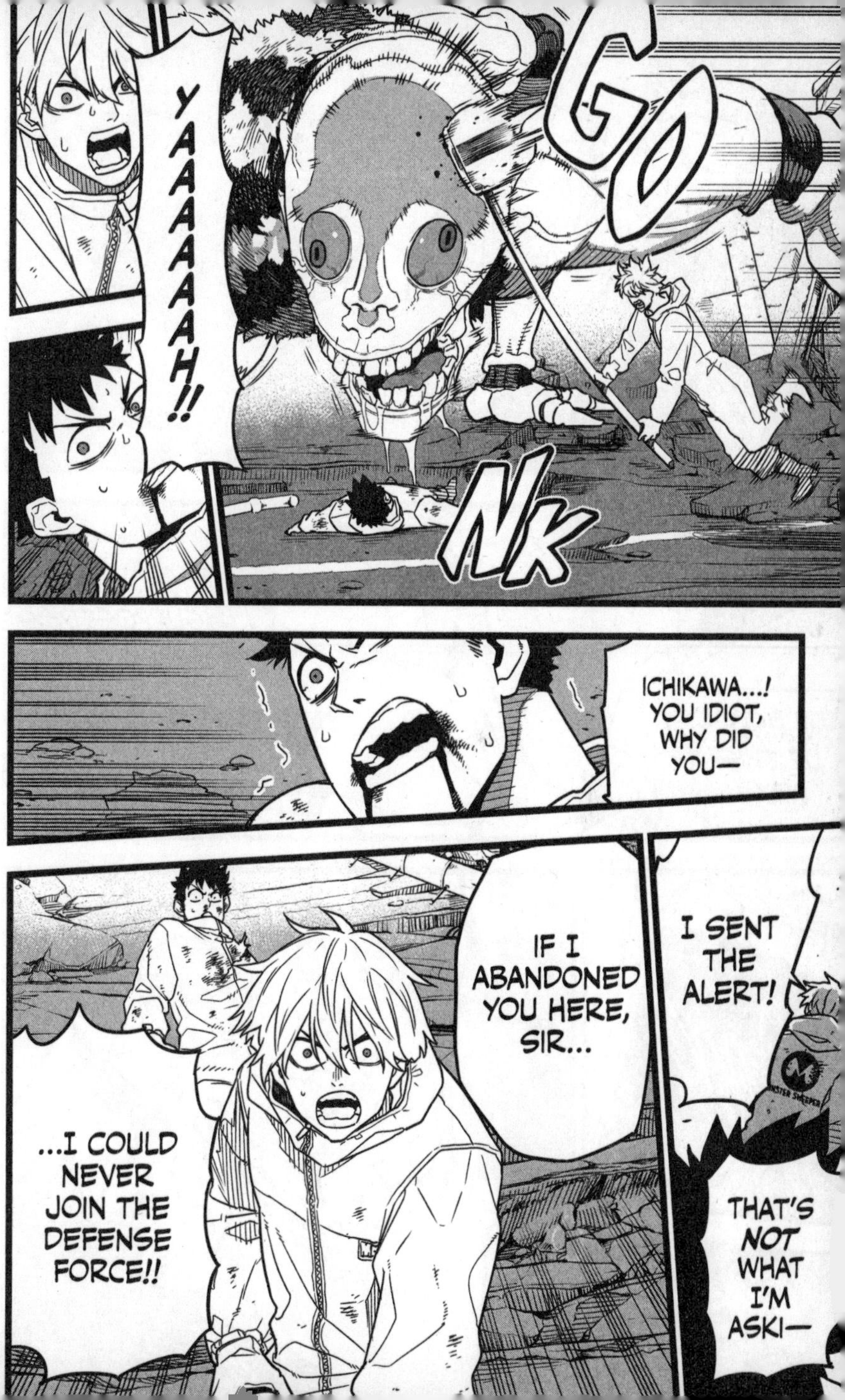
GO
Nk
YAAAAAAAH!!
ICHIKAWA...! YOU IDIOT, WHY DID YOU—
I SENT THE ALERT!
THAT'S *NOT* WHAT I'M ASKI—
IF I ABANDONED YOU HERE, SIR...
...I COULD NEVER JOIN THE DEFENSE FORCE!!

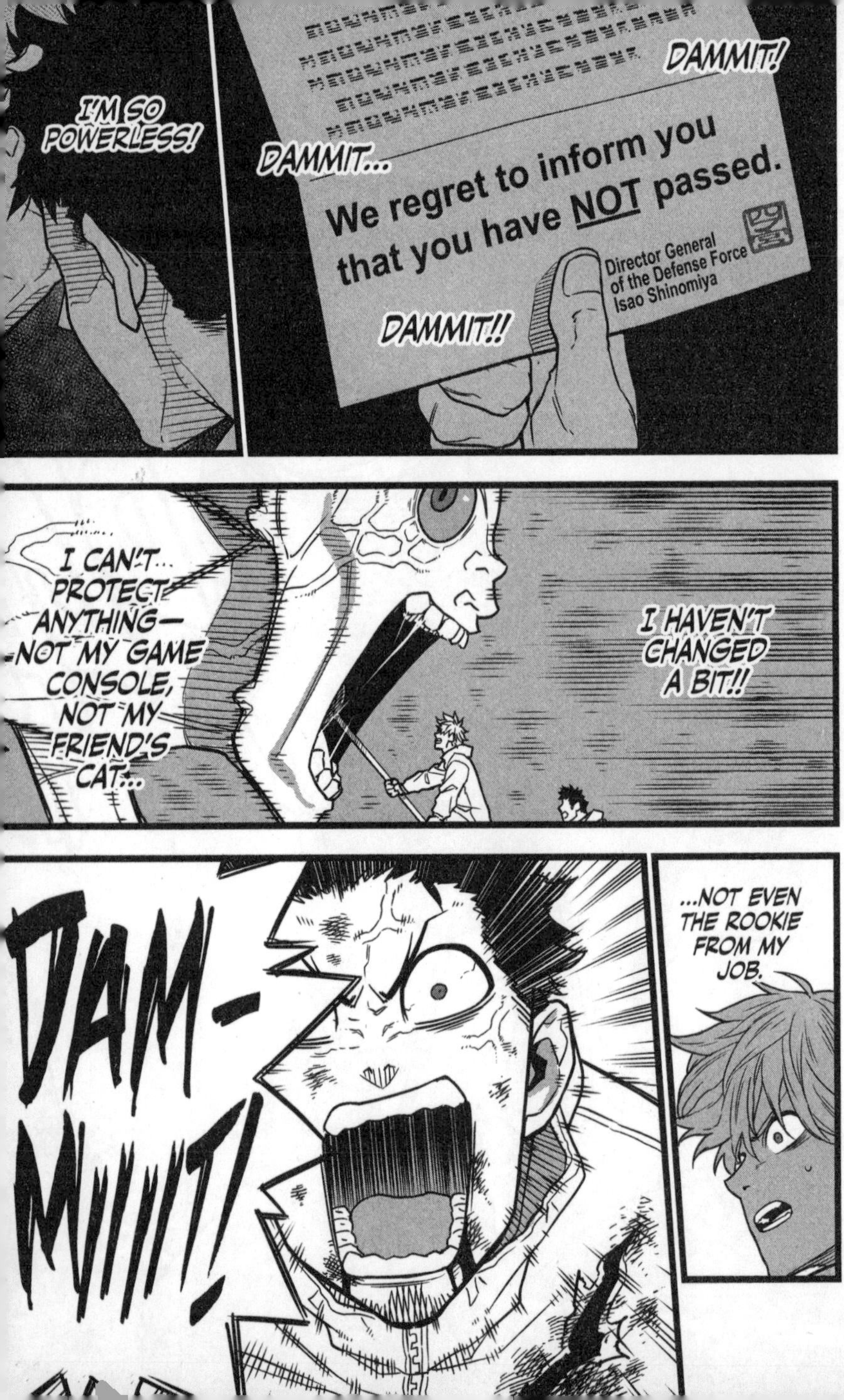
DAMMIT!
DAMMIT...
We regret to inform you that you have NOT passed.
Director General of the Defense Force Isao Shinomiya
DAMMIT!!
I'M SO POWERLESS!
I HAVEN'T CHANGED A BIT!!
I CAN'T... PROTECT ANYTHING— NOT MY GAME CONSOLE, NOT MY FRIEND'S CAT...
...NOT EVEN THE ROOKIE FROM MY JOB.
DAM-MIIIT!

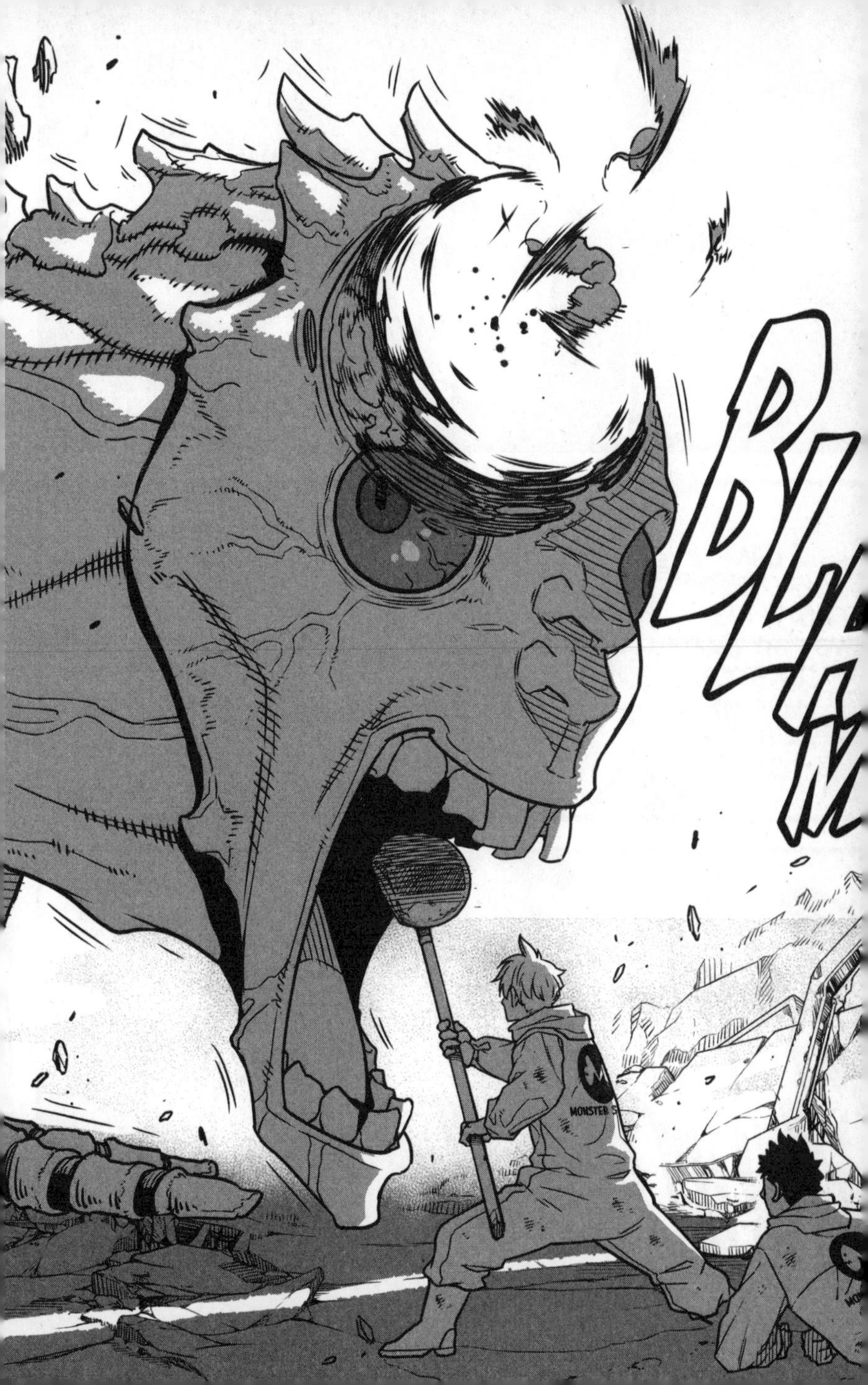
BLAM

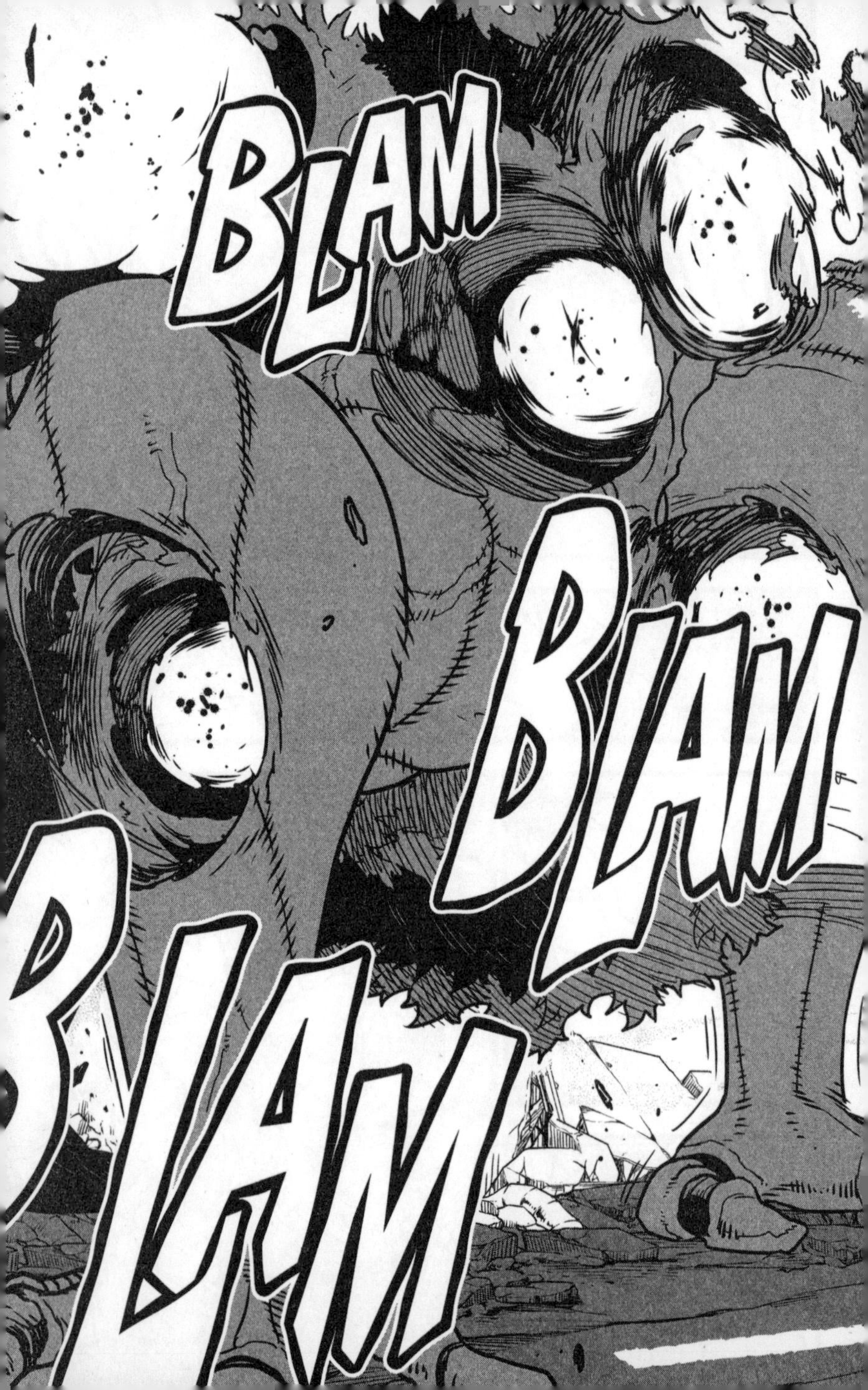
BLAM
BLAM
BLAM

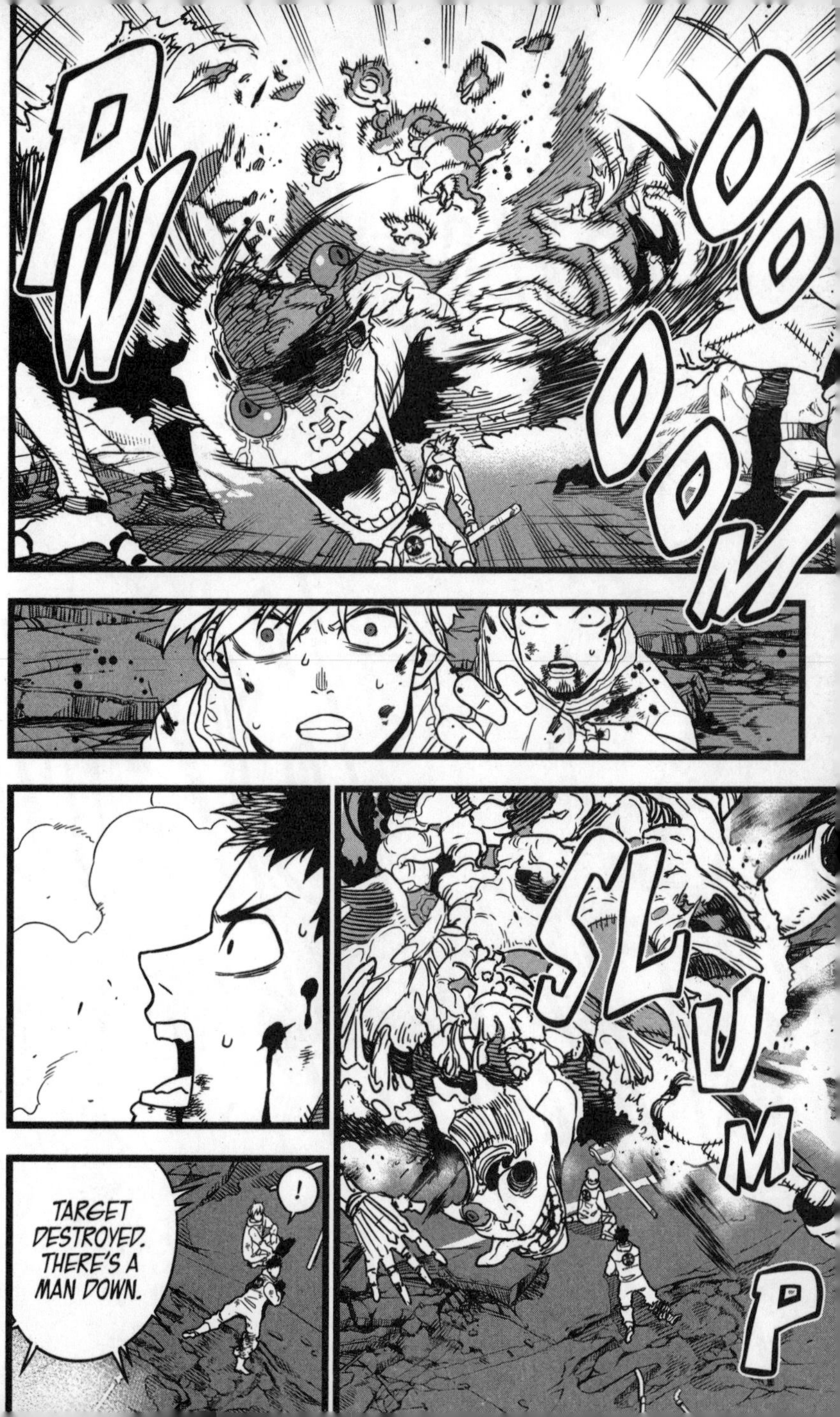
DOOOM
POW
SLUMP
!
TARGET DESTROYED. THERE'S A MAN DOWN.

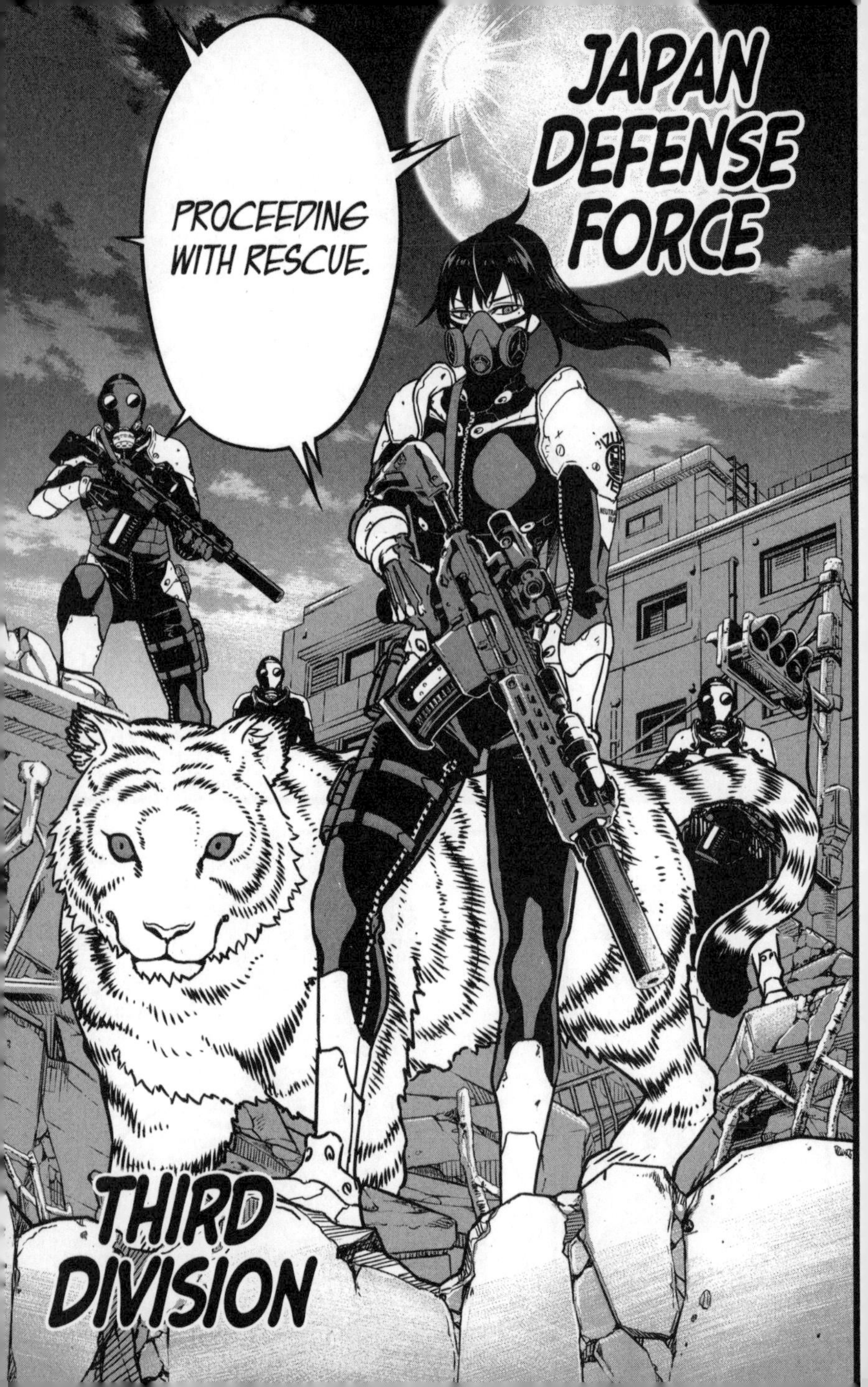
JAPAN DEFENSE FORCE
PROCEEDING WITH RESCUE.
THIRD DIVISION

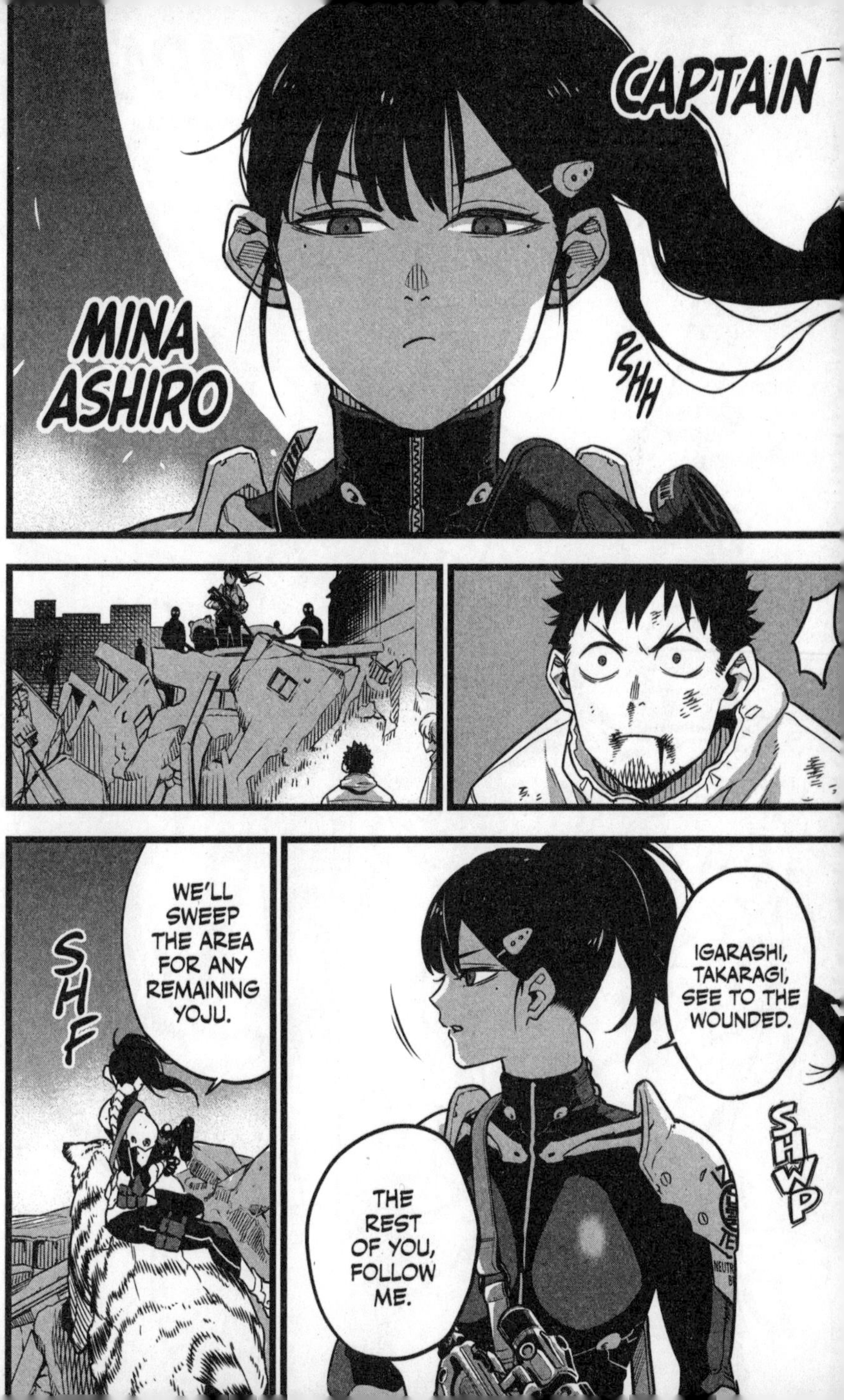
CAPTAIN
MINA ASHIRO
PSHH
!
IGARASHI, TAKARAGI, SEE TO THE WOUNDED.
SHWP
THE REST OF YOU, FOLLOW ME.
WE'LL SWEEP THE AREA FOR ANY REMAINING YOJU.
SHF

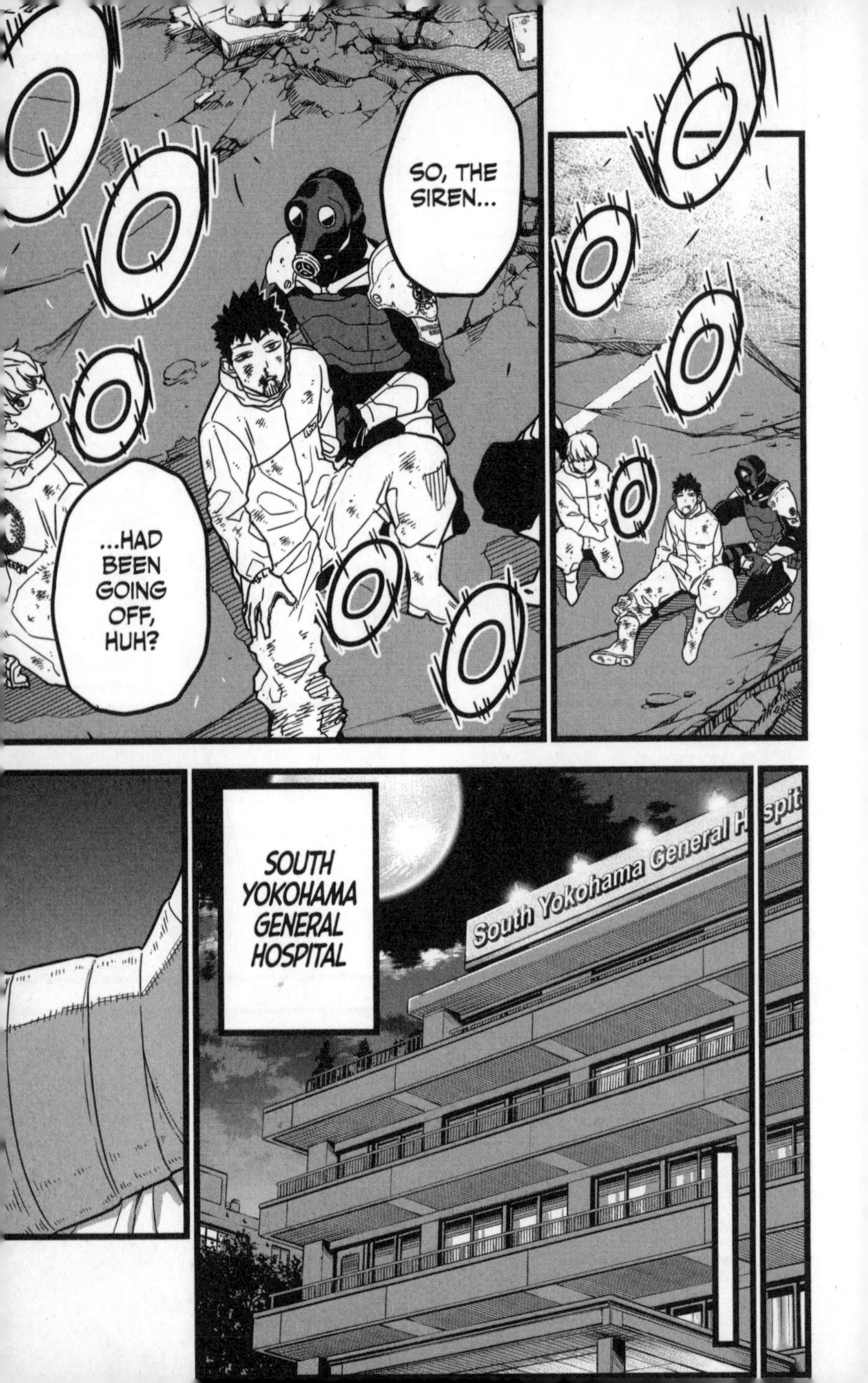
SO, THE SIREN...
...HAD BEEN GOING OFF, HUH?
SOUTH YOKOHAMA GENERAL HOSPITAL
South Yokohama General H spit

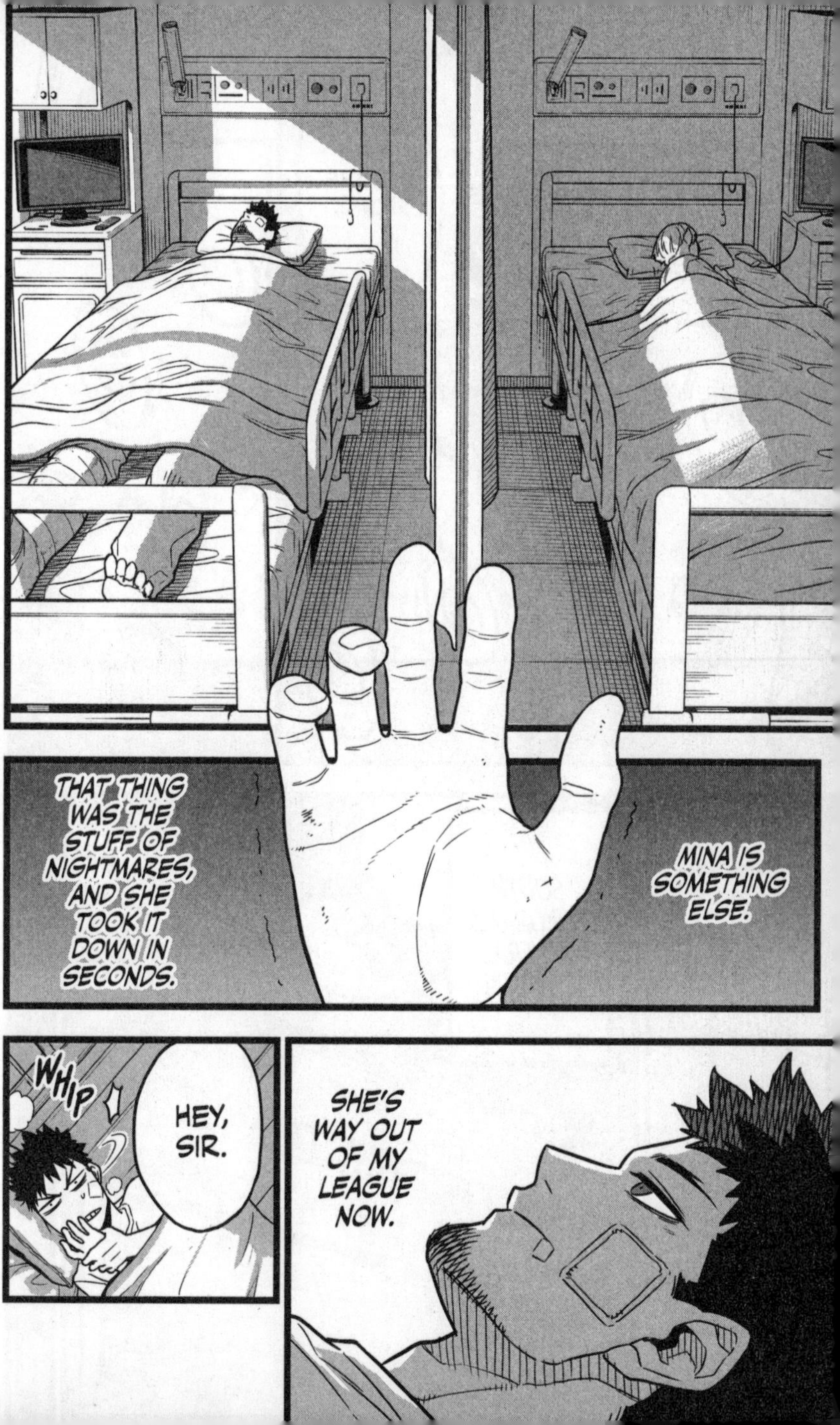
MINA IS SOMETHING ELSE.
THAT THING WAS THE STUFF OF NIGHTMARES, AND SHE TOOK IT DOWN IN SECONDS.
SHE'S WAY OUT OF MY LEAGUE NOW.
HEY, SIR.
WHIP

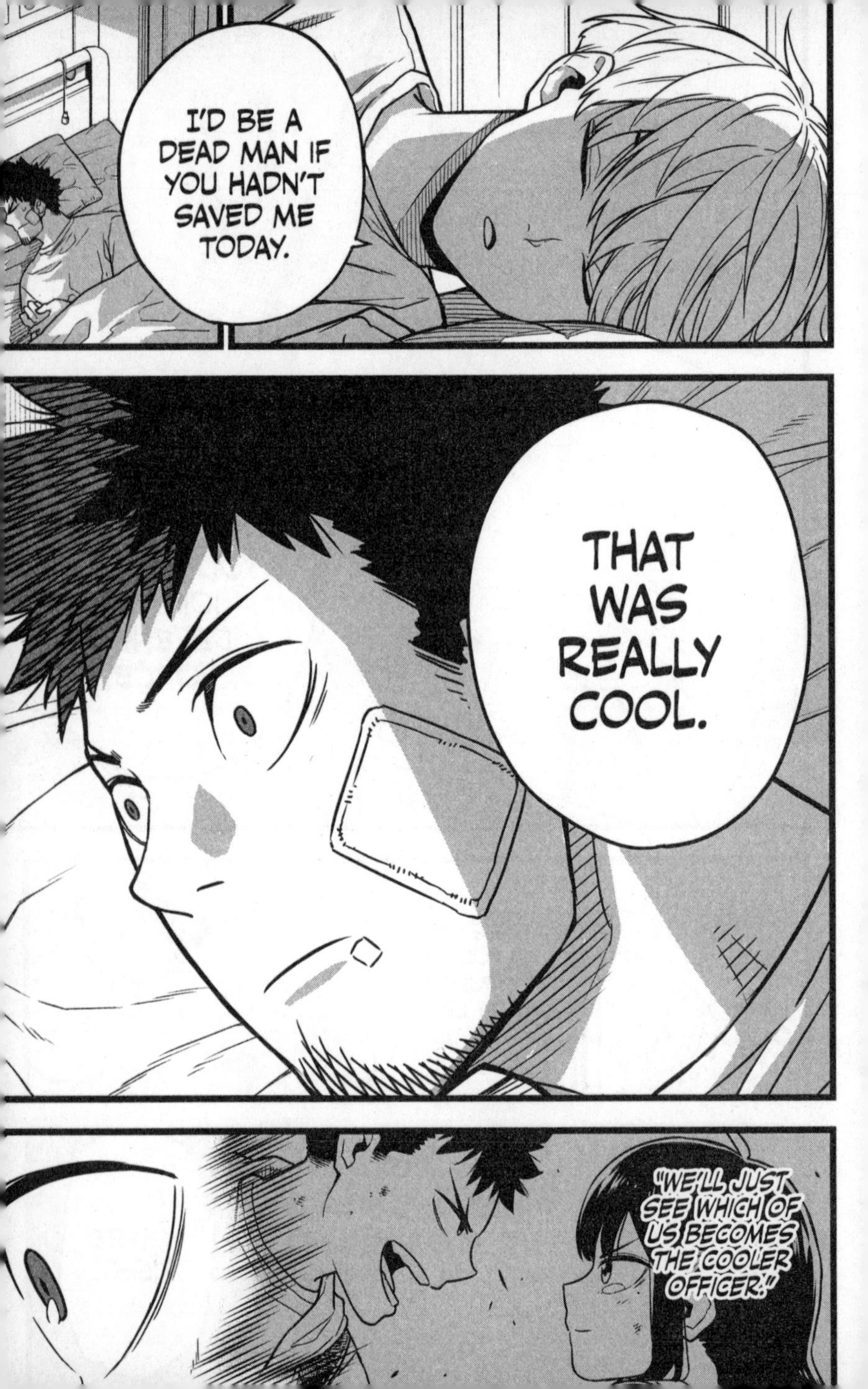
I'D BE A DEAD MAN IF YOU HADN'T SAVED ME TODAY.
THAT WAS REALLY COOL.
"WE'LL JUST SEE WHICH OF US BECOMES THE COOLER OFFICER."

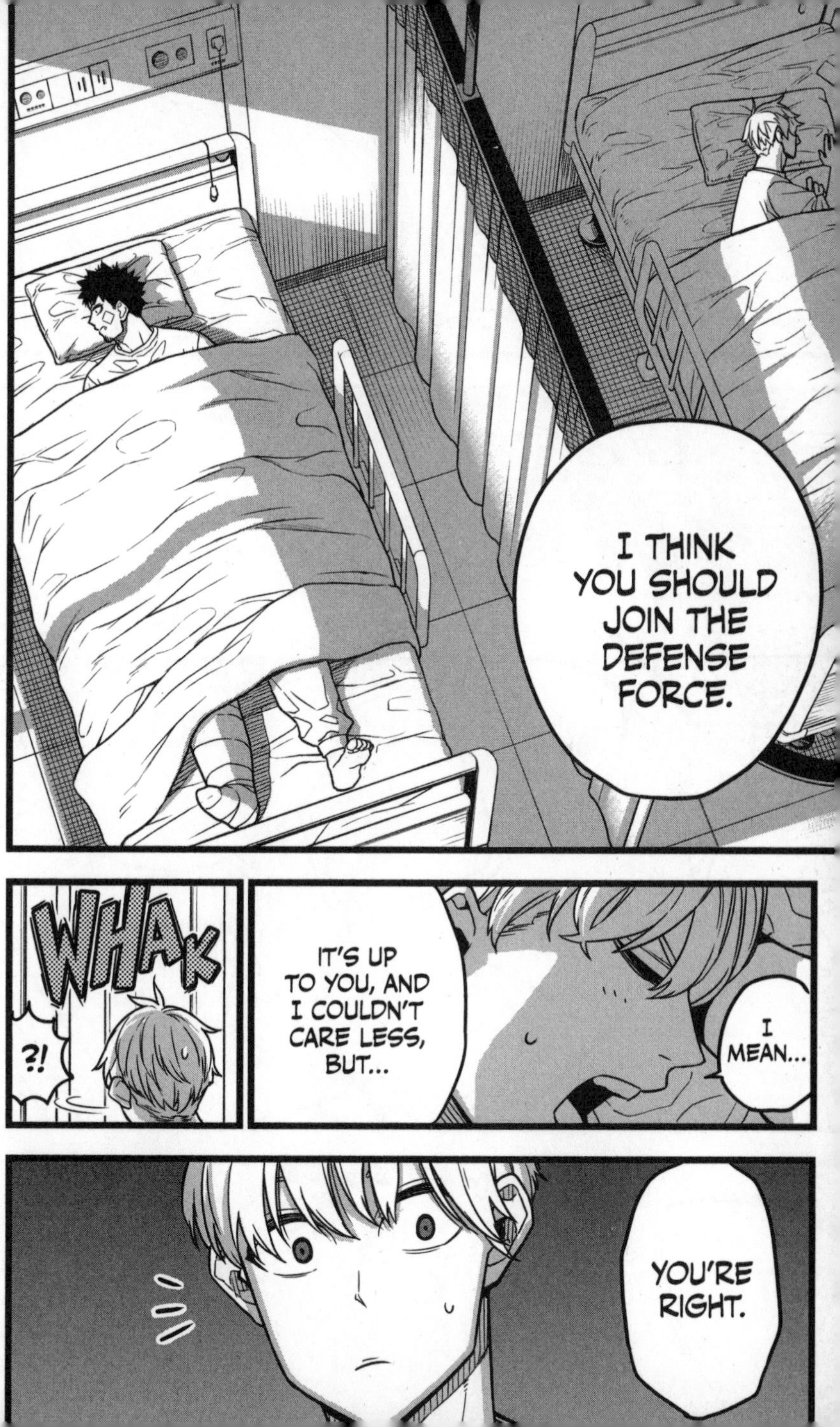
I THINK YOU SHOULD JOIN THE DEFENSE FORCE.
I MEAN...
IT'S UP TO YOU, AND I COULDN'T CARE LESS, BUT...
WHAK
?!
YOU'RE RIGHT.

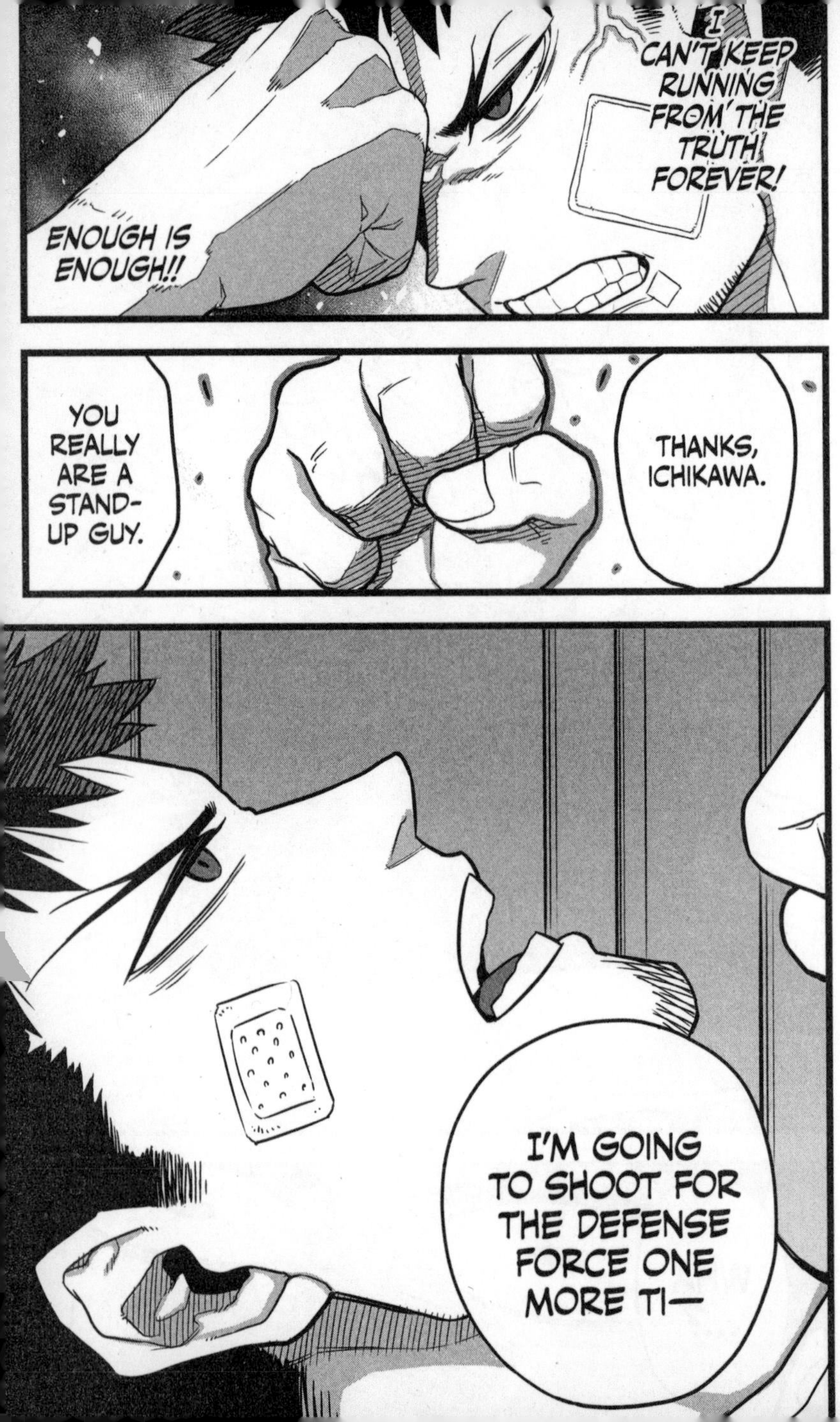
I CAN'T KEEP RUNNING FROM THE TRUTH FOREVER!
ENOUGH IS ENOUGH!!
THANKS, ICHIKAWA.
YOU REALLY ARE A STAND-UP GUY.
I'M GOING TO SHOOT FOR THE DEFENSE FORCE ONE MORE TI—

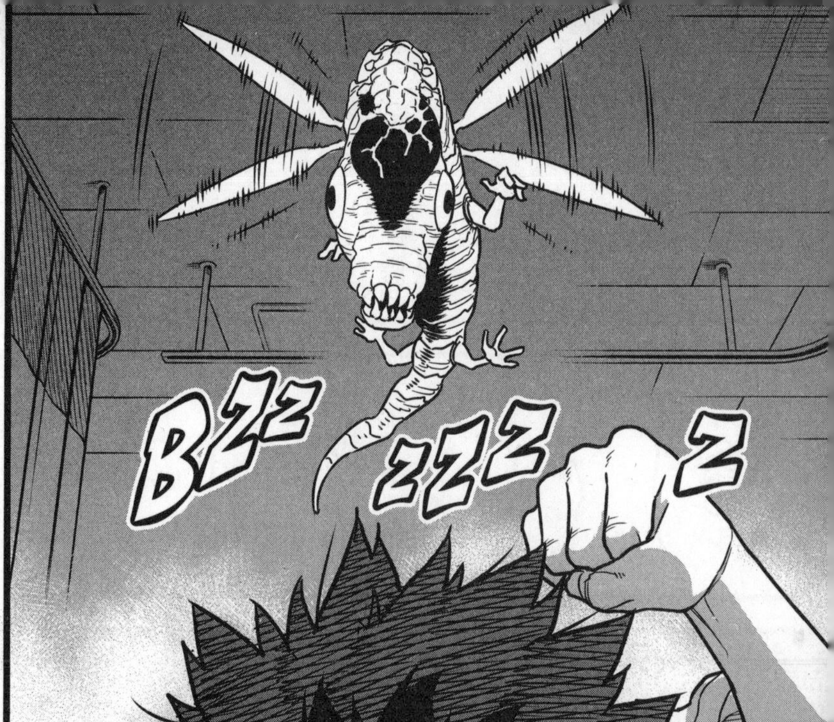
BZZ
ZZZ
Z
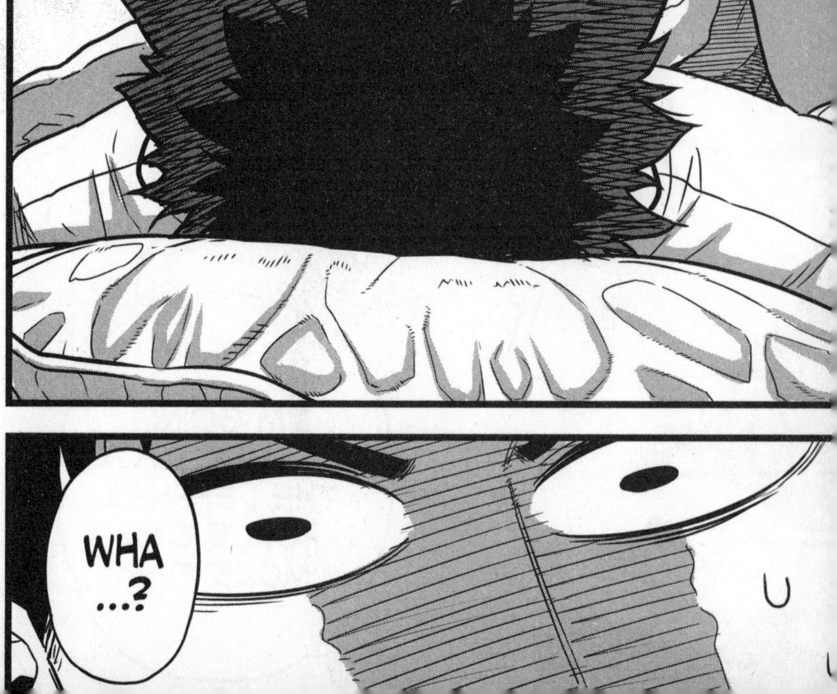
WHA ...?
U

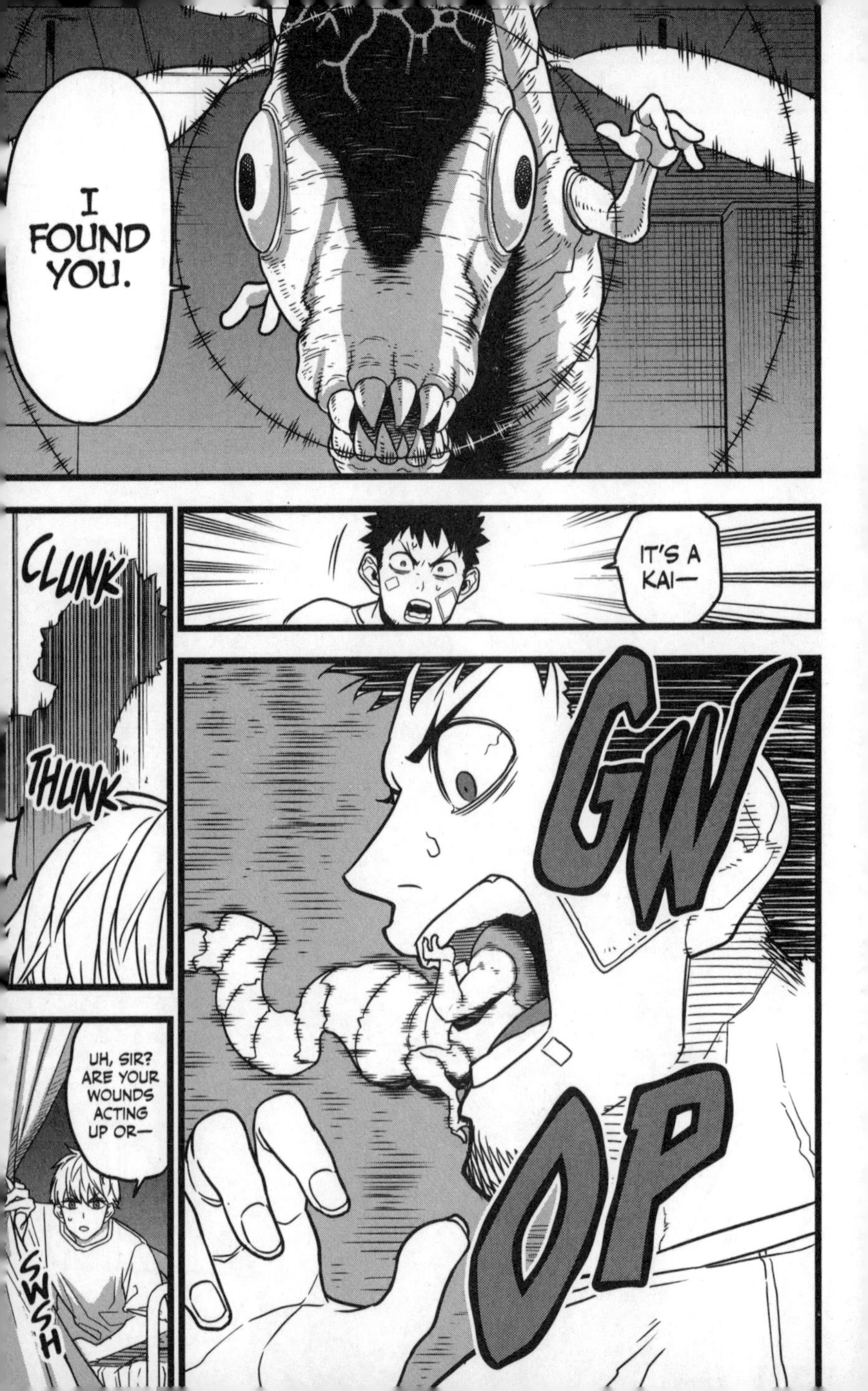
I FOUND YOU.
IT'S A KAI—
GWOOP
CLUNK
THUNK
UH, SIR? ARE YOUR WOUNDS ACTING UP OR—
SWSH

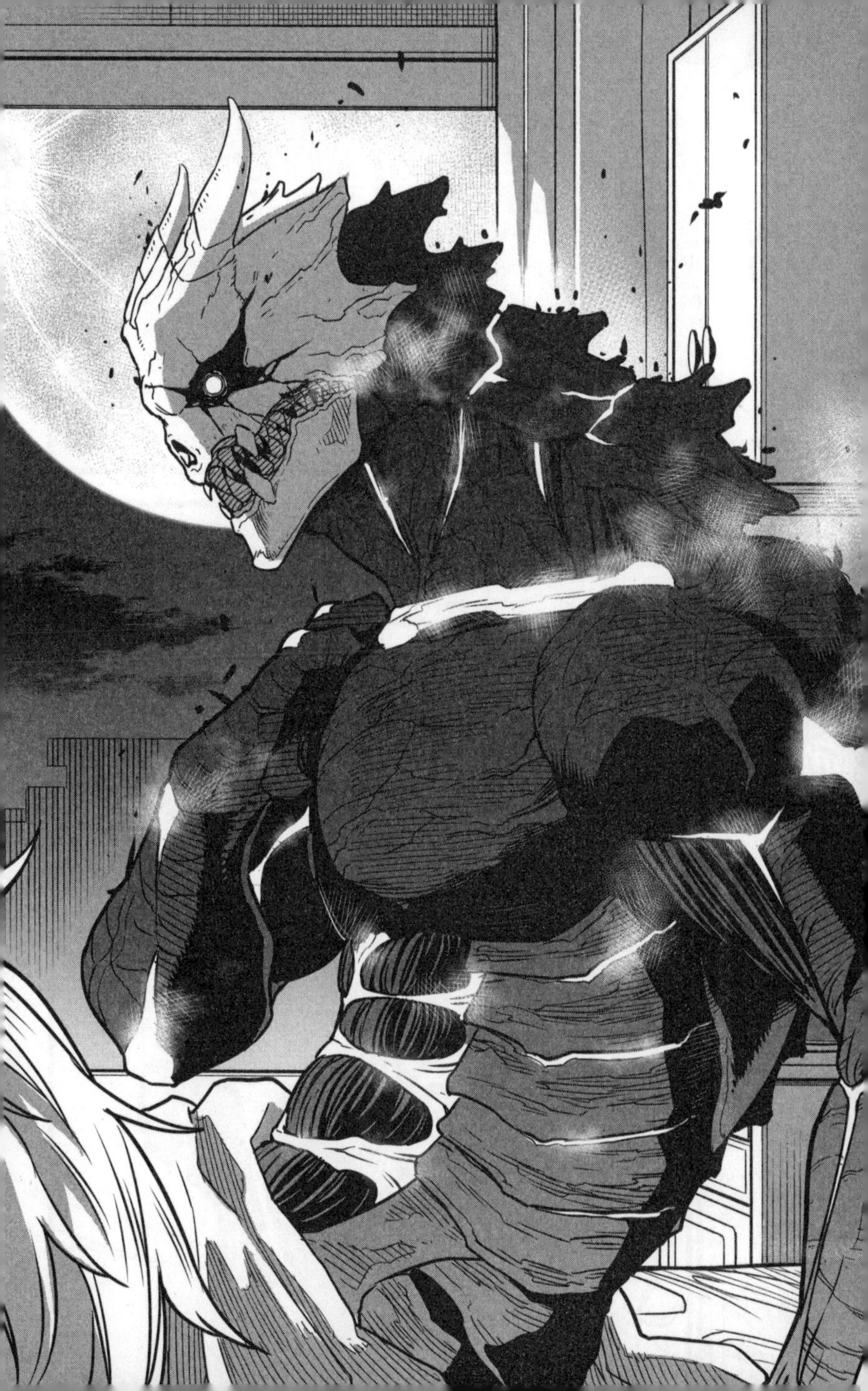

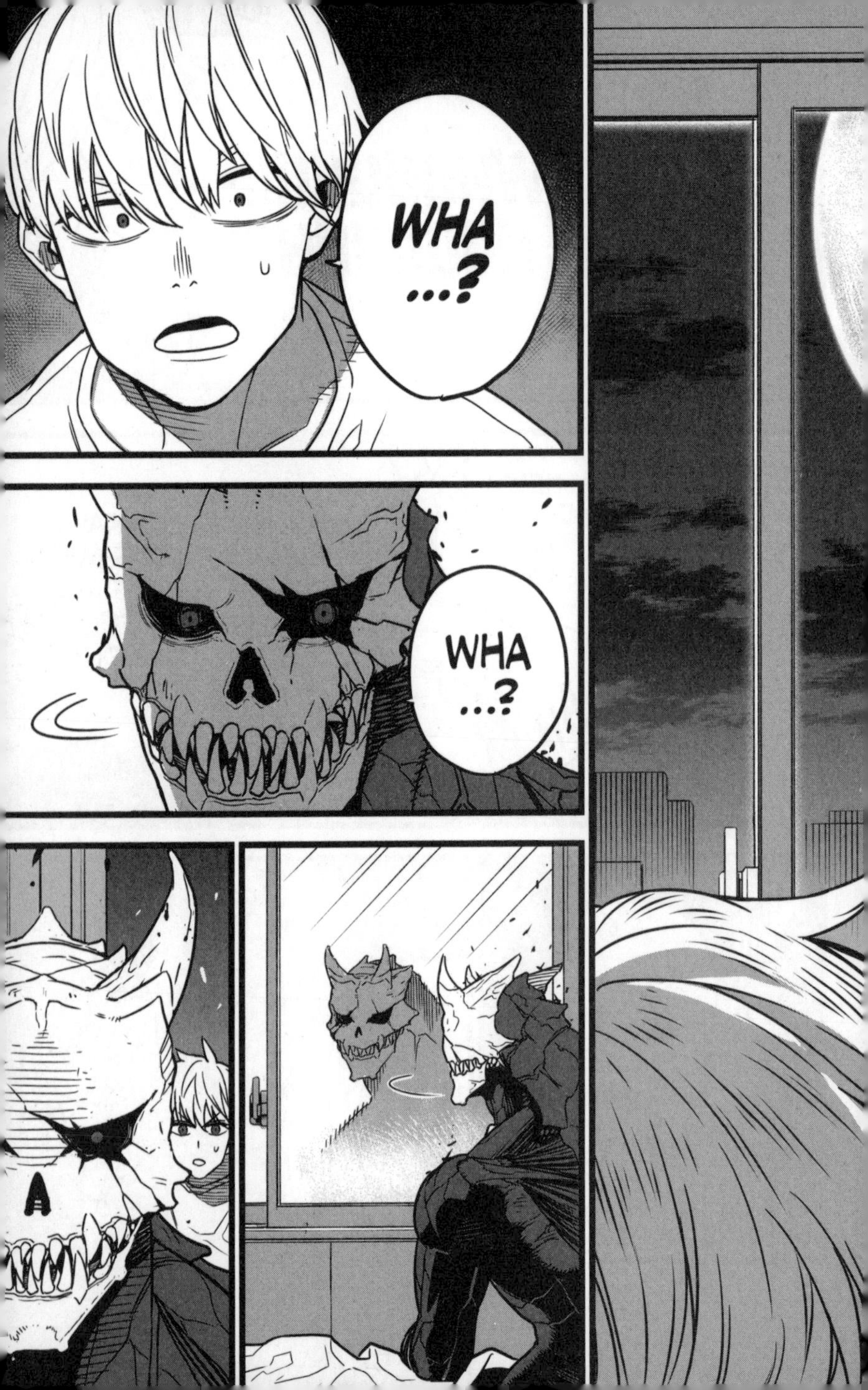
WHA ...?
WHA ...?

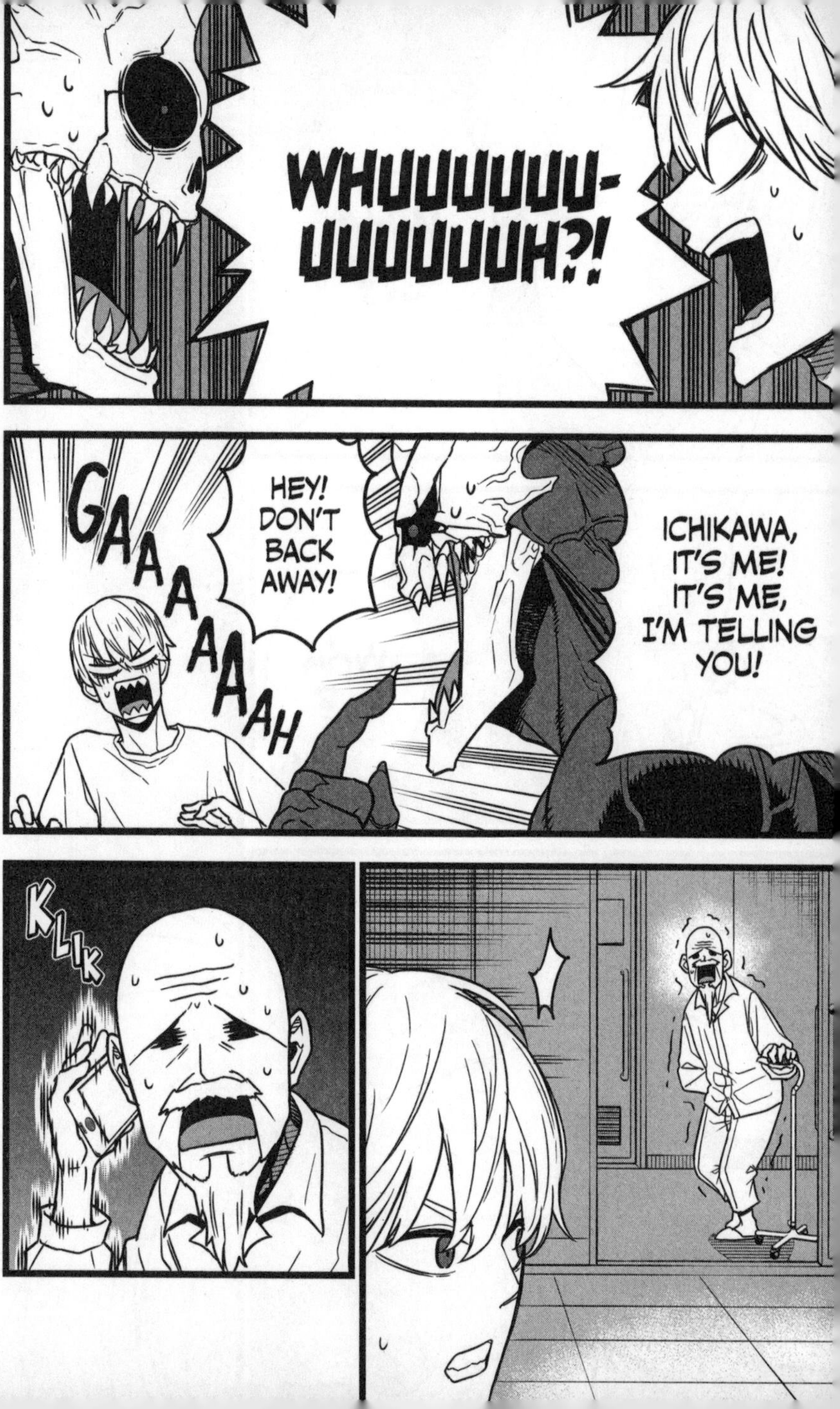
WHUUUUUUU-
UUUUUUUUH?!
ICHIKAWA, IT'S ME! IT'S ME, I'M TELLING YOU!
HEY! DON'T BACK AWAY!
GAAAAAAH
KLIK

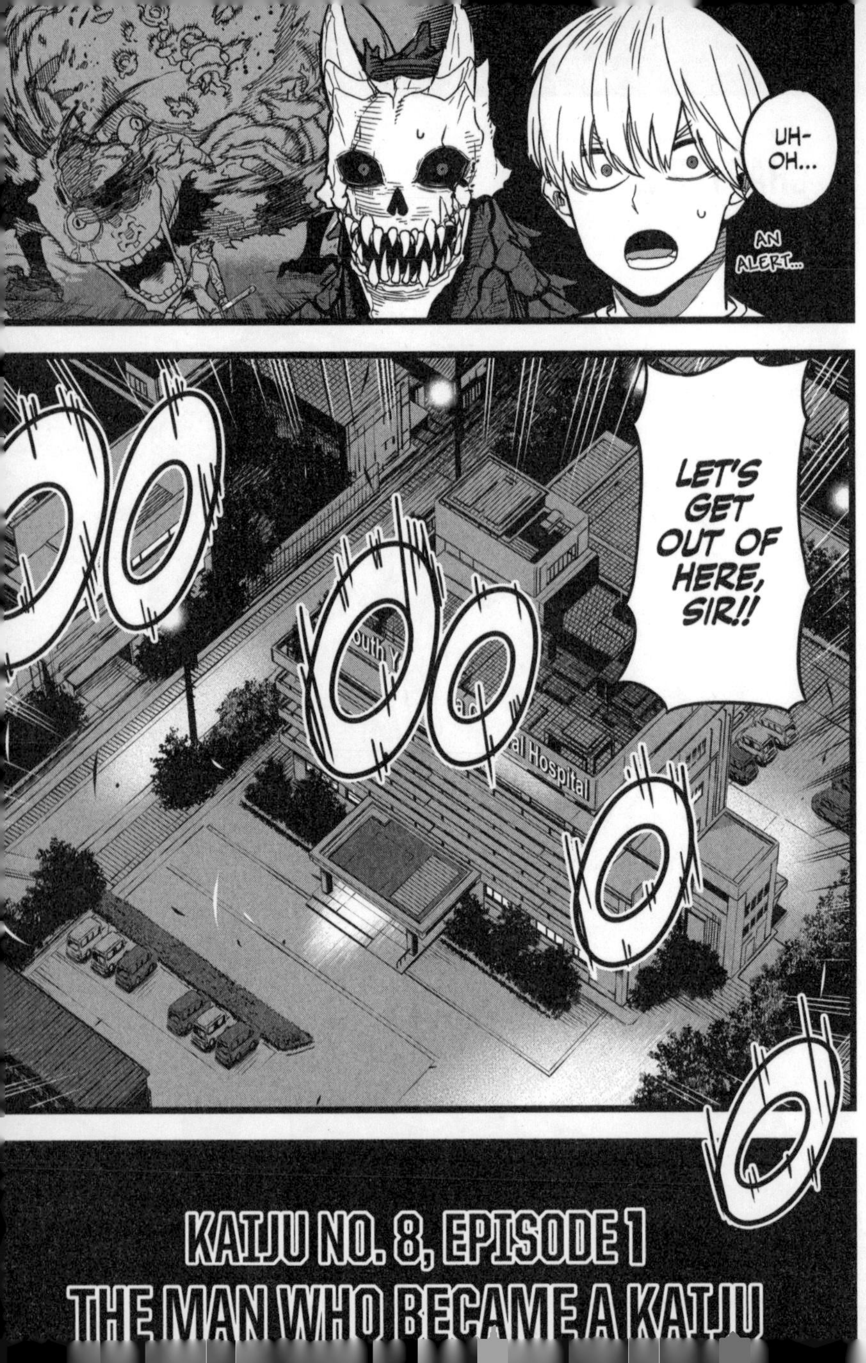
UH-OH...
AN ALERT...
LET'S GET OUT OF HERE, SIR!!
KAIJU NO. 8, EPISODE 1
THE MAN WHO BECAME A KAIJU

# CHAPTER 2

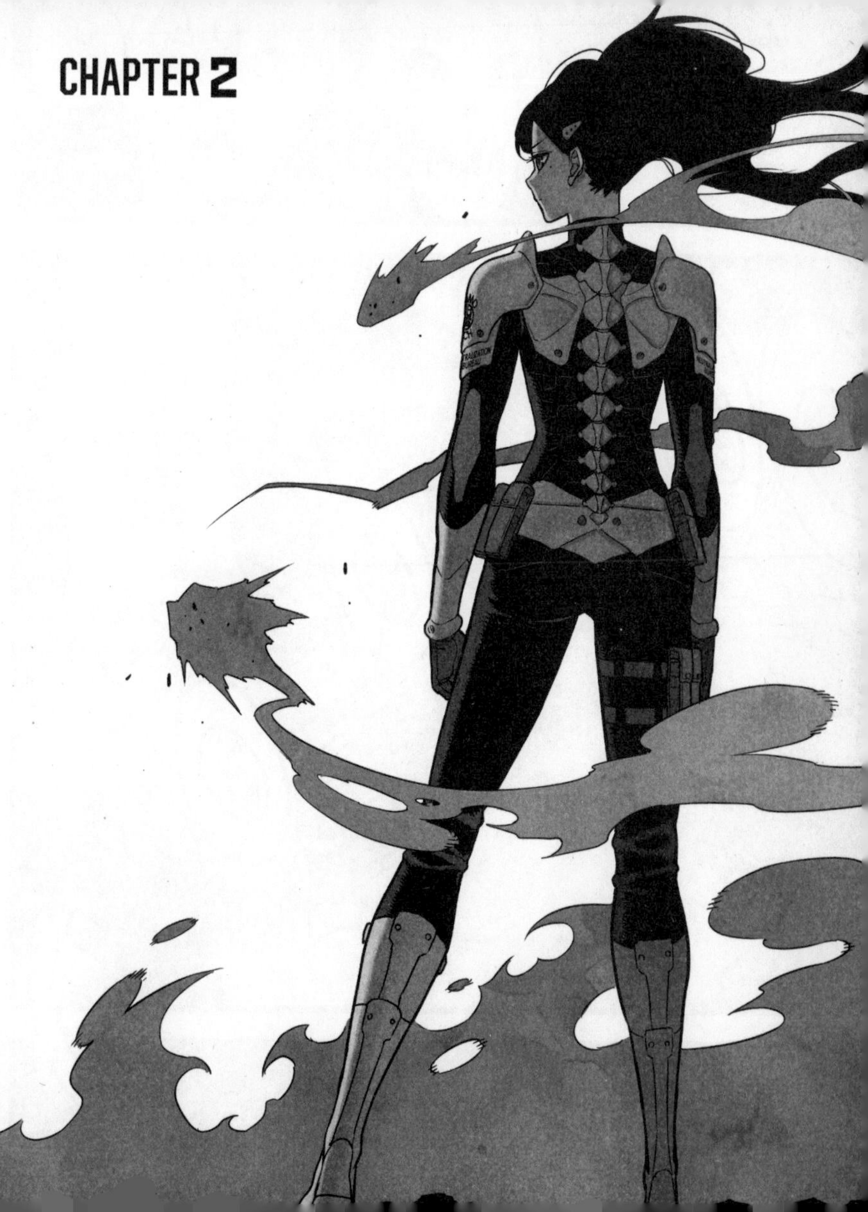

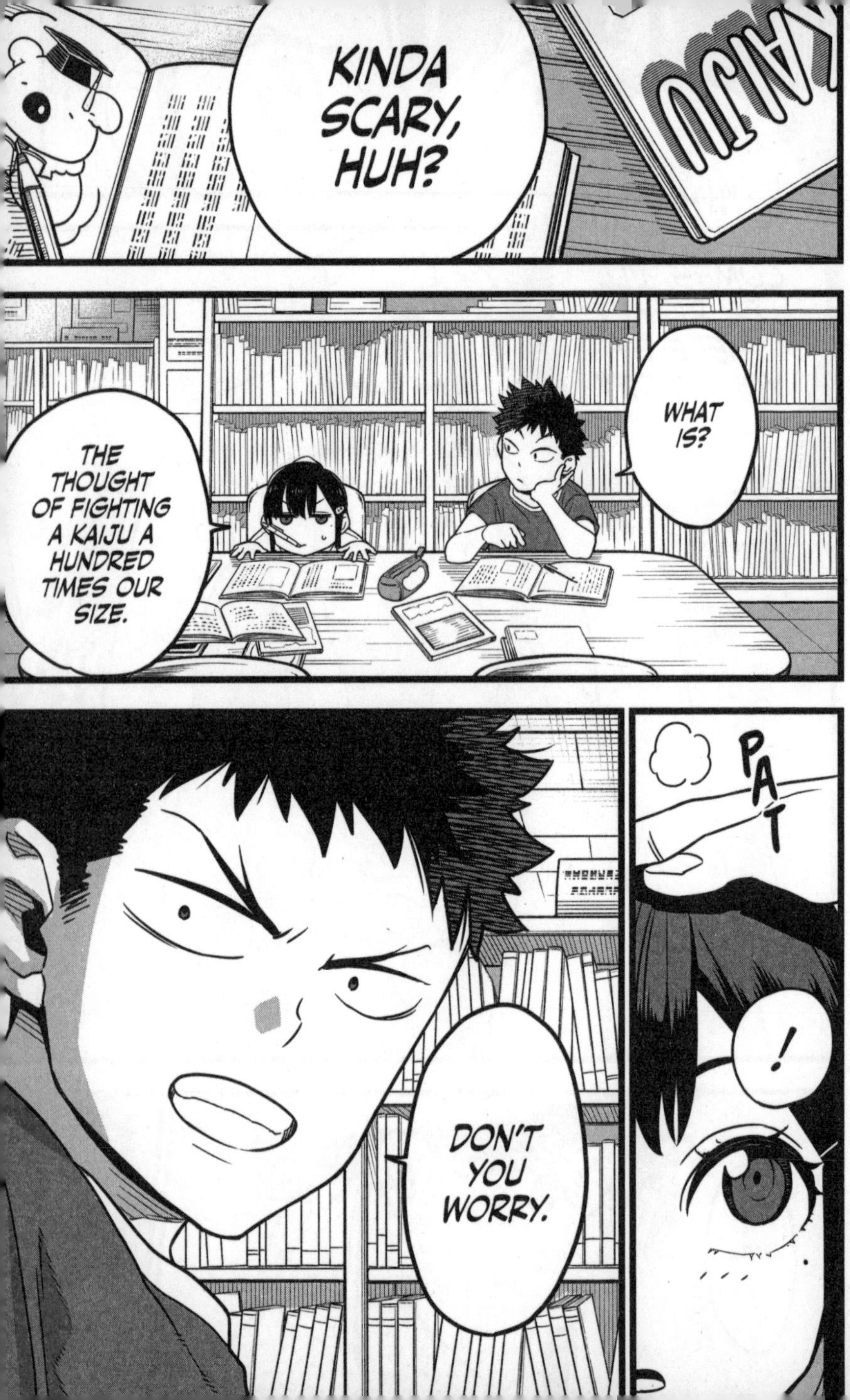
KAIJU
KINDA SCARY, HUH?
WHAT IS?
THE THOUGHT OF FIGHTING A KAIJU A HUNDRED TIMES OUR SIZE.
PAT
!
DON'T YOU WORRY.

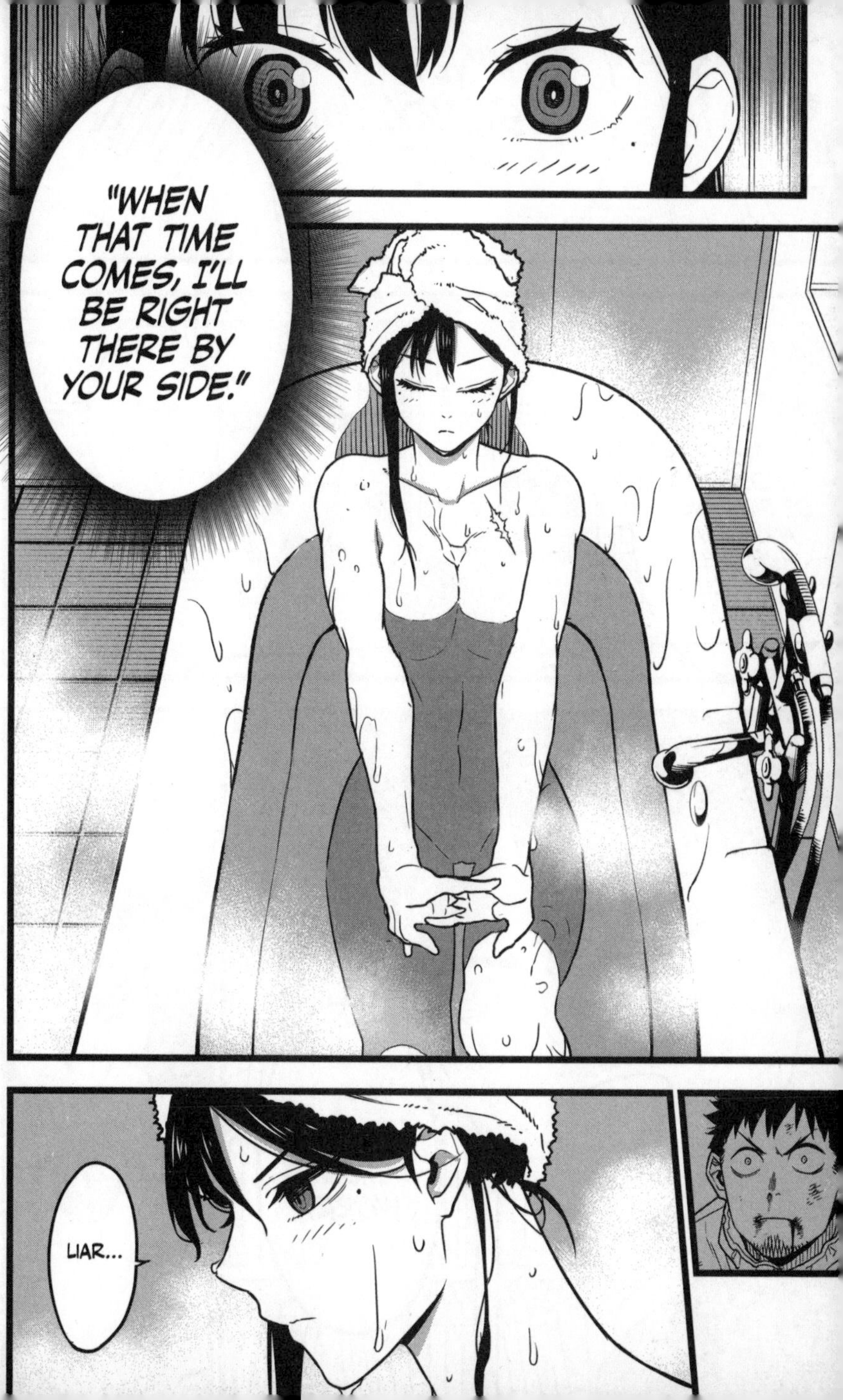
"WHEN THAT TIME COMES, I'LL BE RIGHT THERE BY YOUR SIDE."
LIAR...

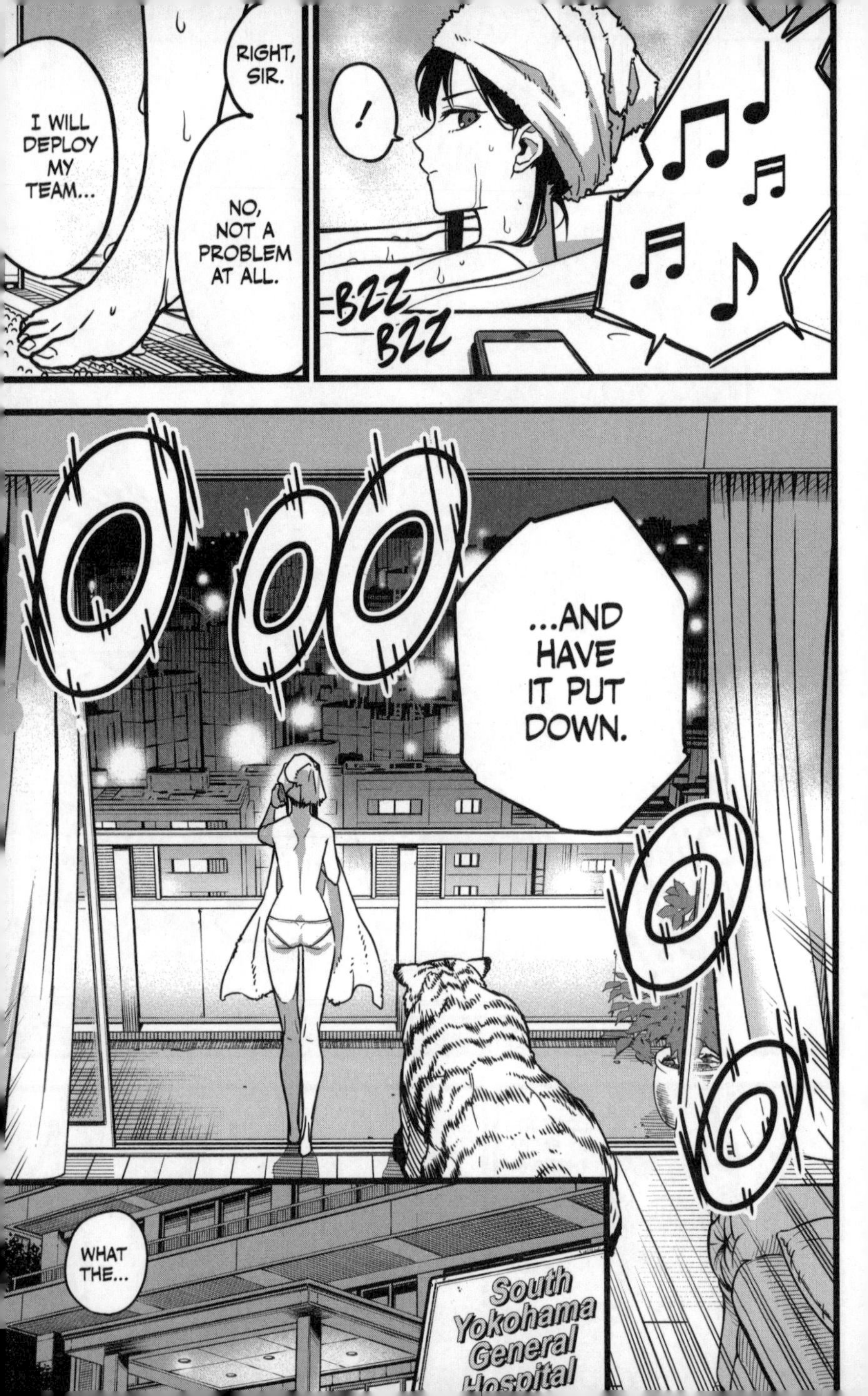
!
BZZ
BZZ
RIGHT, SIR.
NO, NOT A PROBLEM AT ALL.
I WILL DEPLOY MY TEAM...
...AND HAVE IT PUT DOWN.
WHAT THE...
South Yokohama General Hospital

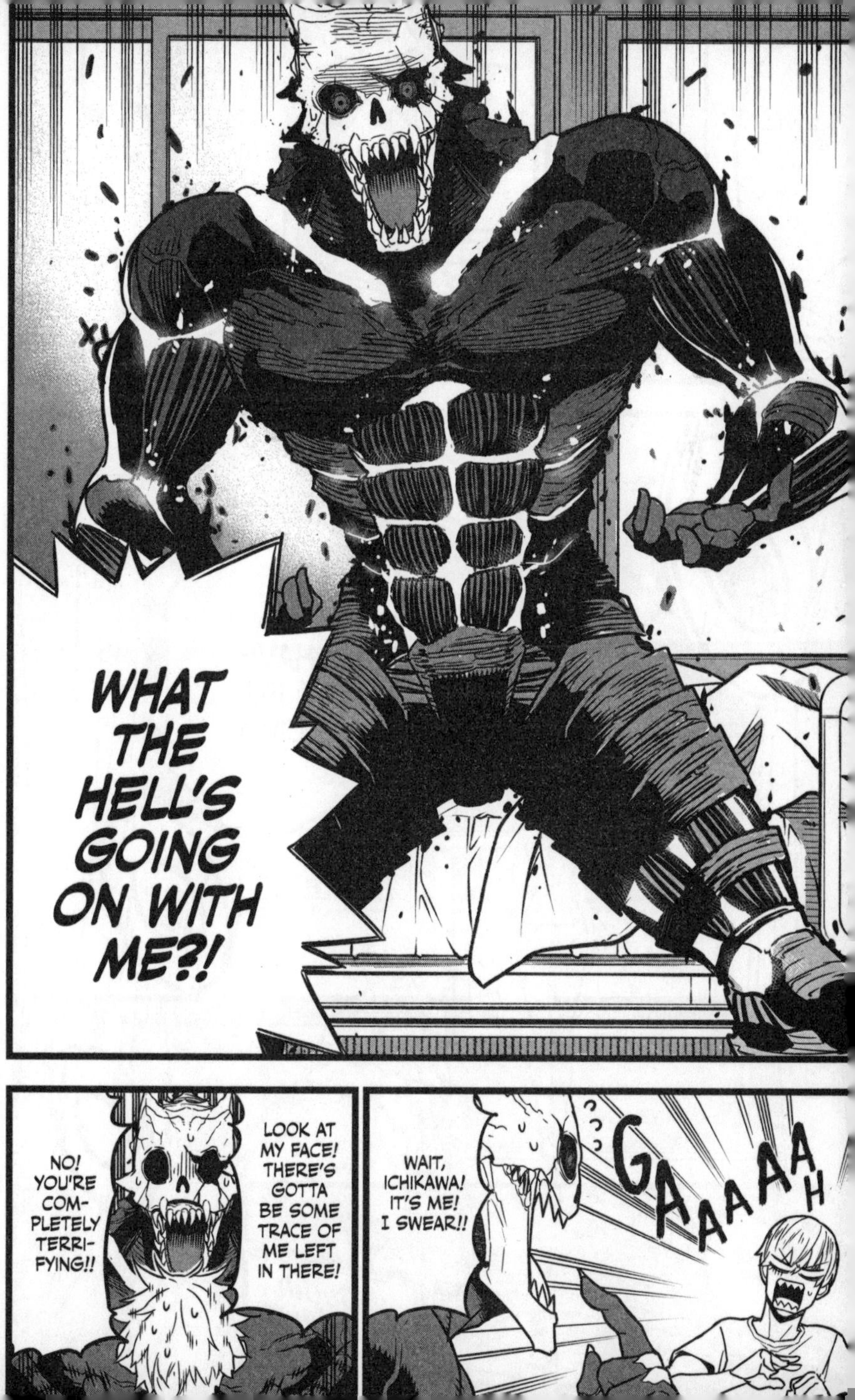
WHAT THE HELL'S GOING ON WITH ME?!
GAAAAAAH
WAIT, ICHIKAWA! IT'S ME! I SWEAR!!
LOOK AT MY FACE! THERE'S GOTTA BE SOME TRACE OF ME LEFT IN THERE!
NO! YOU'RE COM-PLETELY TERRI-FYING!!

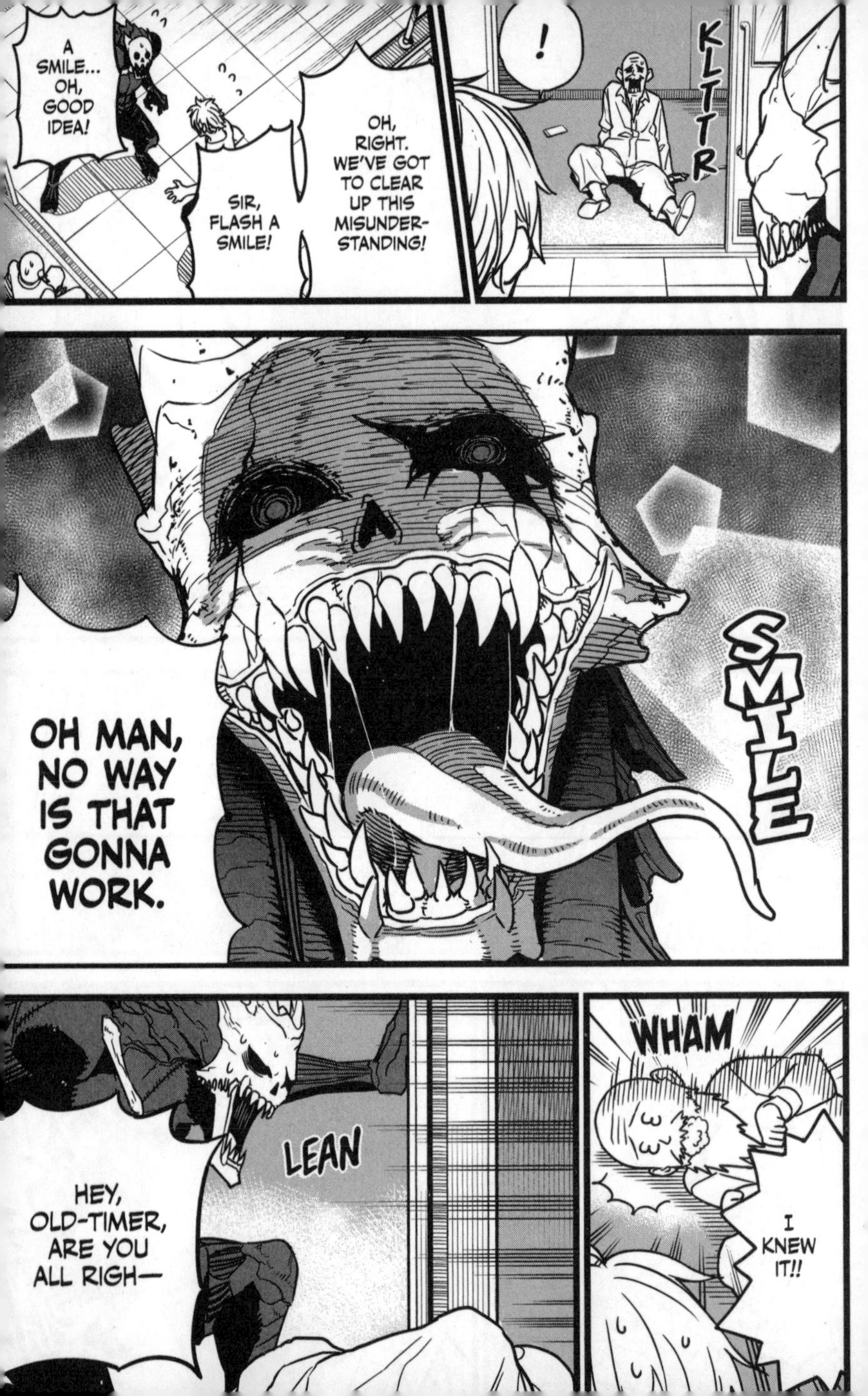
!
KLTTTR
OH, RIGHT. WE'VE GOT TO CLEAR UP THIS MISUNDER-STANDING!
SIR, FLASH A SMILE!
A SMILE... OH, GOOD IDEA!
SMILE
OH MAN, NO WAY IS THAT GONNA WORK.
WHAM
I KNEW IT!!
LEAN
HEY, OLD-TIMER, ARE YOU ALL RIGH—

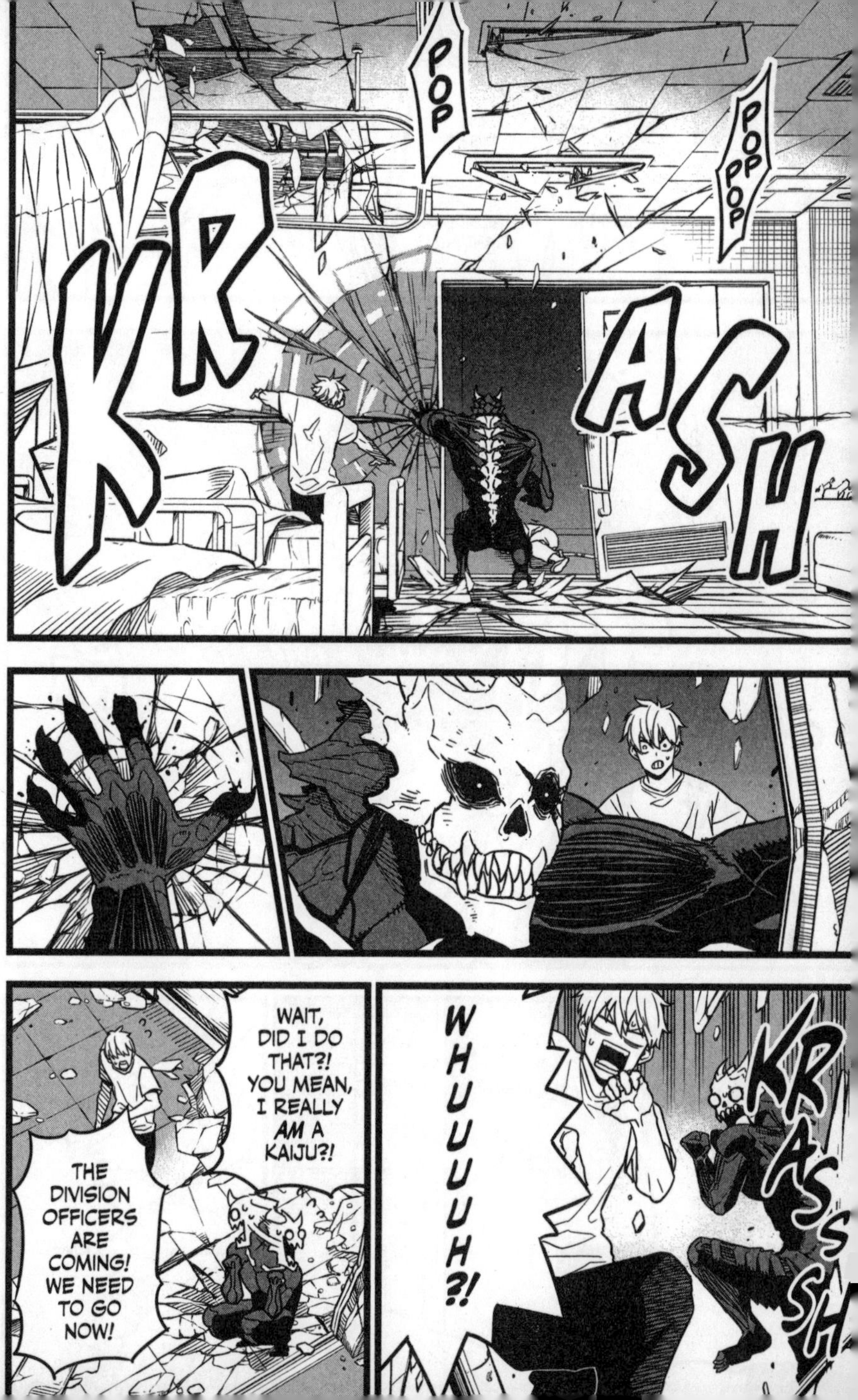
POP POP POP
POP
KRASH
KRASSSH
WHUUUUUH?!
WAIT, DID I DO THAT?! YOU MEAN, I REALLY *AM* A KAIJU?!
THE DIVISION OFFICERS ARE COMING! WE NEED TO GO NOW!

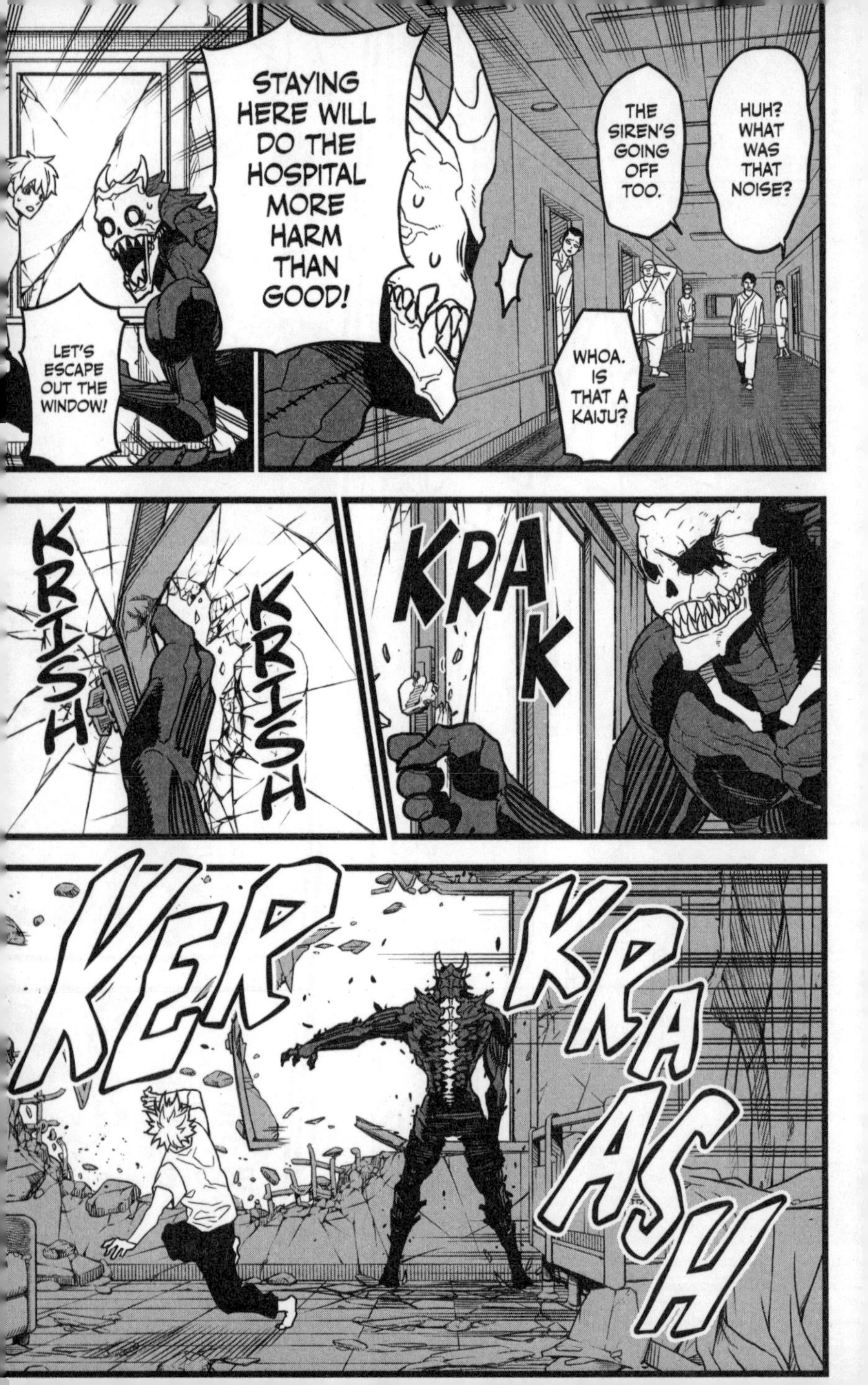
HUH? WHAT WAS THAT NOISE?
THE SIREN'S GOING OFF TOO.
WHOA. IS THAT A KAIJU?
STAYING HERE WILL DO THE HOSPITAL MORE HARM THAN GOOD!
LET'S ESCAPE OUT THE WINDOW!
KRAK
KRISH
KRISH
KERKRAASH

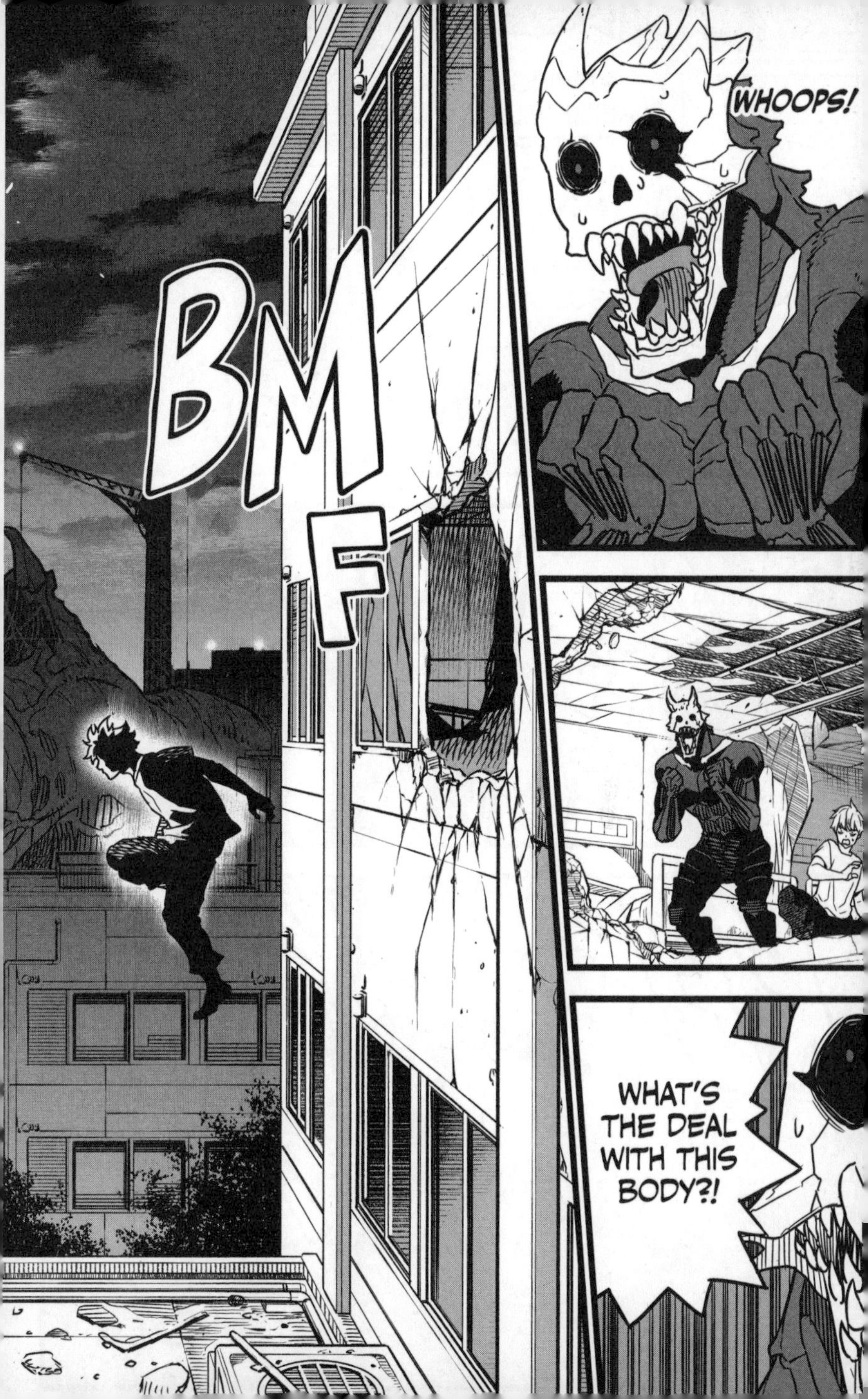
WHOOPS!
WHAT'S THE DEAL WITH THIS BODY?!
BMF

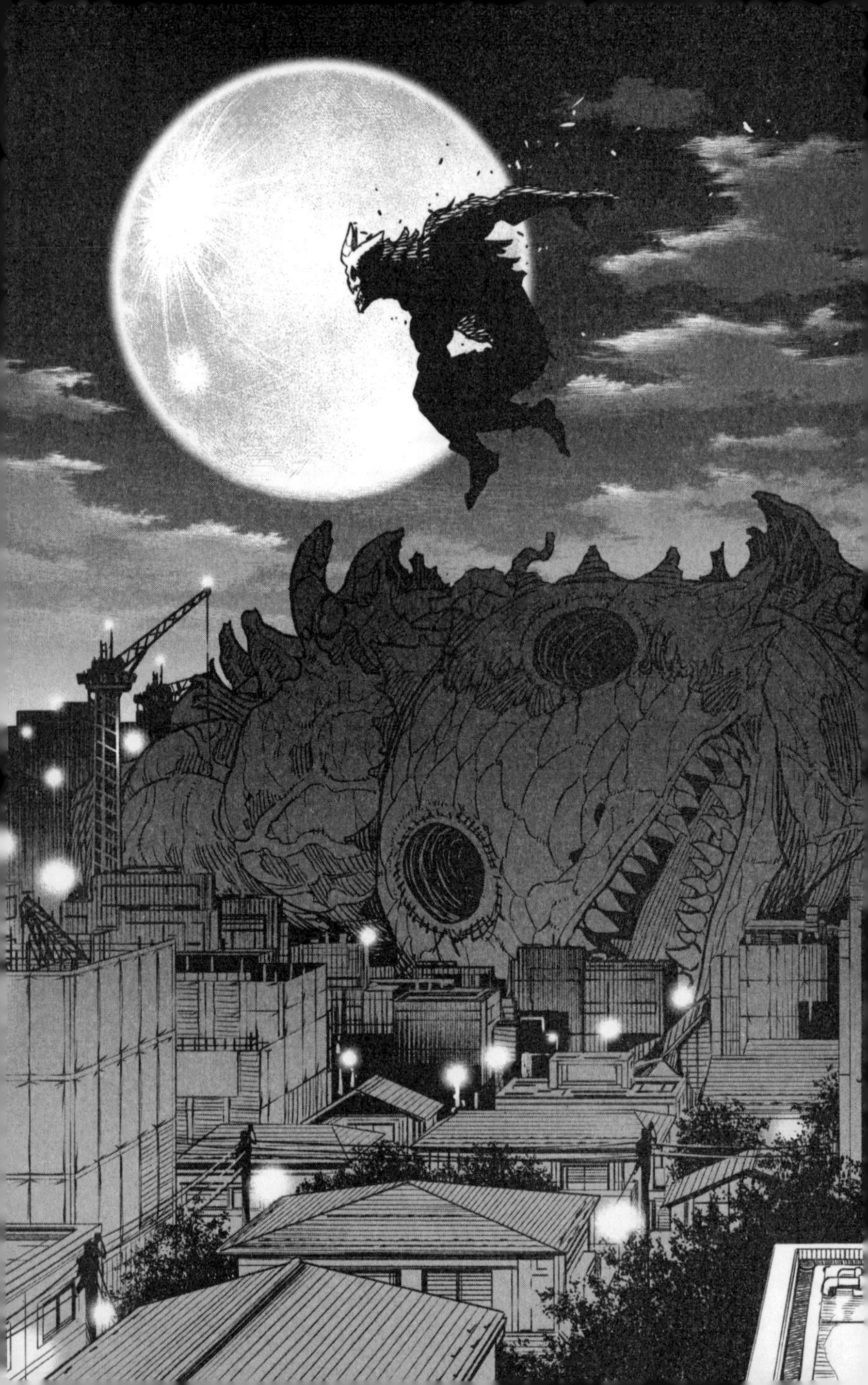

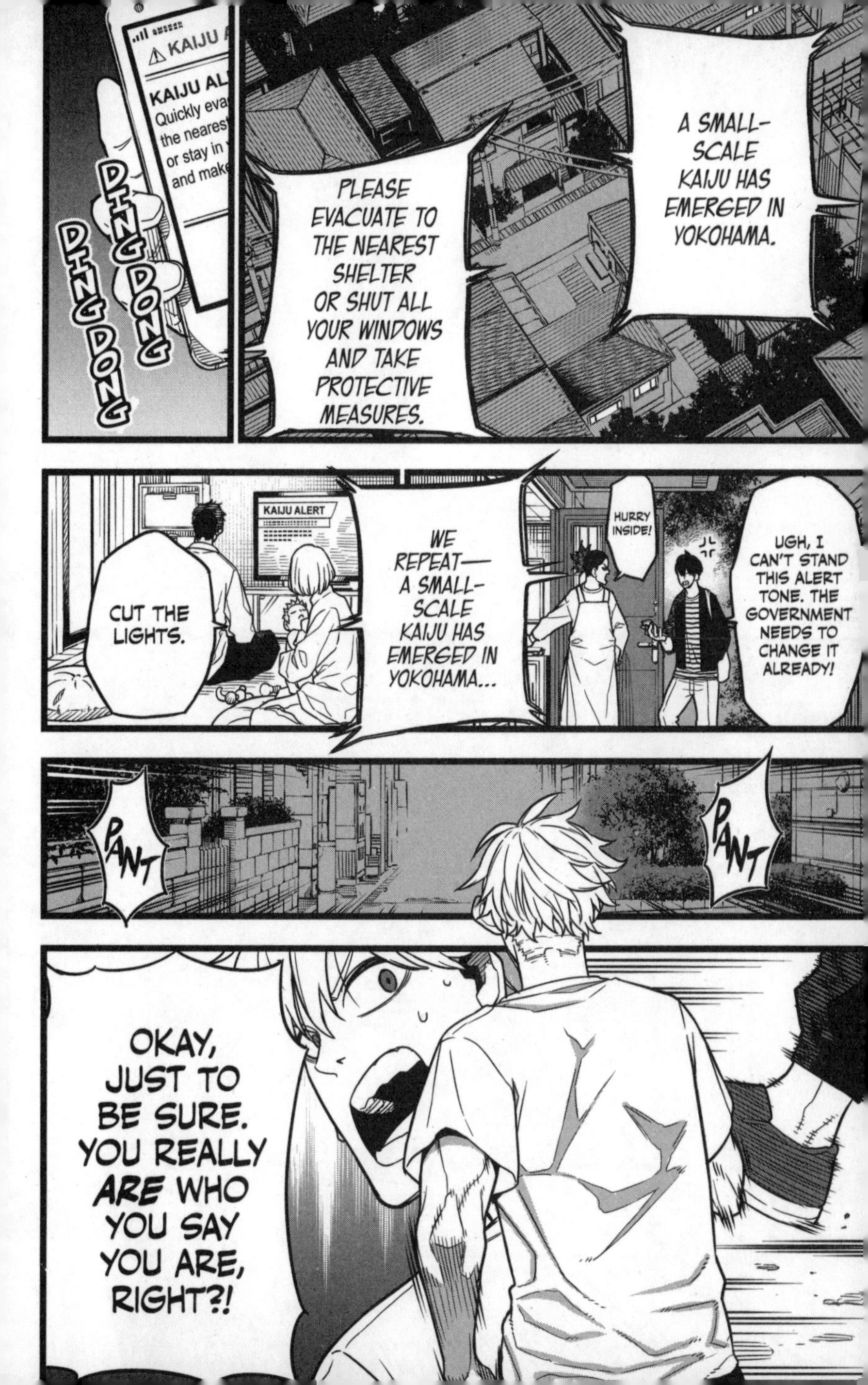
A SMALL-SCALE KAIJU HAS EMERGED IN YOKOHAMA.
PLEASE EVACUATE TO THE NEAREST SHELTER OR SHUT ALL YOUR WINDOWS AND TAKE PROTECTIVE MEASURES.
DING DONG
DING DONG
UGH, I CAN'T STAND THIS ALERT TONE. THE GOVERNMENT NEEDS TO CHANGE IT ALREADY!
HURRY INSIDE!
WE REPEAT—A SMALL-SCALE KAIJU HAS EMERGED IN YOKOHAMA...
KAIJU ALERT
CUT THE LIGHTS.
PANT
PANT
OKAY, JUST TO BE SURE. YOU REALLY ARE WHO YOU SAY YOU ARE, RIGHT?!

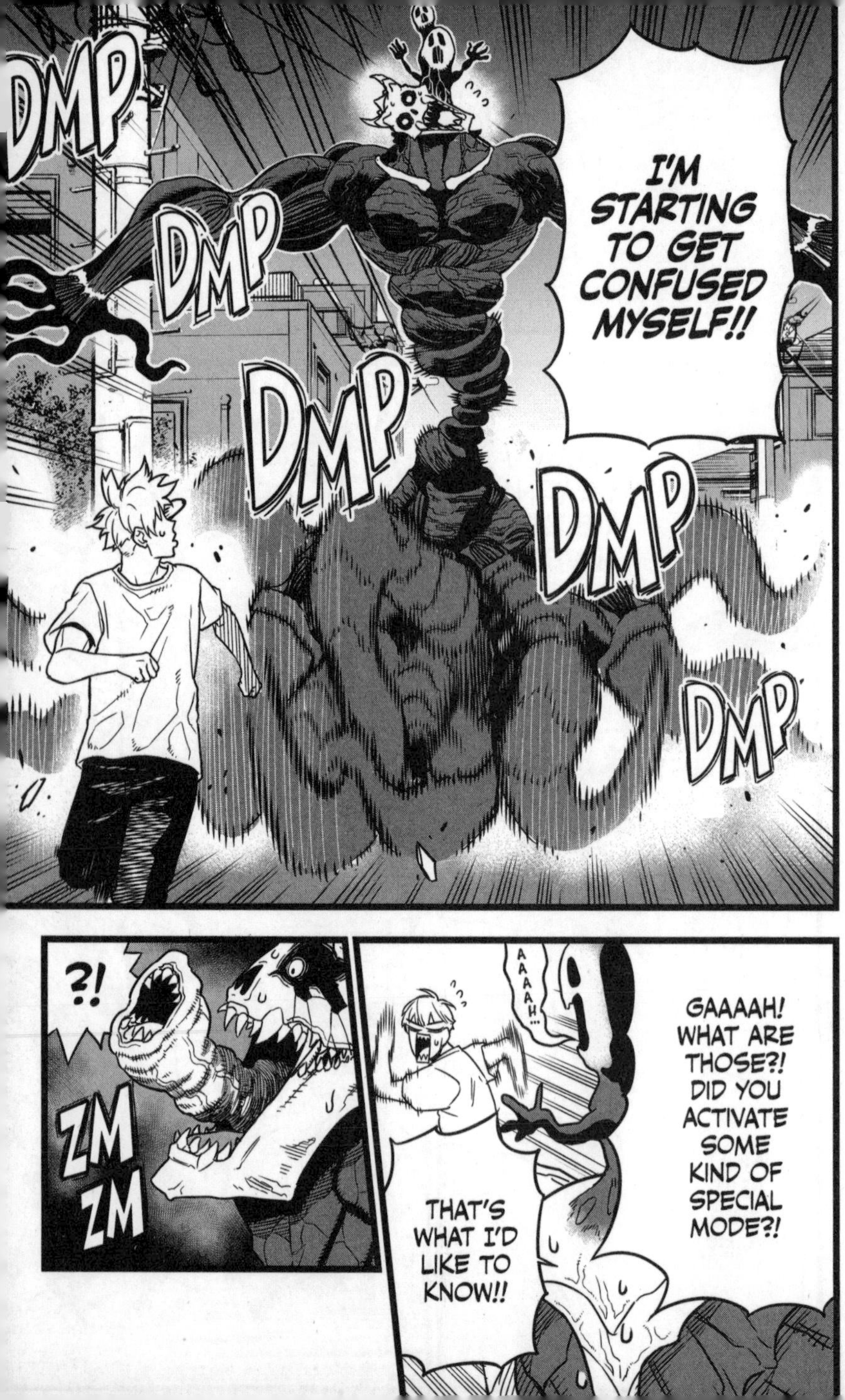
DMP
DMP
DMP
DMP
DMP
I'M STARTING TO GET CONFUSED MYSELF!!
GAAAAH! WHAT ARE THOSE?! DID YOU ACTIVATE SOME KIND OF SPECIAL MODE?!
AAAAH...
THAT'S WHAT I'D LIKE TO KNOW!!
?!
ZM ZM

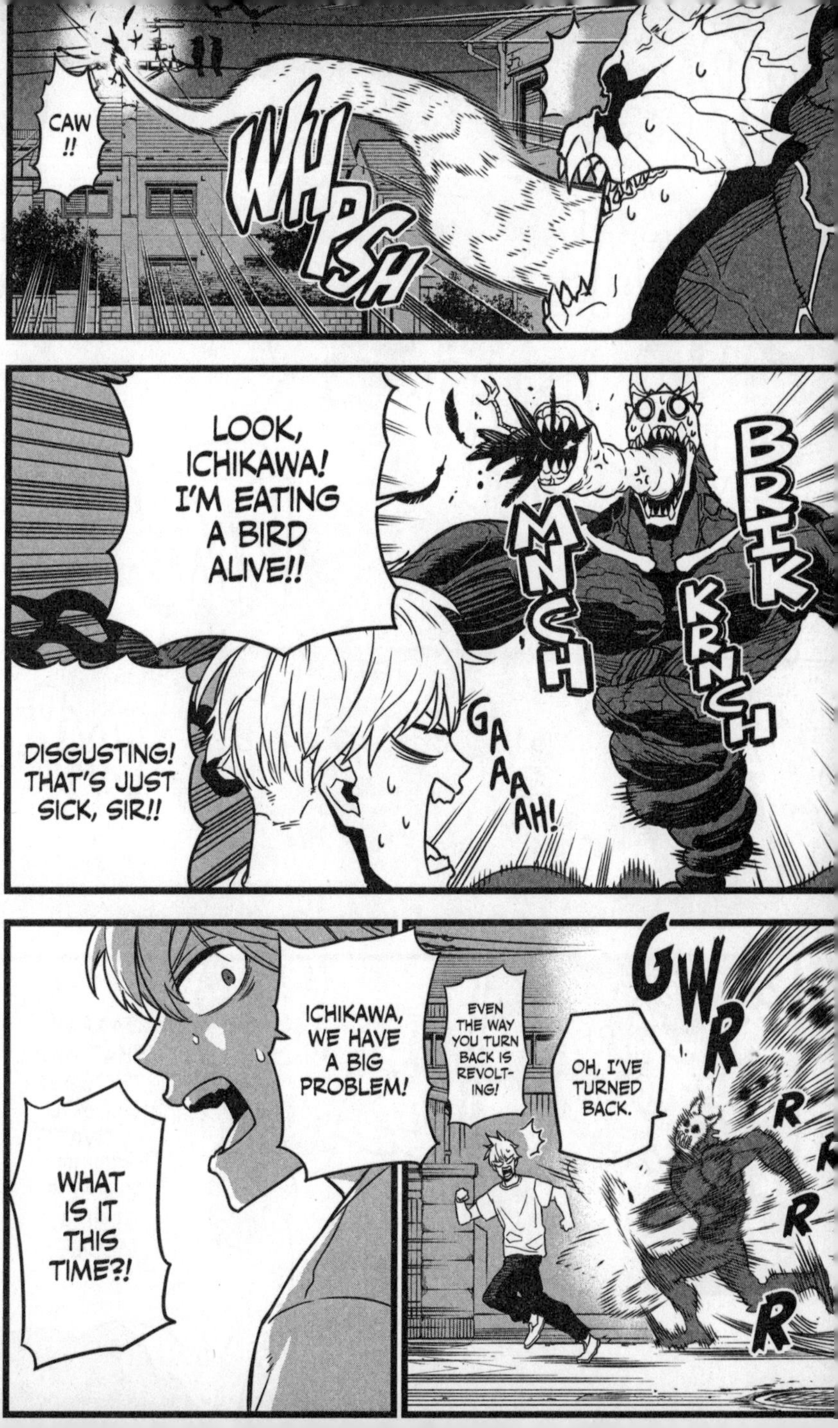
WHPSH
CAW!!
BRIK
KRNCH
MNCH
LOOK, ICHIKAWA! I'M EATING A BIRD ALIVE!!
GAAAAH!
DISGUSTING! THAT'S JUST SICK, SIR!!
GWRRRRRRR
OH, I'VE TURNED BACK.
EVEN THE WAY YOU TURN BACK IS REVOLTING!
ICHIKAWA, WE HAVE A BIG PROBLEM!
WHAT IS IT THIS TIME?!

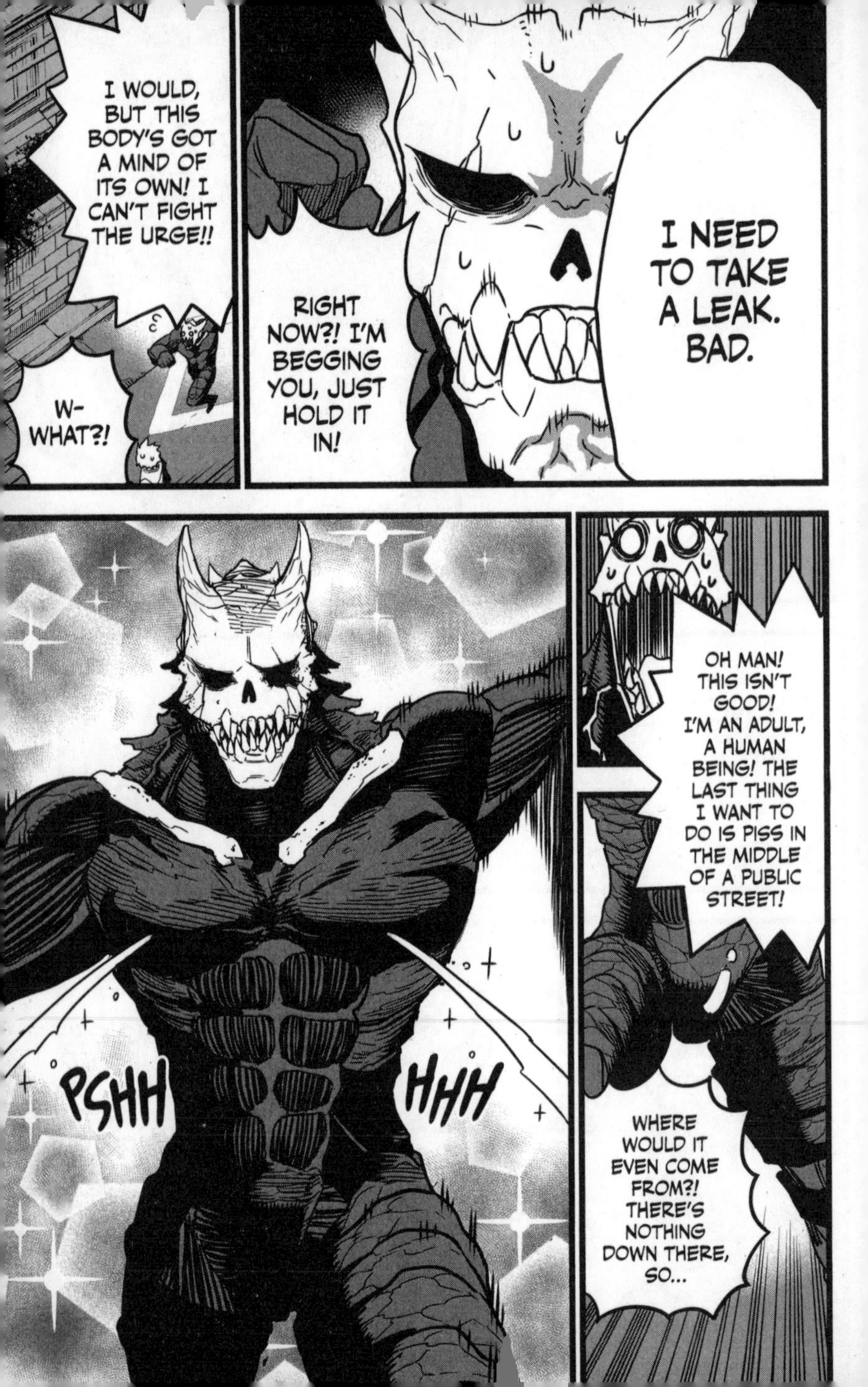
I NEED TO TAKE A LEAK. BAD.
RIGHT NOW?! I'M BEGGING YOU, JUST HOLD IT IN!
I WOULD, BUT THIS BODY'S GOT A MIND OF ITS OWN! I CAN'T FIGHT THE URGE!!
W-WHAT?!
OH MAN! THIS ISN'T GOOD! I'M AN ADULT, A HUMAN BEING! THE LAST THING I WANT TO DO IS PISS IN THE MIDDLE OF A PUBLIC STREET!
WHERE WOULD IT EVEN COME FROM?! THERE'S NOTHING DOWN THERE, SO...
PSHHHHH

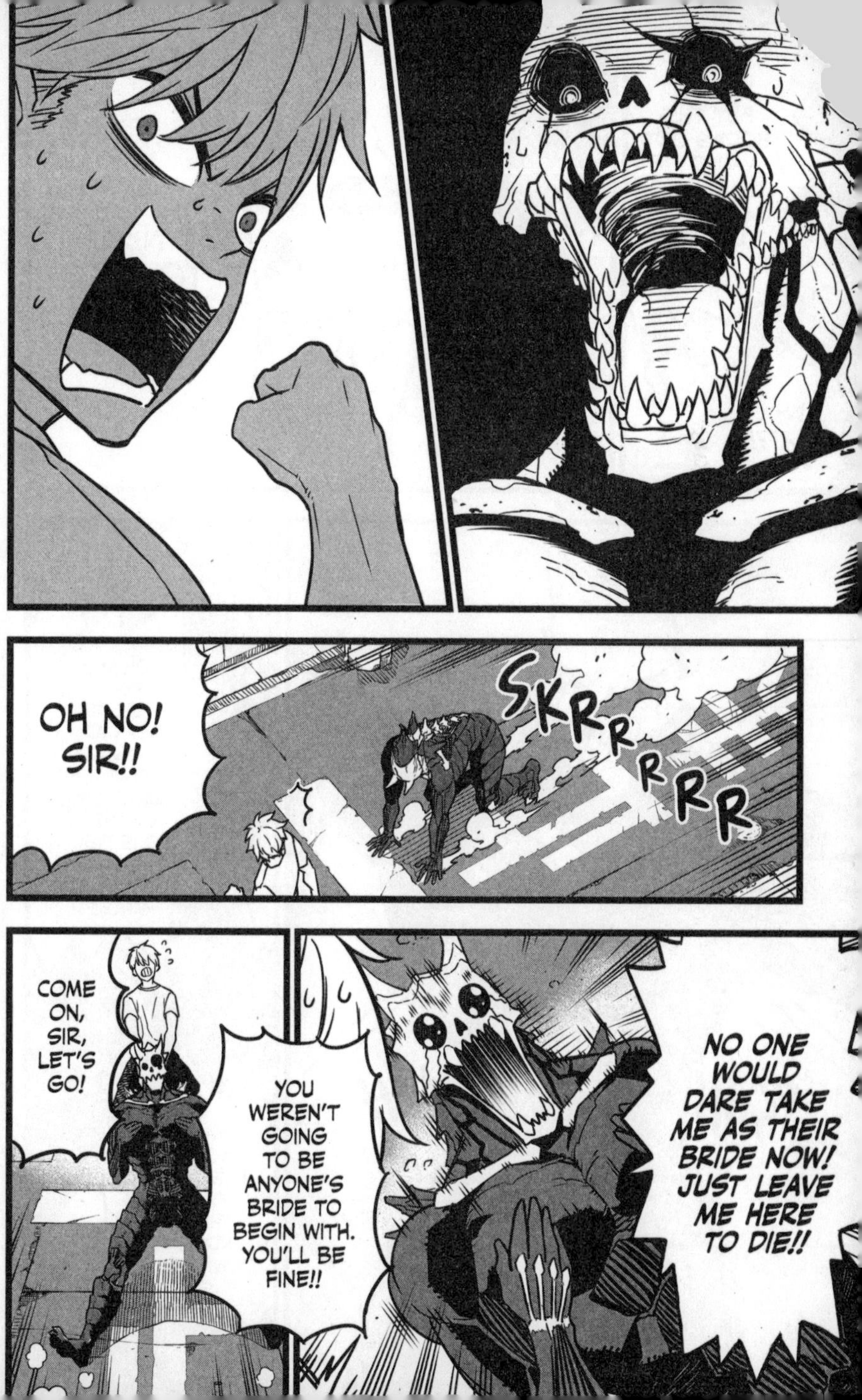
SKRRRRR
OH NO! SIR!!
NO ONE WOULD DARE TAKE ME AS THEIR BRIDE NOW! JUST LEAVE ME HERE TO DIE!!
YOU WEREN'T GOING TO BE ANYONE'S BRIDE TO BEGIN WITH. YOU'LL BE FINE!!
COME ON, SIR, LET'S GO!

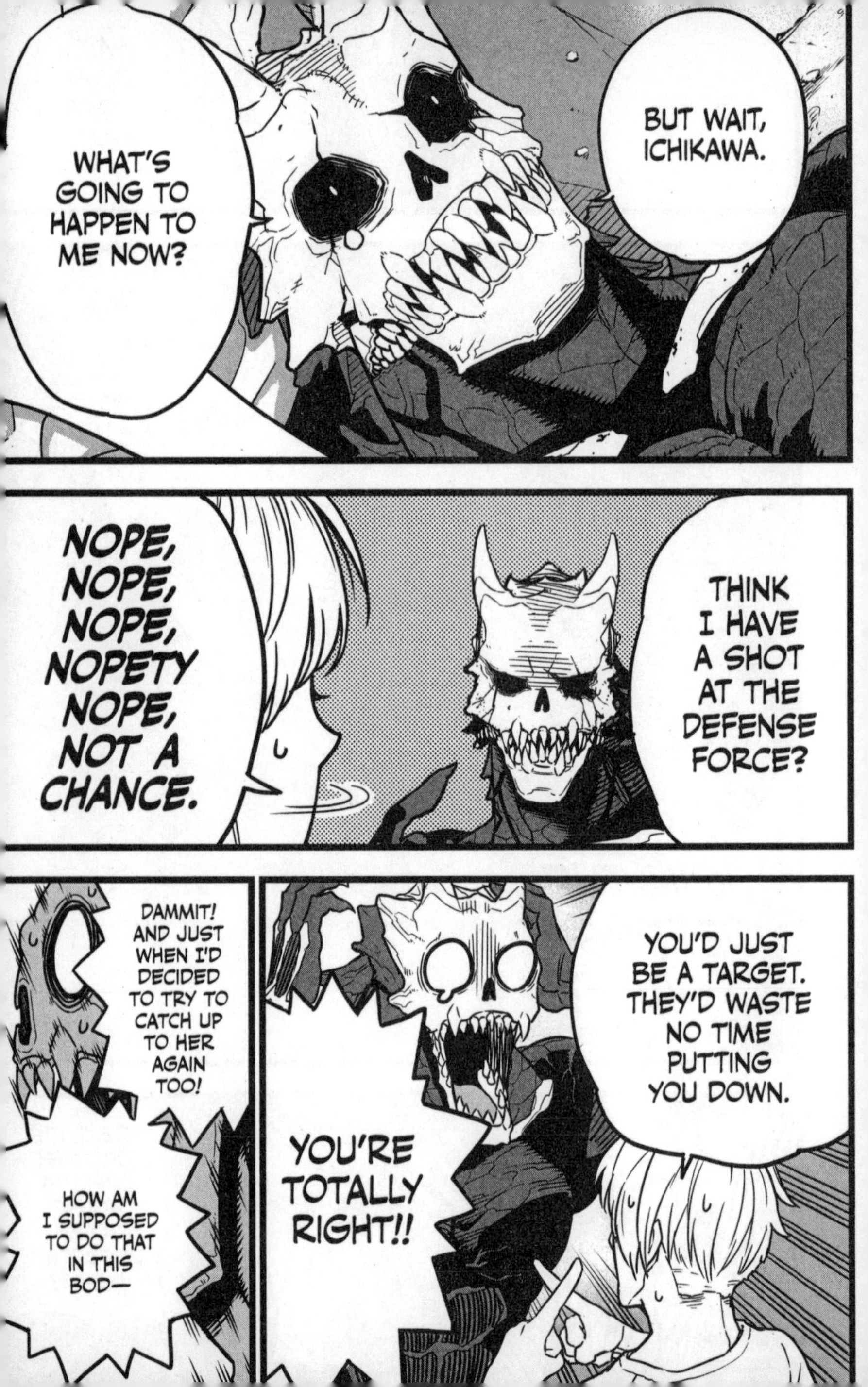
BUT WAIT, ICHIKAWA.
WHAT'S GOING TO HAPPEN TO ME NOW?
THINK I HAVE A SHOT AT THE DEFENSE FORCE?
NOPE, NOPE, NOPE, NOPETY NOPE, NOT A CHANCE.
YOU'D JUST BE A TARGET. THEY'D WASTE NO TIME PUTTING YOU DOWN.
YOU'RE TOTALLY RIGHT!!
DAMMIT! AND JUST WHEN I'D DECIDED TO TRY TO CATCH UP TO HER AGAIN TOO!
HOW AM I SUPPOSED TO DO THAT IN THIS BOD—

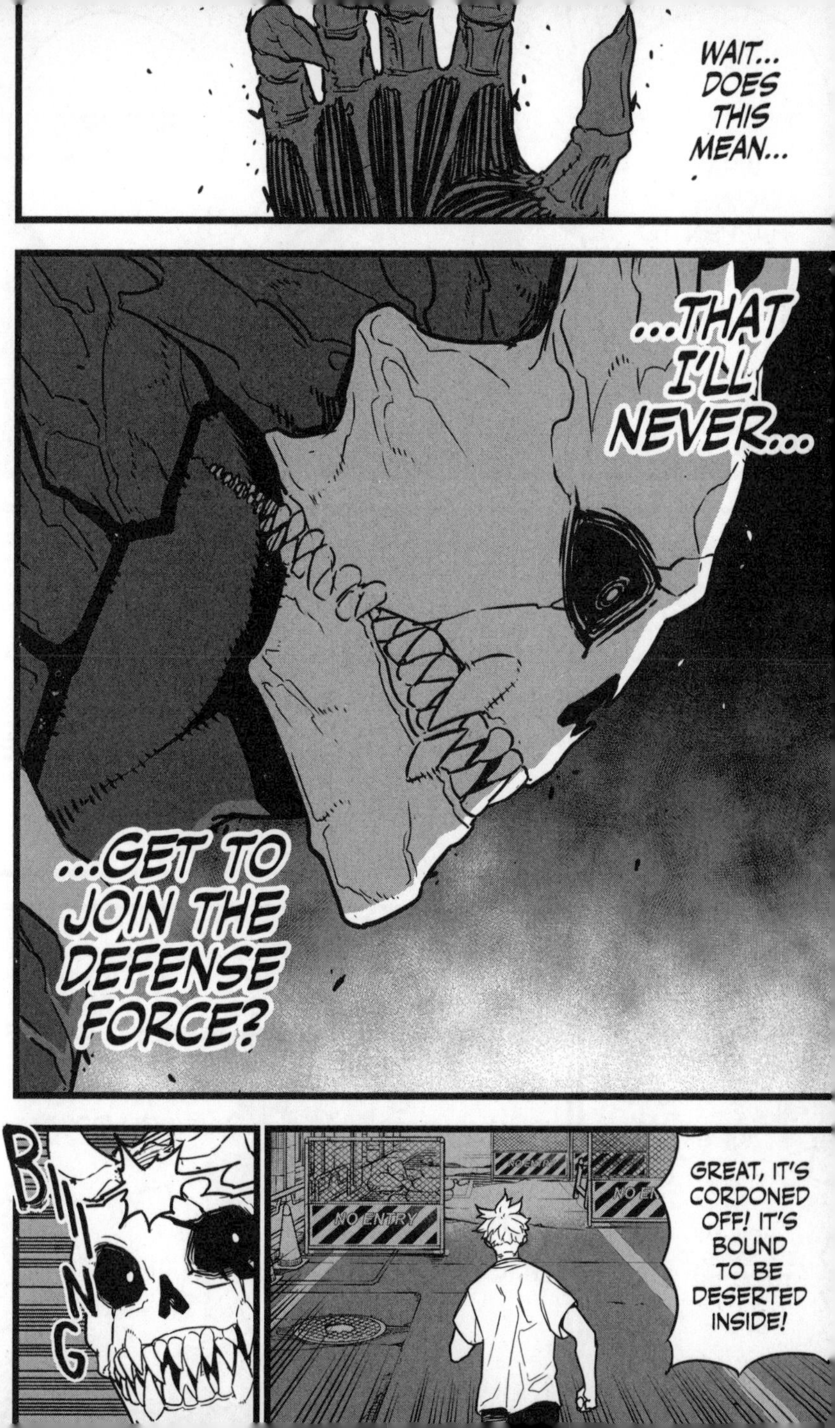
WAIT... DOES THIS MEAN...
...THAT I'LL NEVER...
...GET TO JOIN THE DEFENSE FORCE?
GREAT, IT'S CORDONED OFF! IT'S BOUND TO BE DESERTED INSIDE!
NO ENTRY
NO ENTRY
BIIING

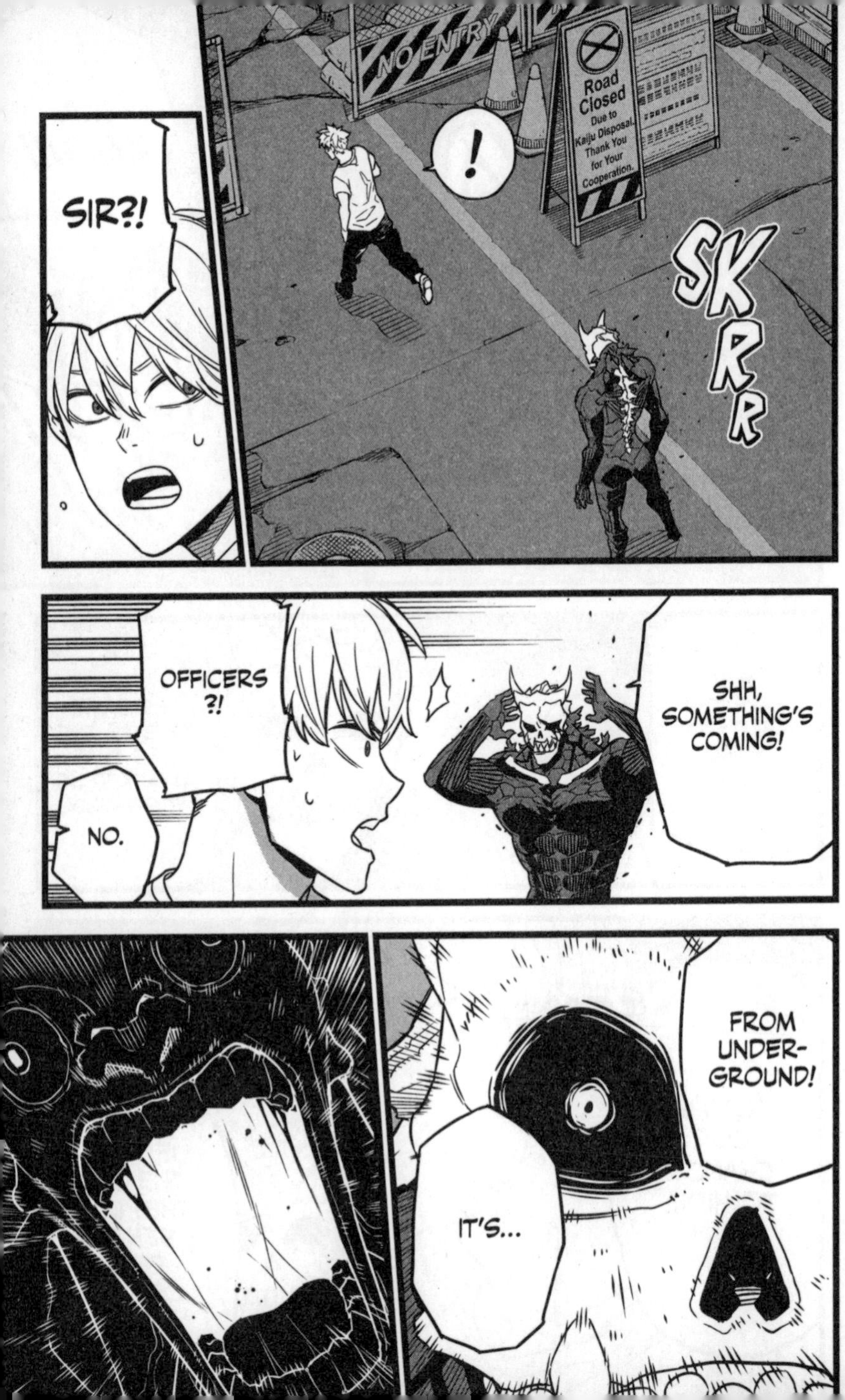
NO ENTRY
Road Closed
Due to Kaiju Disposal. Thank You for Your Cooperation.
!
SKRR
SIR?!
SHH, SOMETHING'S COMING!
OFFICERS ?!
NO.
FROM UNDER-GROUND!
IT'S...

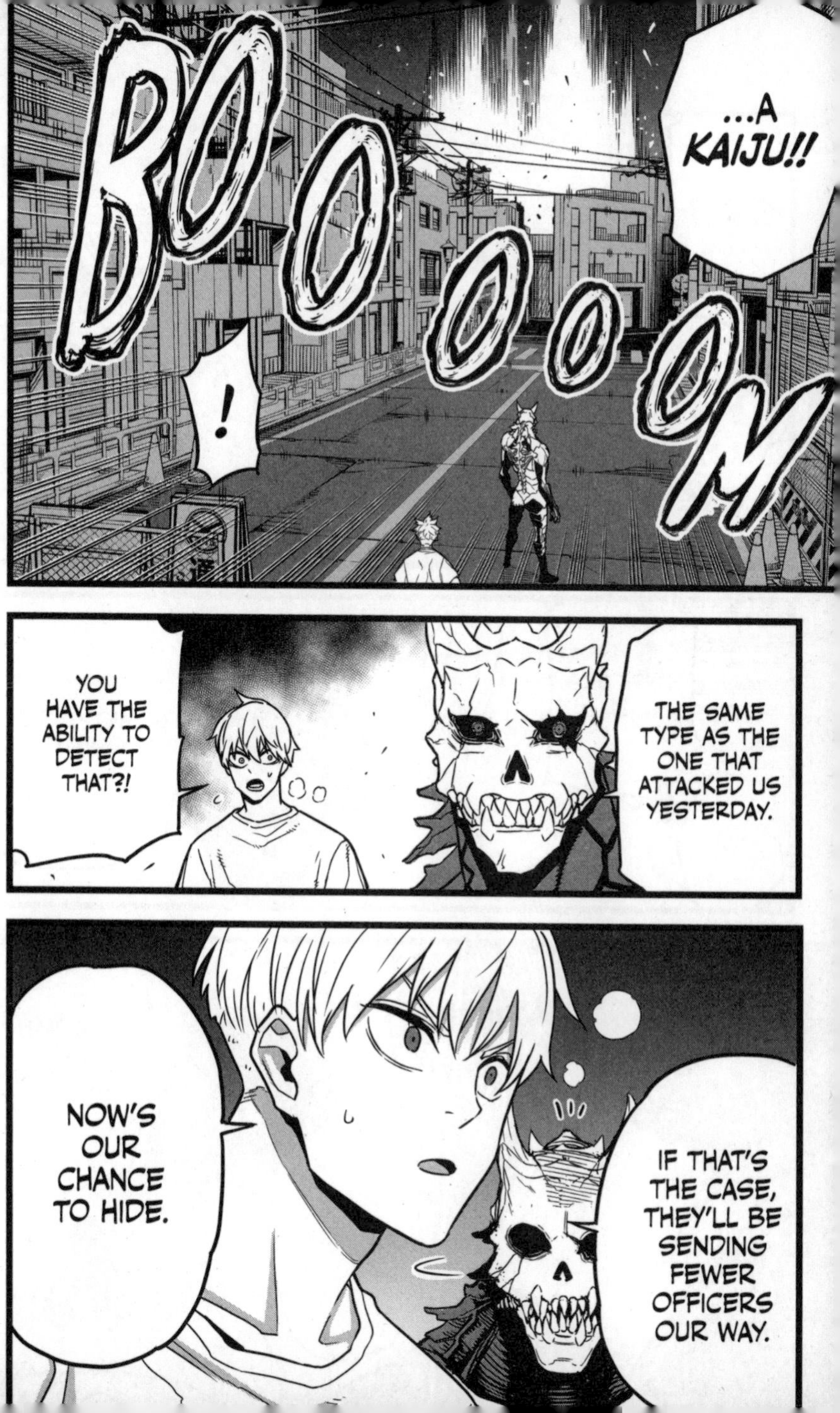

...A KAIJU!!
BOOOOOOOM
!
THE SAME TYPE AS THE ONE THAT ATTACKED US YESTERDAY.
YOU HAVE THE ABILITY TO DETECT THAT?!
IF THAT'S THE CASE, THEY'LL BE SENDING FEWER OFFICERS OUR WAY.
NOW'S OUR CHANCE TO HIDE.

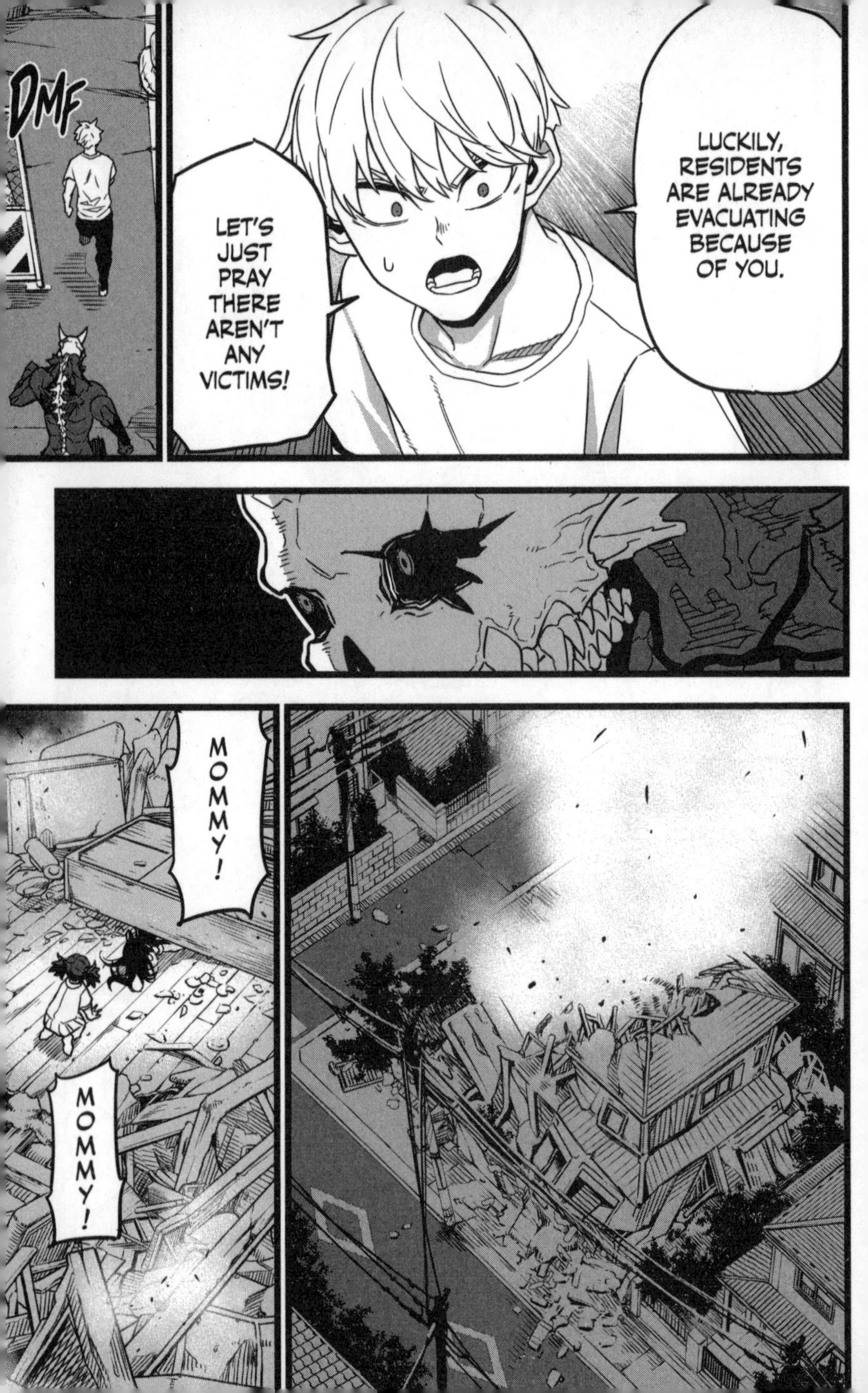
LUCKILY, RESIDENTS ARE ALREADY EVACUATING BECAUSE OF YOU.
LET'S JUST PRAY THERE AREN'T ANY VICTIMS!
DMF
MOMMY!
MOMMY!

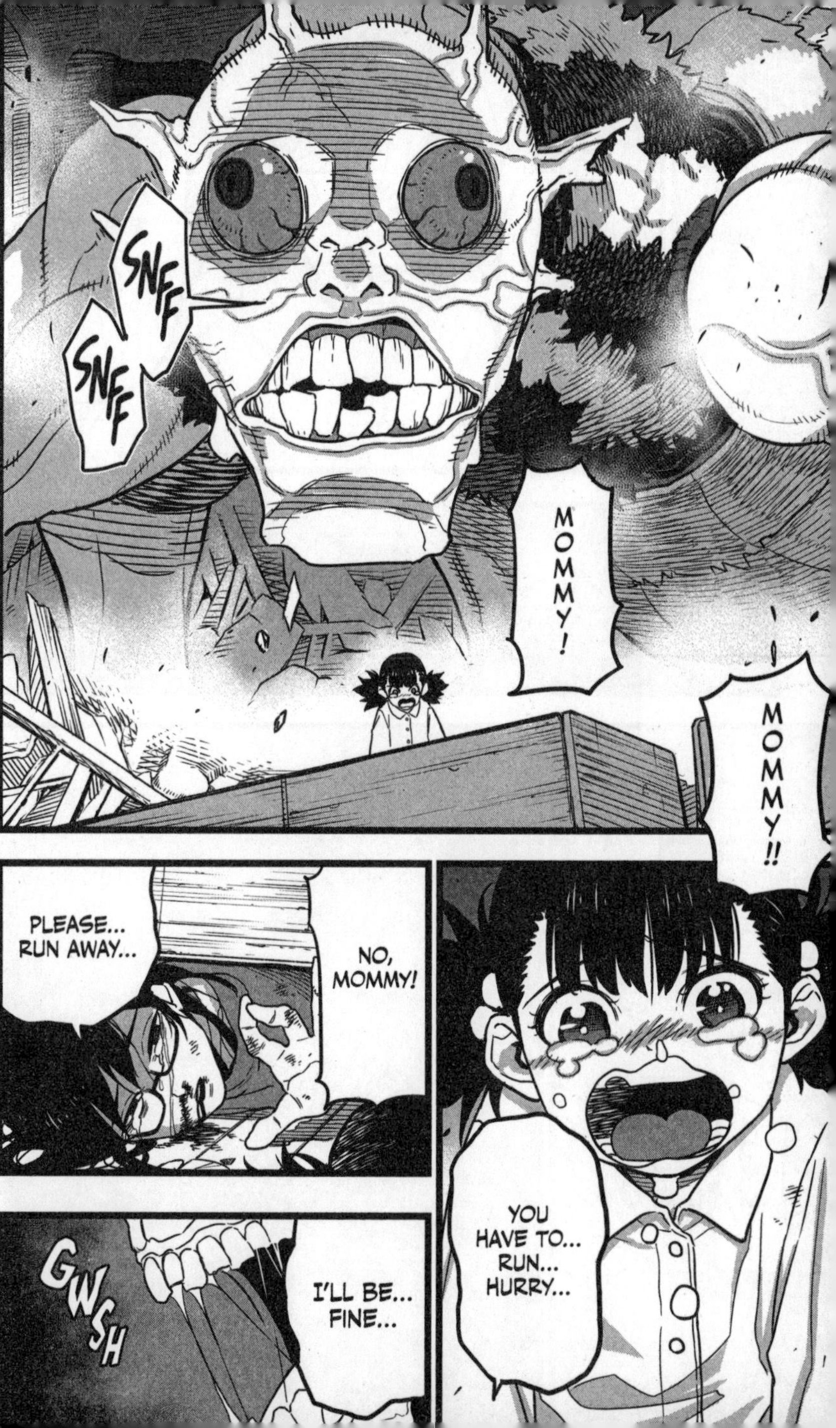
SNFF
SNFF
MOMMY!
MOMMY!!
YOU HAVE TO... RUN... HURRY...
NO, MOMMY!
PLEASE... RUN AWAY...
I'LL BE... FINE...
GWSH

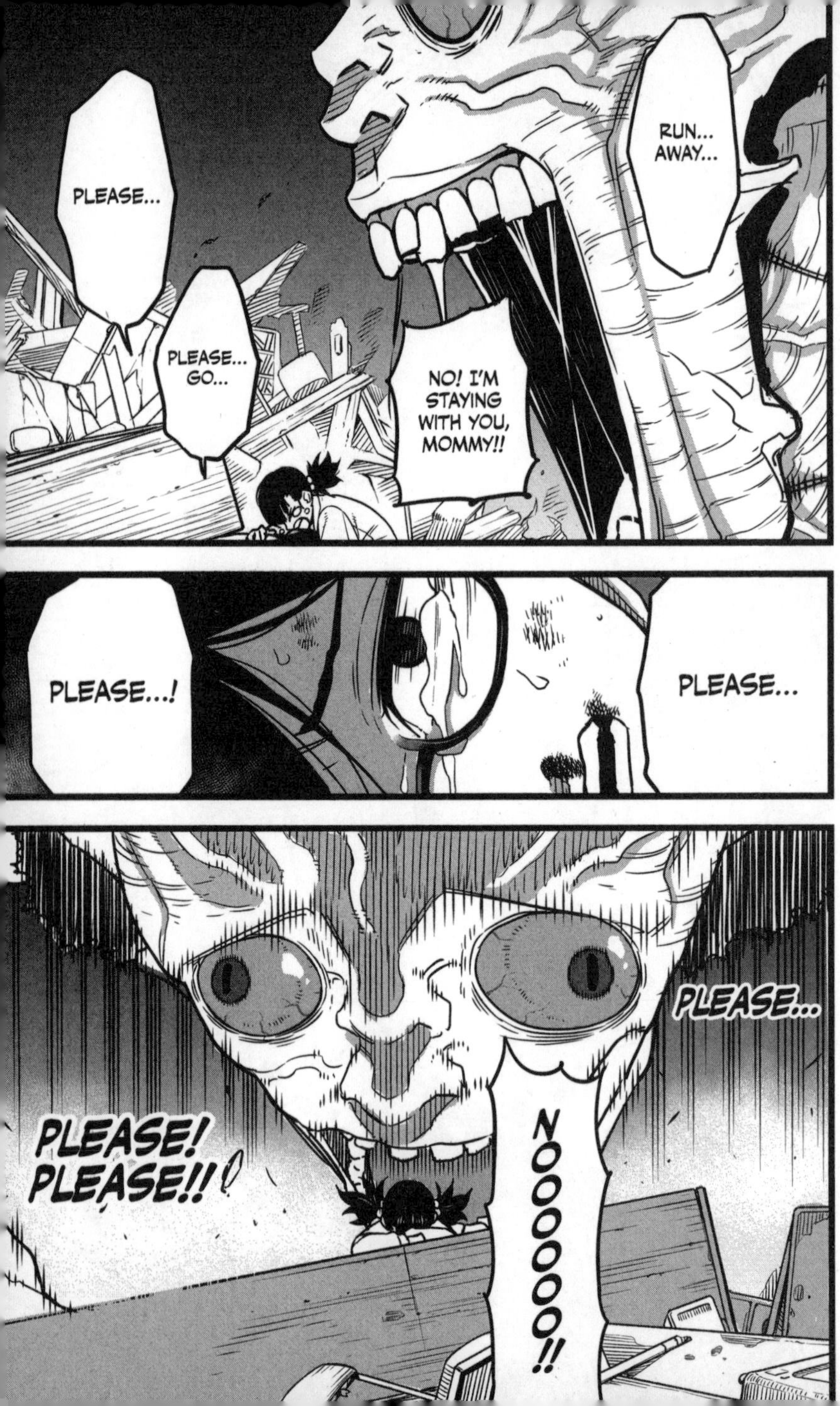
RUN... AWAY...
NO! I'M STAYING WITH YOU, MOMMY!!
PLEASE...
PLEASE... GO...
PLEASE...
PLEASE...!
PLEASE...
NOOOOOOO!!
PLEASE! PLEASE!!

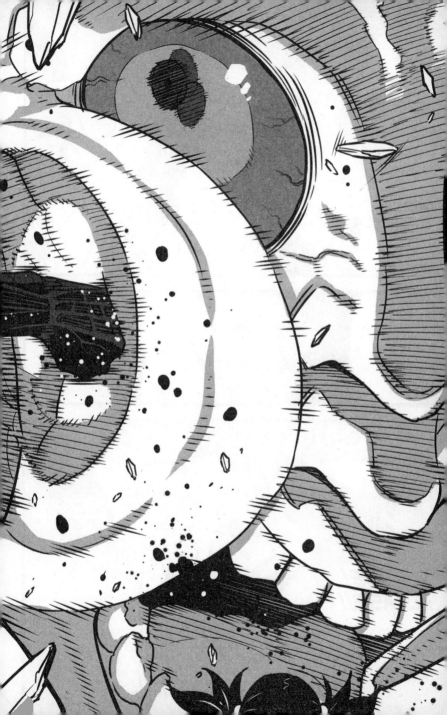

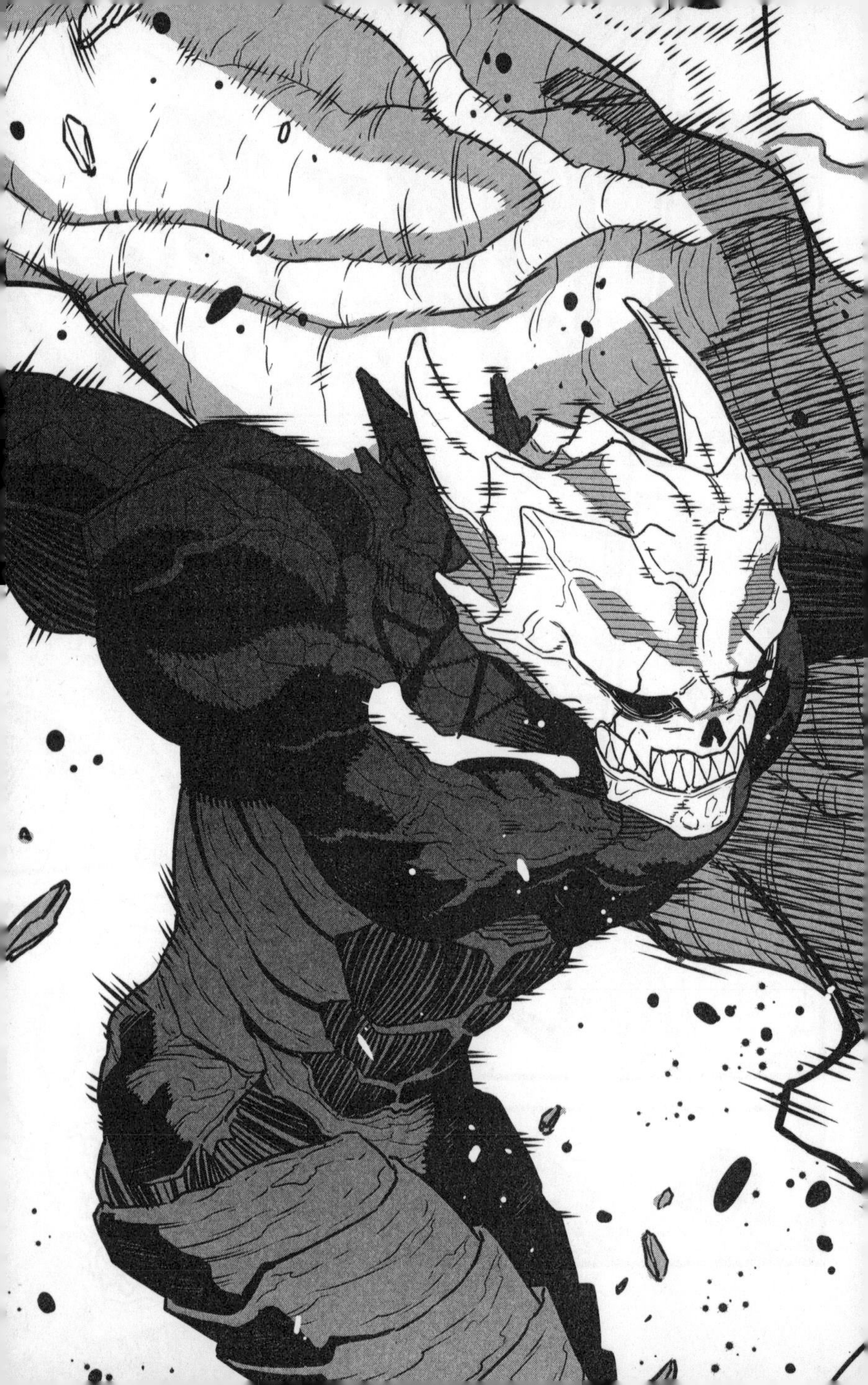

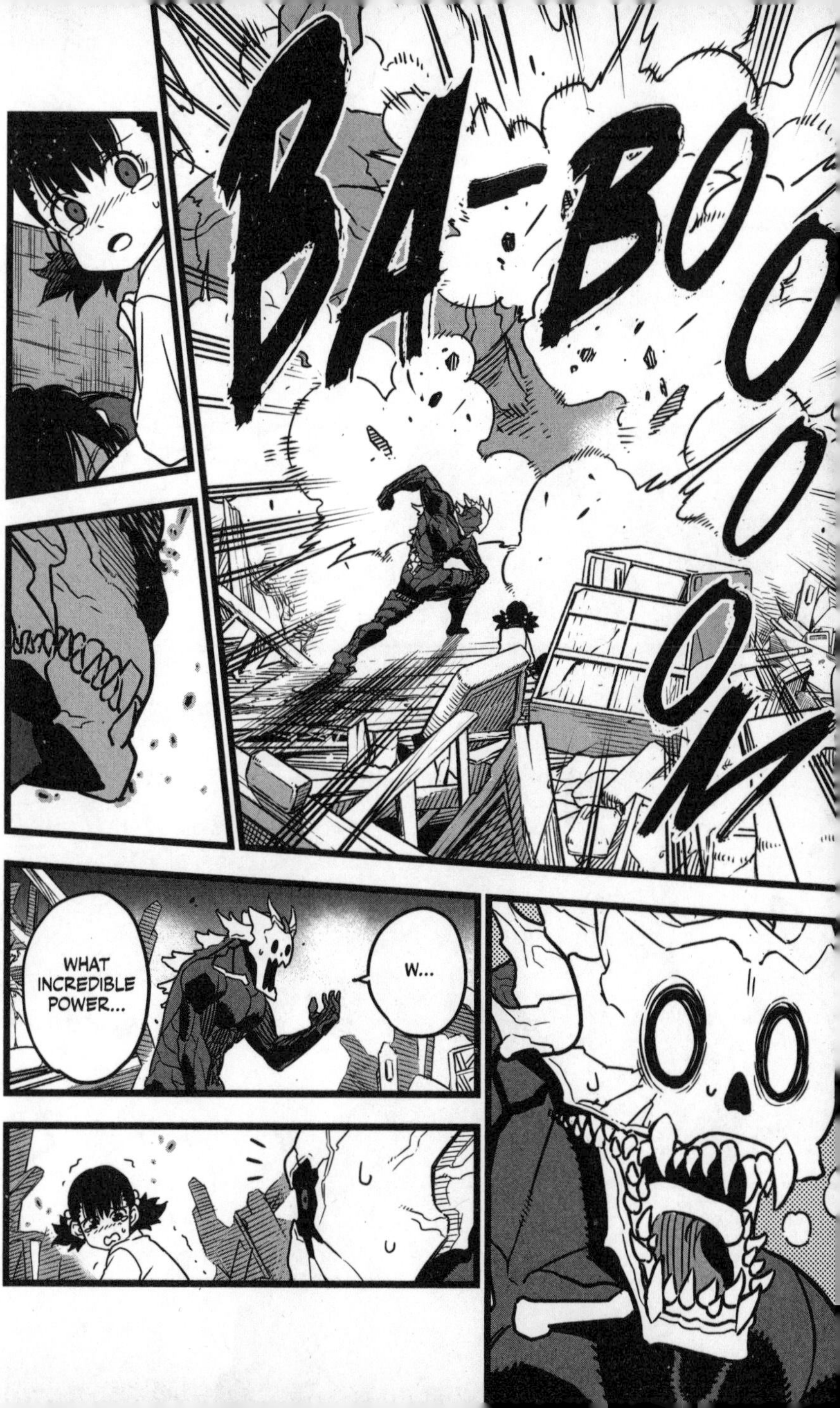
BA-BOOOOM
W...
WHAT INCREDIBLE POWER...

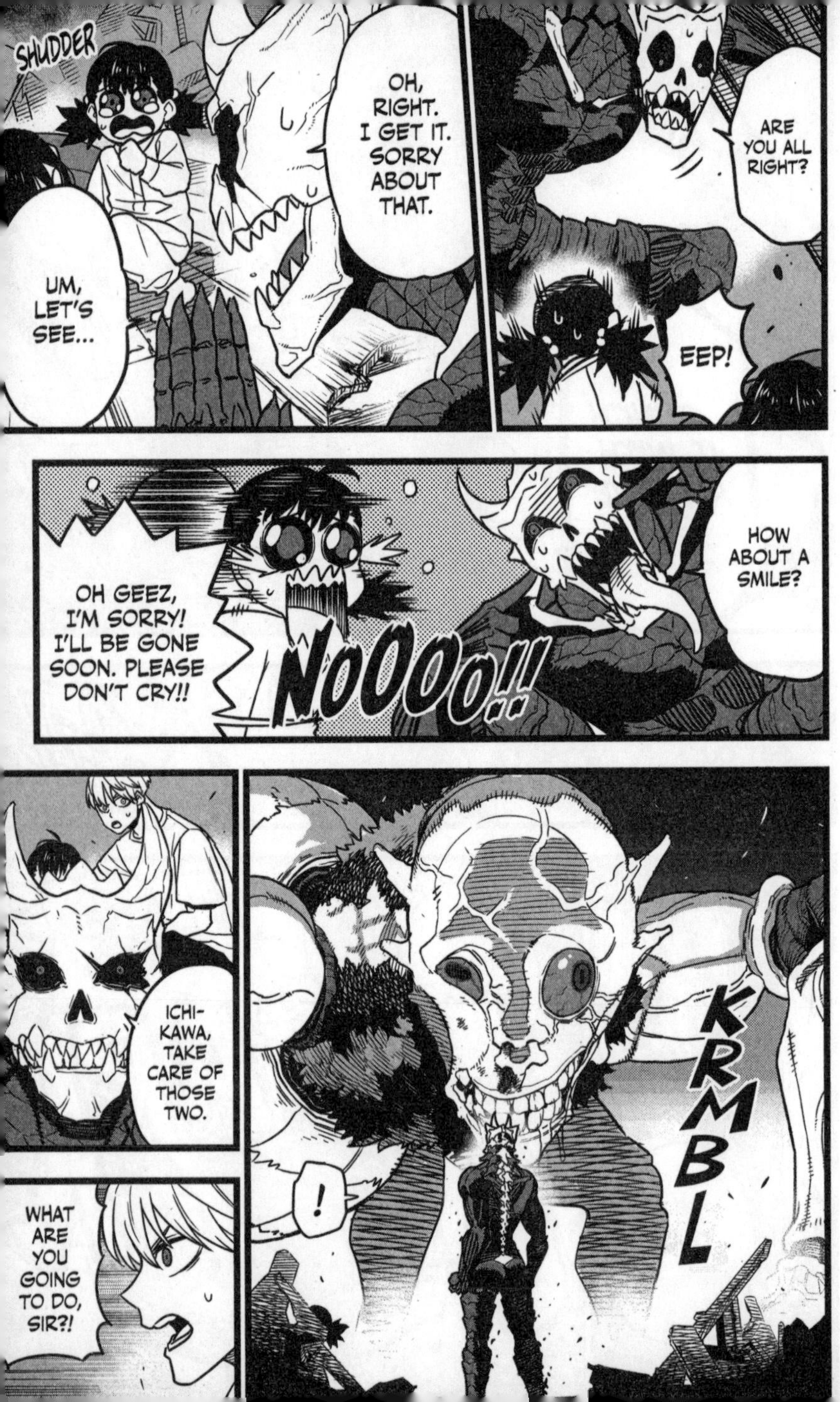
ARE YOU ALL RIGHT?
EEP!
OH, RIGHT. I GET IT. SORRY ABOUT THAT.
SHUDDER
UM, LET'S SEE...
HOW ABOUT A SMILE?
NOOOO!!
OH GEEZ, I'M SORRY! I'LL BE GONE SOON. PLEASE DON'T CRY!!
KRMBL
!
ICHIKAWA, TAKE CARE OF THOSE TWO.
WHAT ARE YOU GOING TO DO, SIR?!

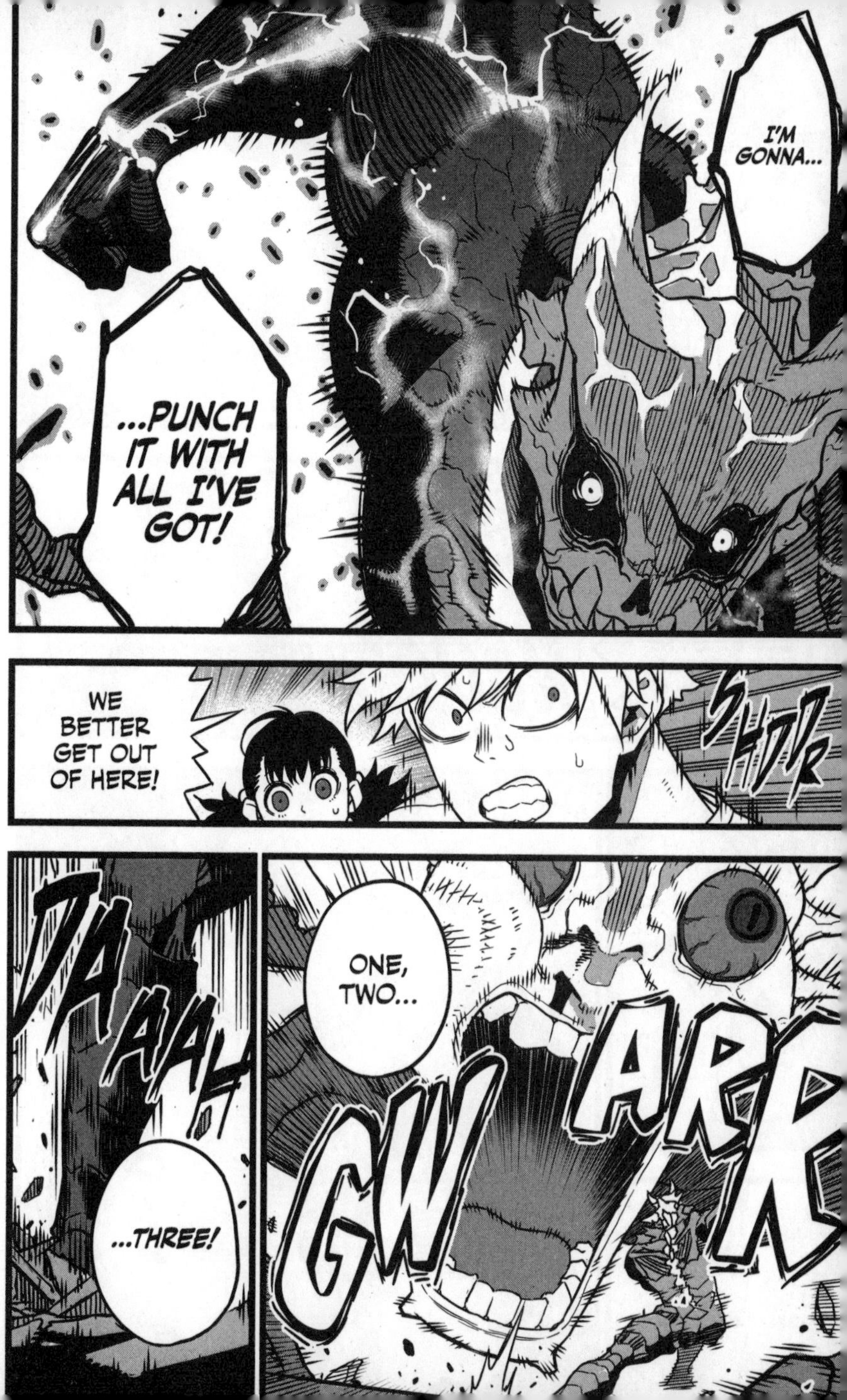
I'M GONNA...
...PUNCH IT WITH ALL I'VE GOT!
WE BETTER GET OUT OF HERE!
ONE, TWO...
...THREE!

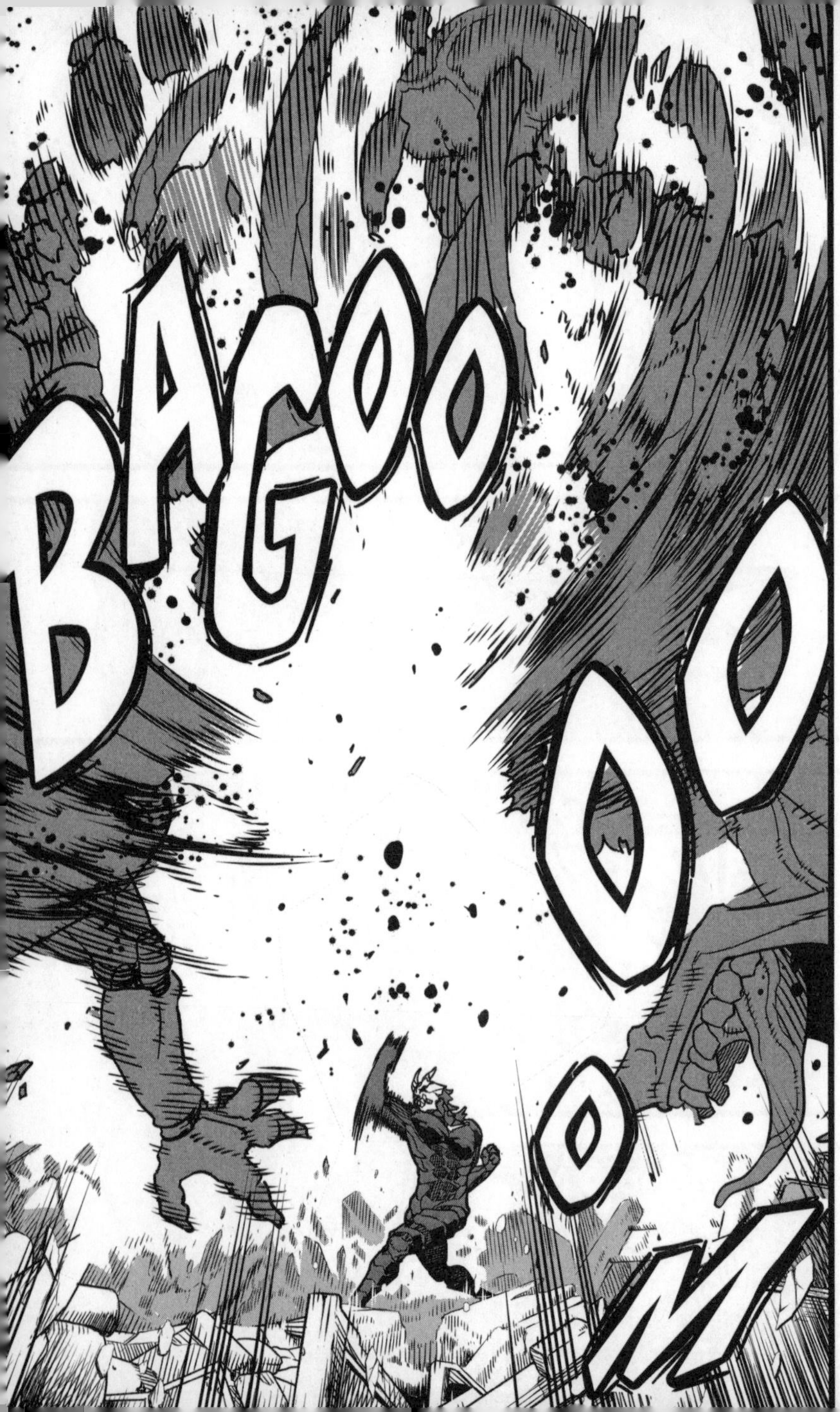
BAGOOOOOOM

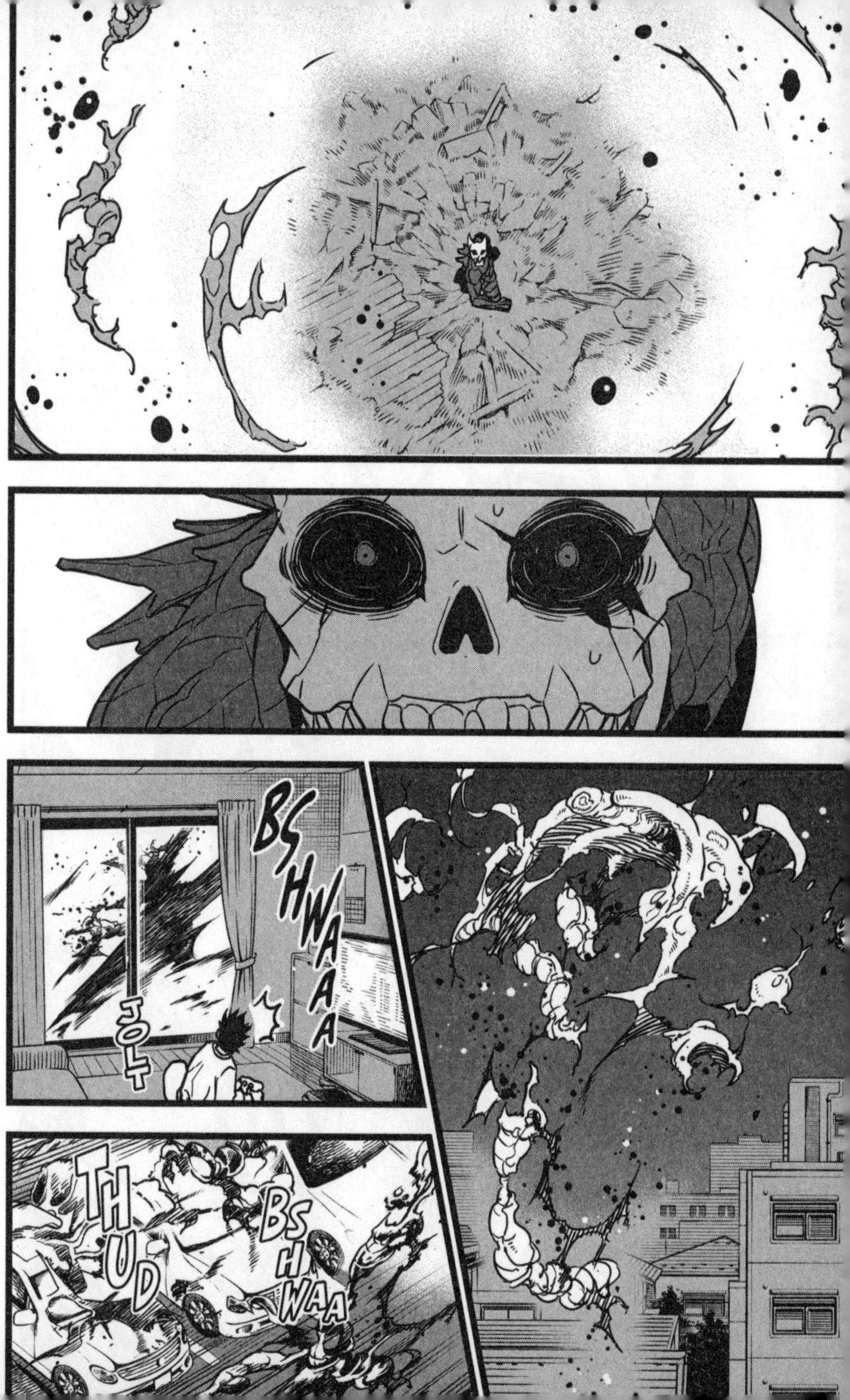
BSHWAAA
JOLT
BSHWAA
THUD

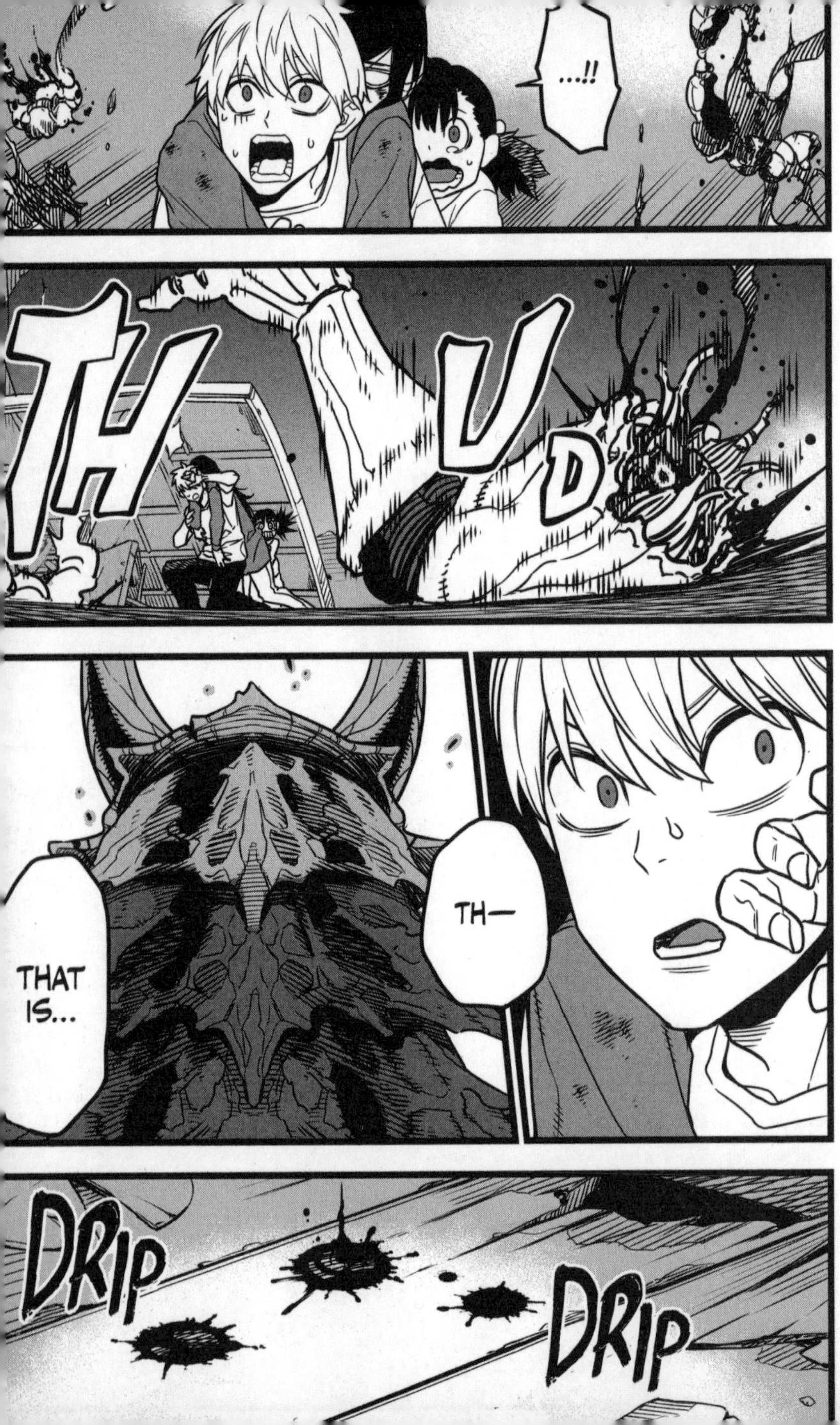
...!!
THUD
TH—
THAT IS...
DRIP
DRIP

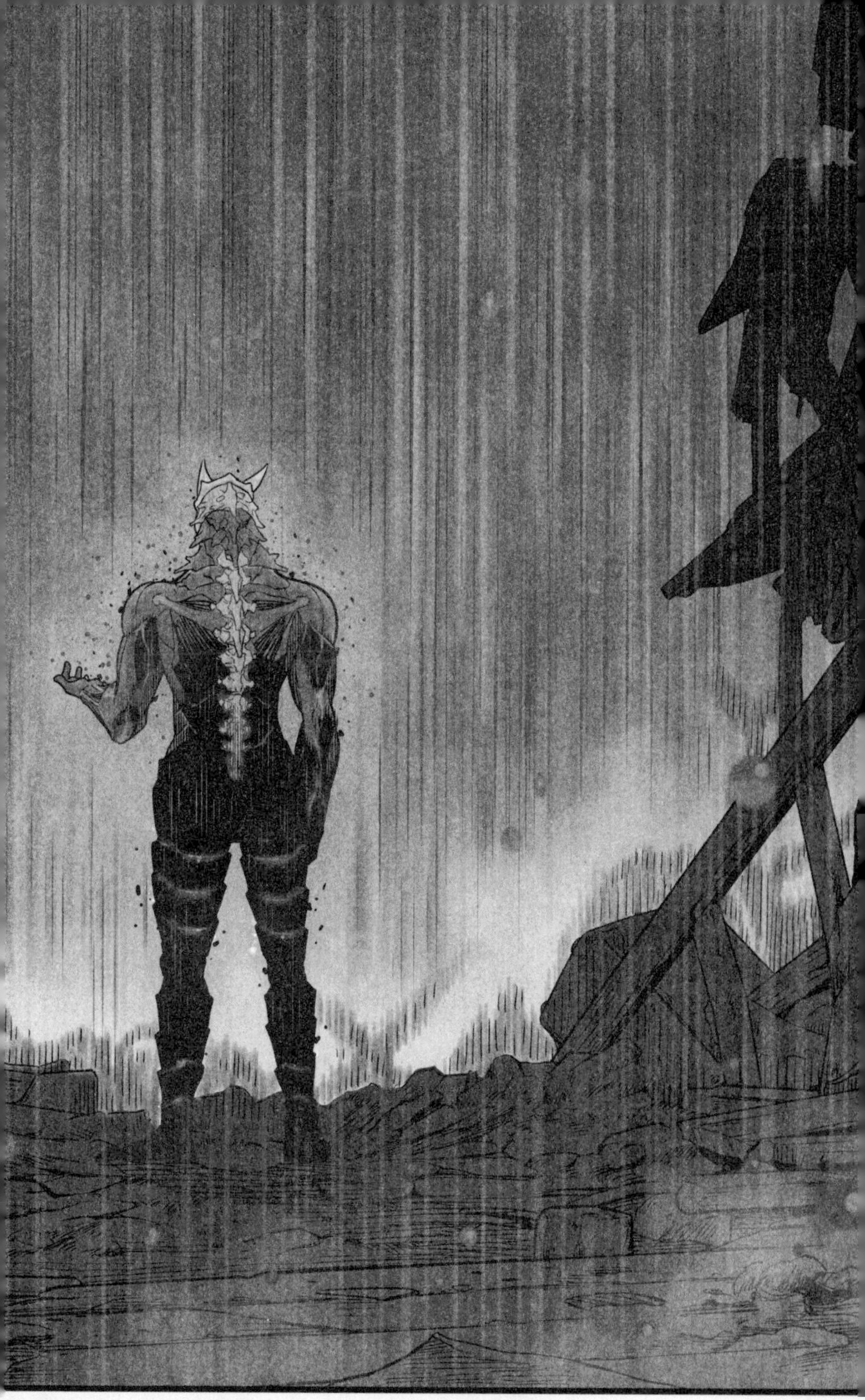

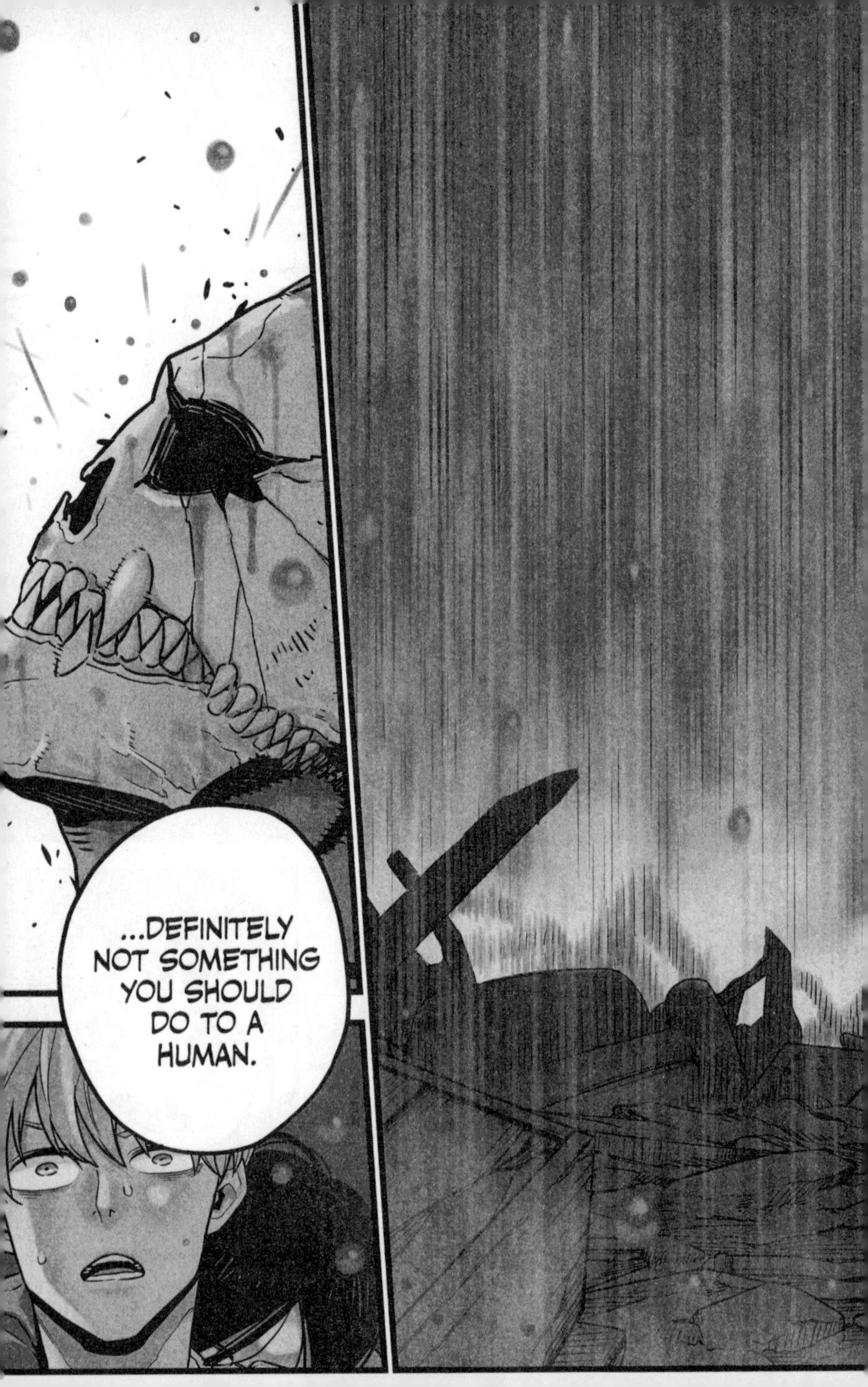
...DEFINITELY NOT SOMETHING YOU SHOULD DO TO A HUMAN.

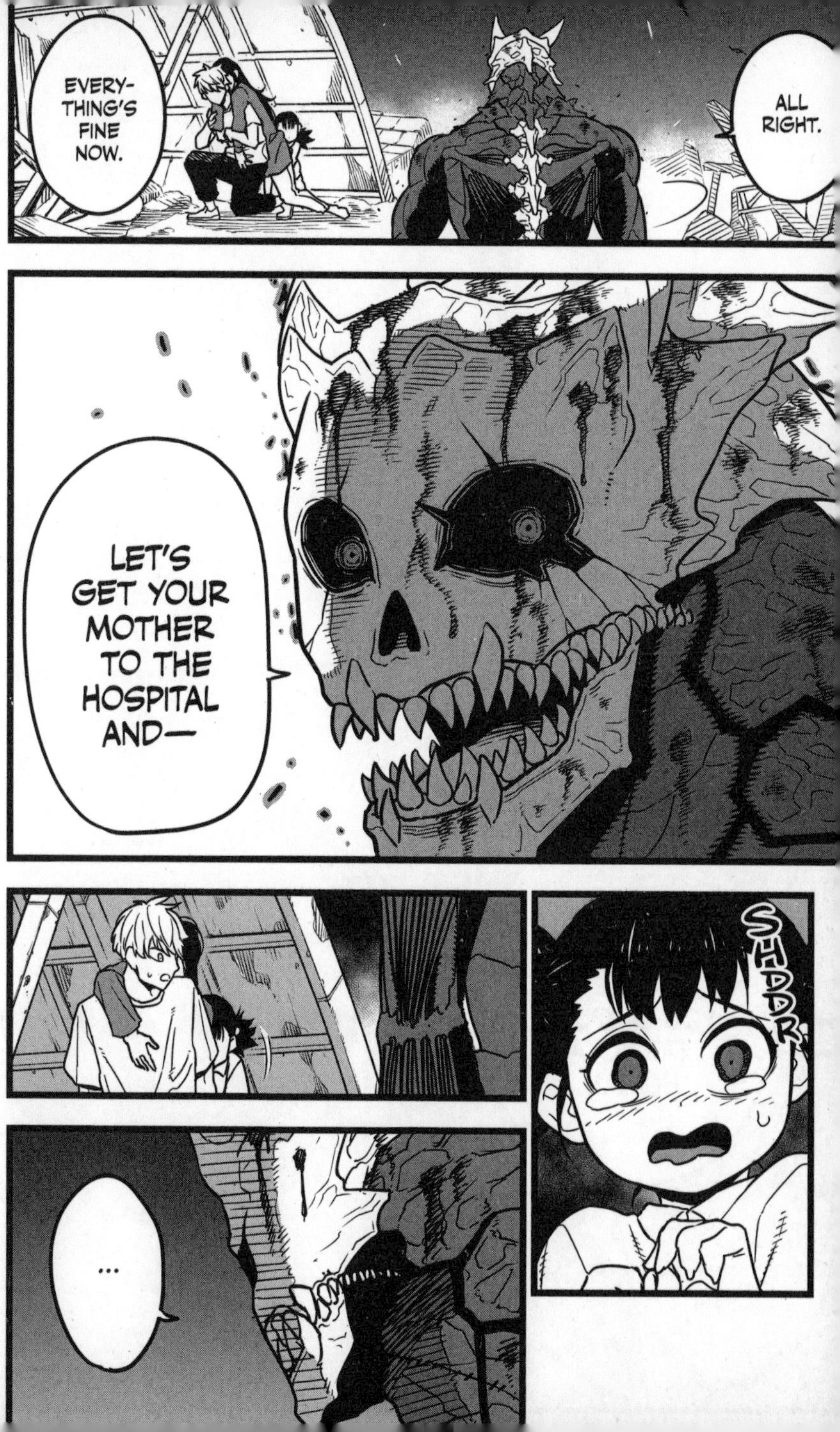
ALL RIGHT.
EVERY-THING'S FINE NOW.
LET'S GET YOUR MOTHER TO THE HOSPITAL AND—
SHDDR
...

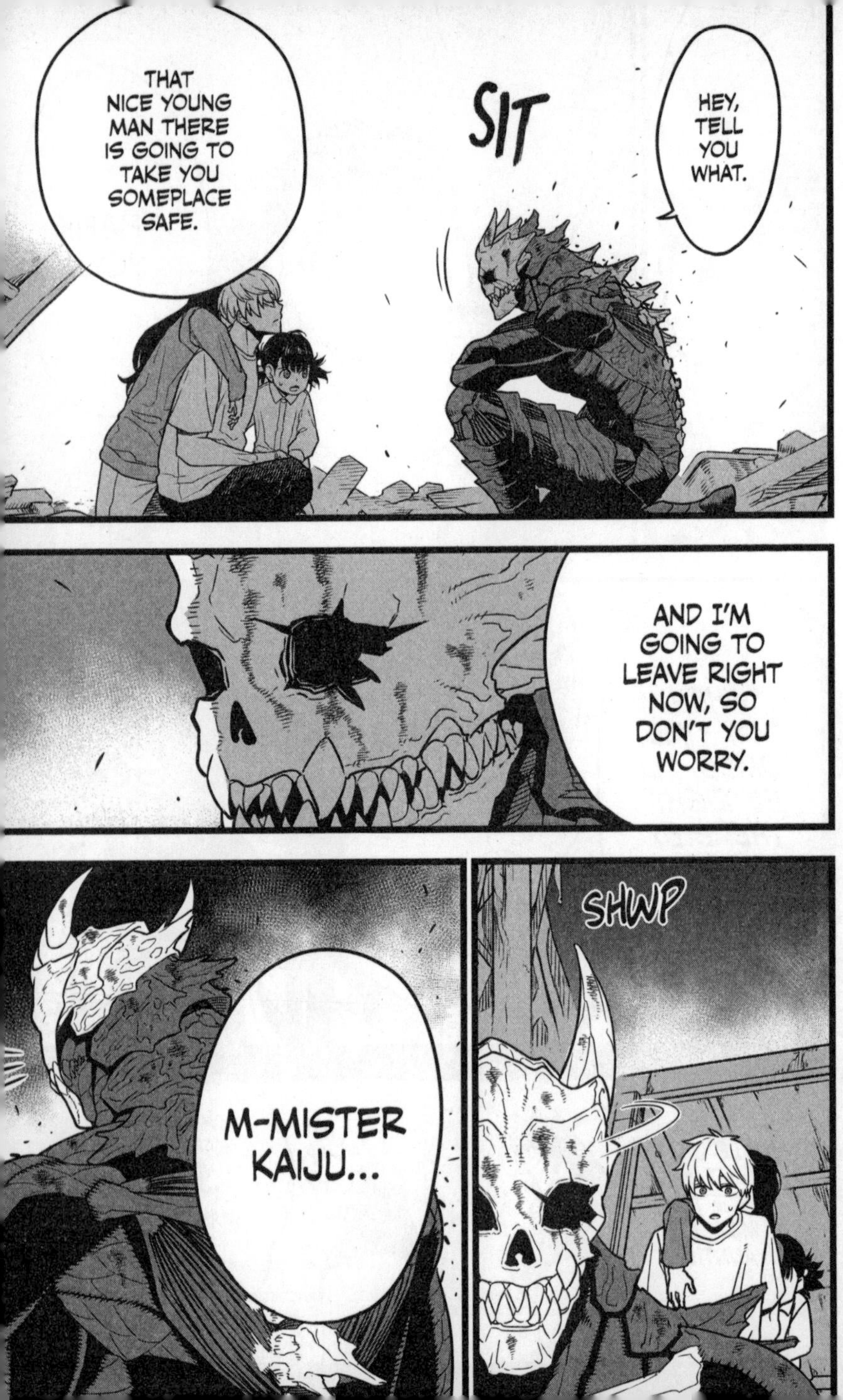
HEY, TELL YOU WHAT.
SIT
THAT NICE YOUNG MAN THERE IS GOING TO TAKE YOU SOMEPLACE SAFE.
AND I'M GOING TO LEAVE RIGHT NOW, SO DON'T YOU WORRY.
SHWP
M-MISTER KAIJU...

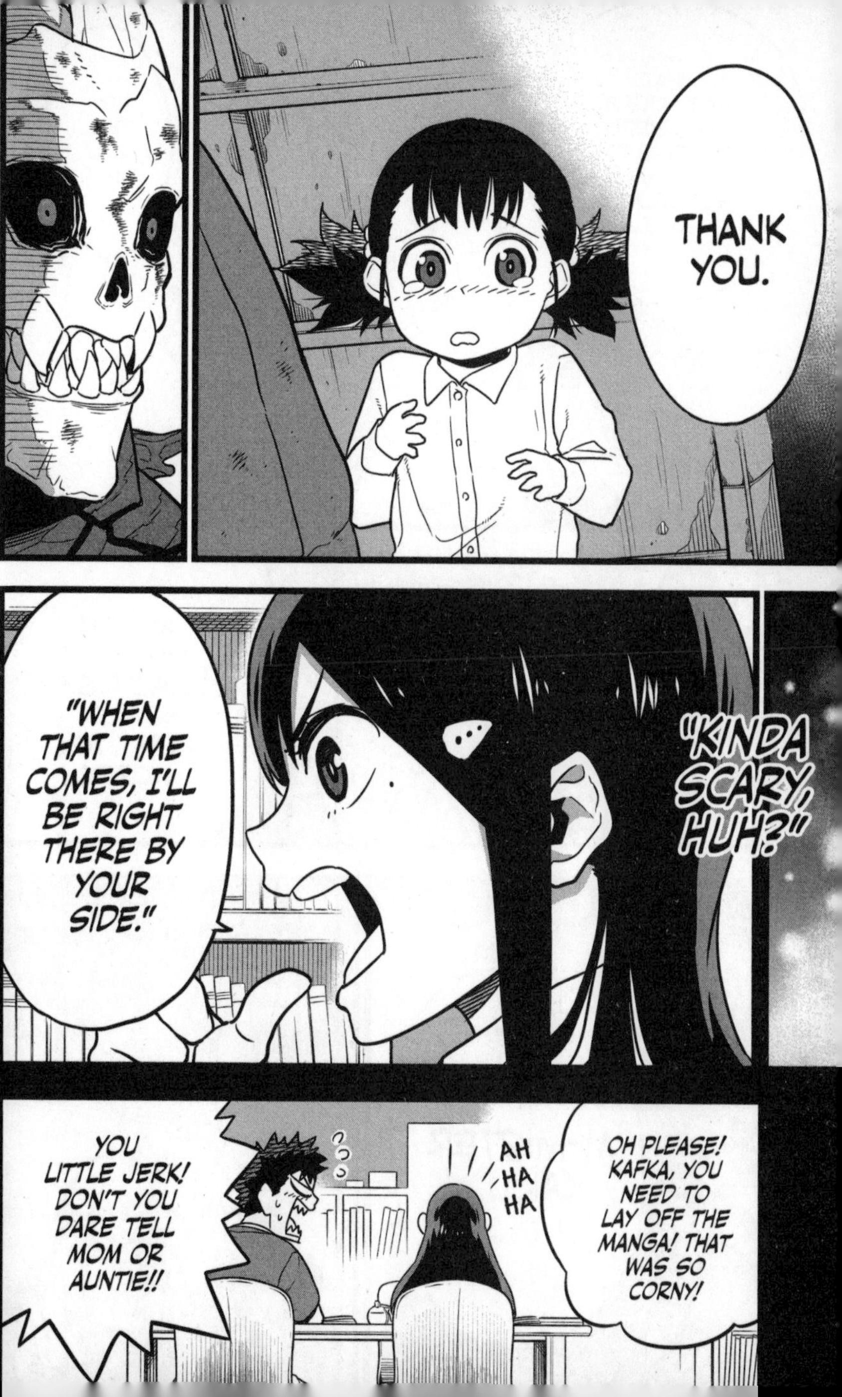
THANK YOU.
"KINDA SCARY, HUH?"
"WHEN THAT TIME COMES, I'LL BE RIGHT THERE BY YOUR SIDE."
OH PLEASE! KAFKA, YOU NEED TO LAY OFF THE MANGA! THAT WAS SO CORNY!
AH HA HA
YOU LITTLE JERK! DON'T YOU DARE TELL MOM OR AUNTIE!!

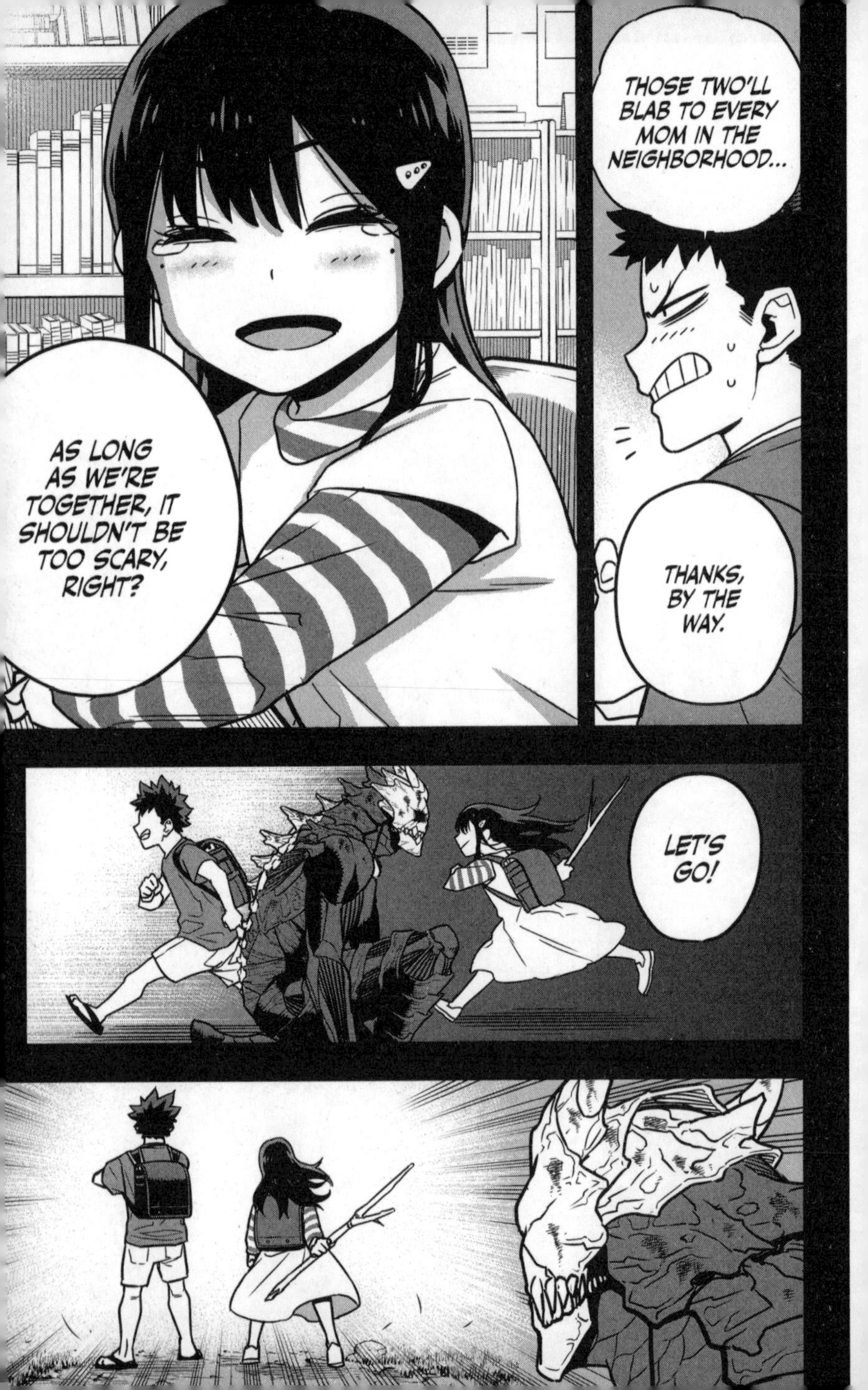
THOSE TWO'LL BLAB TO EVERY MOM IN THE NEIGHBORHOOD...
THANKS, BY THE WAY.
AS LONG AS WE'RE TOGETHER, IT SHOULDN'T BE TOO SCARY, RIGHT?
LET'S GO!

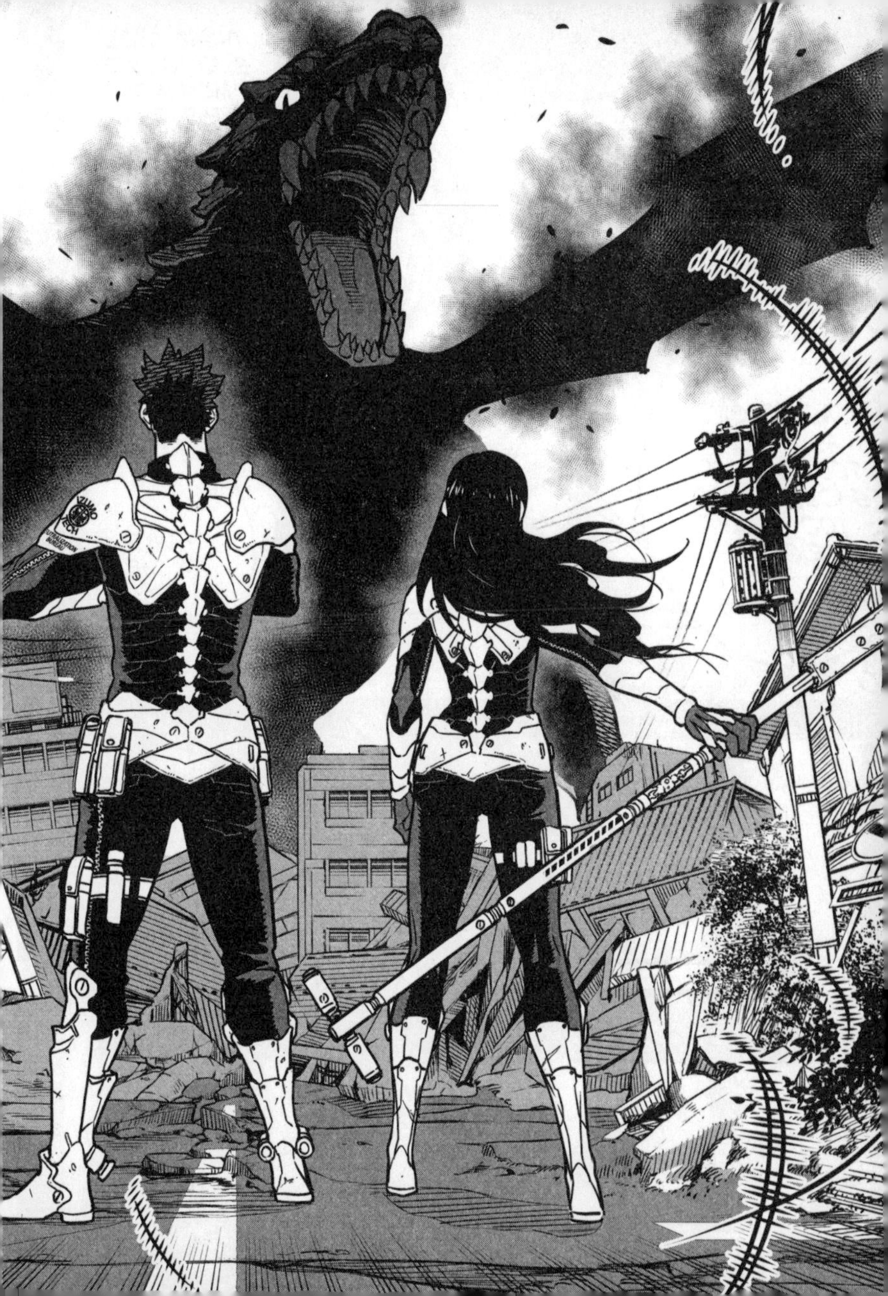

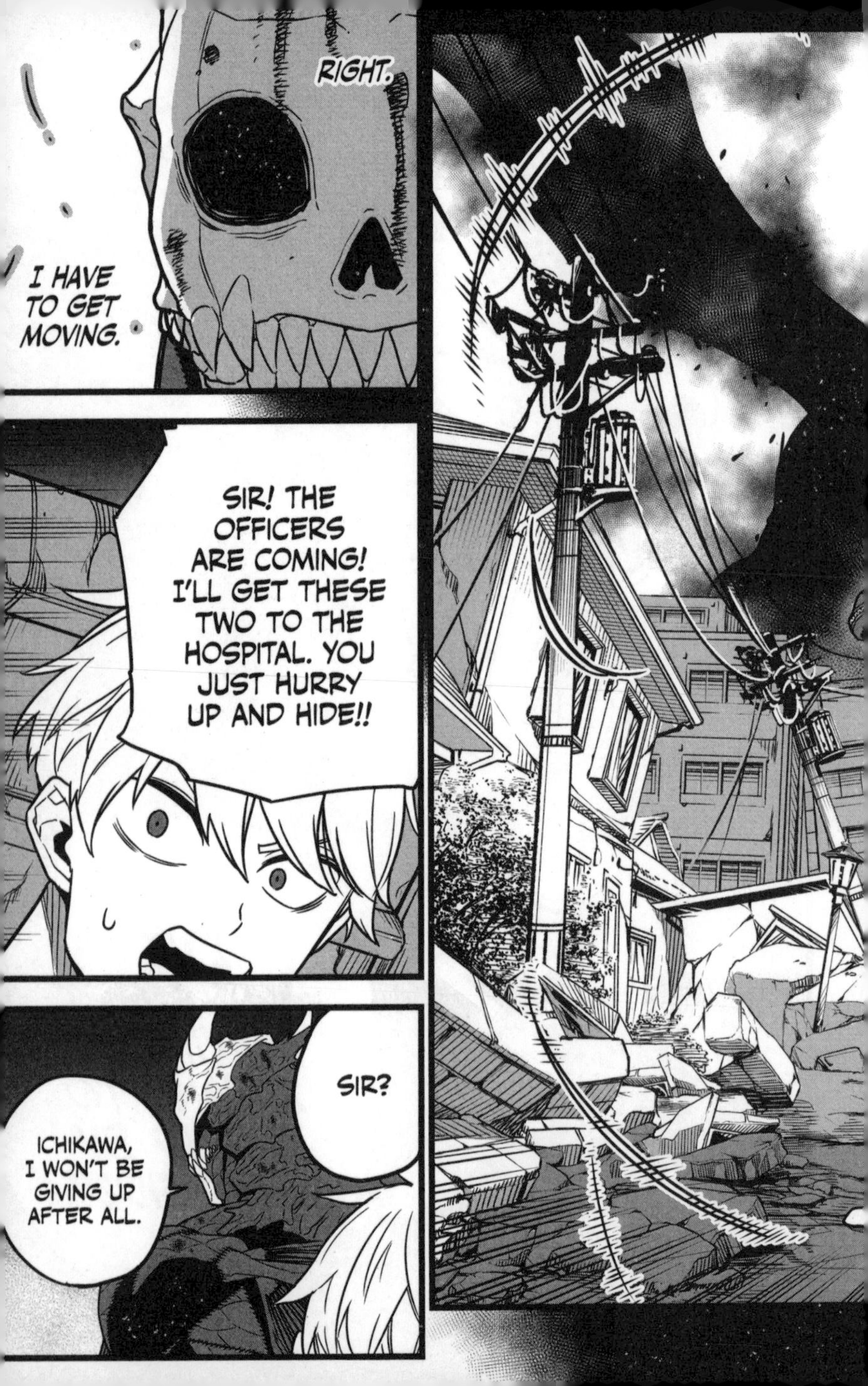
RIGHT.
I HAVE TO GET MOVING.
SIR! THE OFFICERS ARE COMING! I'LL GET THESE TWO TO THE HOSPITAL. YOU JUST HURRY UP AND HIDE!!
SIR?
ICHIKAWA, I WON'T BE GIVING UP AFTER ALL.

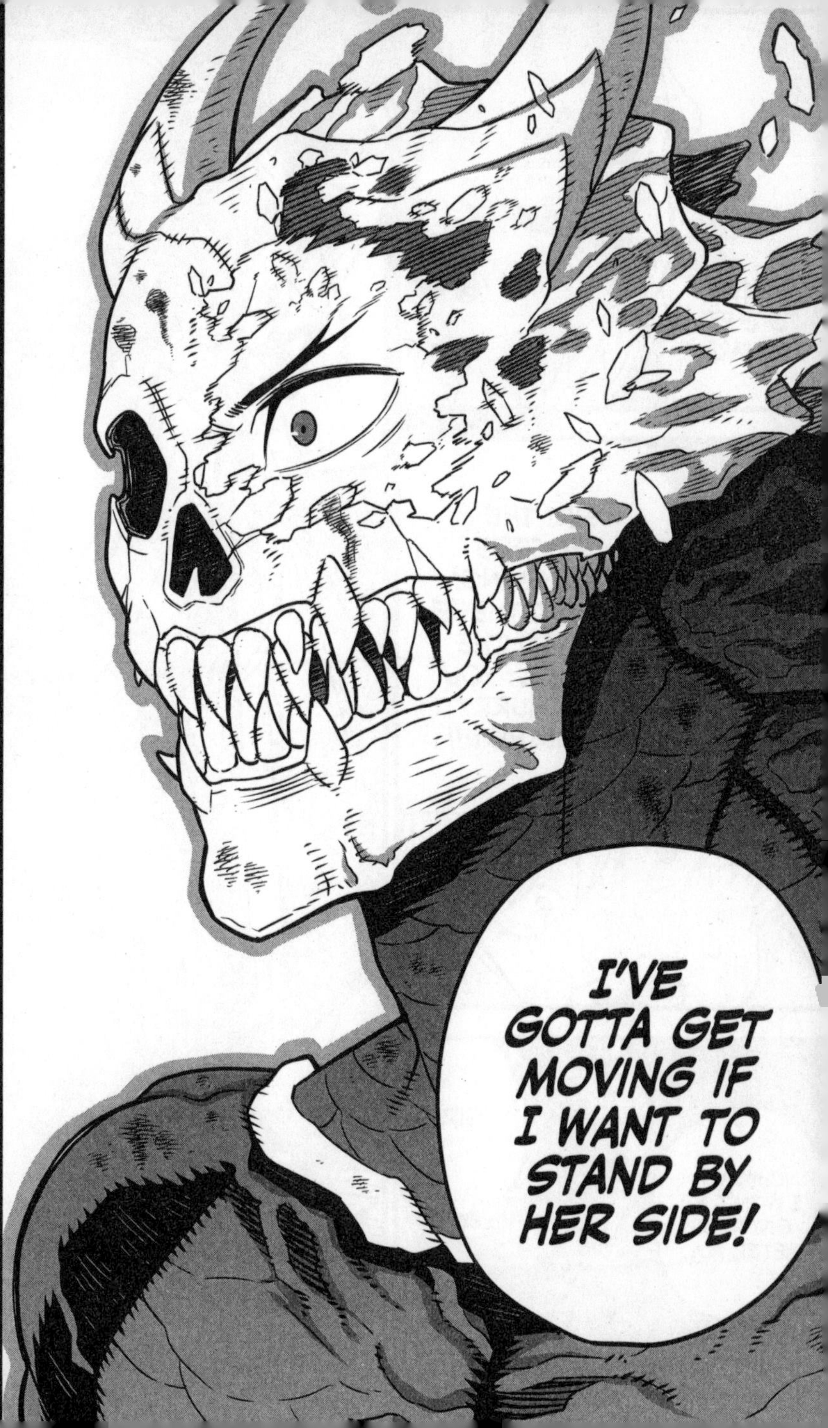
I'VE GOTTA GET MOVING IF I WANT TO STAND BY HER SIDE!

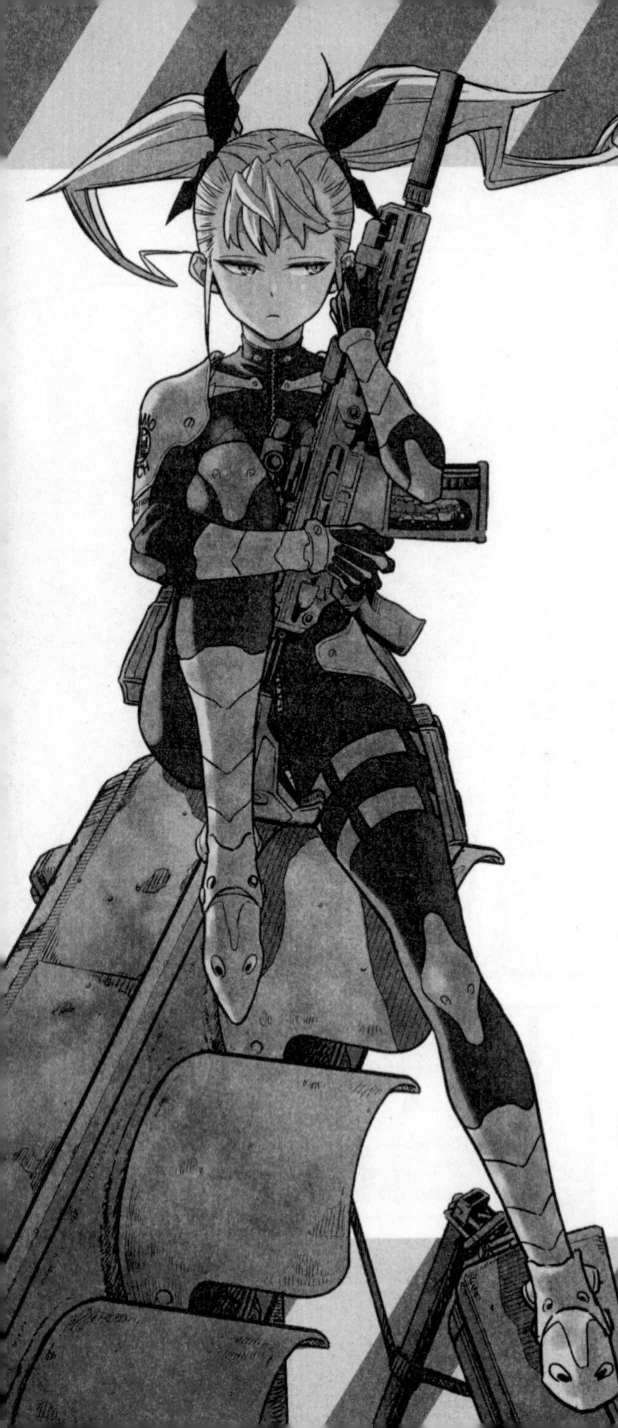

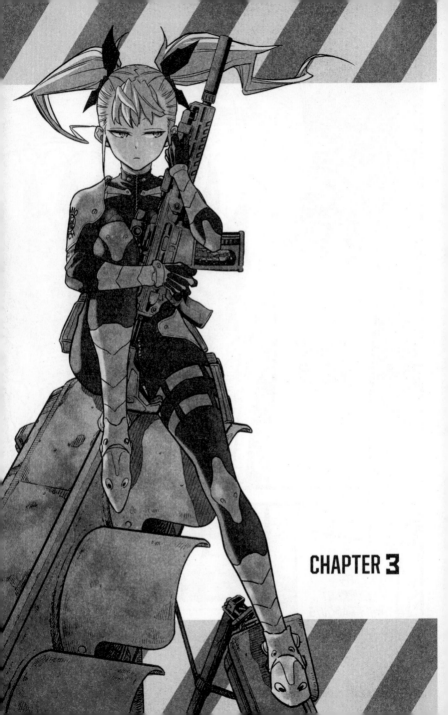

# CHAPTER 3

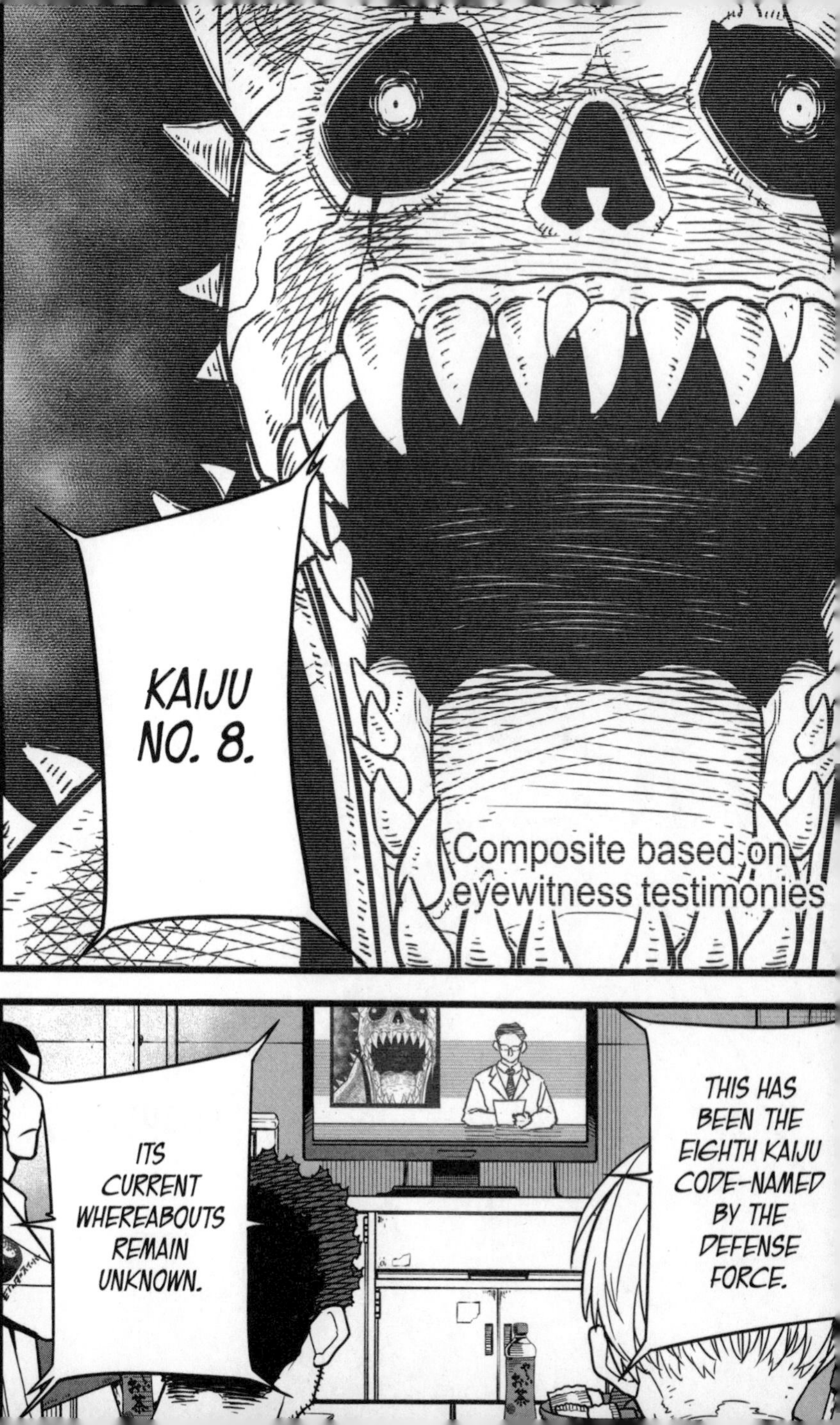
KAIJU NO. 8.
Composite based on eyewitness testimonies
THIS HAS BEEN THE EIGHTH KAIJU CODE-NAMED BY THE DEFENSE FORCE.
ITS CURRENT WHEREABOUTS REMAIN UNKNOWN.

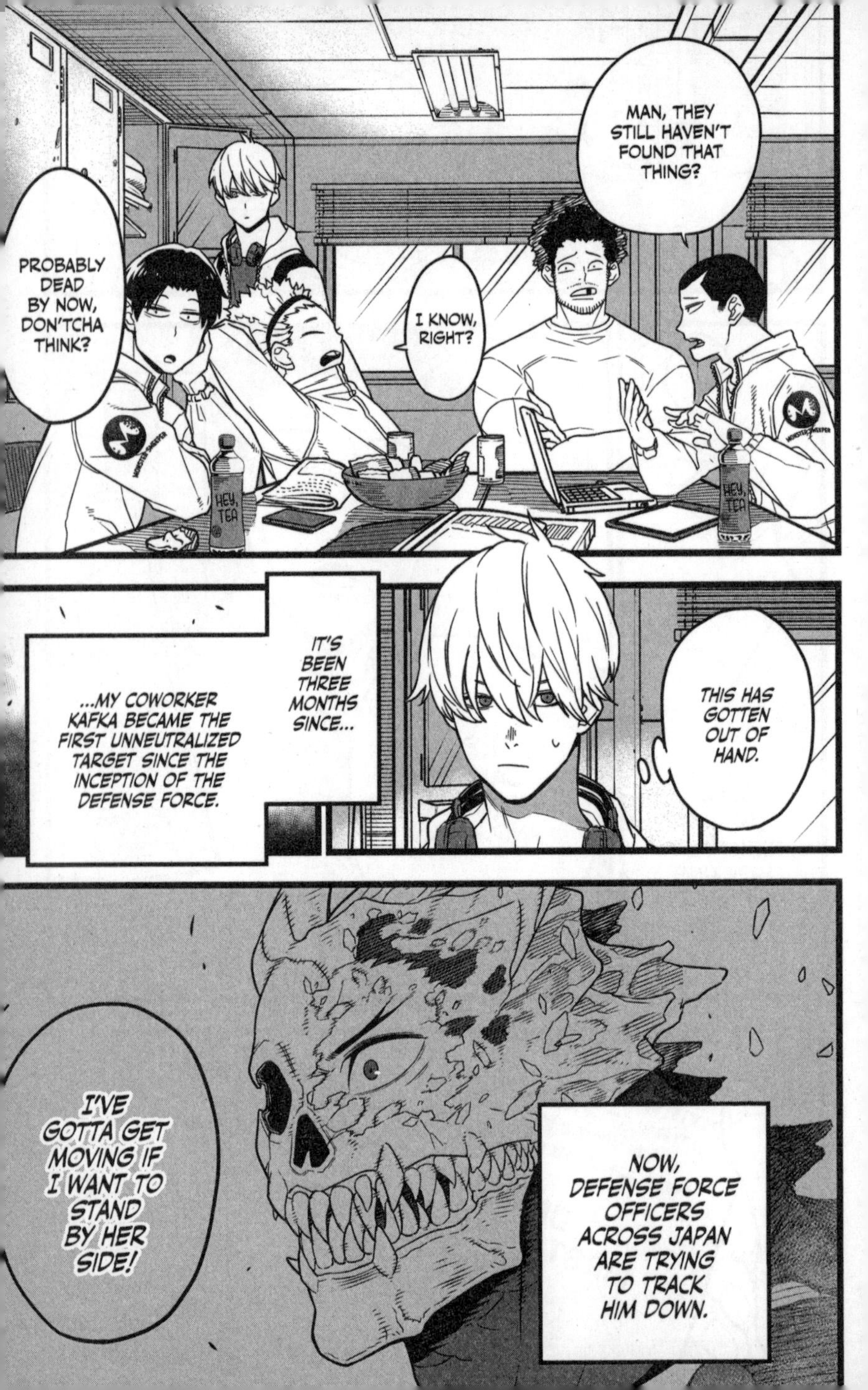
MAN, THEY STILL HAVEN'T FOUND THAT THING?
I KNOW, RIGHT?
PROBABLY DEAD BY NOW, DON'TCHA THINK?
HEY, TEA
HEY, TEA
THIS HAS GOTTEN OUT OF HAND.
IT'S BEEN THREE MONTHS SINCE...
...MY COWORKER KAFKA BECAME THE FIRST UNNEUTRALIZED TARGET SINCE THE INCEPTION OF THE DEFENSE FORCE.
NOW, DEFENSE FORCE OFFICERS ACROSS JAPAN ARE TRYING TO TRACK HIM DOWN.
I'VE GOTTA GET MOVING IF I WANT TO STAND BY HER SIDE!

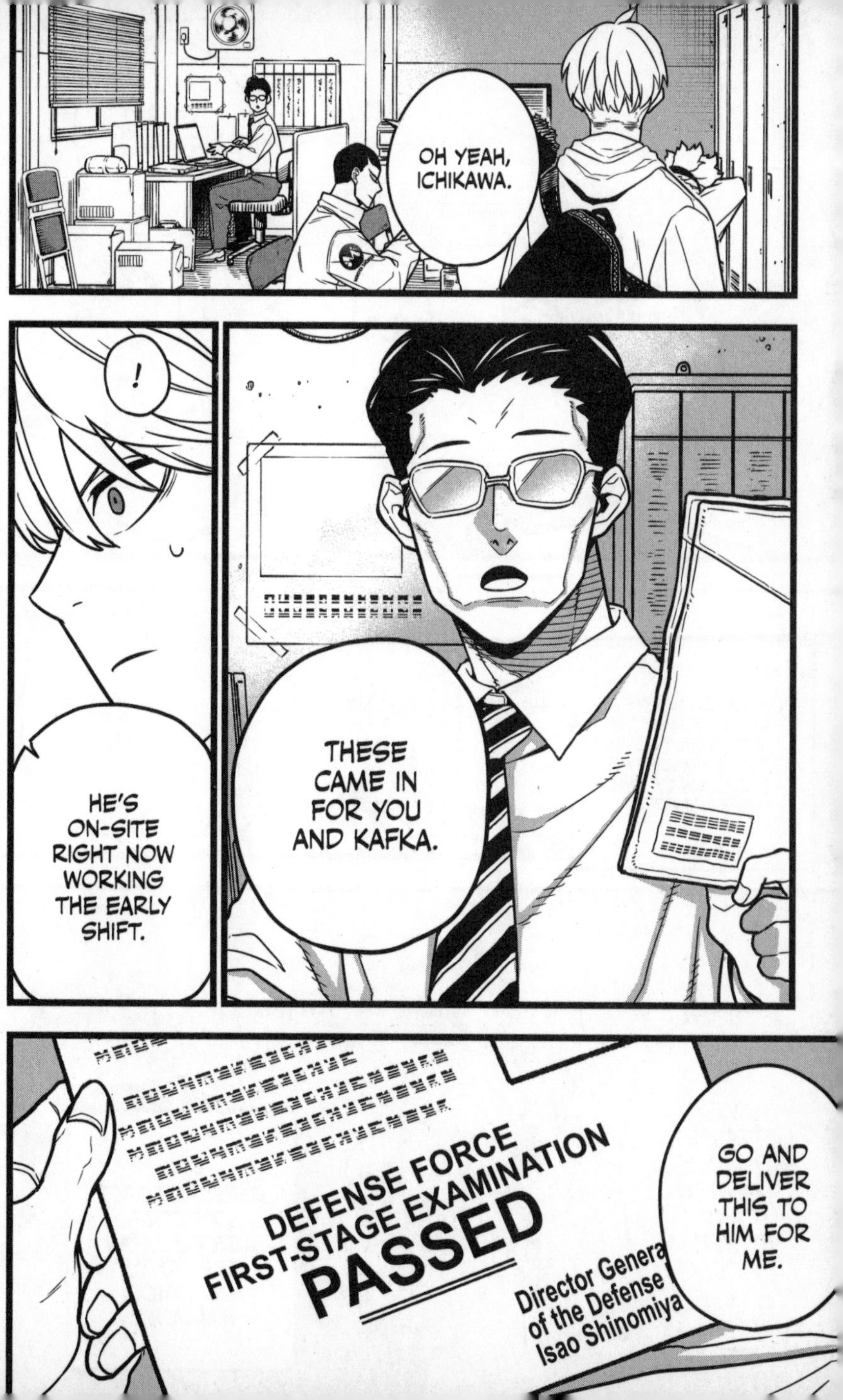

OH YEAH, ICHIKAWA.
THESE CAME IN FOR YOU AND KAFKA.
!
HE'S ON-SITE RIGHT NOW WORKING THE EARLY SHIFT.
GO AND DELIVER THIS TO HIM FOR ME.
DEFENSE FORCE FIRST-STAGE EXAMINATION
PASSED
Director Genera
of the Defense
Isao Shinomiya

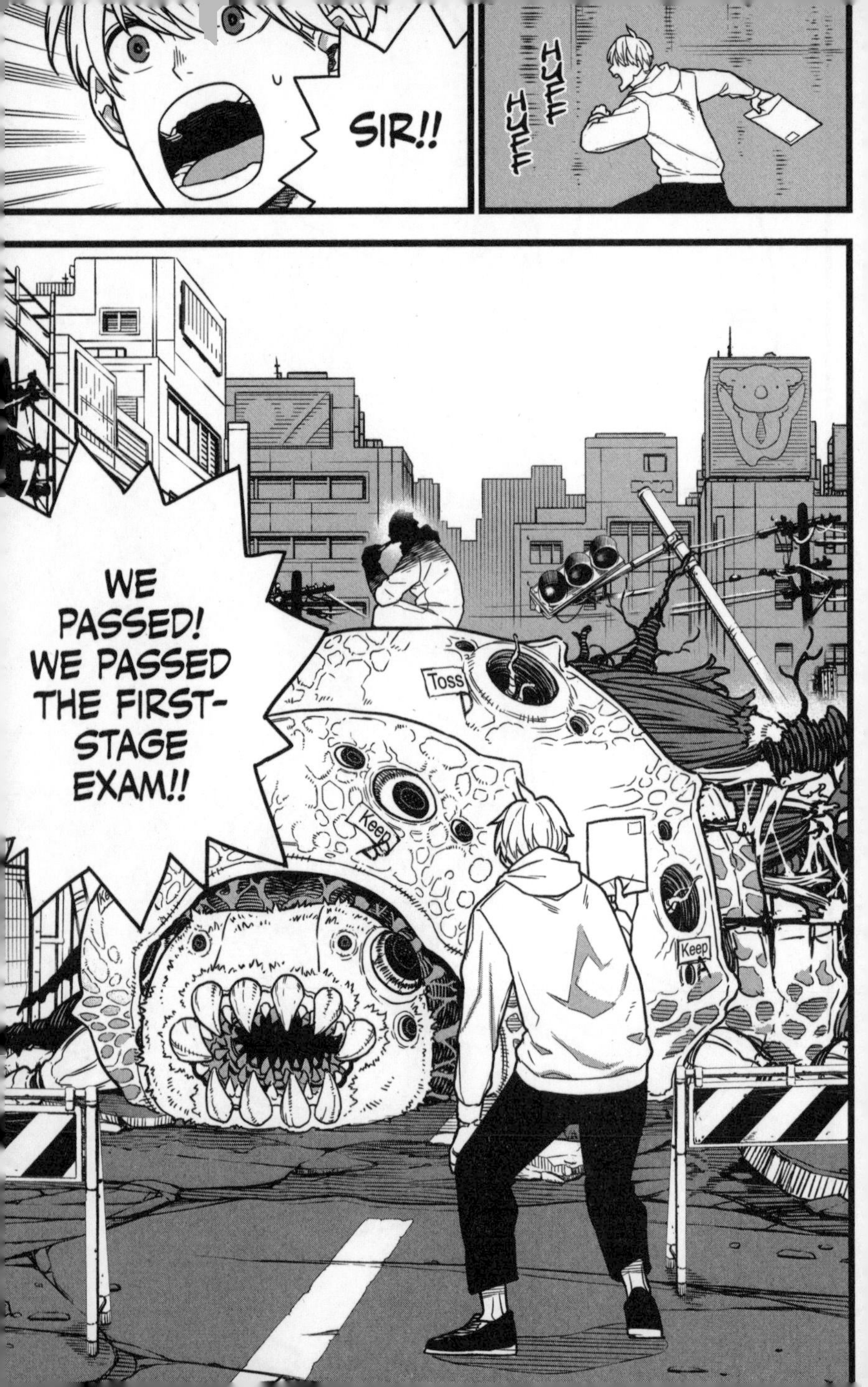
HUFF
HUFF
SIR!!
WE PASSED! WE PASSED THE FIRST-STAGE EXAM!!
Toss
Keep
Keep

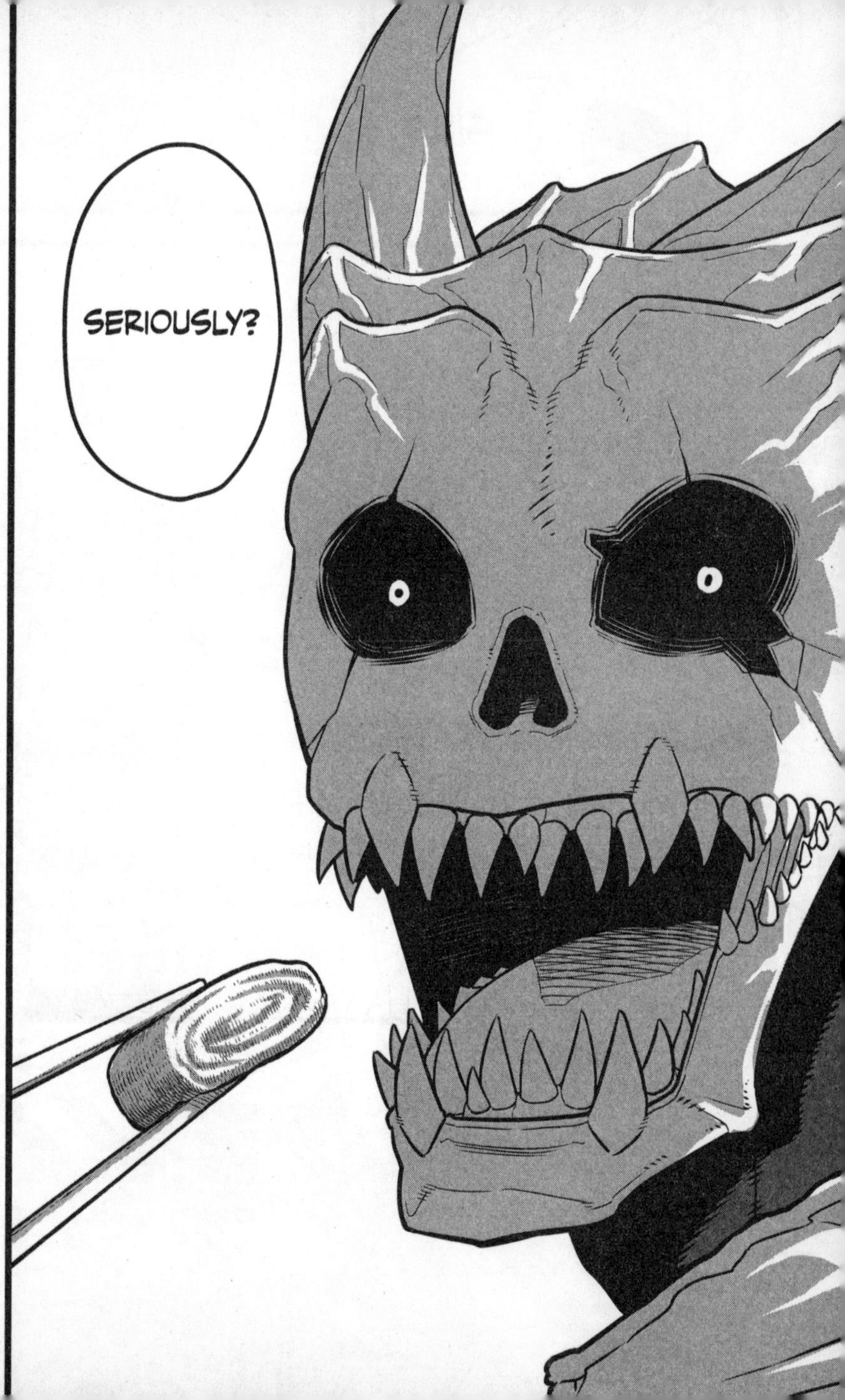
SERIOUSLY?

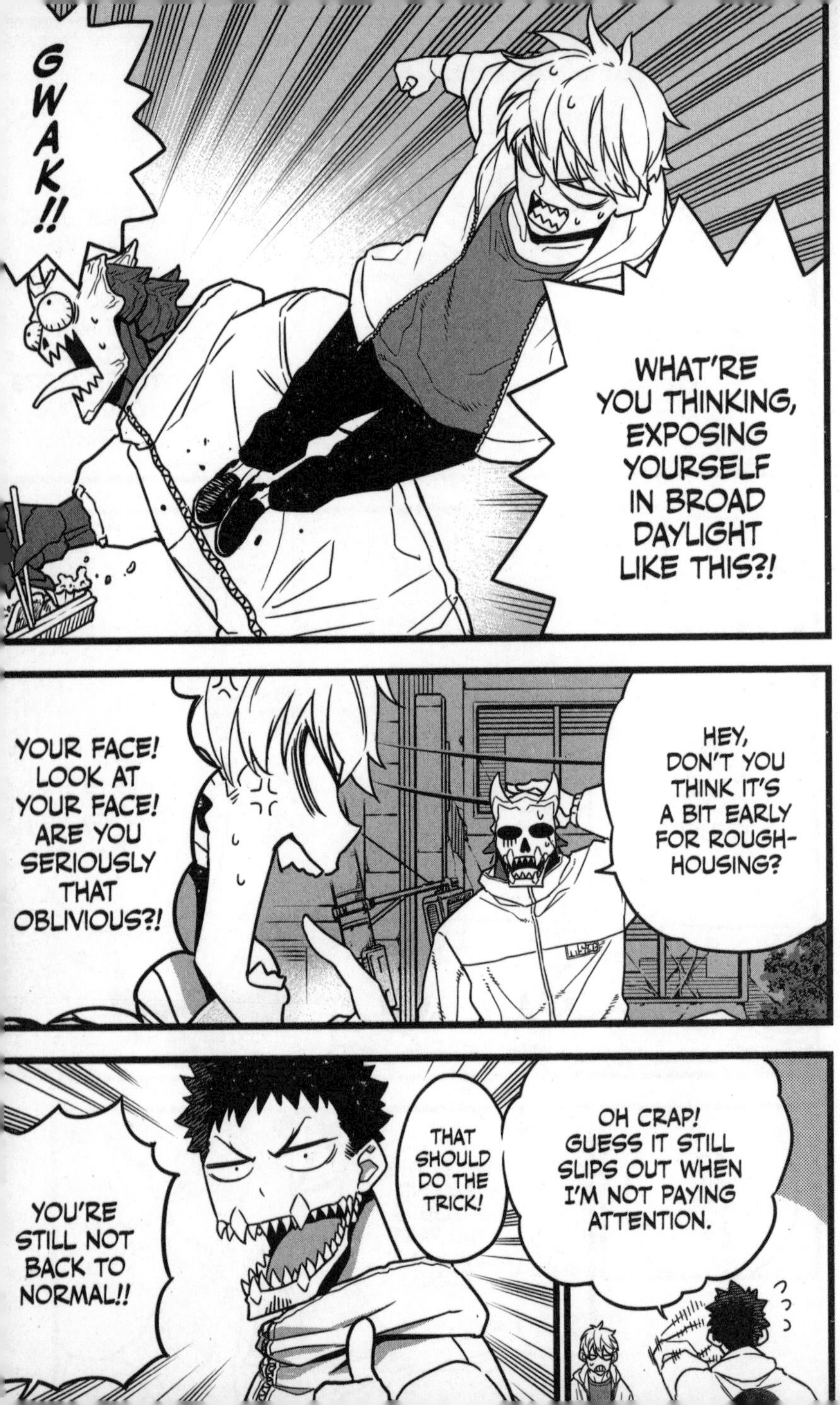
GWAK!!
WHAT'RE YOU THINKING, EXPOSING YOURSELF IN BROAD DAYLIGHT LIKE THIS?!
HEY, DON'T YOU THINK IT'S A BIT EARLY FOR ROUGH-HOUSING?
YOUR FACE! LOOK AT YOUR FACE! ARE YOU SERIOUSLY THAT OBLIVIOUS?!
OH CRAP! GUESS IT STILL SLIPS OUT WHEN I'M NOT PAYING ATTENTION.
THAT SHOULD DO THE TRICK!
YOU'RE STILL NOT BACK TO NORMAL!!

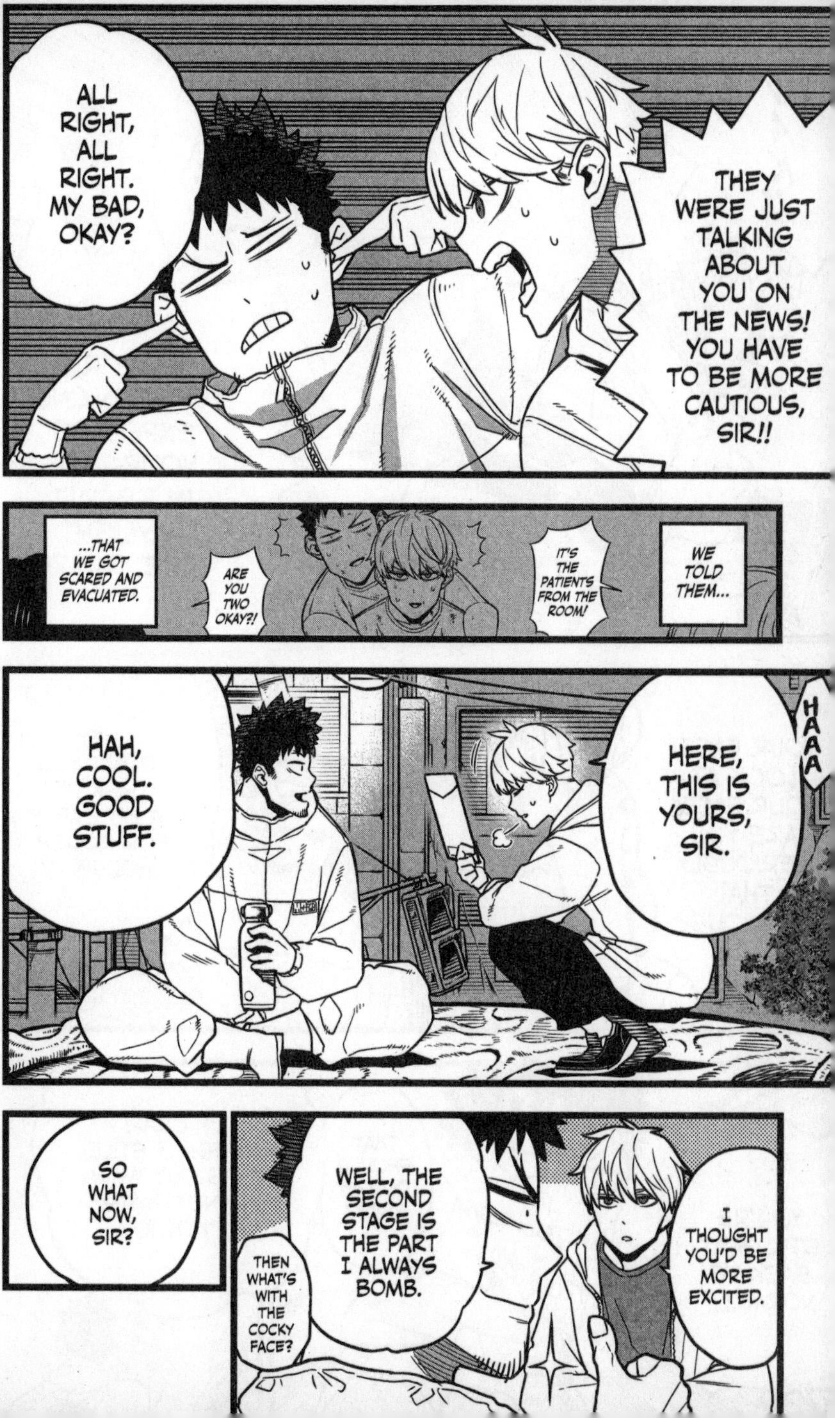
THEY WERE JUST TALKING ABOUT YOU ON THE NEWS! YOU HAVE TO BE MORE CAUTIOUS, SIR!!
ALL RIGHT, ALL RIGHT. MY BAD, OKAY?
WE TOLD THEM...
IT'S THE PATIENTS FROM THE ROOM!
ARE YOU TWO OKAY?!
...THAT WE GOT SCARED AND EVACUATED.
HAAA
HERE, THIS IS YOURS, SIR.
HAH, COOL. GOOD STUFF.
I THOUGHT YOU'D BE MORE EXCITED.
WELL, THE SECOND STAGE IS THE PART I ALWAYS BOMB.
THEN WHAT'S WITH THE COCKY FACE?
SO WHAT NOW, SIR?

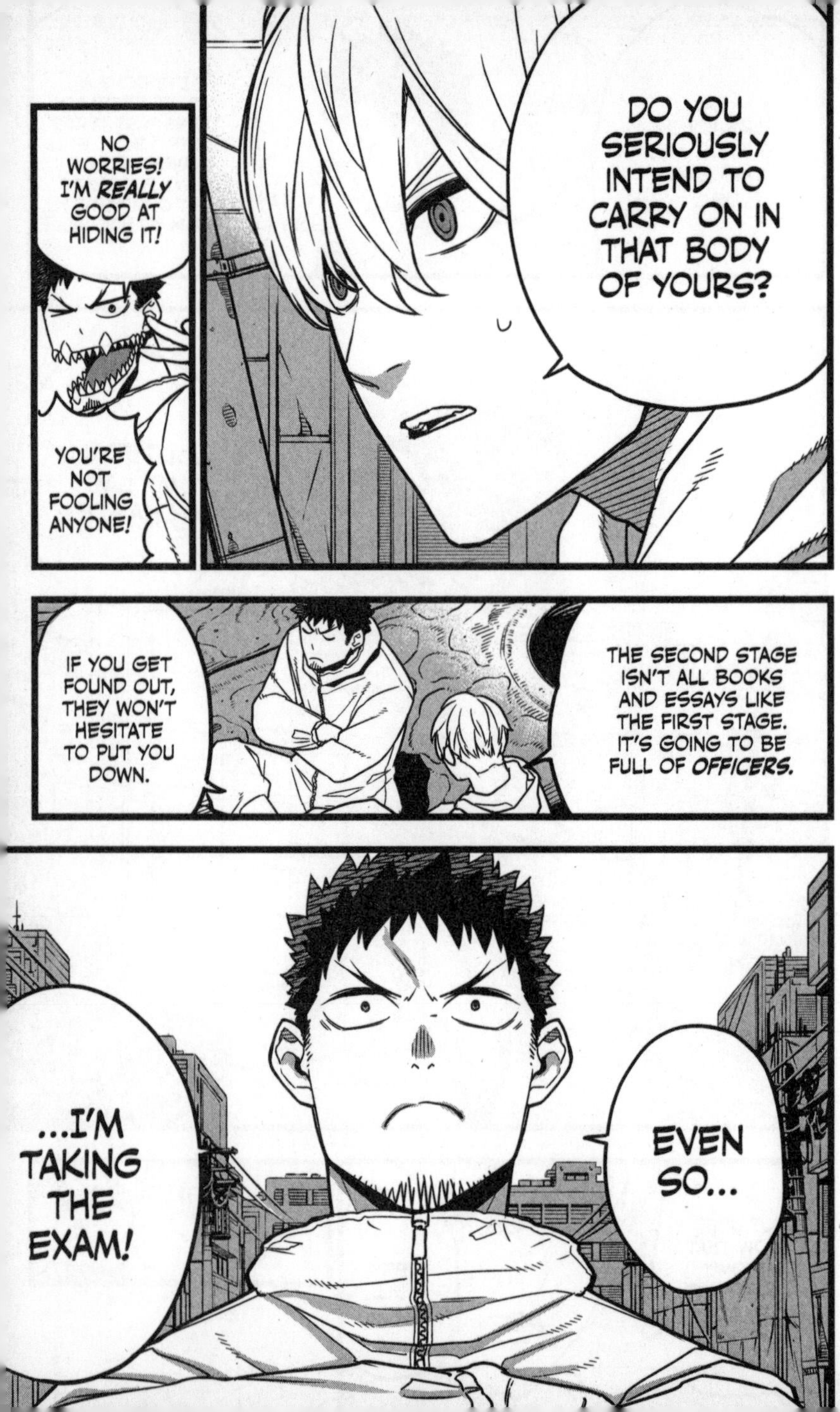
DO YOU SERIOUSLY INTEND TO CARRY ON IN THAT BODY OF YOURS?
NO WORRIES! I'M *REALLY* GOOD AT HIDING IT!
YOU'RE NOT FOOLING ANYONE!
THE SECOND STAGE ISN'T ALL BOOKS AND ESSAYS LIKE THE FIRST STAGE. IT'S GOING TO BE FULL OF *OFFICERS.*
IF YOU GET FOUND OUT, THEY WON'T HESITATE TO PUT YOU DOWN.
EVEN SO...
...I'M TAKING THE EXAM!

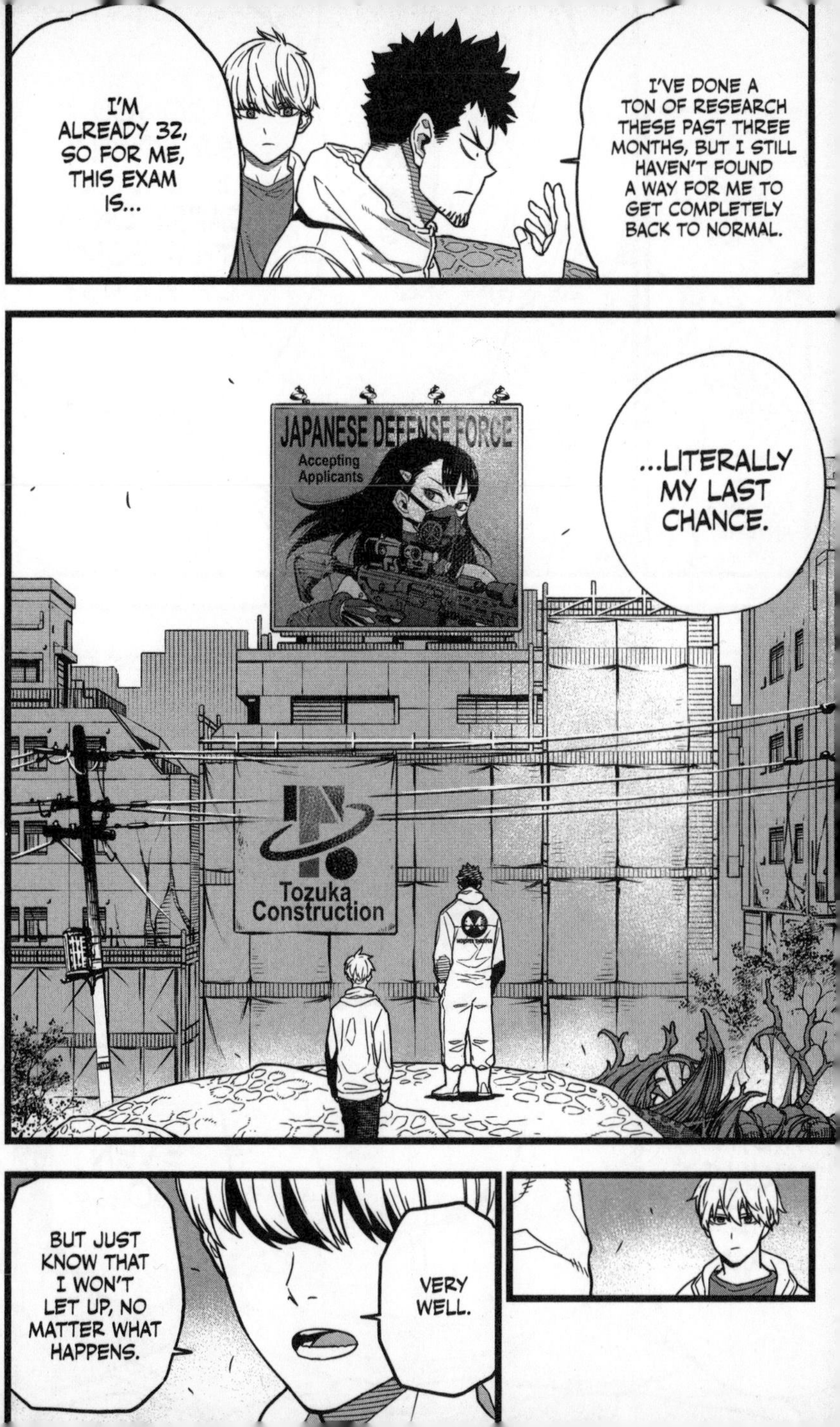
I'VE DONE A TON OF RESEARCH THESE PAST THREE MONTHS, BUT I STILL HAVEN'T FOUND A WAY FOR ME TO GET COMPLETELY BACK TO NORMAL.
I'M ALREADY 32, SO FOR ME, THIS EXAM IS...
...LITERALLY MY LAST CHANCE.
JAPANESE DEFENSE FORCE
Accepting Applicants
Tozuka Construction
VERY WELL.
BUT JUST KNOW THAT I WON'T LET UP, NO MATTER WHAT HAPPENS.

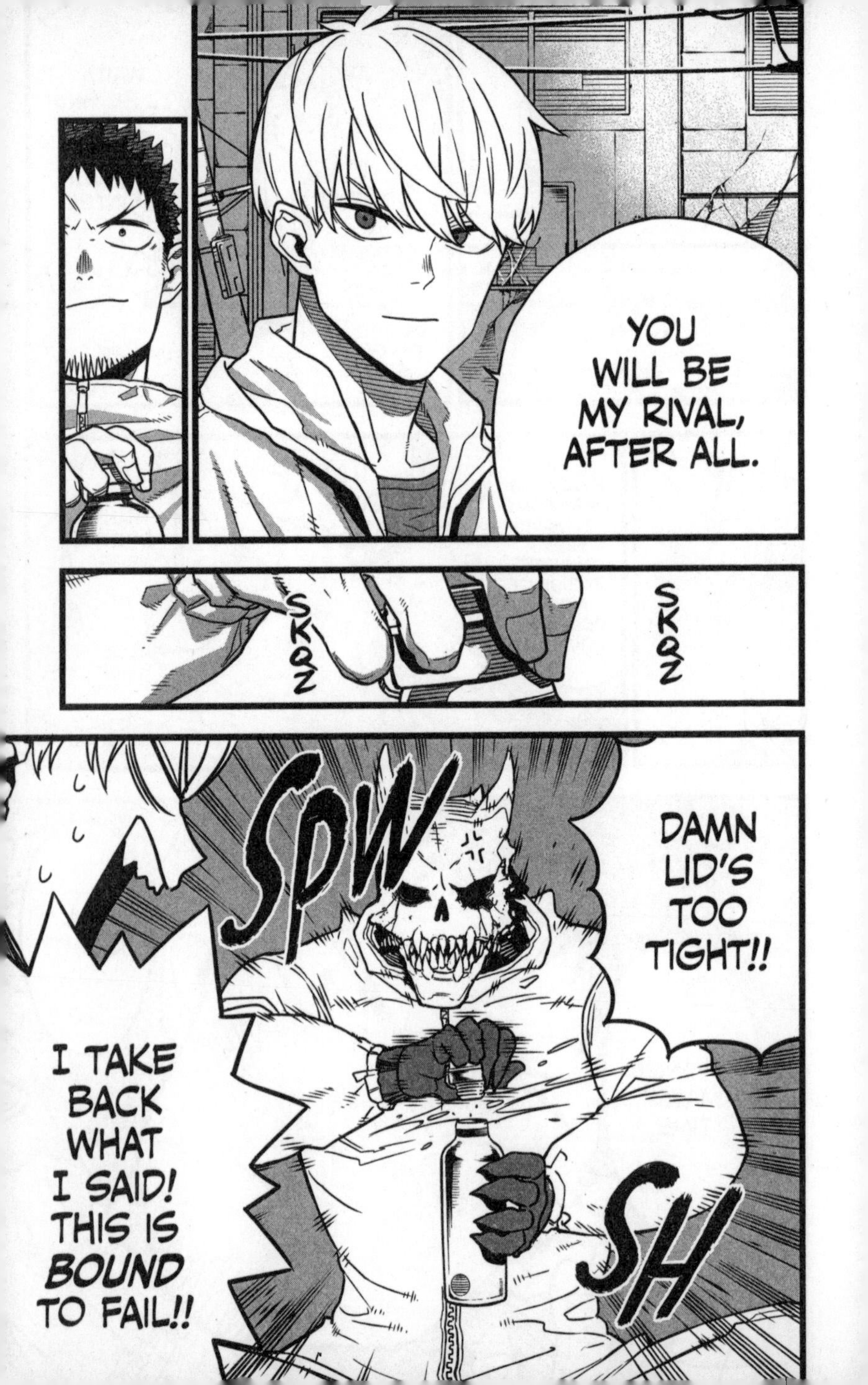

YOU WILL BE MY RIVAL, AFTER ALL.
SKQZ
SKQZ
DAMN LID'S TOO TIGHT!!
SPW
SH
I TAKE BACK WHAT I SAID! THIS IS *BOUND* TO FAIL!!

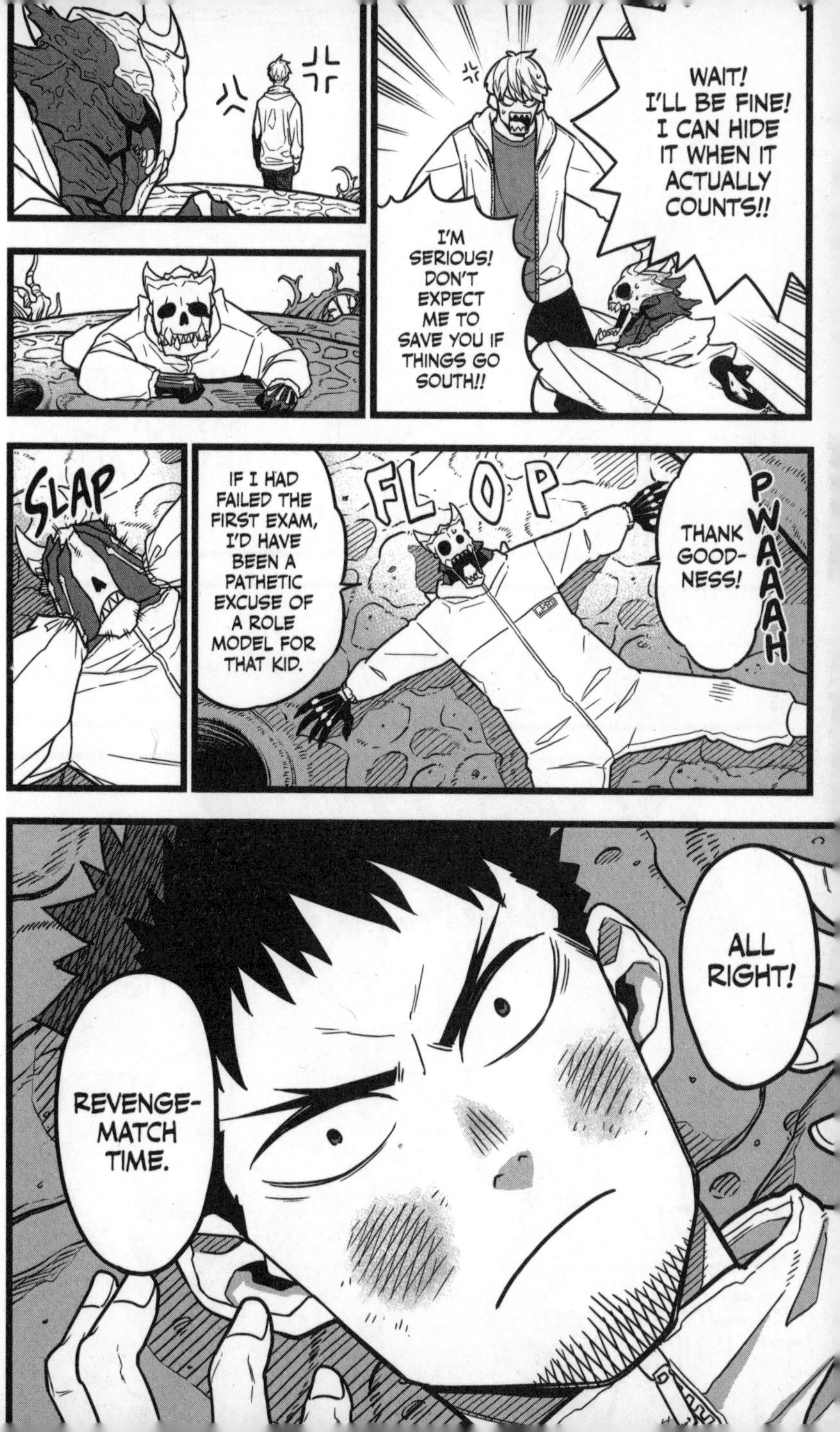
WAIT! I'LL BE FINE! I CAN HIDE IT WHEN IT ACTUALLY COUNTS!!
I'M SERIOUS! DON'T EXPECT ME TO SAVE YOU IF THINGS GO SOUTH!!
PWAAAH
THANK GOOD-NESS!
FLOP
IF I HAD FAILED THE FIRST EXAM, I'D HAVE BEEN A PATHETIC EXCUSE OF A ROLE MODEL FOR THAT KID.
SLAP
ALL RIGHT!
REVENGE-MATCH TIME.

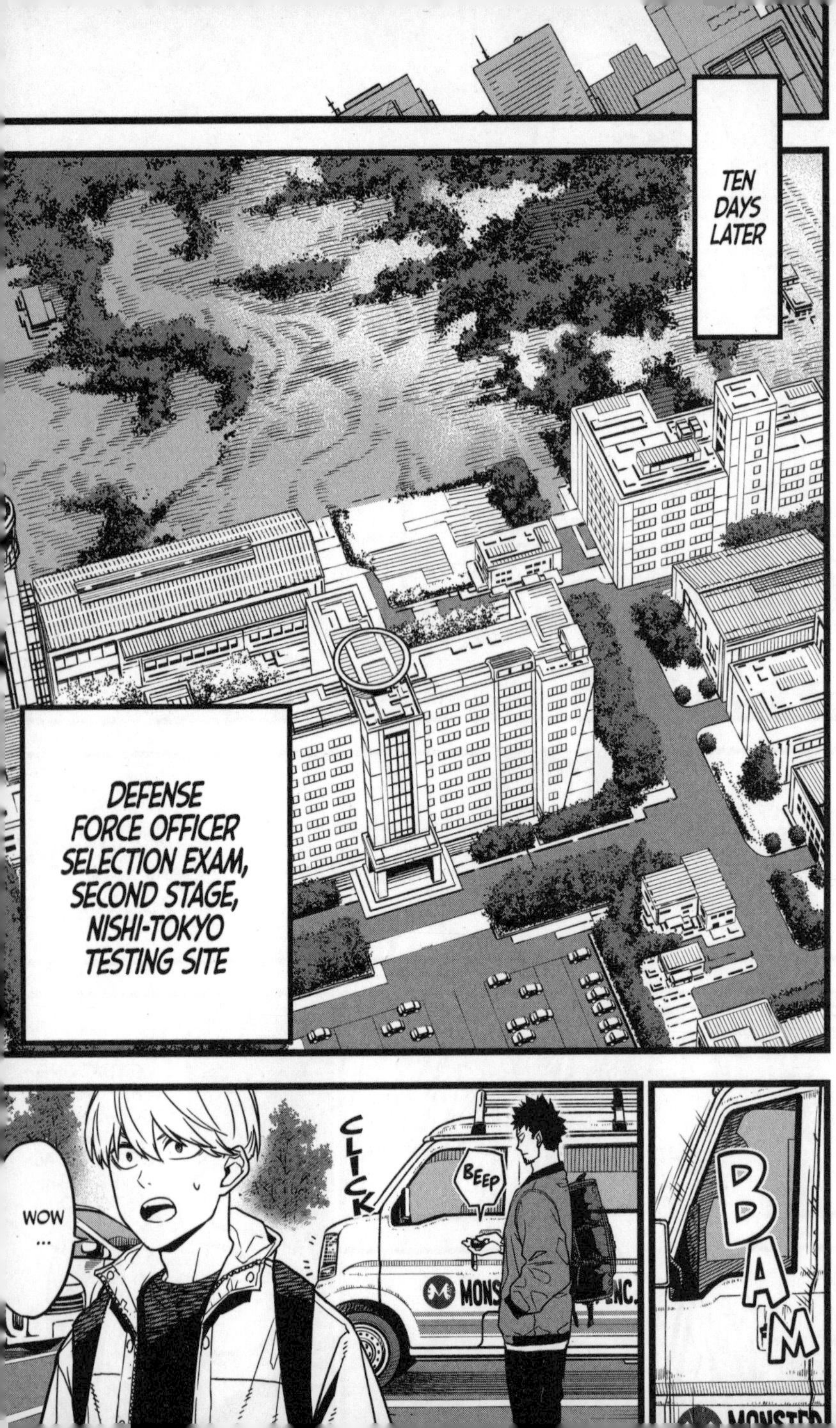
TEN DAYS LATER
DEFENSE FORCE OFFICER SELECTION EXAM, SECOND STAGE, NISHI-TOKYO TESTING SITE
BAM
CLICK
BEEP
WOW...

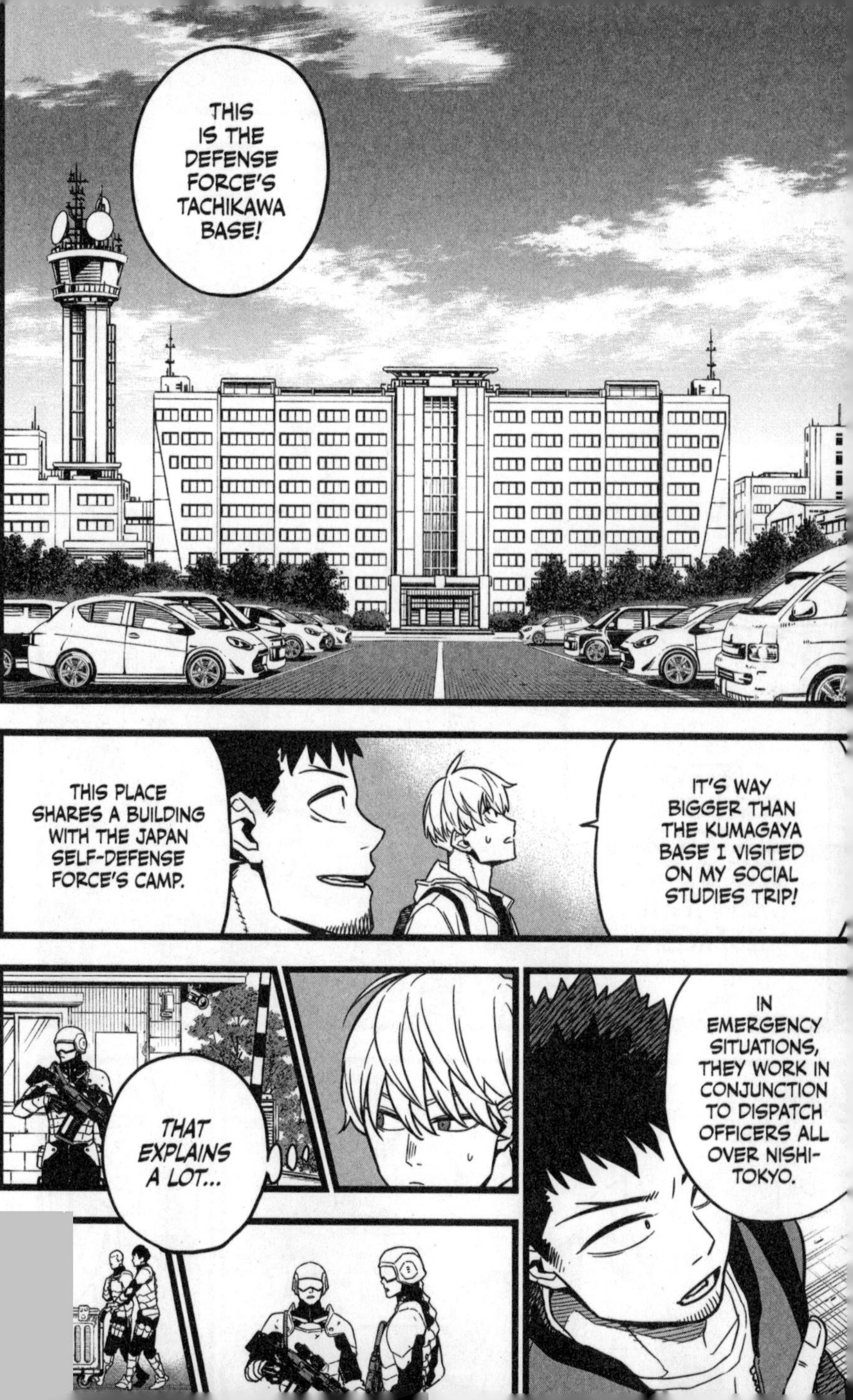
THIS IS THE DEFENSE FORCE'S TACHIKAWA BASE!
IT'S WAY BIGGER THAN THE KUMAGAYA BASE I VISITED ON MY SOCIAL STUDIES TRIP!
THIS PLACE SHARES A BUILDING WITH THE JAPAN SELF-DEFENSE FORCE'S CAMP.
IN EMERGENCY SITUATIONS, THEY WORK IN CONJUNCTION TO DISPATCH OFFICERS ALL OVER NISHI-TOKYO.
THAT EXPLAINS A LOT...

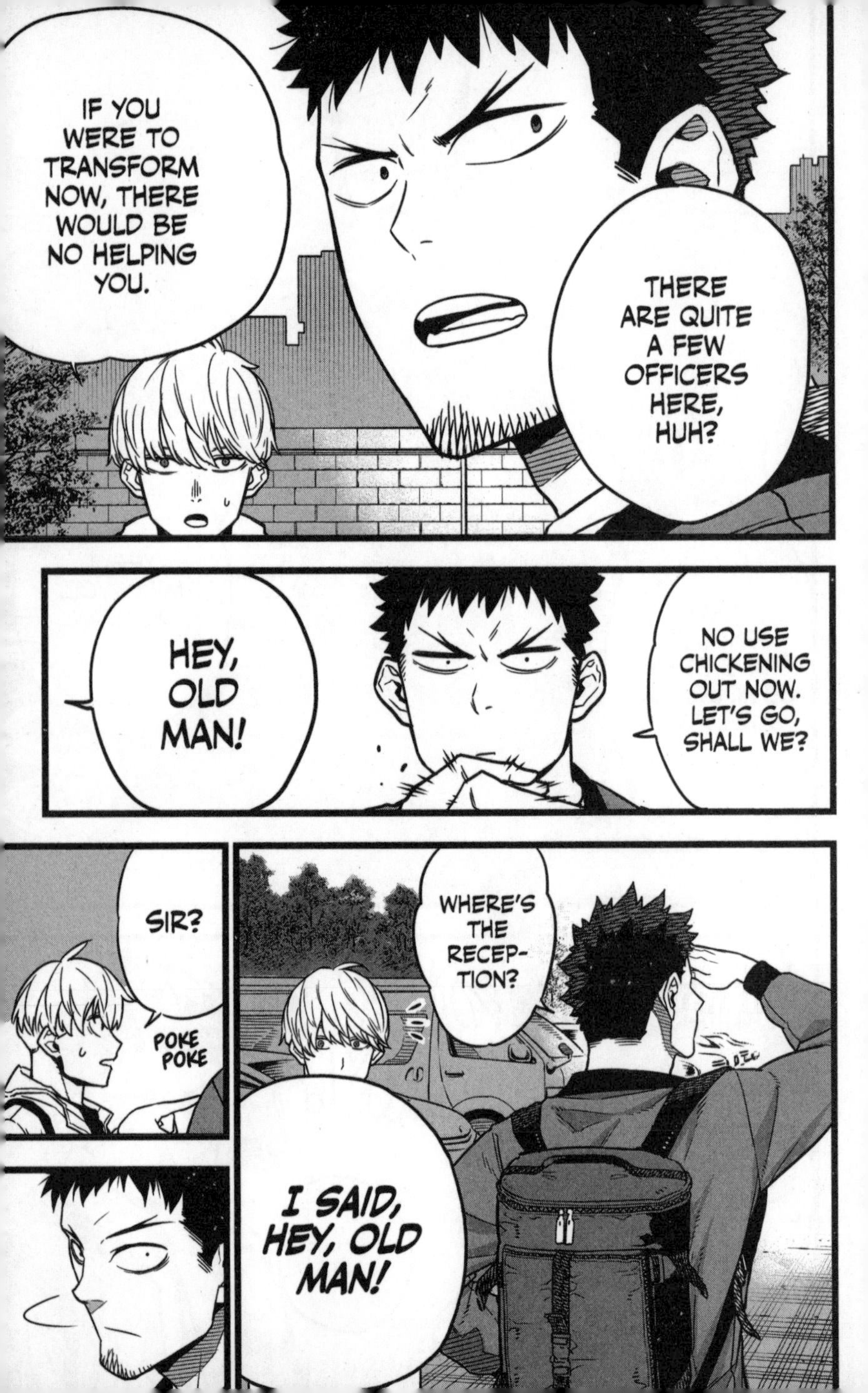
THERE ARE QUITE A FEW OFFICERS HERE, HUH?
IF YOU WERE TO TRANSFORM NOW, THERE WOULD BE NO HELPING YOU.
NO USE CHICKENING OUT NOW. LET'S GO, SHALL WE?
HEY, OLD MAN!
WHERE'S THE RECEPTION?
SIR?
POKE POKE
I SAID, HEY, OLD MAN!

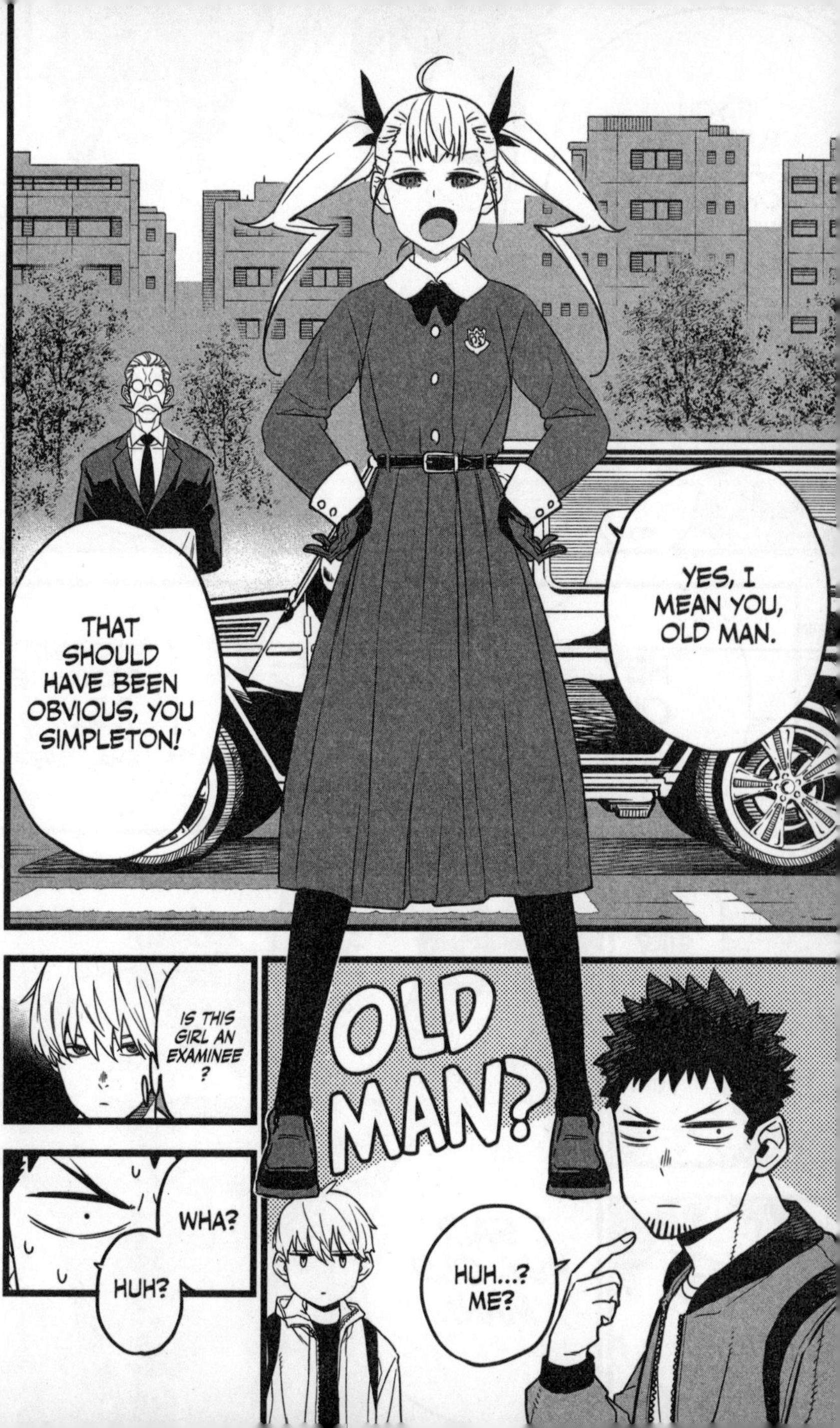
YES, I MEAN YOU, OLD MAN.
THAT SHOULD HAVE BEEN OBVIOUS, YOU SIMPLETON!
OLD MAN?
HUH...? ME?
IS THIS GIRL AN EXAMINEE?
WHA?
HUH?

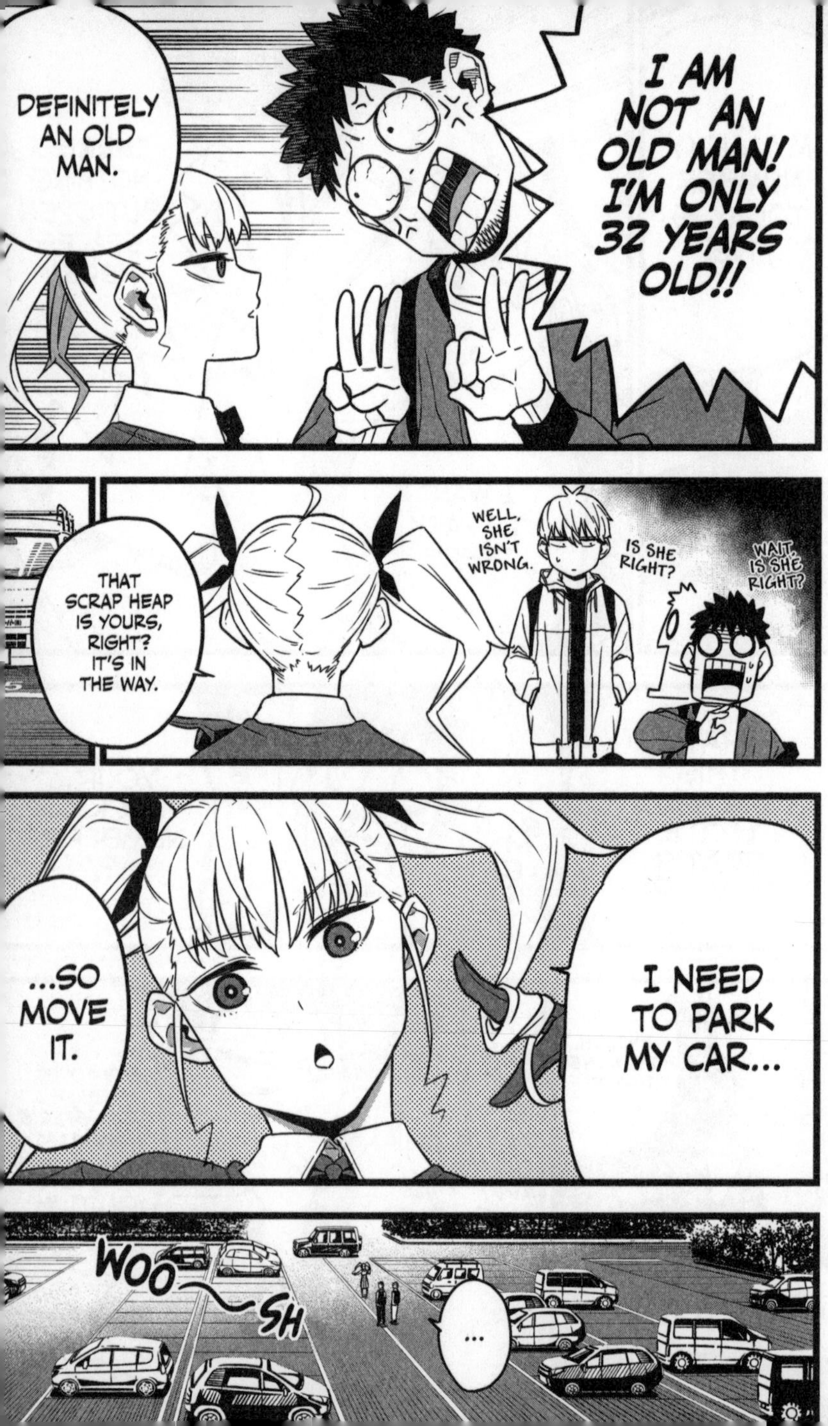
I AM NOT AN OLD MAN! I'M ONLY 32 YEARS OLD!!
DEFINITELY AN OLD MAN.
WAIT, IS SHE RIGHT?
IS SHE RIGHT?
WELL, SHE ISN'T WRONG.
THAT SCRAP HEAP IS YOURS, RIGHT? IT'S IN THE WAY.
I NEED TO PARK MY CAR...
...SO MOVE IT.
...
WOO~SH

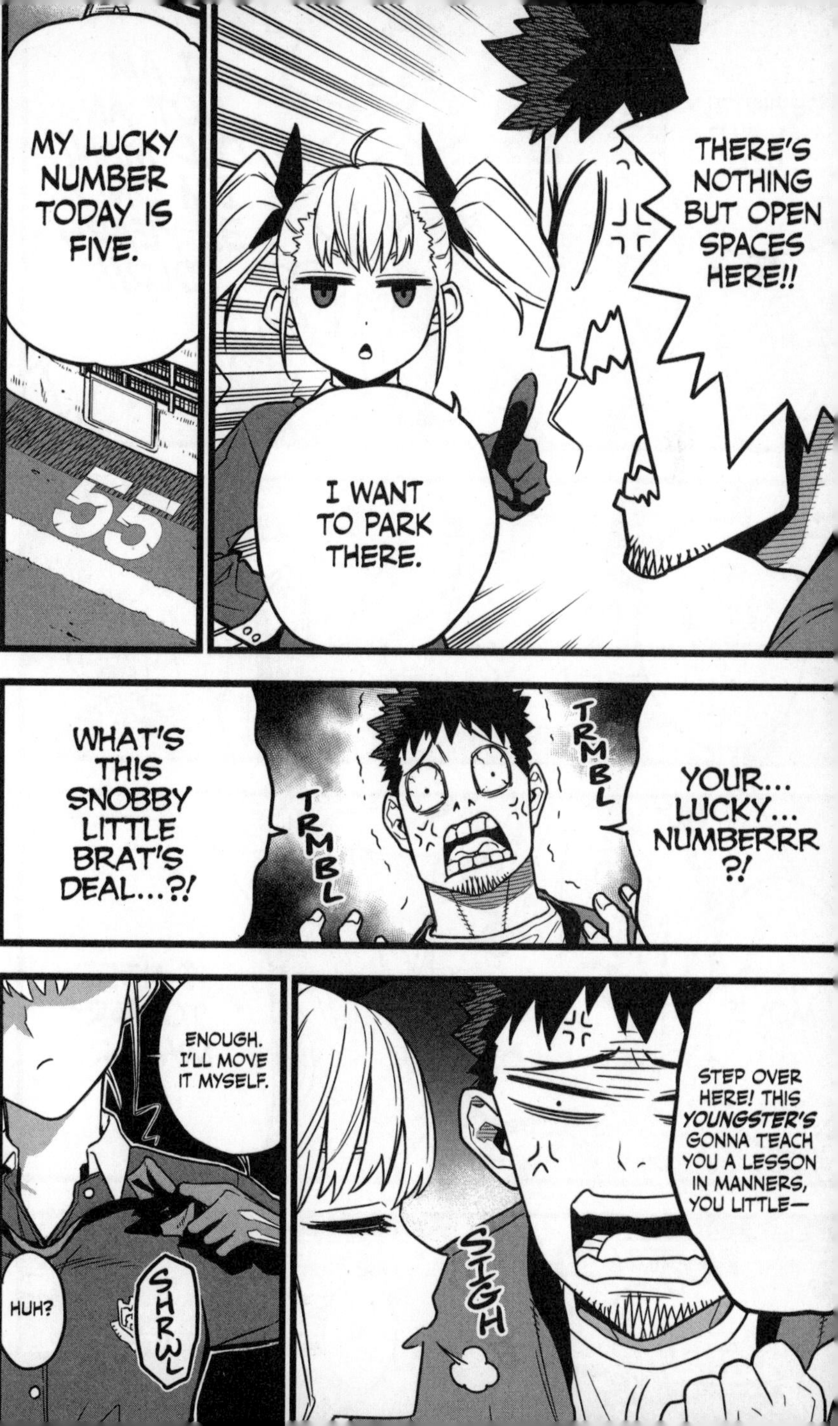
THERE'S NOTHING BUT OPEN SPACES HERE!!
I WANT TO PARK THERE.
MY LUCKY NUMBER TODAY IS FIVE.
55
YOUR... LUCKY... NUMBERRR?!
TRMBL
TRMBL
WHAT'S THIS SNOBBY LITTLE BRAT'S DEAL...?!
STEP OVER HERE! THIS YOUNGSTER'S GONNA TEACH YOU A LESSON IN MANNERS, YOU LITTLE—
SIGH
ENOUGH. I'LL MOVE IT MYSELF.
SHRWL
HUH?

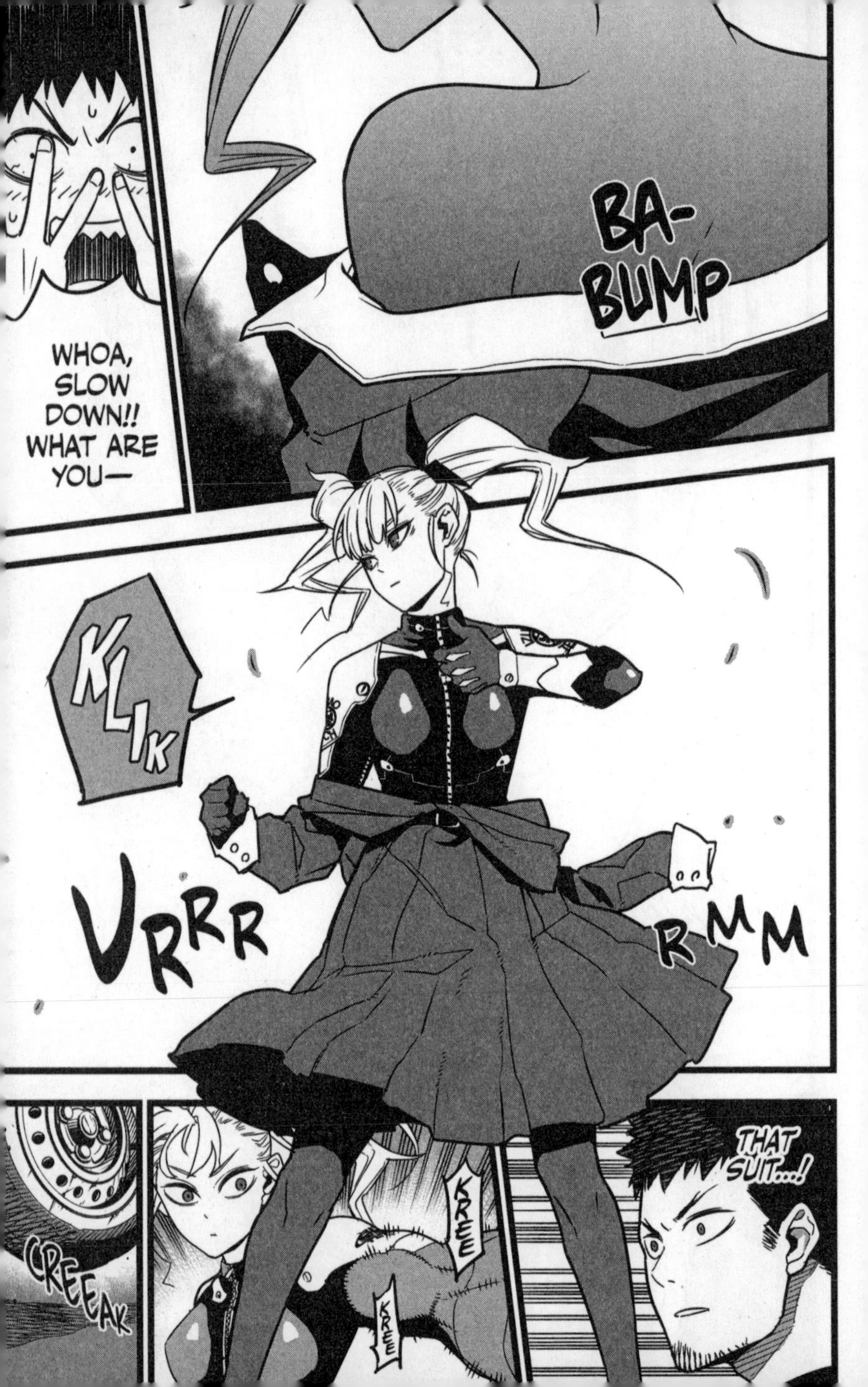
BA-
BUMP
WHOA, SLOW DOWN!! WHAT ARE YOU—
KLIK
VRRR
RMM
THAT SUIT...!
KREE
KREE
CREEEAK

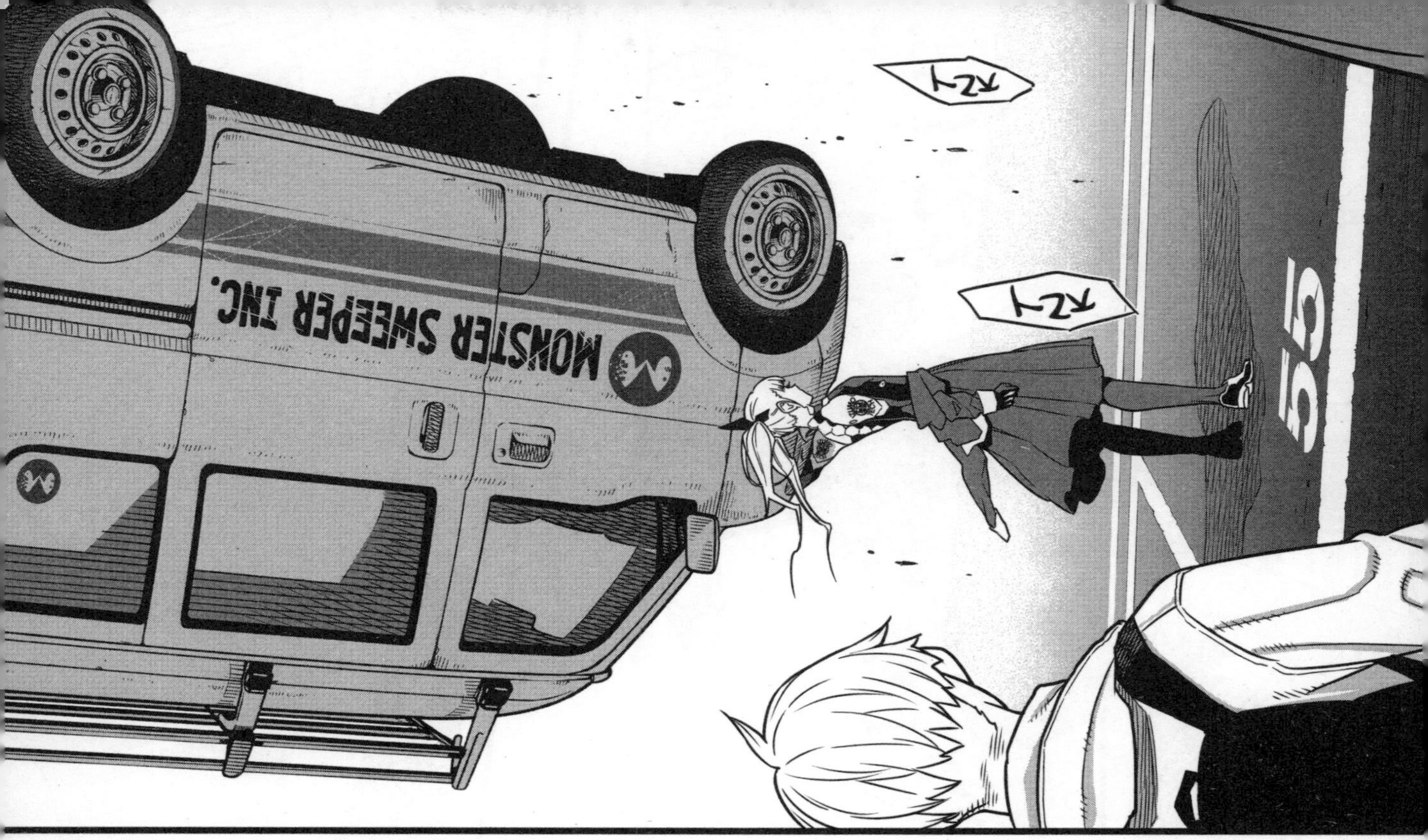
MONSTER SWEEPER INC.
ズン
ズン
55

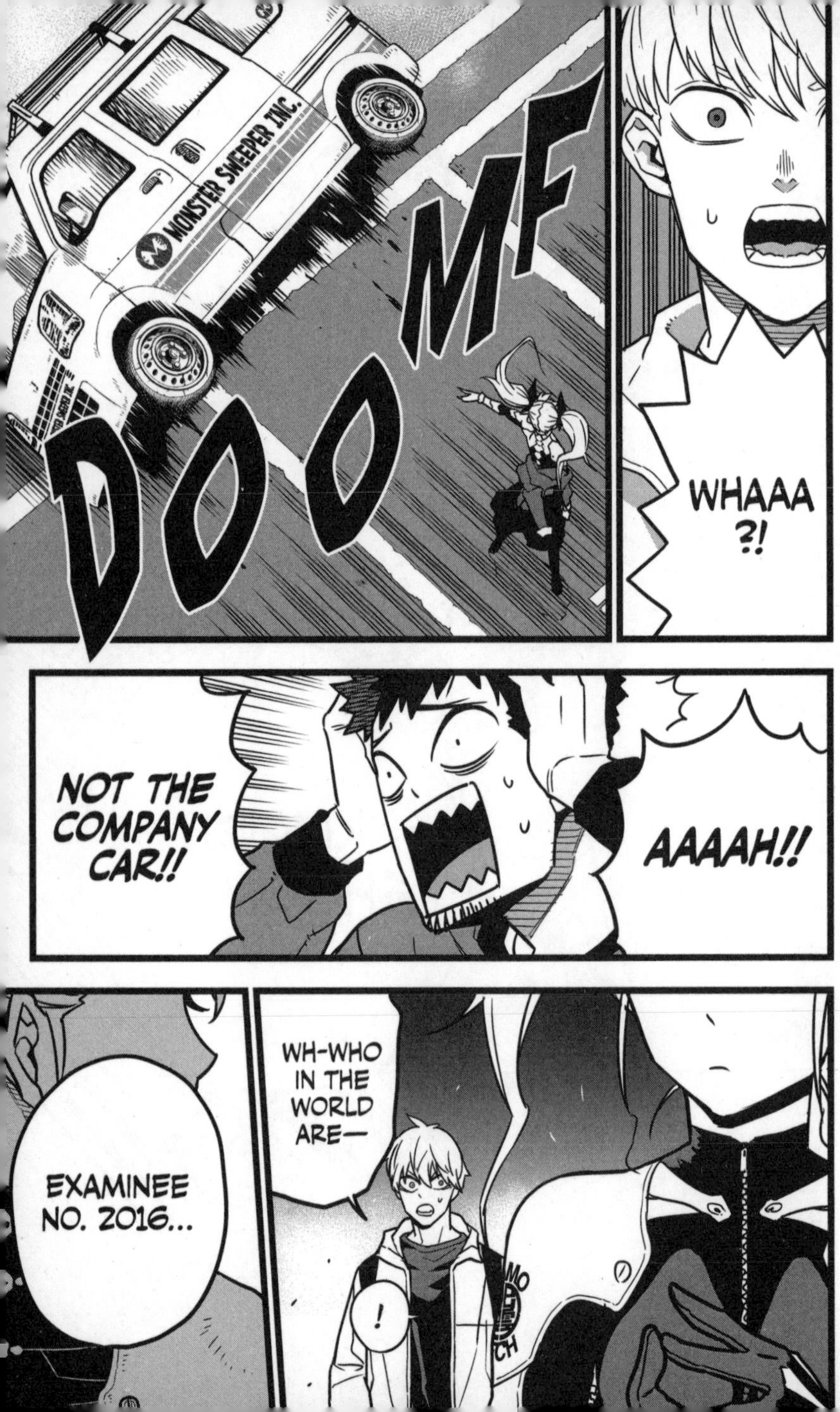
WHAAA ?!
MONSTER SWEEPER INC.
DOOOMF
AAAAH!!
NOT THE COMPANY CAR!!
WH-WHO IN THE WORLD ARE—
!
EXAMINEE NO. 2016...

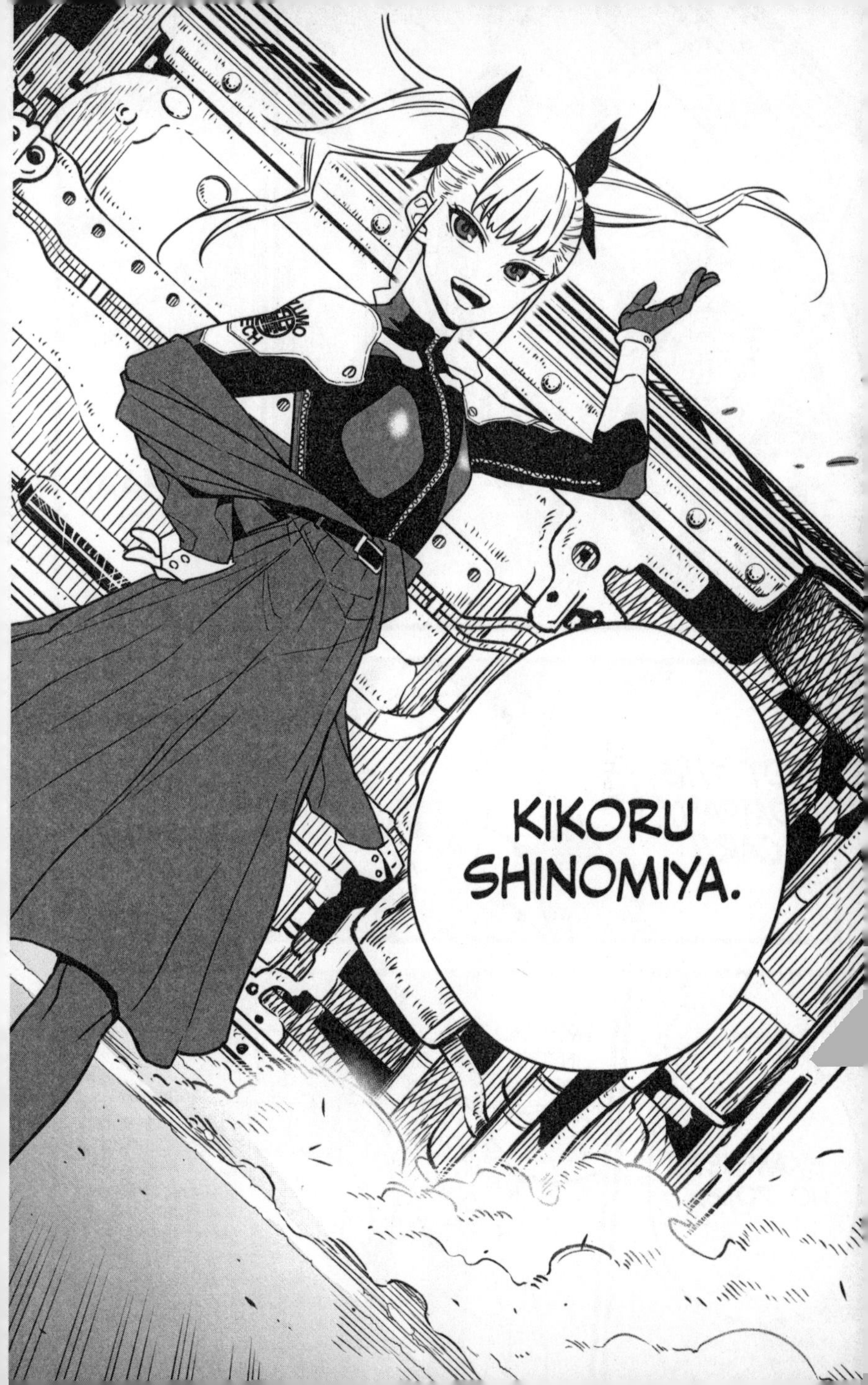
KIKORU SHINOMIYA.

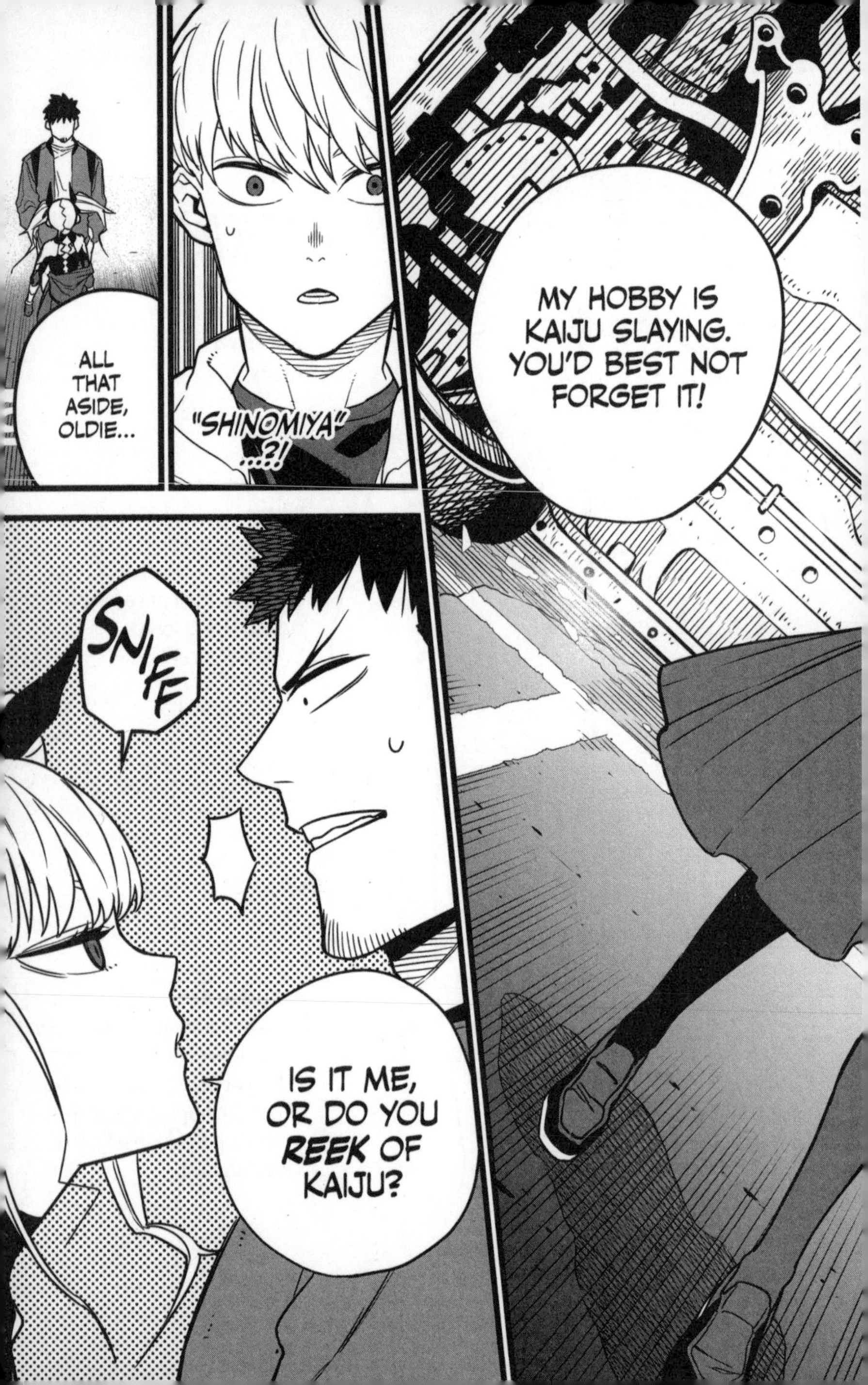
MY HOBBY IS KAIJU SLAYING. YOU'D BEST NOT FORGET IT!
"SHINOMIYA" ...?!
ALL THAT ASIDE, OLDIE...
SNIFF
IS IT ME, OR DO YOU REEK OF KAIJU?

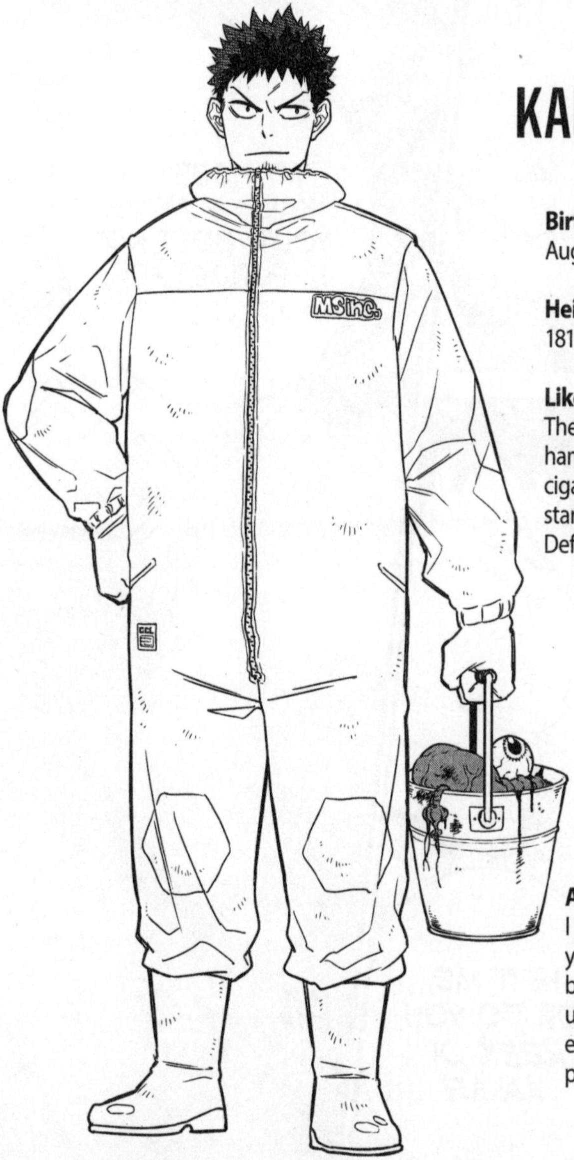
MSinc.

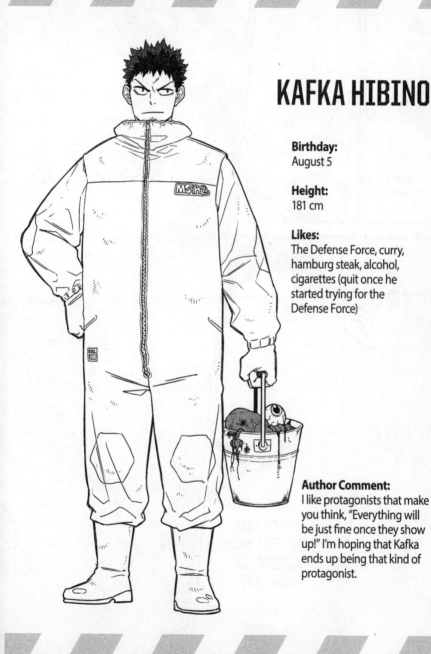

# KAFKA HIBINO

**Birthday:**
August 5

**Height:**
181 cm

**Likes:**
The Defense Force, curry, hamburg steak, alcohol, cigarettes (quit once he started trying for the Defense Force)

**Author Comment:**
I like protagonists that make you think, "Everything will be just fine once they show up!" I'm hoping that Kafka ends up being that kind of protagonist.

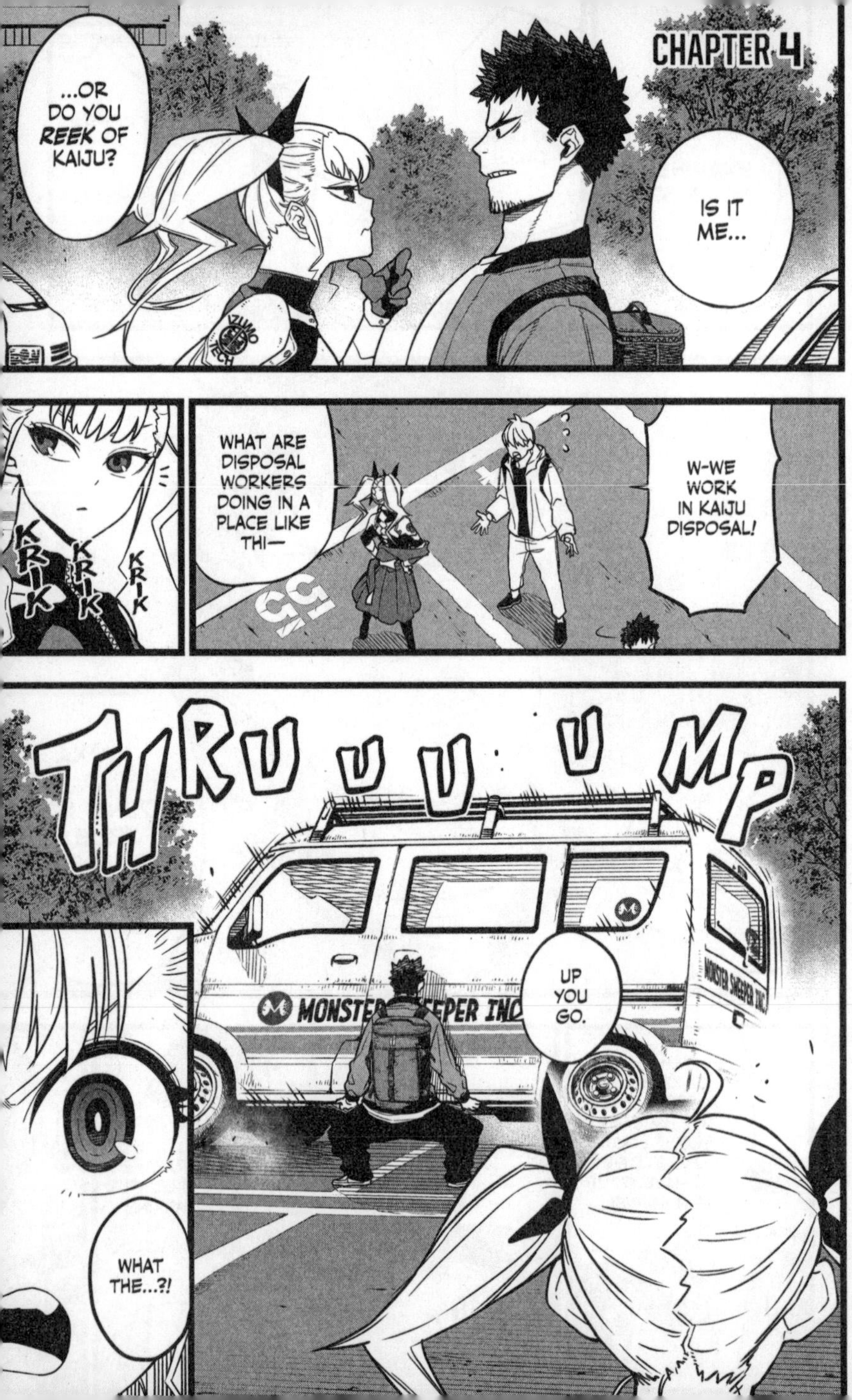
CHAPTER 4
IS IT ME...
...OR DO YOU REEK OF KAIJU?
IZUMO TECH
W-WE WORK IN KAIJU DISPOSAL!
WHAT ARE DISPOSAL WORKERS DOING IN A PLACE LIKE THI—
KRIK KRIK KRIK
THRUUUUMP
MONSTER SWEEPER INC.
UP YOU GO.
WHAT THE...?!

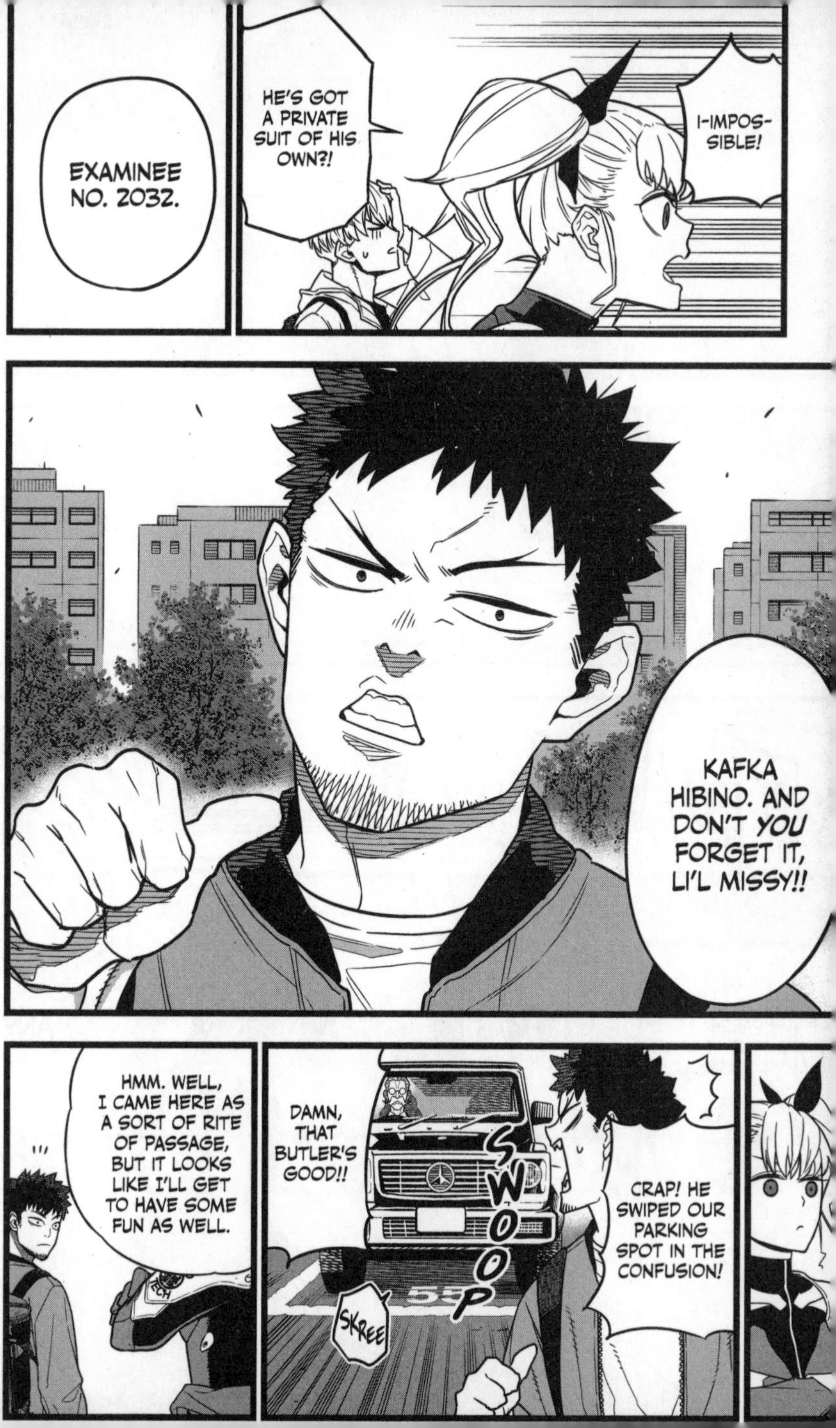
I-IMPOS-SIBLE!
HE'S GOT A PRIVATE SUIT OF HIS OWN?!
EXAMINEE NO. 2032.
KAFKA HIBINO. AND DON'T *YOU* FORGET IT, LI'L MISSY!!
CRAP! HE SWIPED OUR PARKING SPOT IN THE CONFUSION!
SWOOP
SKREE
DAMN, THAT BUTLER'S GOOD!!
HMM. WELL, I CAME HERE AS A SORT OF RITE OF PASSAGE, BUT IT LOOKS LIKE I'LL GET TO HAVE SOME FUN AS WELL.

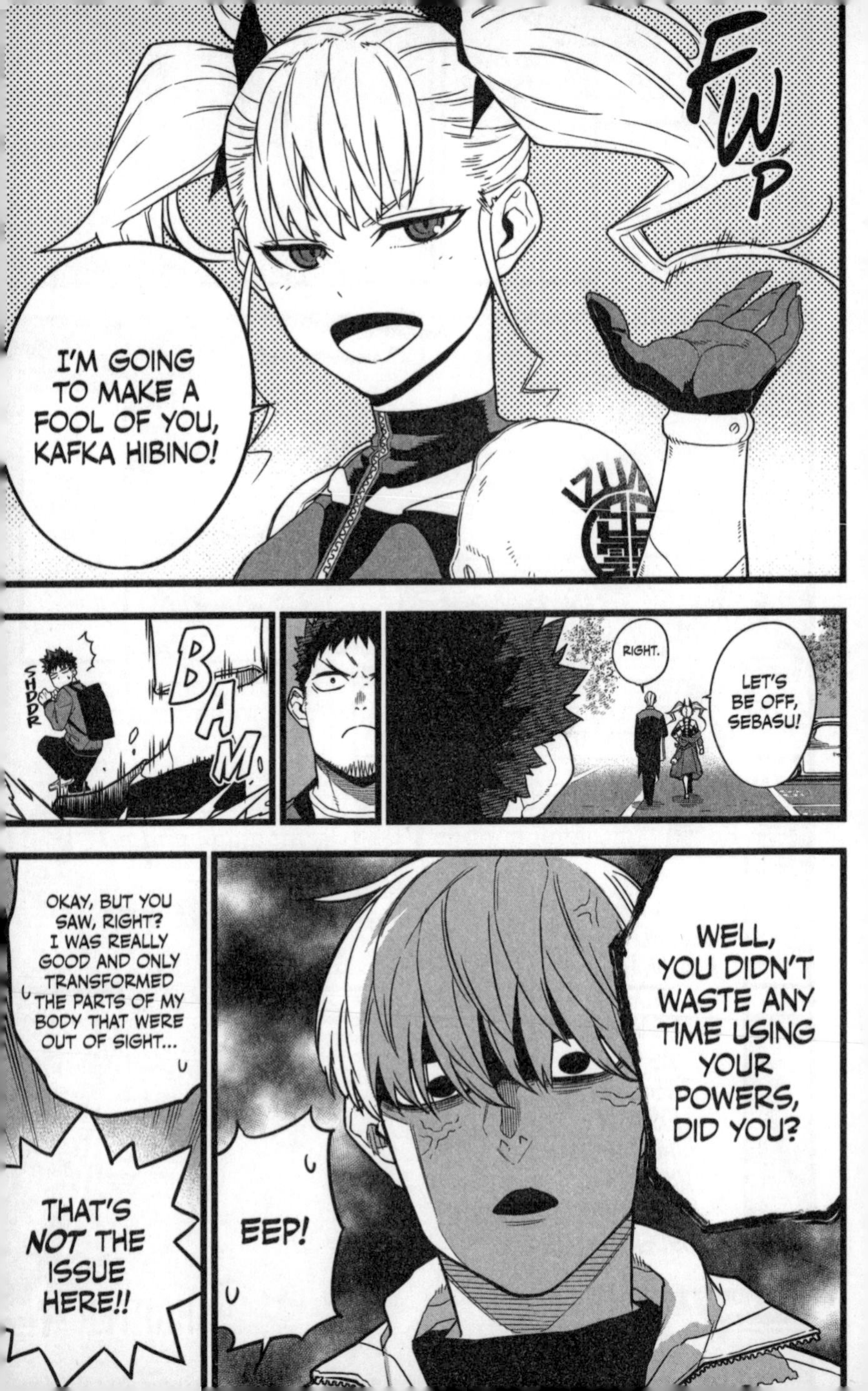
FWP
I'M GOING TO MAKE A FOOL OF YOU, KAFKA HIBINO!
LET'S BE OFF, SEBASU!
RIGHT.
BAM
SHDDR
WELL, YOU DIDN'T WASTE ANY TIME USING YOUR POWERS, DID YOU?
EEP!
OKAY, BUT YOU SAW, RIGHT? I WAS REALLY GOOD AND ONLY TRANSFORMED THE PARTS OF MY BODY THAT WERE OUT OF SIGHT...
THAT'S *NOT* THE ISSUE HERE!!

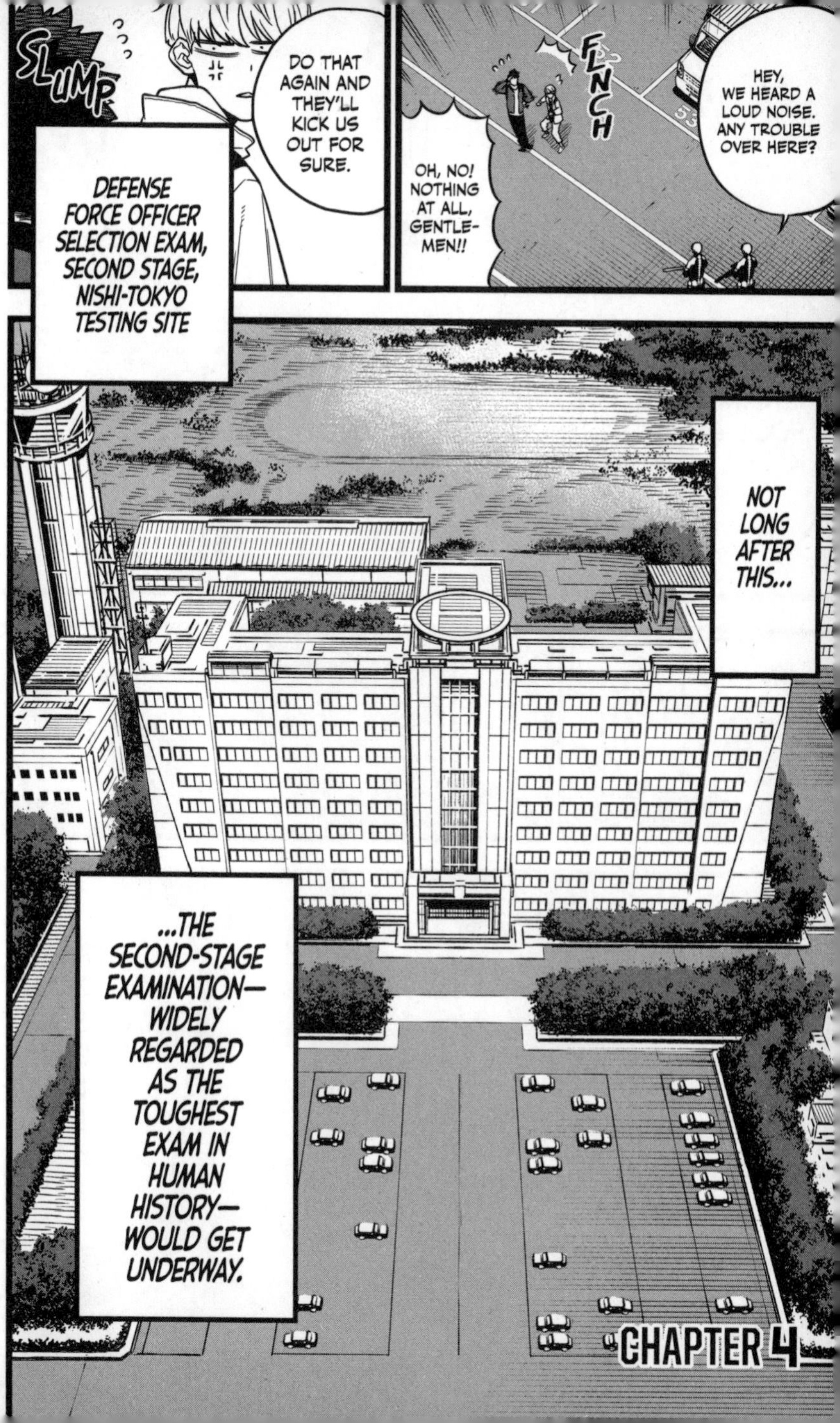
HEY, WE HEARD A LOUD NOISE. ANY TROUBLE OVER HERE?
FLNCH
OH, NO! NOTHING AT ALL, GENTLE-MEN!!
DO THAT AGAIN AND THEY'LL KICK US OUT FOR SURE.
SLUMP
DEFENSE FORCE OFFICER SELECTION EXAM, SECOND STAGE, NISHI-TOKYO TESTING SITE
NOT LONG AFTER THIS...
...THE SECOND-STAGE EXAMINATION—WIDELY REGARDED AS THE TOUGHEST EXAM IN HUMAN HISTORY—WOULD GET UNDERWAY.
CHAPTER 4

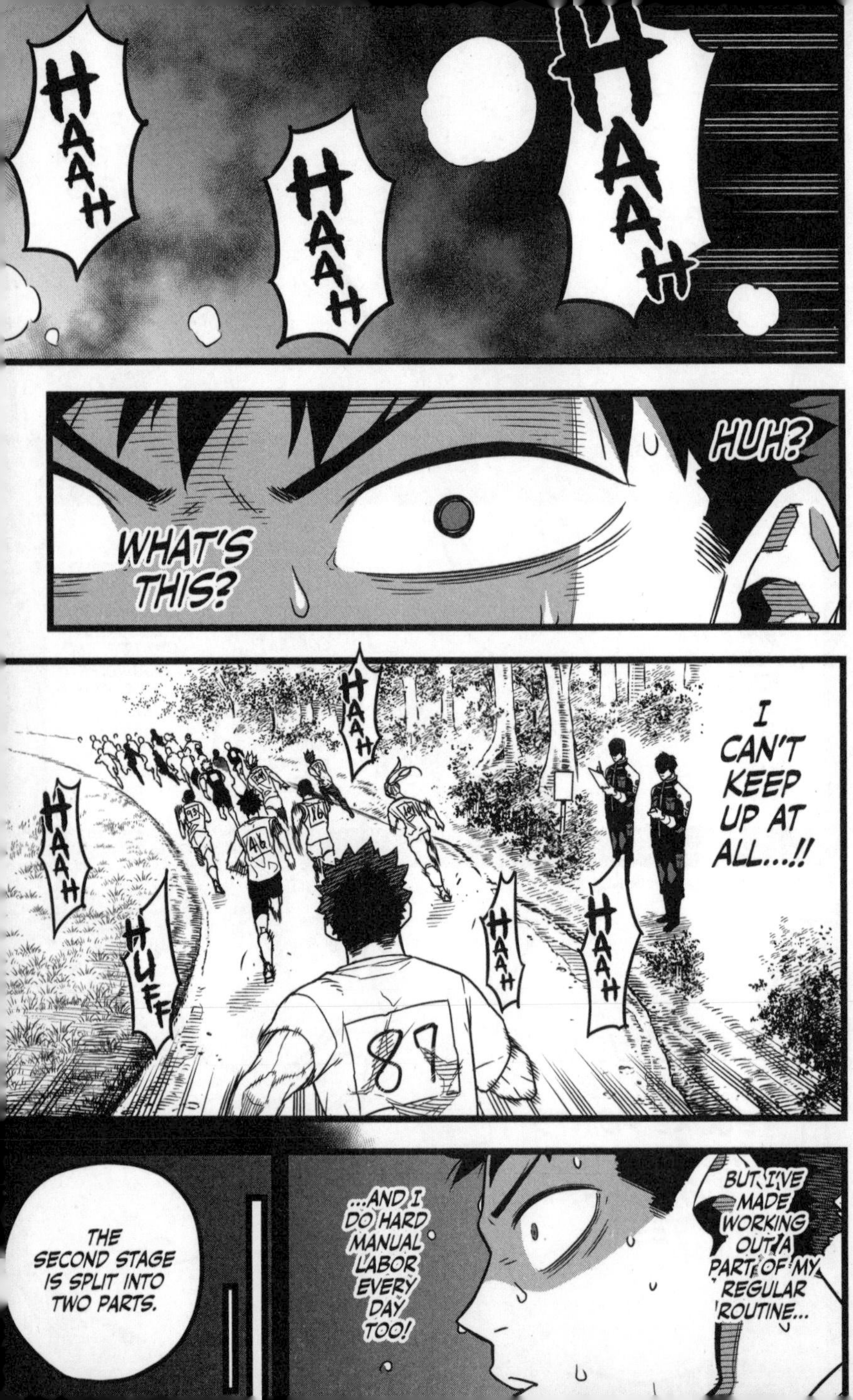
HAAH
HAAAH
HAAH
HUH?
WHAT'S THIS?
I CAN'T KEEP UP AT ALL...!!
HAAH
HAAAH
HAAH
HAAAH
HUFF
87
BUT I'VE MADE WORKING OUT A PART OF MY REGULAR ROUTINE...
...AND I DO HARD MANUAL LABOR EVERY DAY TOO!
THE SECOND STAGE IS SPLIT INTO TWO PARTS.

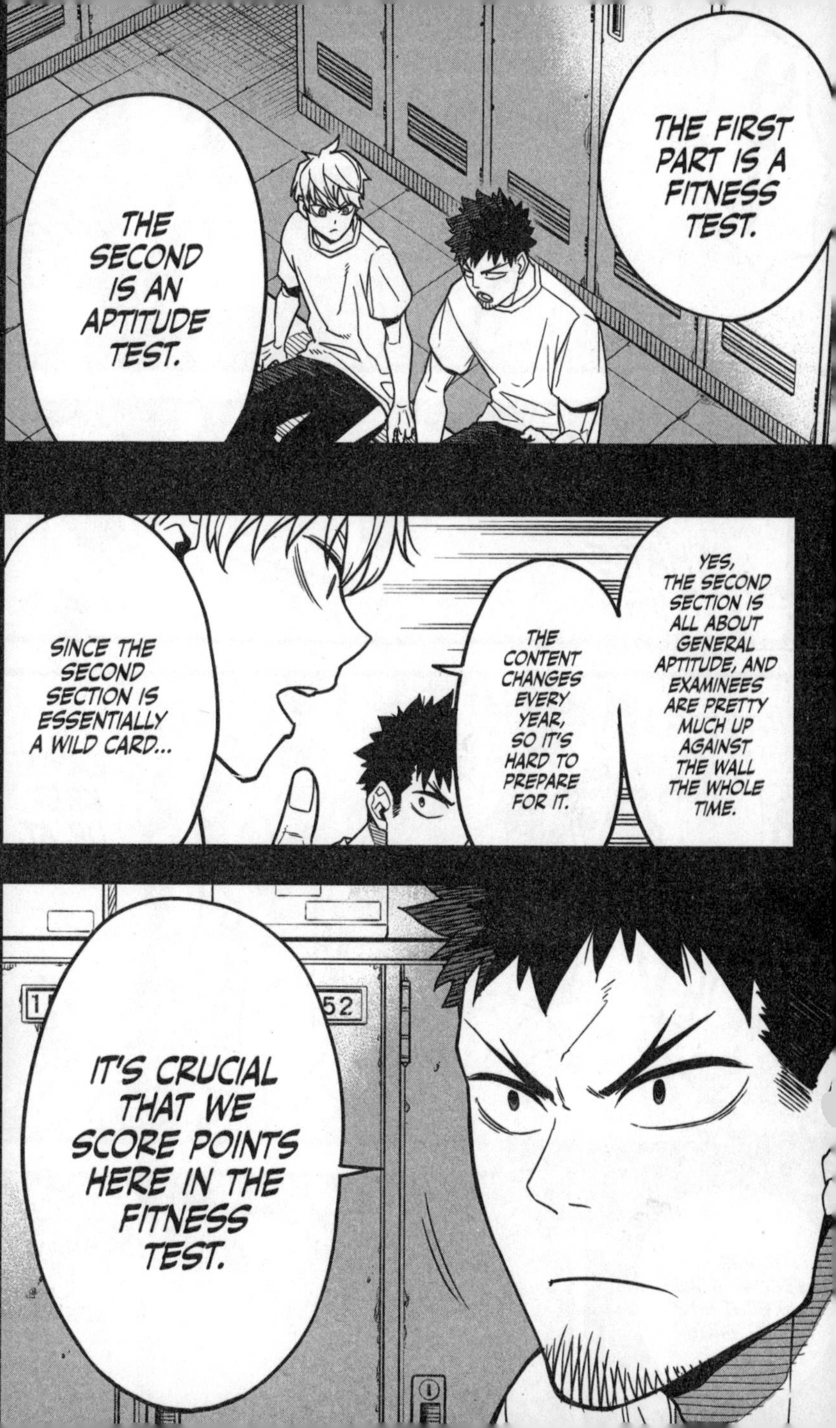
THE FIRST PART IS A FITNESS TEST.
THE SECOND IS AN APTITUDE TEST.
YES, THE SECOND SECTION IS ALL ABOUT GENERAL APTITUDE, AND EXAMINEES ARE PRETTY MUCH UP AGAINST THE WALL THE WHOLE TIME.
THE CONTENT CHANGES EVERY YEAR, SO IT'S HARD TO PREPARE FOR IT.
SINCE THE SECOND SECTION IS ESSENTIALLY A WILD CARD...
IT'S CRUCIAL THAT WE SCORE POINTS HERE IN THE FITNESS TEST.

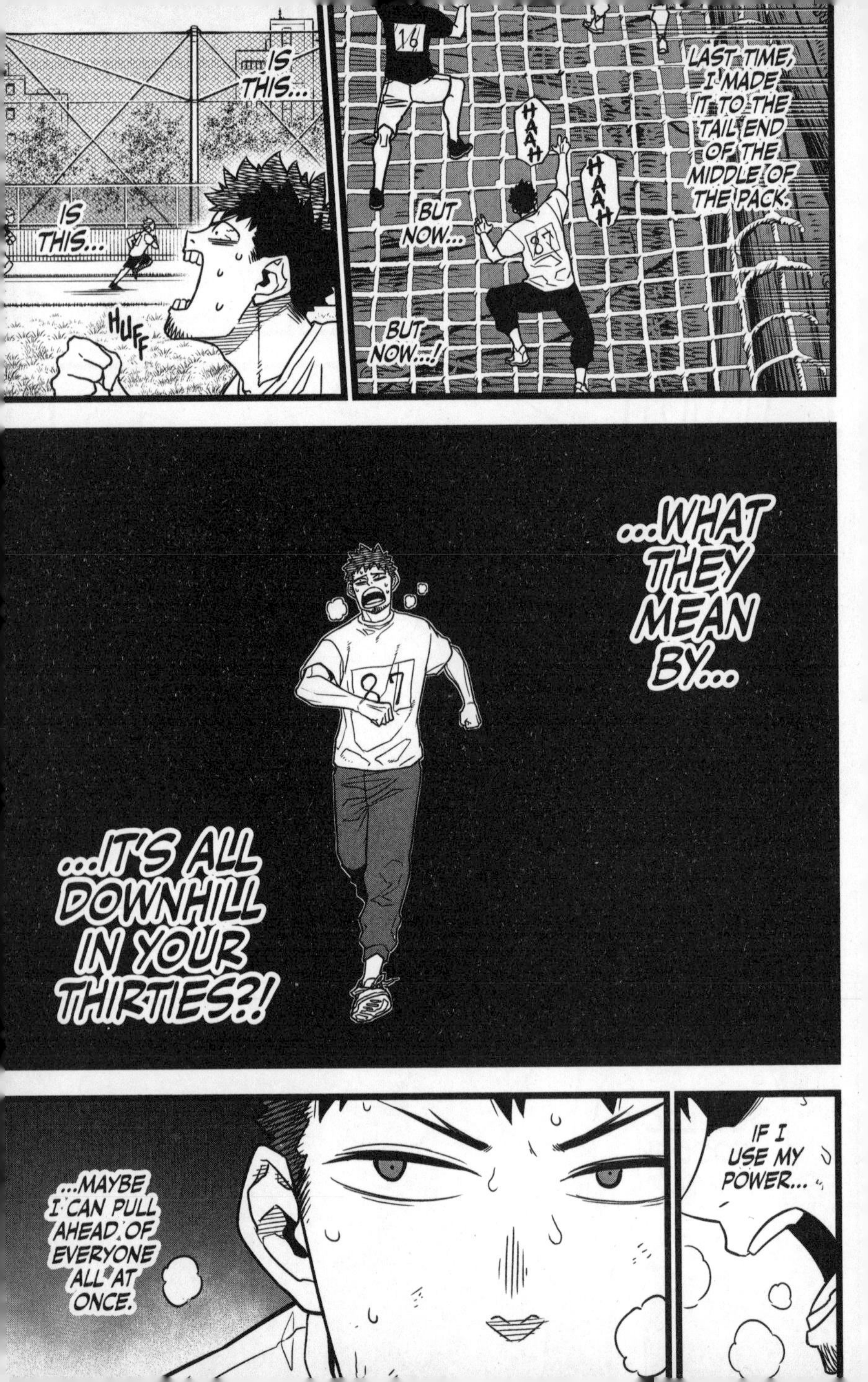
LAST TIME, I MADE IT TO THE TAIL END OF THE MIDDLE OF THE PACK.
HAAH
HAAH
BUT NOW...
BUT NOW...!
IS THIS...
IS THIS...
HUFF
...WHAT THEY MEAN BY...
...IT'S ALL DOWNHILL IN YOUR THIRTIES?!
IF I USE MY POWER...
...MAYBE I CAN PULL AHEAD OF EVERYONE ALL AT ONCE.

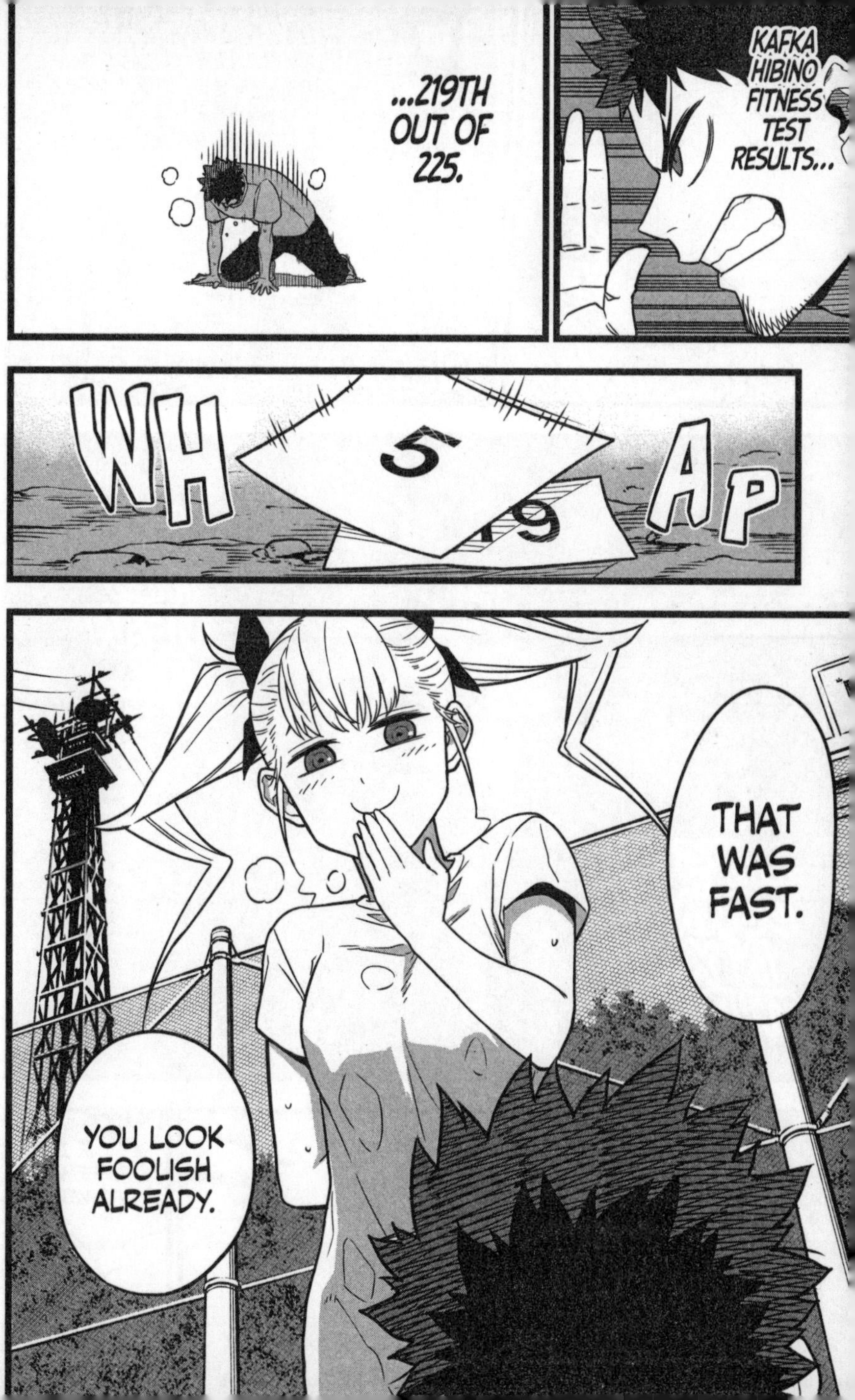
KAFKA HIBINO FITNESS TEST RESULTS...
...219TH OUT OF 225.
WHAP
5
THAT WAS FAST.
YOU LOOK FOOLISH ALREADY.

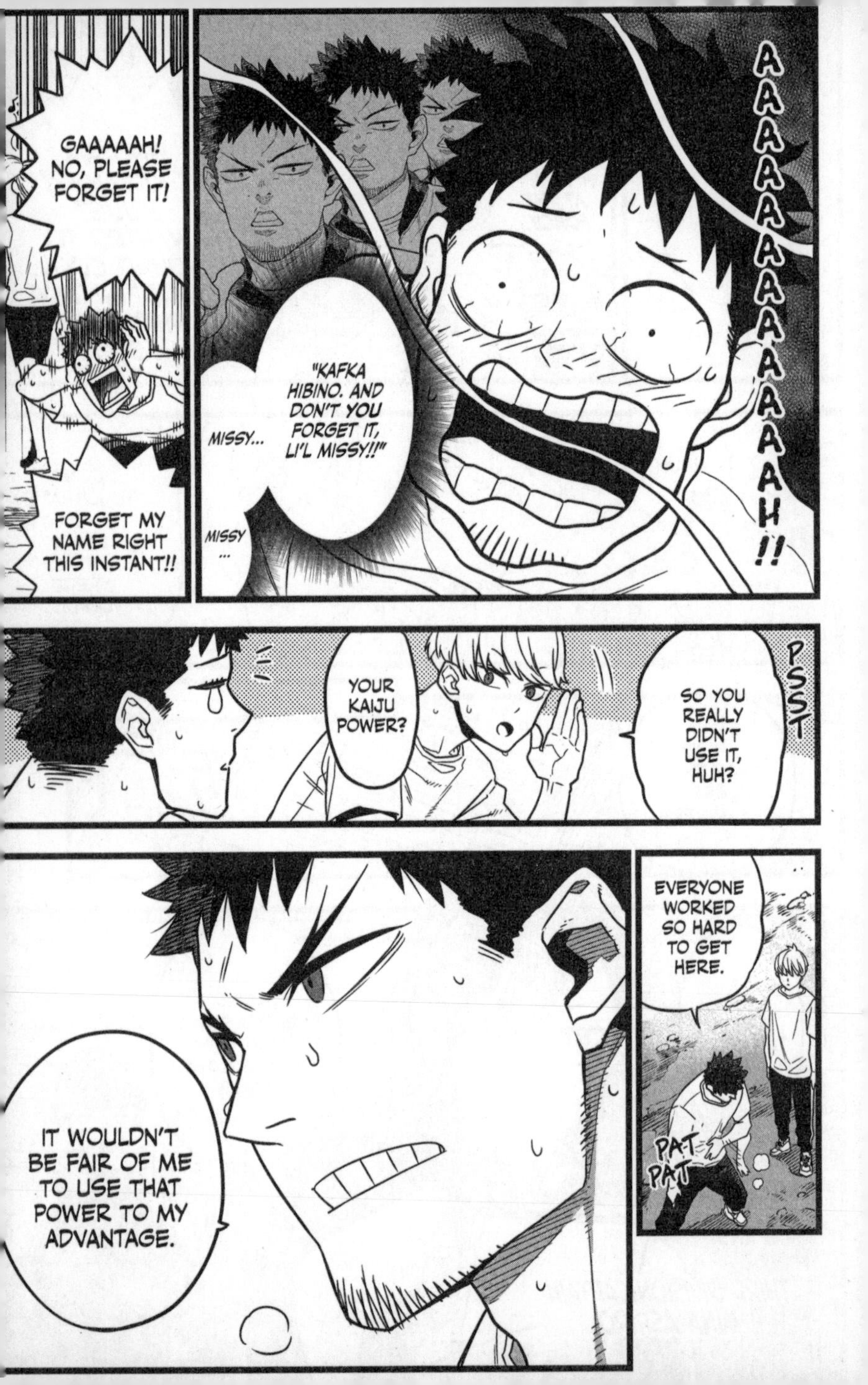
AAAAAAAAAAAH!!
"KAFKA HIBINO. AND DON'T YOU FORGET IT, LI'L MISSY!!"
MISSY...
MISSY ...
GAAAAAH! NO, PLEASE FORGET IT!
FORGET MY NAME RIGHT THIS INSTANT!!
PSST
SO YOU REALLY DIDN'T USE IT, HUH?
YOUR KAIJU POWER?
EVERYONE WORKED SO HARD TO GET HERE.
PAT PAT
IT WOULDN'T BE FAIR OF ME TO USE THAT POWER TO MY ADVANTAGE.

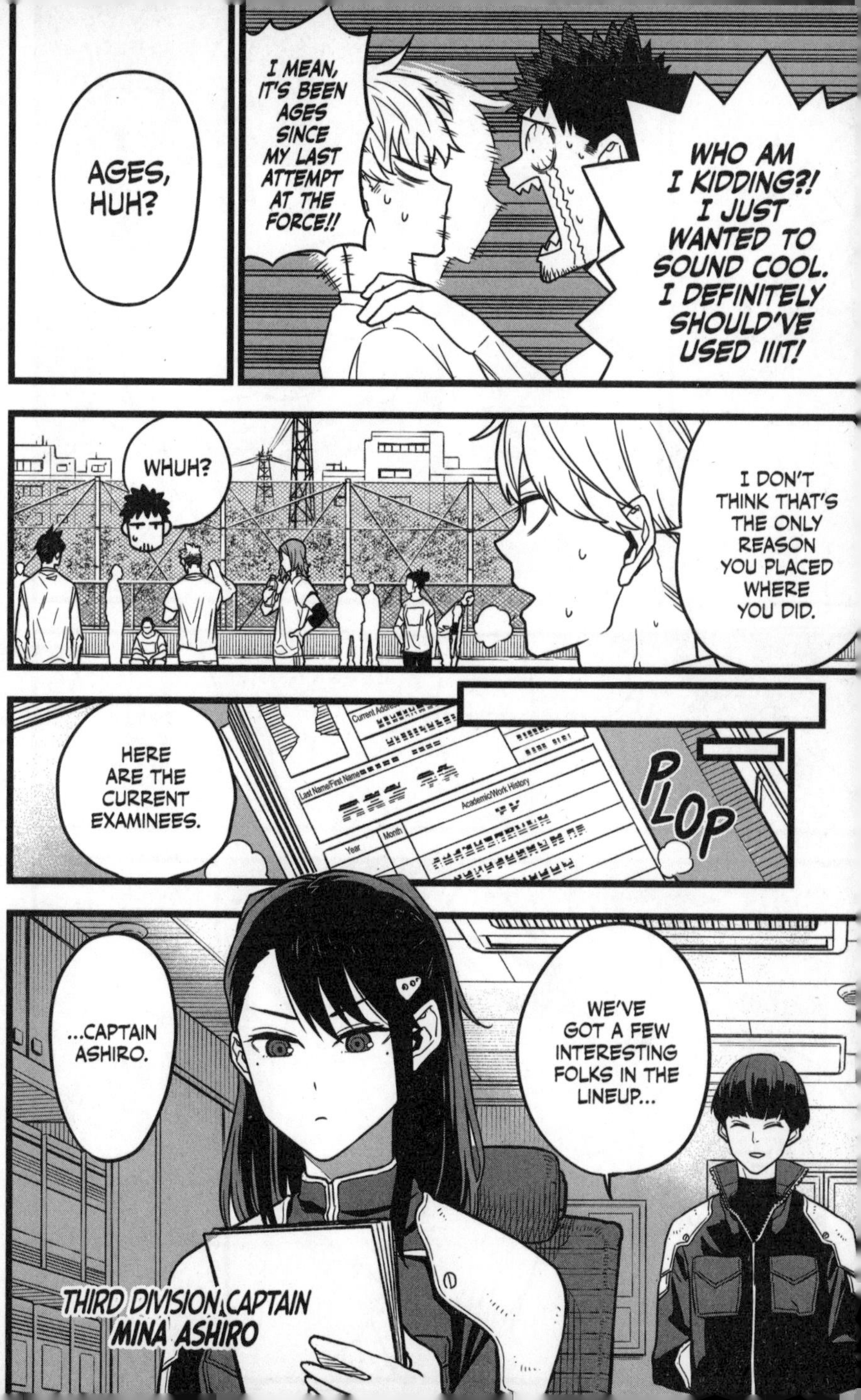
I MEAN, IT'S BEEN AGES SINCE MY LAST ATTEMPT AT THE FORCE!!
WHO AM I KIDDING?! I JUST WANTED TO SOUND COOL. I DEFINITELY SHOULD'VE USED IIIT!
AGES, HUH?
I DON'T THINK THAT'S THE ONLY REASON YOU PLACED WHERE YOU DID.
WHUH?
PLOP
Current Address
Last Name/First Name
Academic/Work History
Year
Month
HERE ARE THE CURRENT EXAMINEES.
WE'VE GOT A FEW INTERESTING FOLKS IN THE LINEUP...
...CAPTAIN ASHIRO.
THIRD DIVISION CAPTAIN MINA ASHIRO

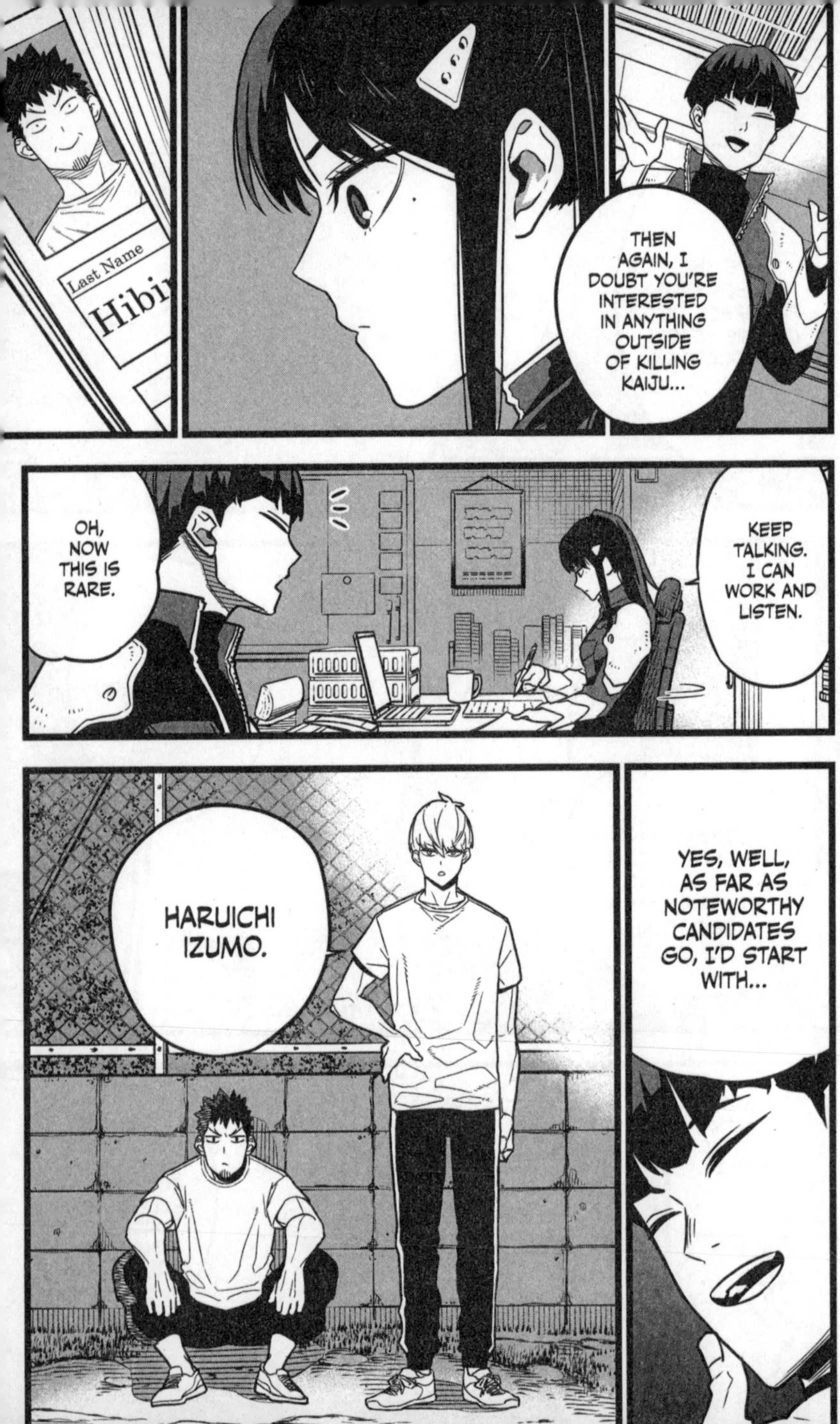
THEN AGAIN, I DOUBT YOU'RE INTERESTED IN ANYTHING OUTSIDE OF KILLING KAIJU...
Last Name
Hibi
KEEP TALKING. I CAN WORK AND LISTEN.
OH, NOW THIS IS RARE.
YES, WELL, AS FAR AS NOTEWORTHY CANDIDATES GO, I'D START WITH...
HARUICHI IZUMO.

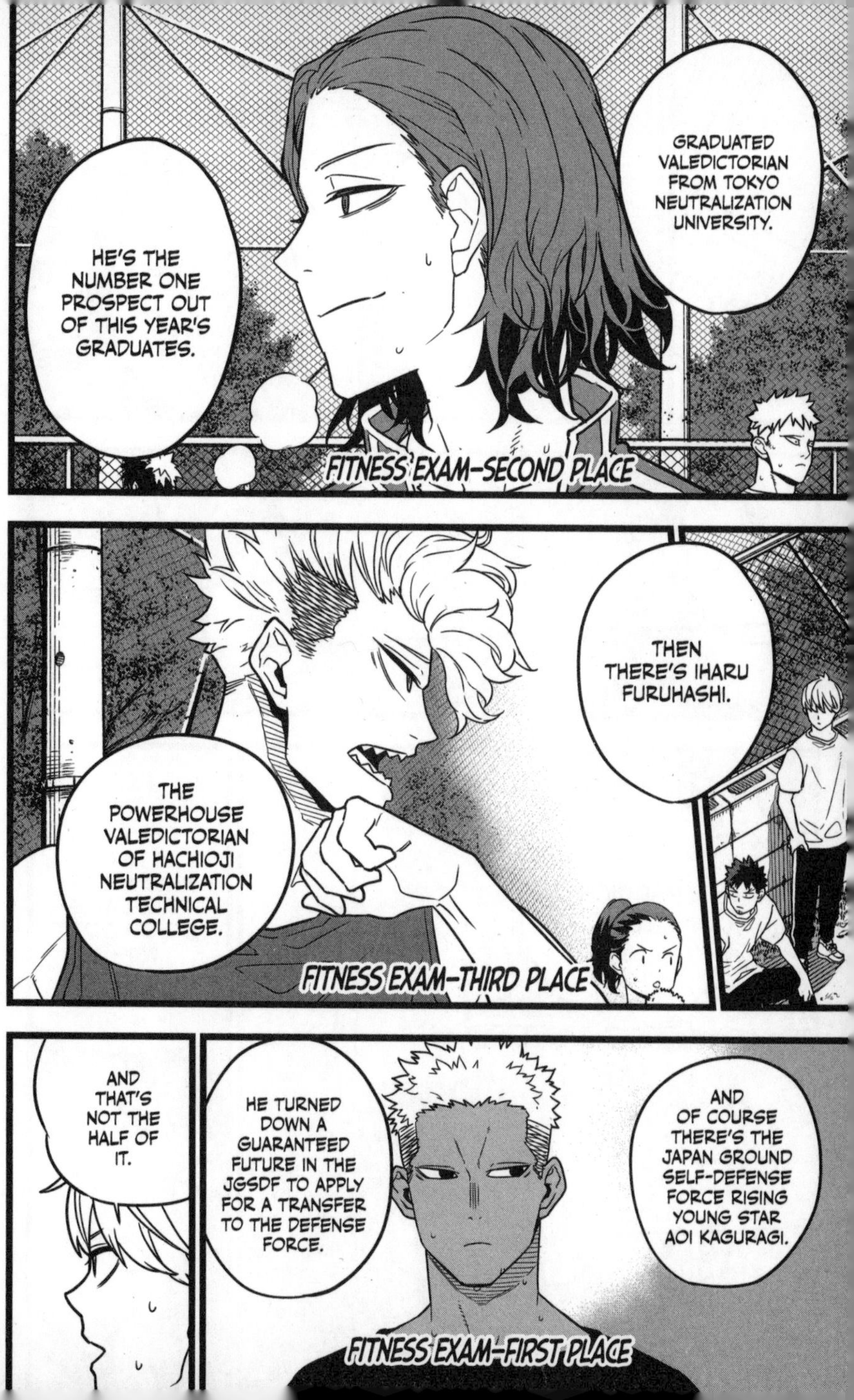
GRADUATED VALEDICTORIAN FROM TOKYO NEUTRALIZATION UNIVERSITY.
HE'S THE NUMBER ONE PROSPECT OUT OF THIS YEAR'S GRADUATES.
FITNESS EXAM—SECOND PLACE
THEN THERE'S IHARU FURUHASHI.
THE POWERHOUSE VALEDICTORIAN OF HACHIOJI NEUTRALIZATION TECHNICAL COLLEGE.
FITNESS EXAM—THIRD PLACE
AND OF COURSE THERE'S THE JAPAN GROUND SELF-DEFENSE FORCE RISING YOUNG STAR AOI KAGURAGI.
HE TURNED DOWN A GUARANTEED FUTURE IN THE JGSDF TO APPLY FOR A TRANSFER TO THE DEFENSE FORCE.
FITNESS EXAM—FIRST PLACE
AND THAT'S NOT THE HALF OF IT.

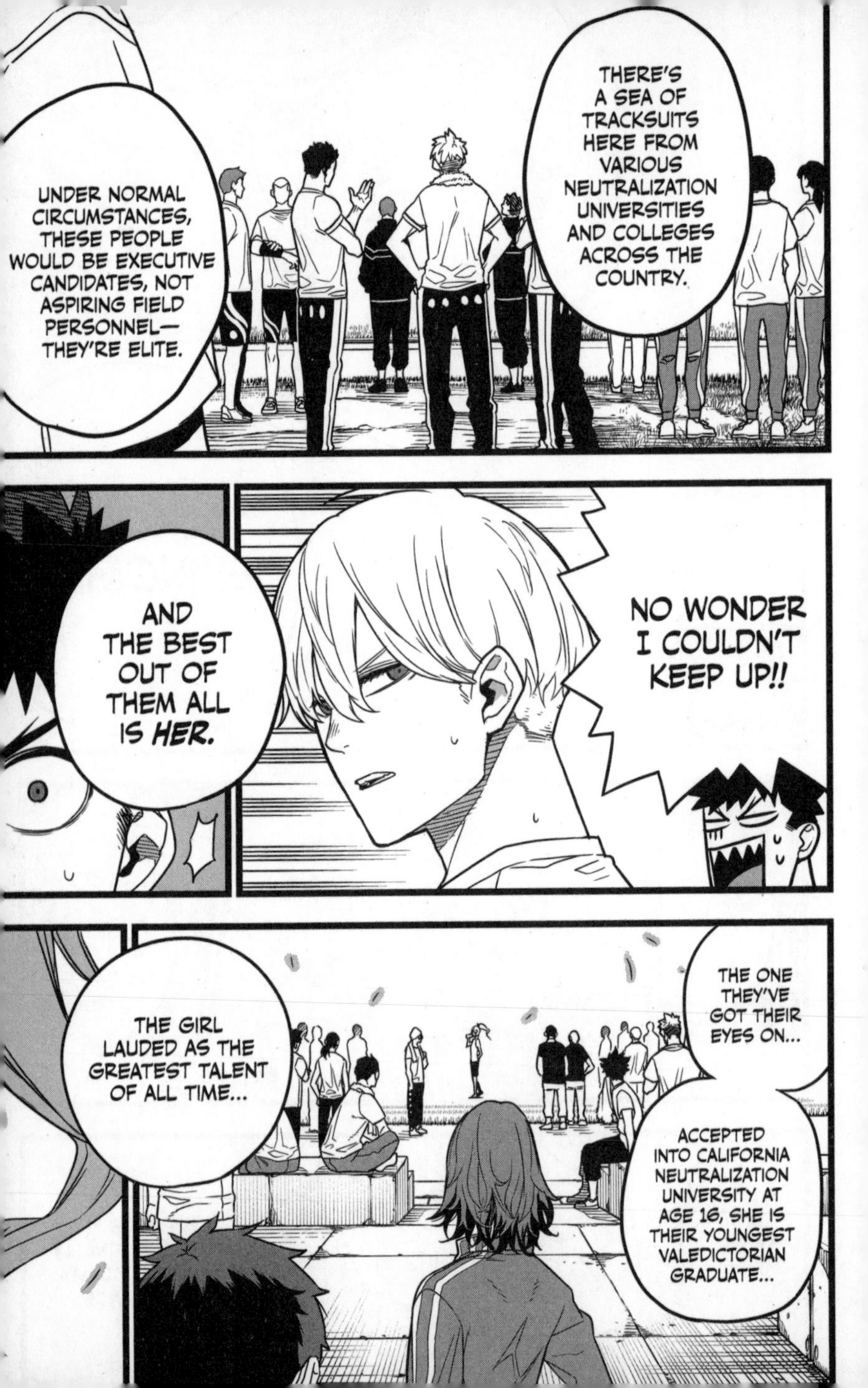
THERE'S A SEA OF TRACKSUITS HERE FROM VARIOUS NEUTRALIZATION UNIVERSITIES AND COLLEGES ACROSS THE COUNTRY.
UNDER NORMAL CIRCUMSTANCES, THESE PEOPLE WOULD BE EXECUTIVE CANDIDATES, NOT ASPIRING FIELD PERSONNEL— THEY'RE ELITE.
NO WONDER I COULDN'T KEEP UP!!
AND THE BEST OUT OF THEM ALL IS *HER.*
THE ONE THEY'VE GOT THEIR EYES ON...
THE GIRL LAUDED AS THE GREATEST TALENT OF ALL TIME...
ACCEPTED INTO CALIFORNIA NEUTRALIZATION UNIVERSITY AT AGE 16, SHE IS THEIR YOUNGEST VALEDICTORIAN GRADUATE...

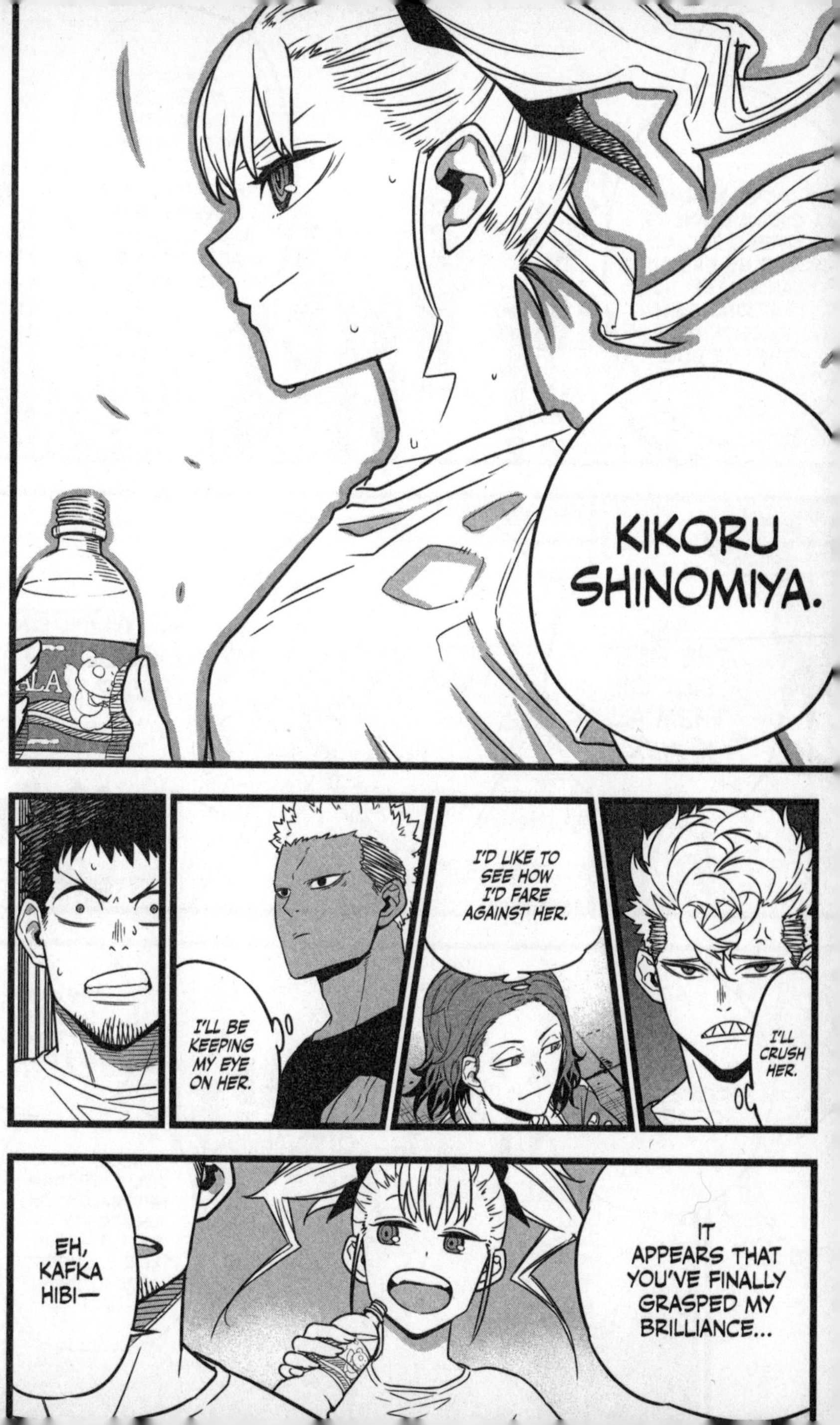
KIKORU SHINOMIYA.
I'LL CRUSH HER.
I'D LIKE TO SEE HOW I'D FARE AGAINST HER.
I'LL BE KEEPING MY EYE ON HER.
IT APPEARS THAT YOU'VE FINALLY GRASPED MY BRILLIANCE...
EH, KAFKA HIBI—

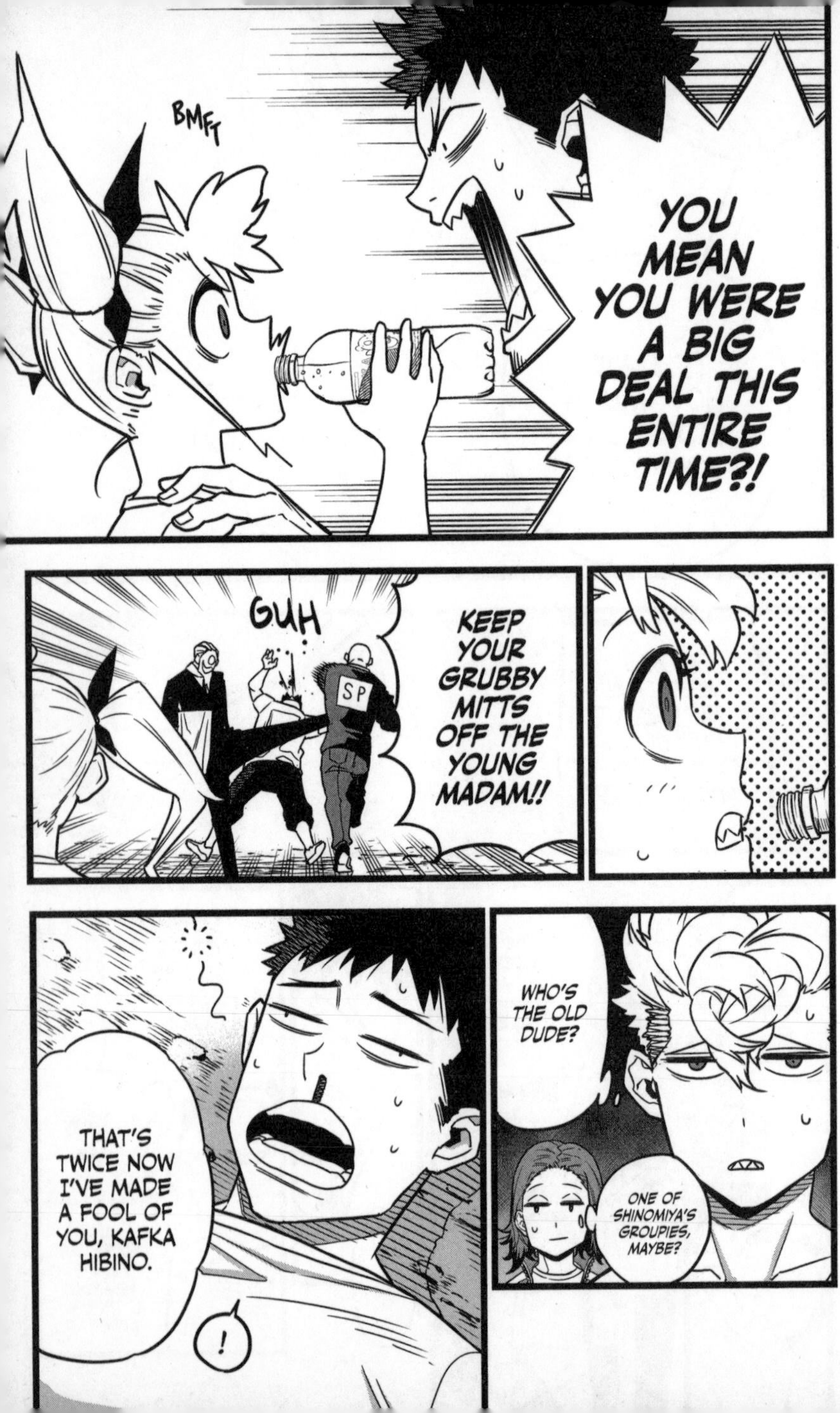
YOU MEAN YOU WERE A BIG DEAL THIS ENTIRE TIME?!
BMFT
KEEP YOUR GRUBBY MITTS OFF THE YOUNG MADAM!!
GUH
SP
WHO'S THE OLD DUDE?
ONE OF SHINOMIYA'S GROUPIES, MAYBE?
THAT'S TWICE NOW I'VE MADE A FOOL OF YOU, KAFKA HIBINO.
!

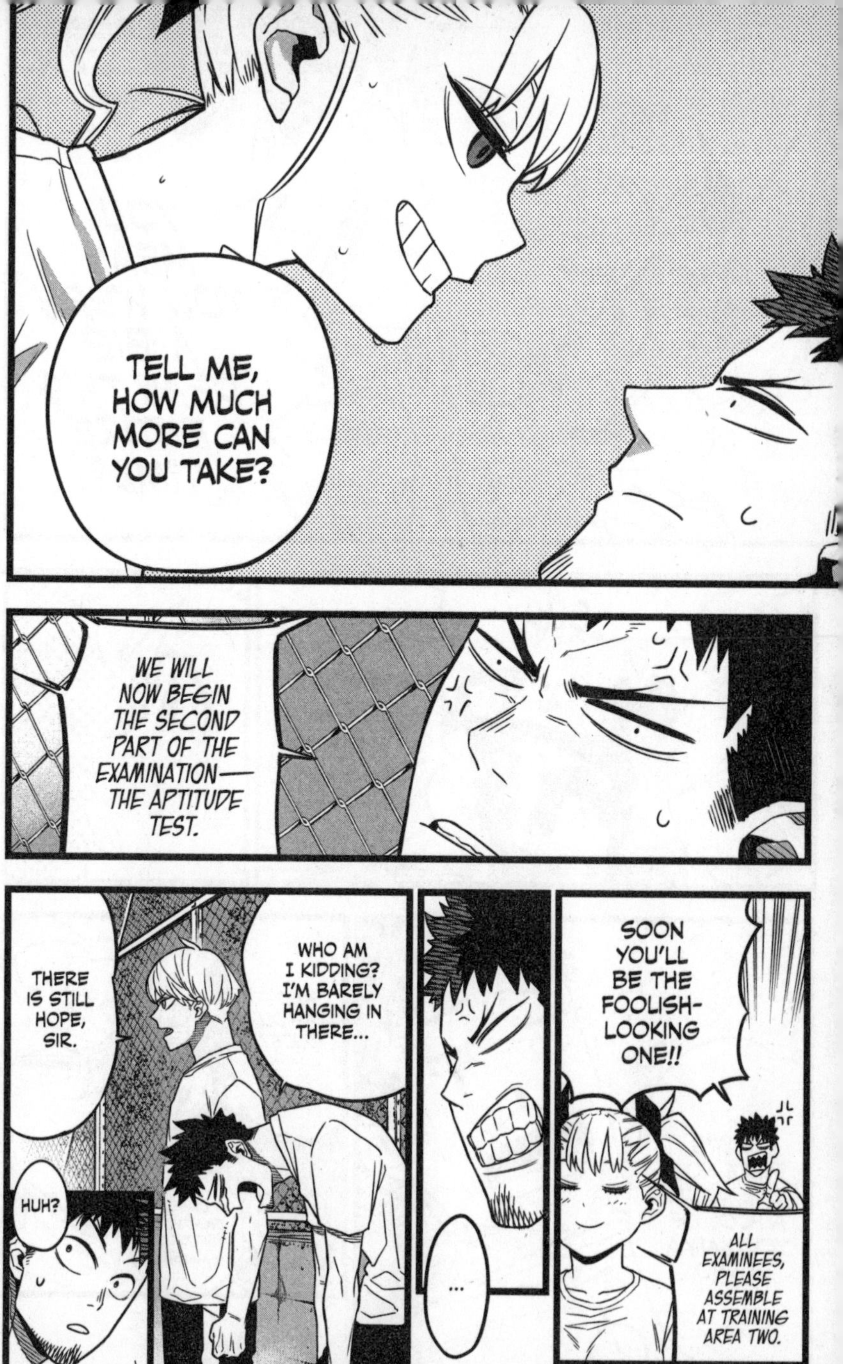

TELL ME, HOW MUCH MORE CAN YOU TAKE?
WE WILL NOW BEGIN THE SECOND PART OF THE EXAMINATION—THE APTITUDE TEST.
SOON YOU'LL BE THE FOOLISH-LOOKING ONE!!
ALL EXAMINEES, PLEASE ASSEMBLE AT TRAINING AREA TWO.
...
WHO AM I KIDDING? I'M BARELY HANGING IN THERE...
THERE IS STILL HOPE, SIR.
HUH?

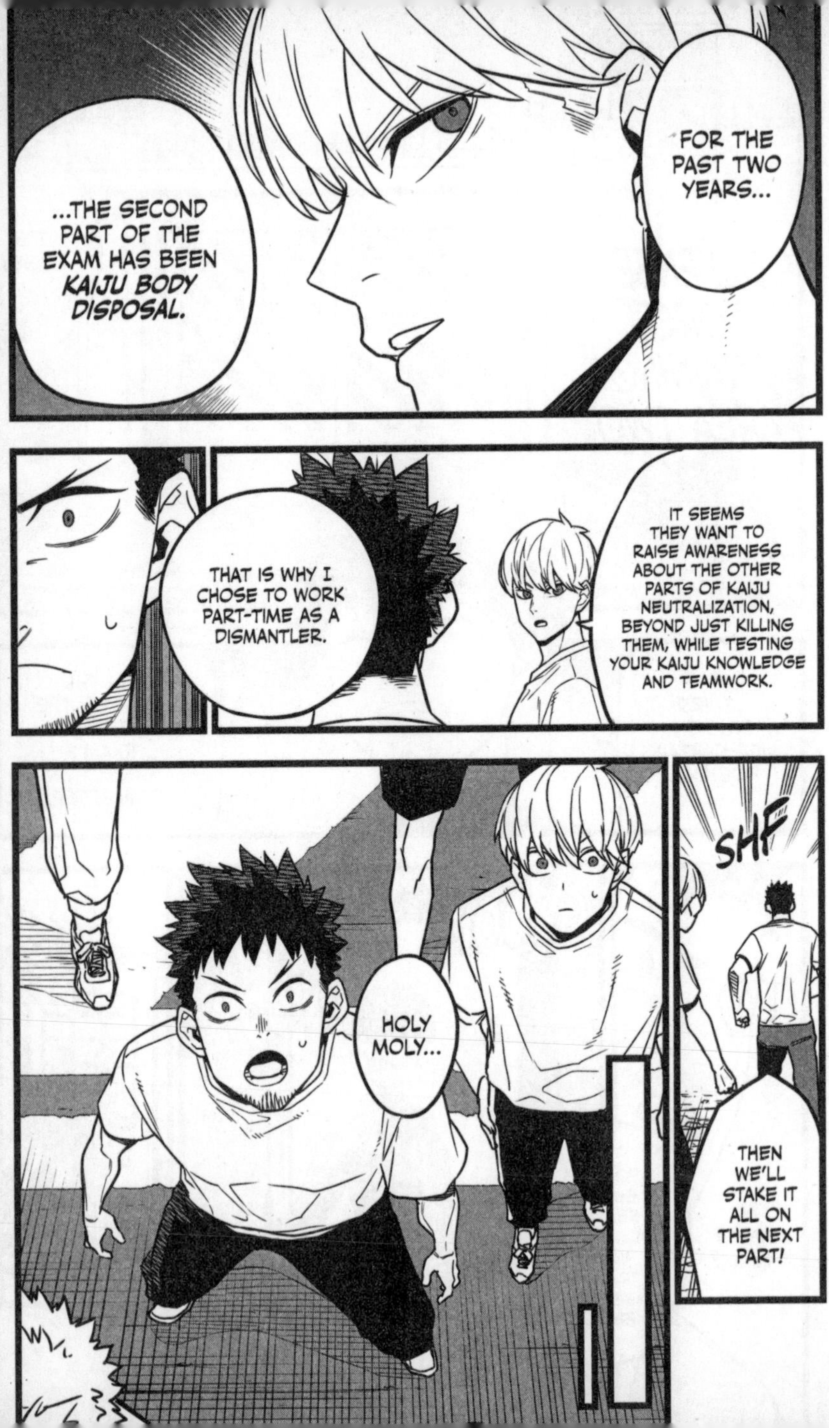
FOR THE PAST TWO YEARS...
...THE SECOND PART OF THE EXAM HAS BEEN *KAIJU BODY DISPOSAL.*
IT SEEMS THEY WANT TO RAISE AWARENESS ABOUT THE OTHER PARTS OF KAIJU NEUTRALIZATION, BEYOND JUST KILLING THEM, WHILE TESTING YOUR KAIJU KNOWLEDGE AND TEAMWORK.
THAT IS WHY I CHOSE TO WORK PART-TIME AS A DISMANTLER.
SHF
THEN WE'LL STAKE IT ALL ON THE NEXT PART!
HOLY MOLY...

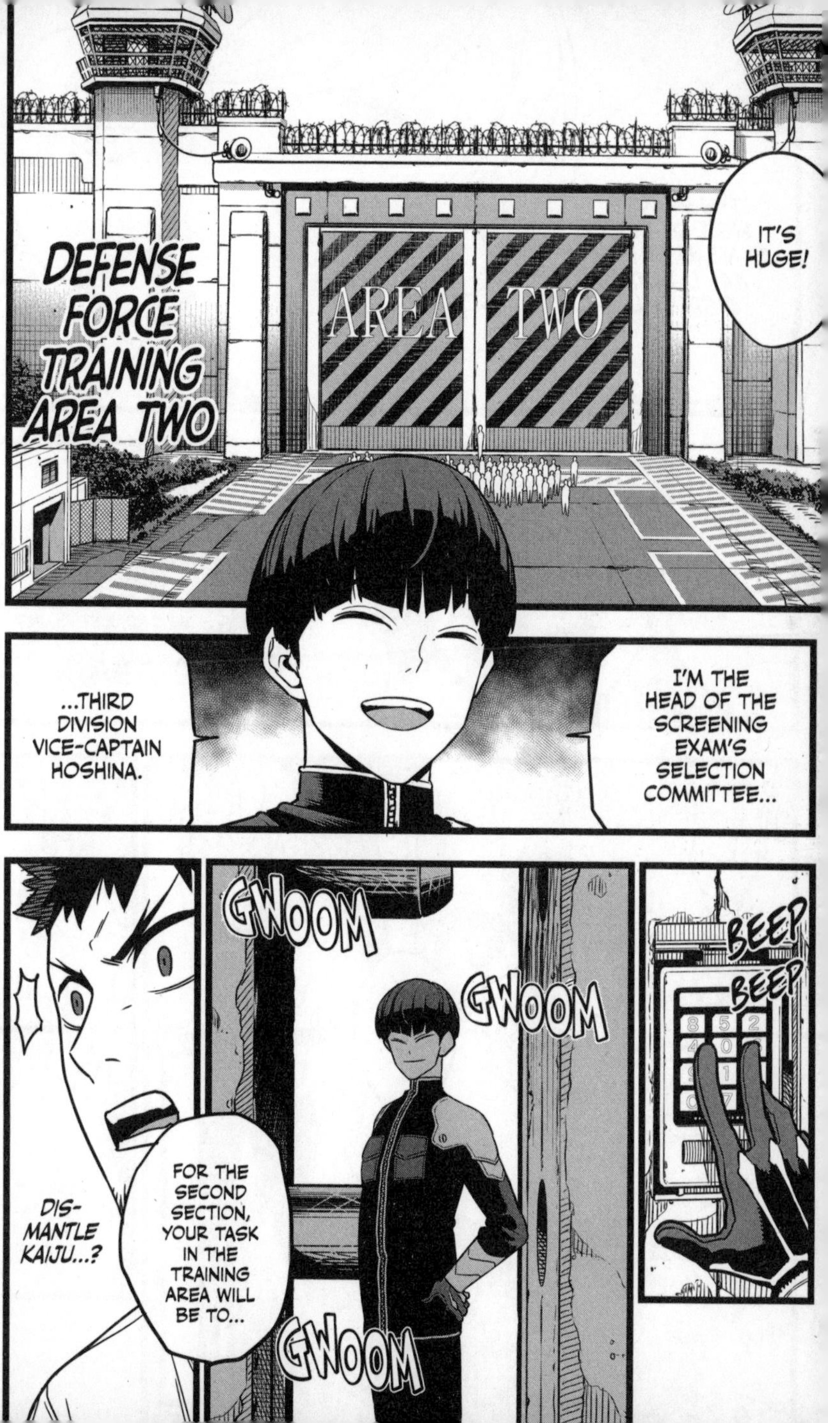
IT'S HUGE!
DEFENSE FORCE TRAINING AREA TWO
AREA TWO
I'M THE HEAD OF THE SCREENING EXAM'S SELECTION COMMITTEE...
...THIRD DIVISION VICE-CAPTAIN HOSHINA.
BEEP
BEEP
8 5 2
4 0
1
7
GWOOM
GWOOM
FOR THE SECOND SECTION, YOUR TASK IN THE TRAINING AREA WILL BE TO...
GWOOM
DIS-MANTLE KAIJU...?

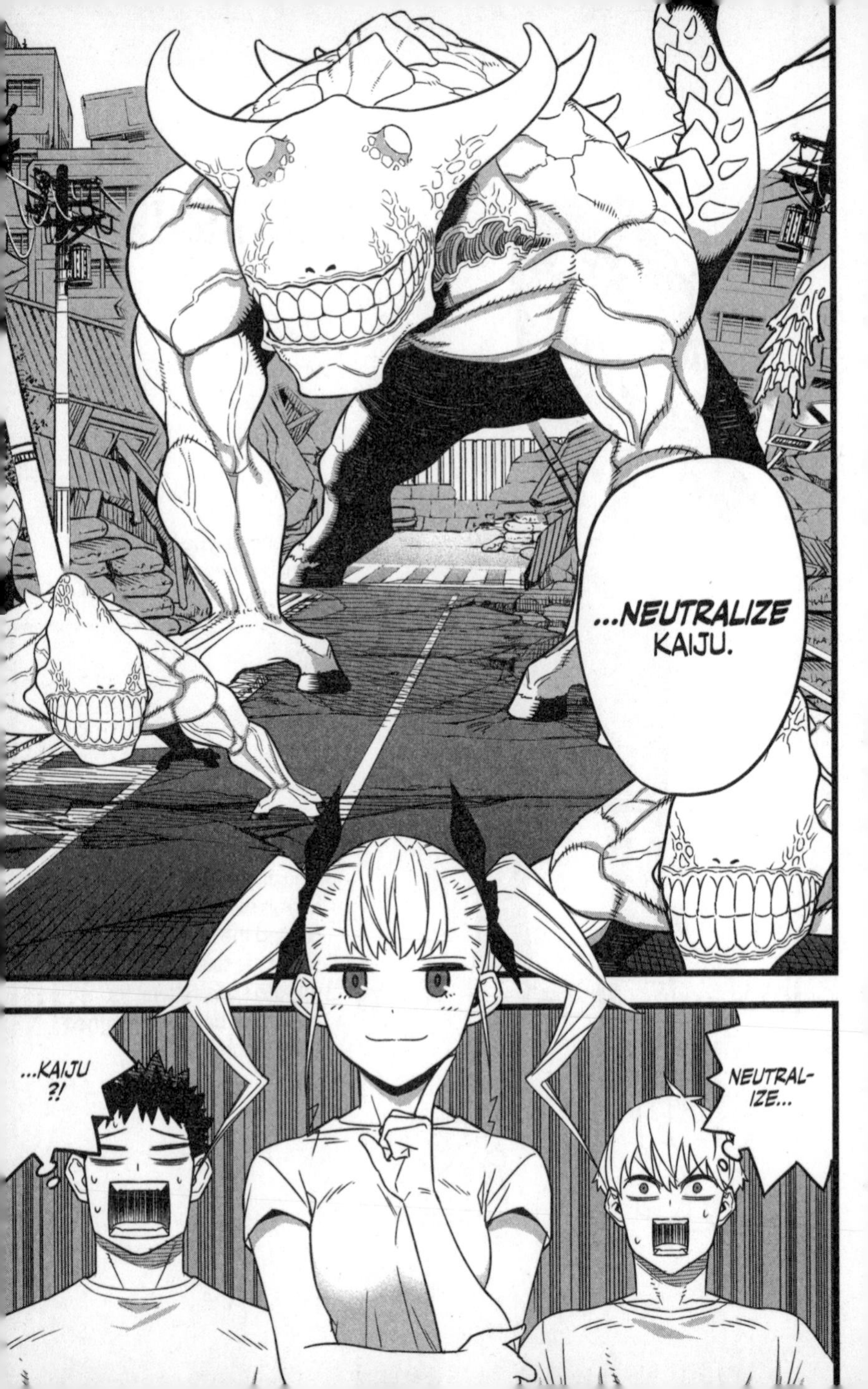
...NEUTRALIZE KAIJU.
NEUTRAL-IZE...
...KAIJU ?!

# MINA ASHIRO

**Birthday:**
June 17

**Height:**
169 cm

**Likes:**
Cats (and maybe feline animals in general?), sweet things, baths, dried cuttlefish

**Author Comment:**
One of our heroines and Kafka's motivation. Since I created the Defense Force suit at the same time I came up with Mina's character design, it's basically designed to look good on her.

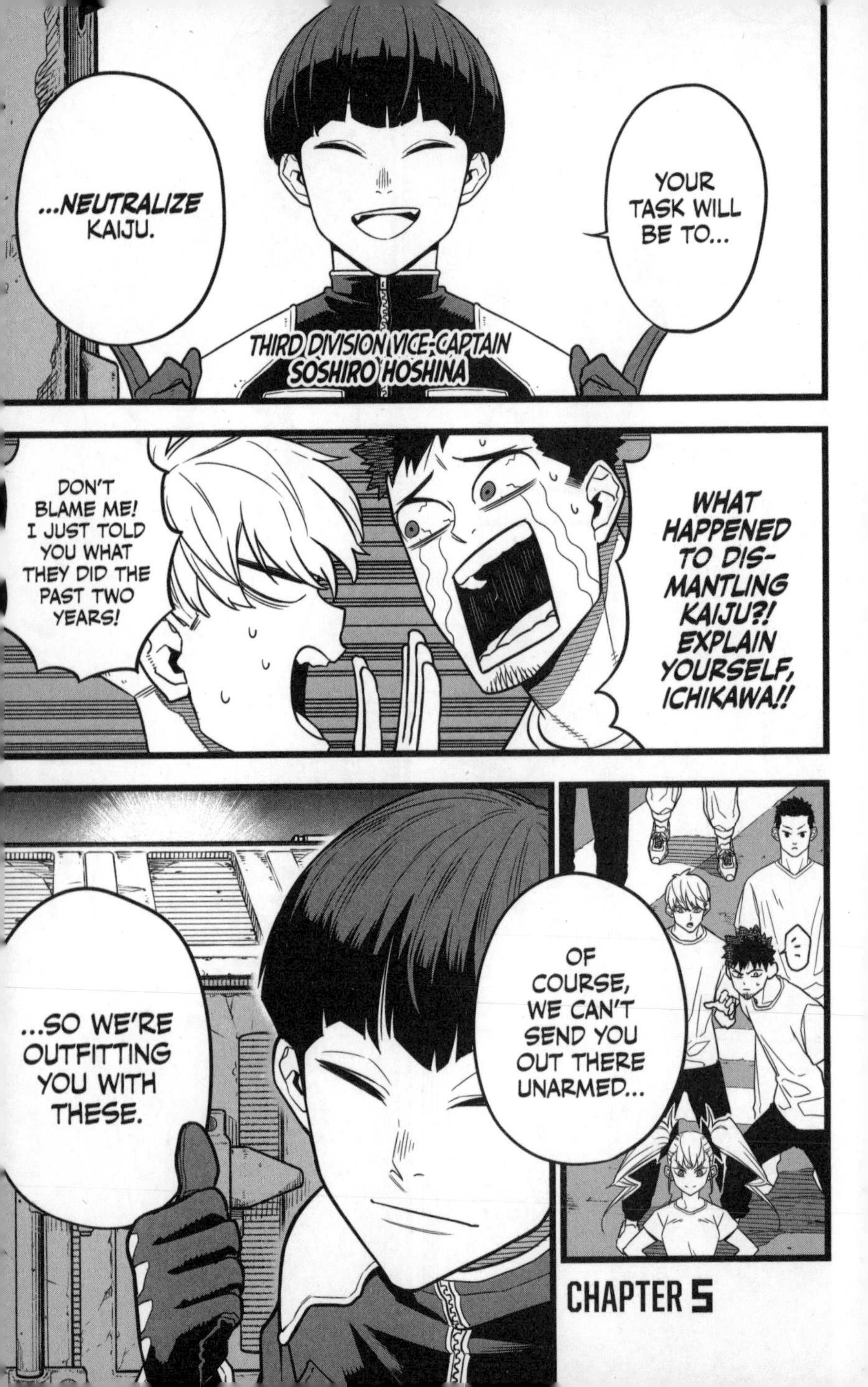
YOUR TASK WILL BE TO...
...NEUTRALIZE KAIJU.
THIRD DIVISION VICE-CAPTAIN SOSHIRO HOSHINA
WHAT HAPPENED TO DIS-MANTLING KAIJU?! EXPLAIN YOURSELF, ICHIKAWA!!
DON'T BLAME ME! I JUST TOLD YOU WHAT THEY DID THE PAST TWO YEARS!
...
OF COURSE, WE CAN'T SEND YOU OUT THERE UNARMED...
...SO WE'RE OUTFITTING YOU WITH THESE.
CHAPTER 5

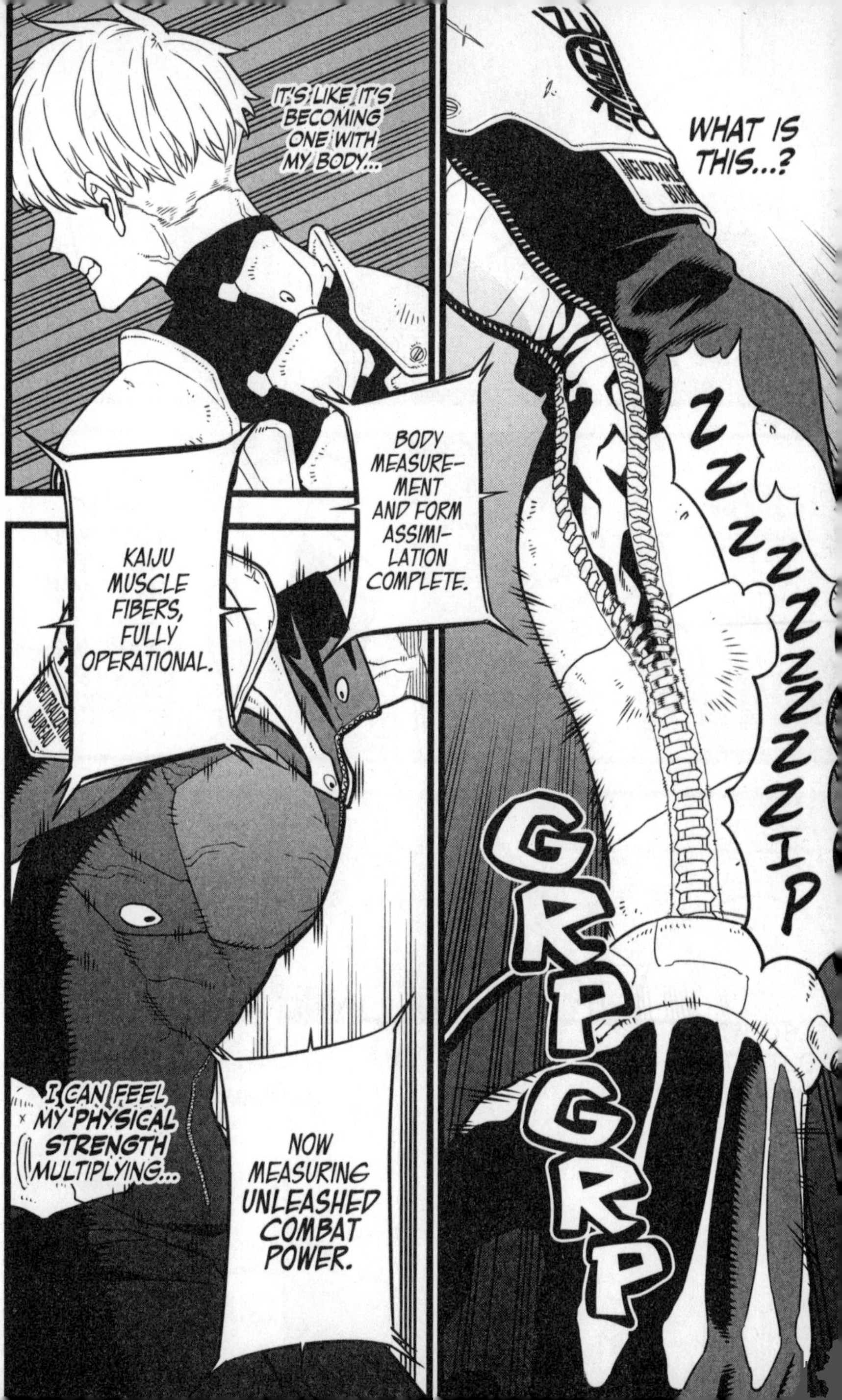
WHAT IS THIS...?
ZZZZZZZZIP
GRPGRP
IT'S LIKE IT'S BECOMING ONE WITH MY BODY...
BODY MEASUREMENT AND FORM ASSIMILATION COMPLETE.
KAIJU MUSCLE FIBERS, FULLY OPERATIONAL.
I CAN FEEL MY PHYSICAL STRENGTH MULTIPLYING...
NOW MEASURING UNLEASHED COMBAT POWER.

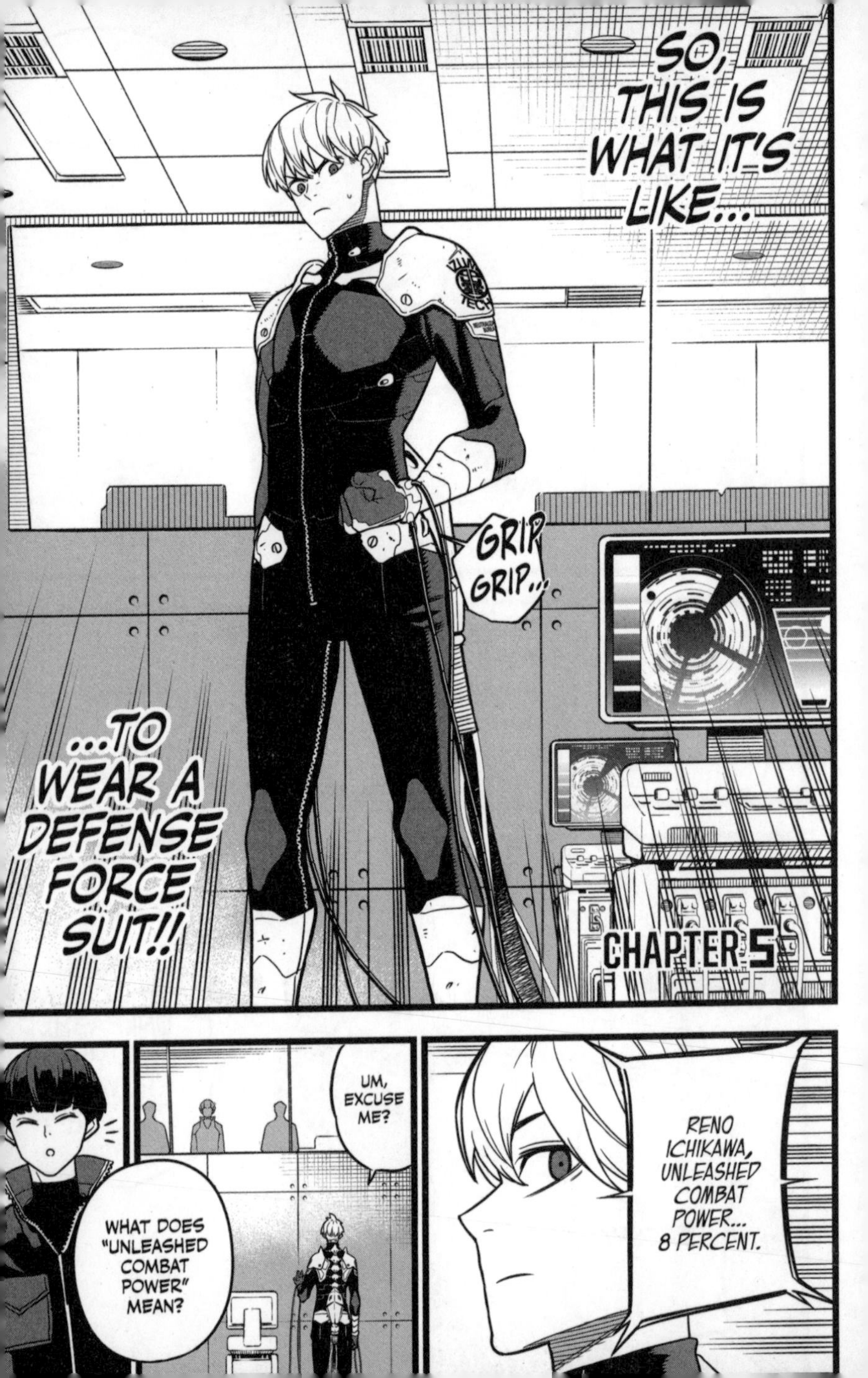
SO, THIS IS WHAT IT'S LIKE...
GRIP GRIP...
...TO WEAR A DEFENSE FORCE SUIT!!
CHAPTER 5
RENO ICHIKAWA, UNLEASHED COMBAT POWER... 8 PERCENT.
UM, EXCUSE ME?
WHAT DOES "UNLEASHED COMBAT POWER" MEAN?

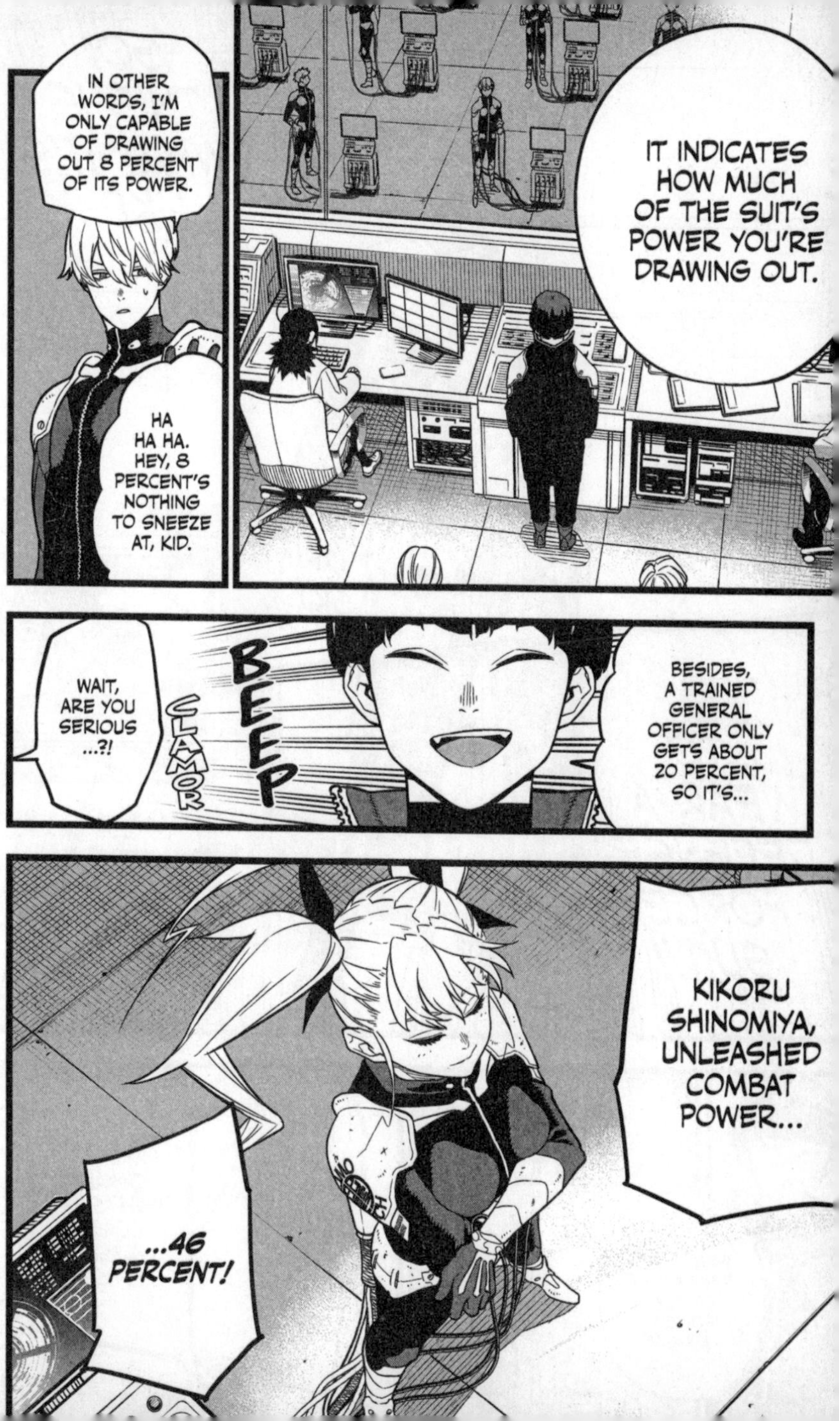
IT INDICATES HOW MUCH OF THE SUIT'S POWER YOU'RE DRAWING OUT.
IN OTHER WORDS, I'M ONLY CAPABLE OF DRAWING OUT 8 PERCENT OF ITS POWER.
HA HA HA. HEY, 8 PERCENT'S NOTHING TO SNEEZE AT, KID.
BESIDES, A TRAINED GENERAL OFFICER ONLY GETS ABOUT 20 PERCENT, SO IT'S...
BEEP
CLAMOR
WAIT, ARE YOU SERIOUS ...?!
KIKORU SHINOMIYA, UNLEASHED COMBAT POWER...
...46 PERCENT!

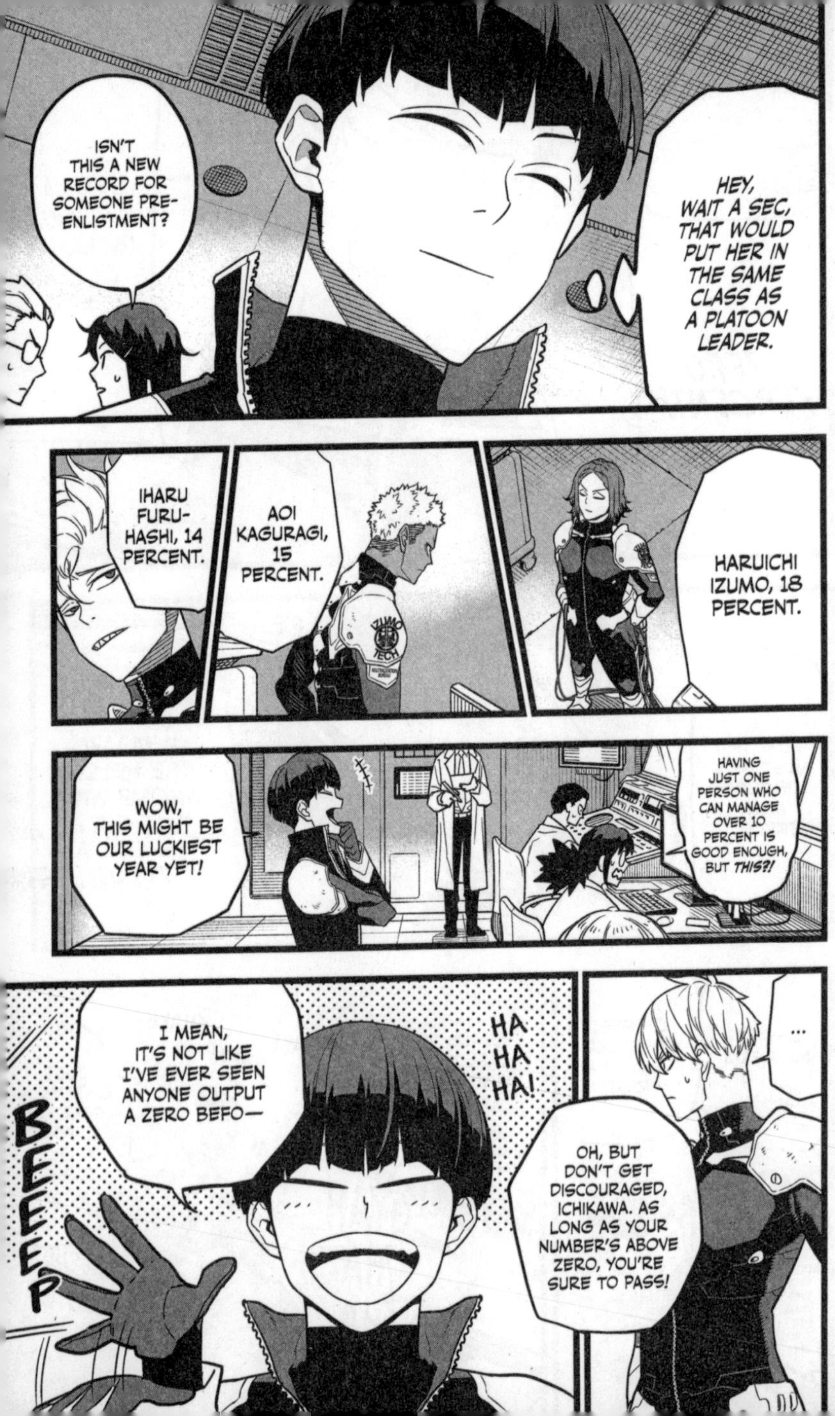
HEY, WAIT A SEC, THAT WOULD PUT HER IN THE SAME CLASS AS A PLATOON LEADER.
ISN'T THIS A NEW RECORD FOR SOMEONE PRE-ENLISTMENT?
HARUICHI IZUMO, 18 PERCENT.
AOI KAGURAGI, 15 PERCENT.
IHARU FURU-HASHI, 14 PERCENT.
HAVING JUST ONE PERSON WHO CAN MANAGE OVER 10 PERCENT IS GOOD ENOUGH, BUT *THIS?!*
WOW, THIS MIGHT BE OUR LUCKIEST YEAR YET!
...
OH, BUT DON'T GET DISCOURAGED, ICHIKAWA. AS LONG AS YOUR NUMBER'S ABOVE ZERO, YOU'RE SURE TO PASS!
HA HA HA!
I MEAN, IT'S NOT LIKE I'VE EVER SEEN ANYONE OUTPUT A ZERO BEFO—
BEEEEP

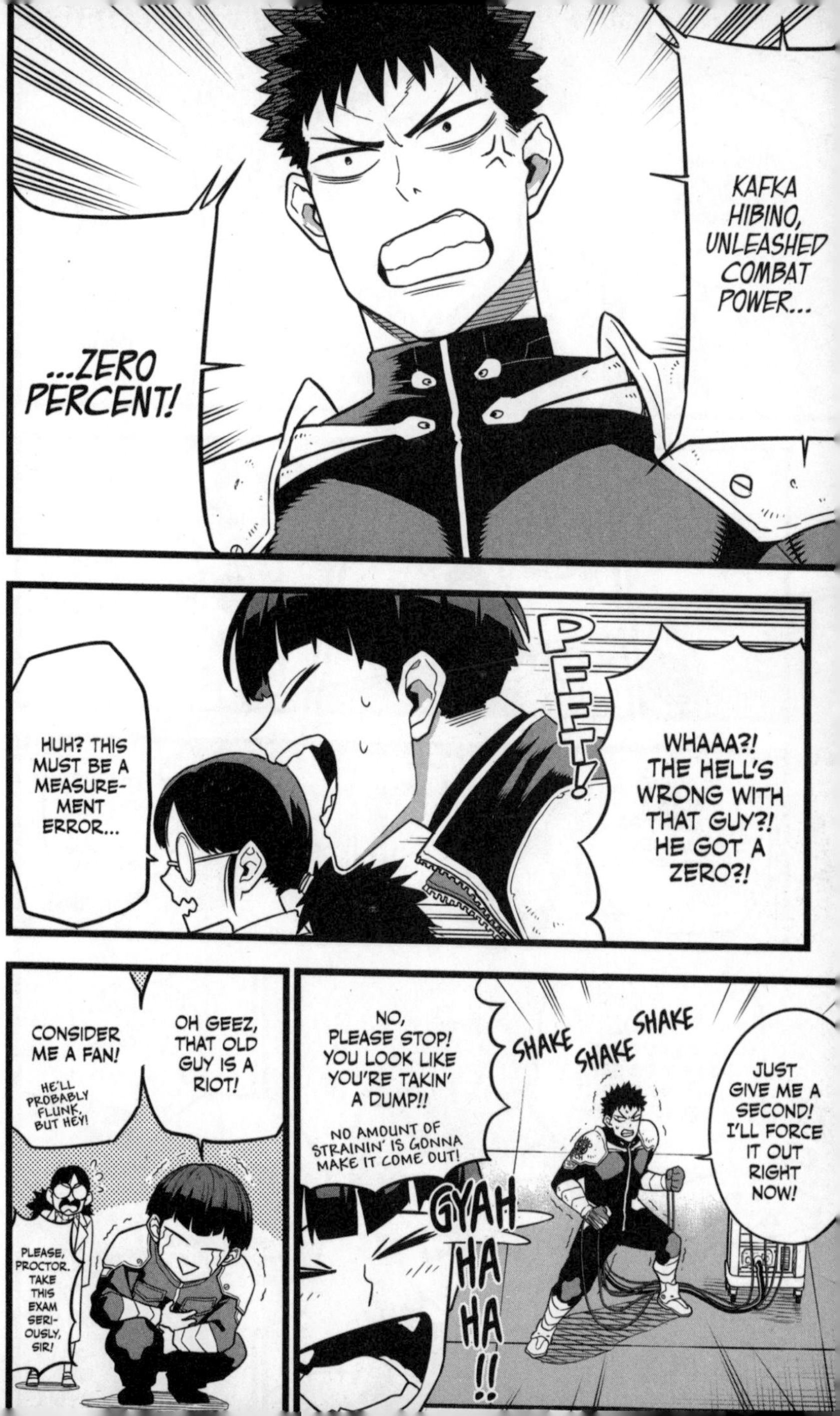
KAFKA HIBINO, UNLEASHED COMBAT POWER...
...ZERO PERCENT!
PFFT!
WHAAA?! THE HELL'S WRONG WITH THAT GUY?! HE GOT A ZERO?!
HUH? THIS MUST BE A MEASUREMENT ERROR...
JUST GIVE ME A SECOND! I'LL FORCE IT OUT RIGHT NOW!
SHAKE SHAKE SHAKE
NO, PLEASE STOP! YOU LOOK LIKE YOU'RE TAKIN' A DUMP!!
NO AMOUNT OF STRAININ' IS GONNA MAKE IT COME OUT!
GYAH HA HA!!
OH GEEZ, THAT OLD GUY IS A RIOT!
CONSIDER ME A FAN!
HE'LL PROBABLY FLUNK, BUT HEY!
PLEASE, PROCTOR. TAKE THIS EXAM SERIOUSLY, SIR!

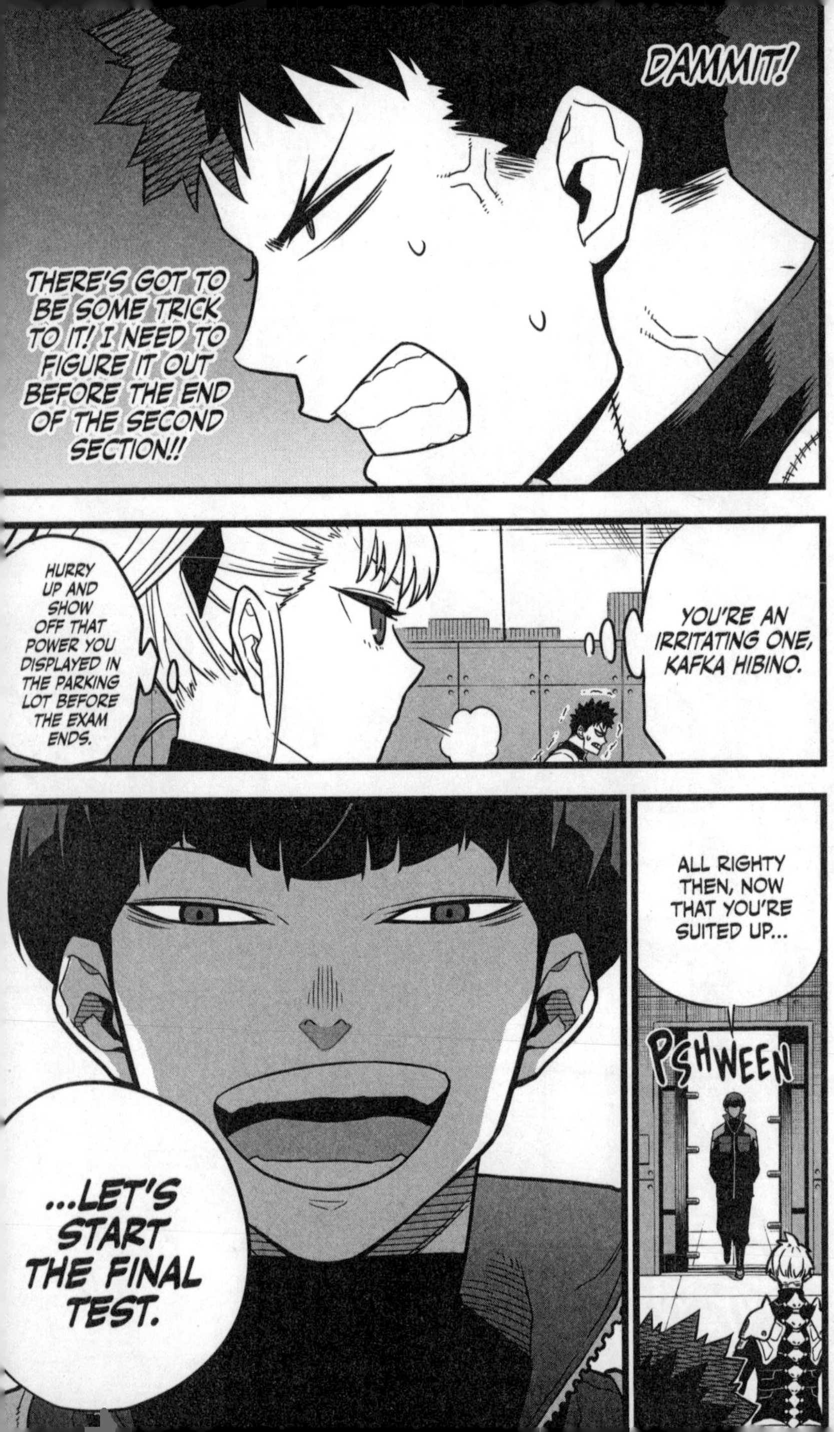
DAMMIT!
THERE'S GOT TO BE SOME TRICK TO IT! I NEED TO FIGURE IT OUT BEFORE THE END OF THE SECOND SECTION!!
YOU'RE AN IRRITATING ONE, KAFKA HIBINO.
HURRY UP AND SHOW OFF THAT POWER YOU DISPLAYED IN THE PARKING LOT BEFORE THE EXAM ENDS.
ALL RIGHTY THEN, NOW THAT YOU'RE SUITED UP...
PSHWEEN
...LET'S START THE FINAL TEST.

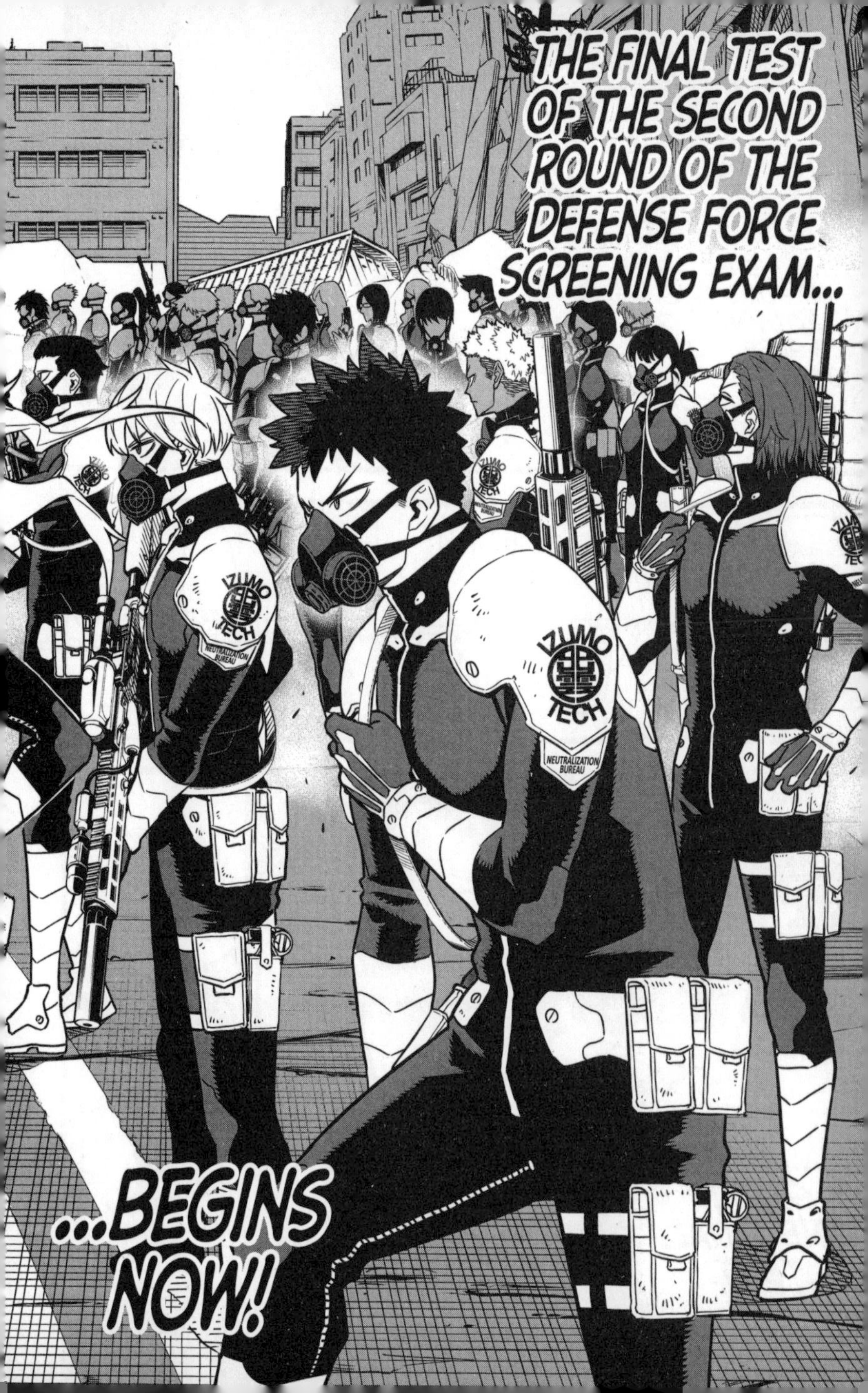
THE FINAL TEST OF THE SECOND ROUND OF THE DEFENSE FORCE SCREENING EXAM...
...BEGINS NOW!
IZUMO TECH
NEUTRALIZATION BUREAU

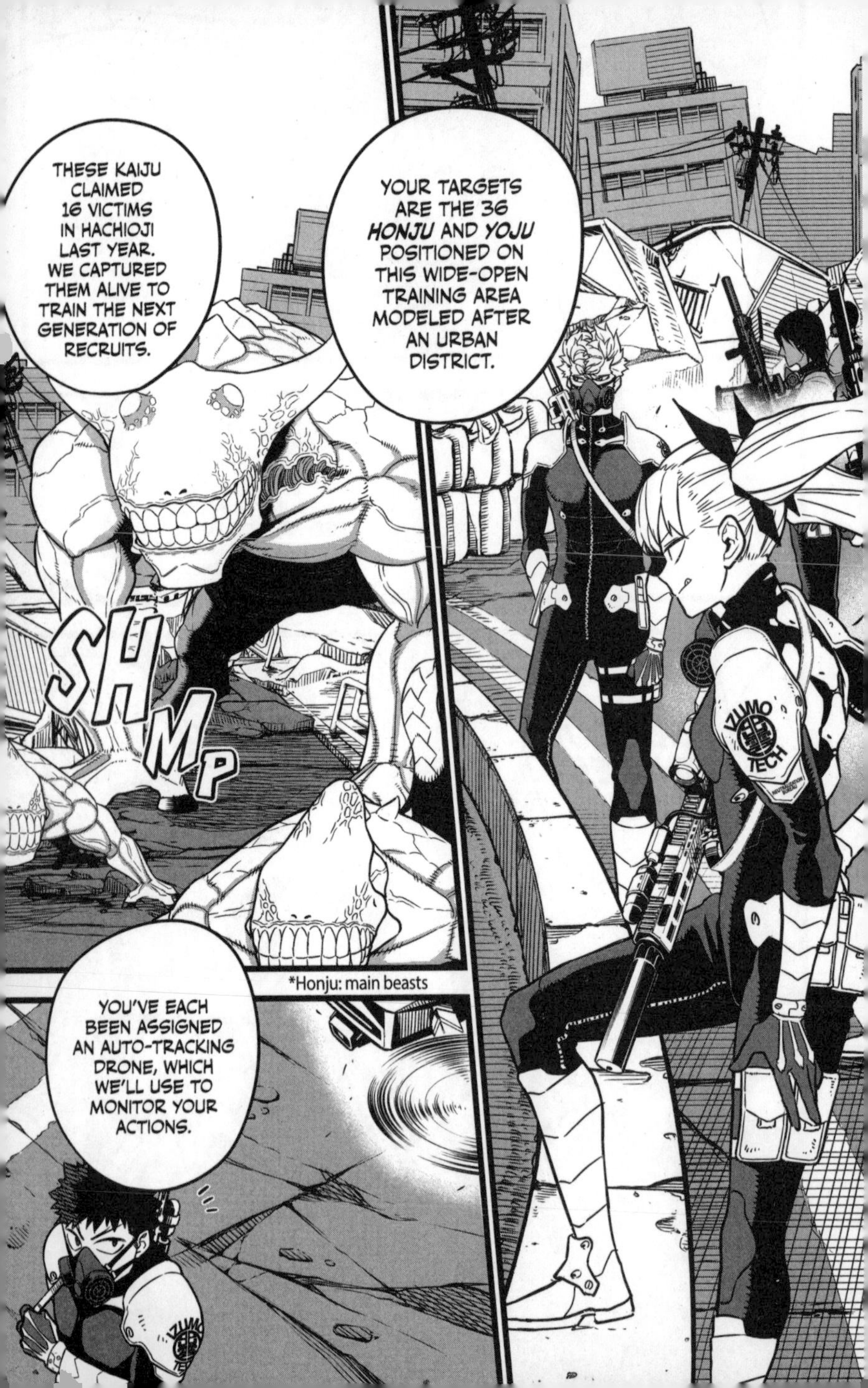
YOUR TARGETS ARE THE 36 *HONJU* AND *YOJU* POSITIONED ON THIS WIDE-OPEN TRAINING AREA MODELED AFTER AN URBAN DISTRICT.
IZUMO TECH
THESE KAIJU CLAIMED 16 VICTIMS IN HACHIOJI LAST YEAR. WE CAPTURED THEM ALIVE TO TRAIN THE NEXT GENERATION OF RECRUITS.
SHMP
*Honju: main beasts
YOU'VE EACH BEEN ASSIGNED AN AUTO-TRACKING DRONE, WHICH WE'LL USE TO MONITOR YOUR ACTIONS.

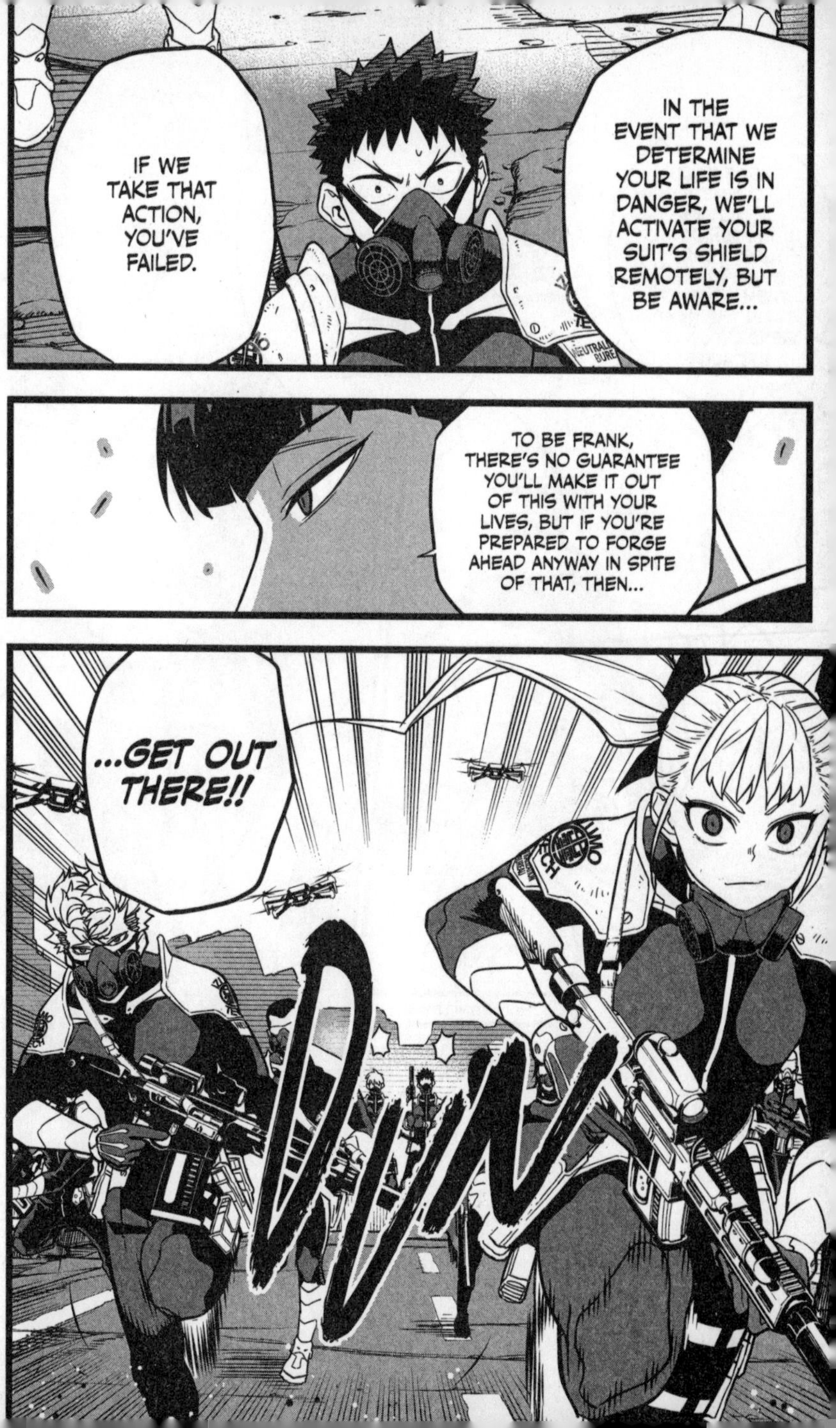
IN THE EVENT THAT WE DETERMINE YOUR LIFE IS IN DANGER, WE'LL ACTIVATE YOUR SUIT'S SHIELD REMOTELY, BUT BE AWARE...
IF WE TAKE THAT ACTION, YOU'VE FAILED.
TO BE FRANK, THERE'S NO GUARANTEE YOU'LL MAKE IT OUT OF THIS WITH YOUR LIVES, BUT IF YOU'RE PREPARED TO FORGE AHEAD ANYWAY IN SPITE OF THAT, THEN...
...GET OUT THERE!!

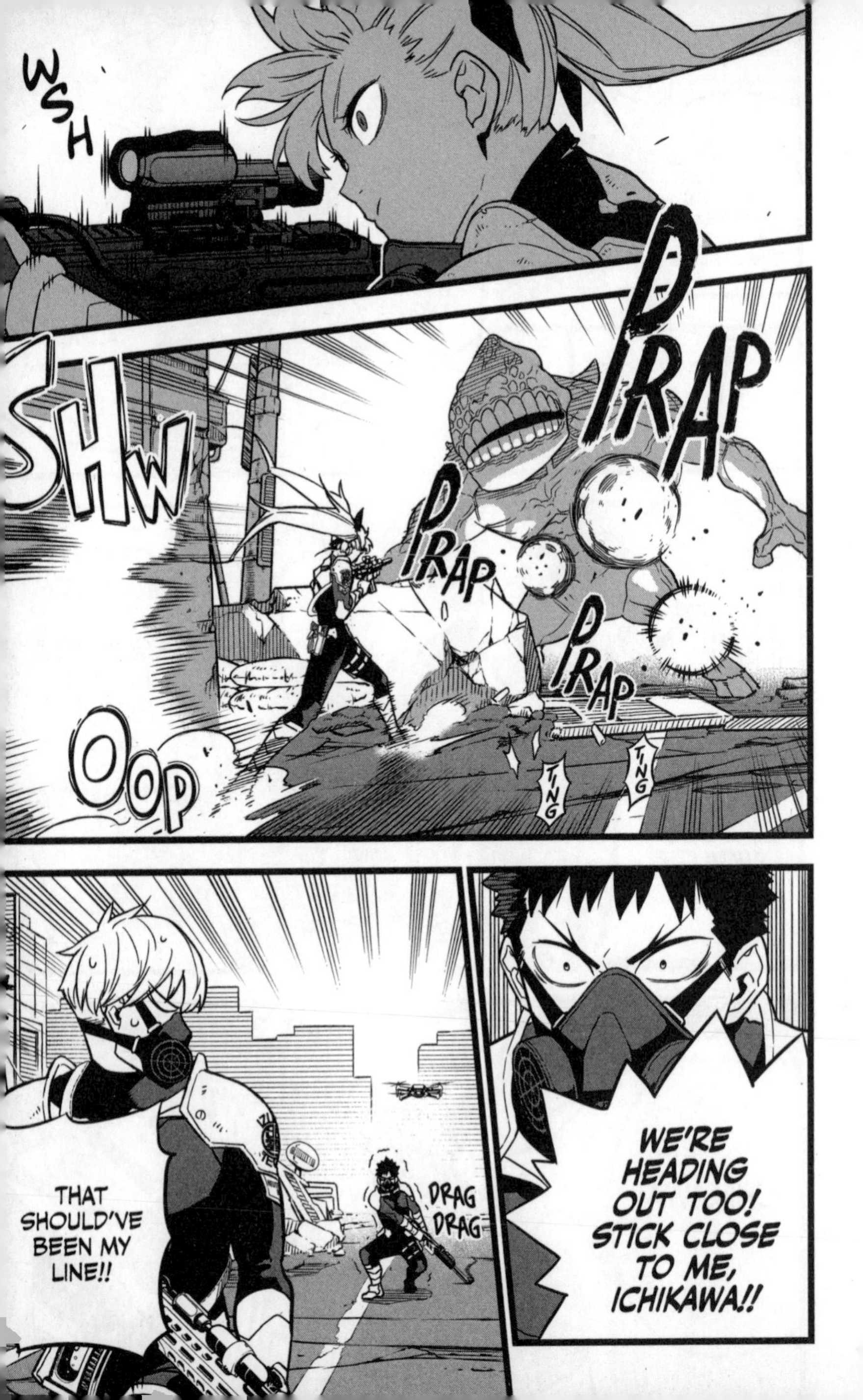
WSH
PRAP
SHW
PRAP
PRAP
OOP
TING
TING
WE'RE HEADING OUT TOO! STICK CLOSE TO ME, ICHIKAWA!!
DRAG DRAG
THAT SHOULD'VE BEEN MY LINE!!

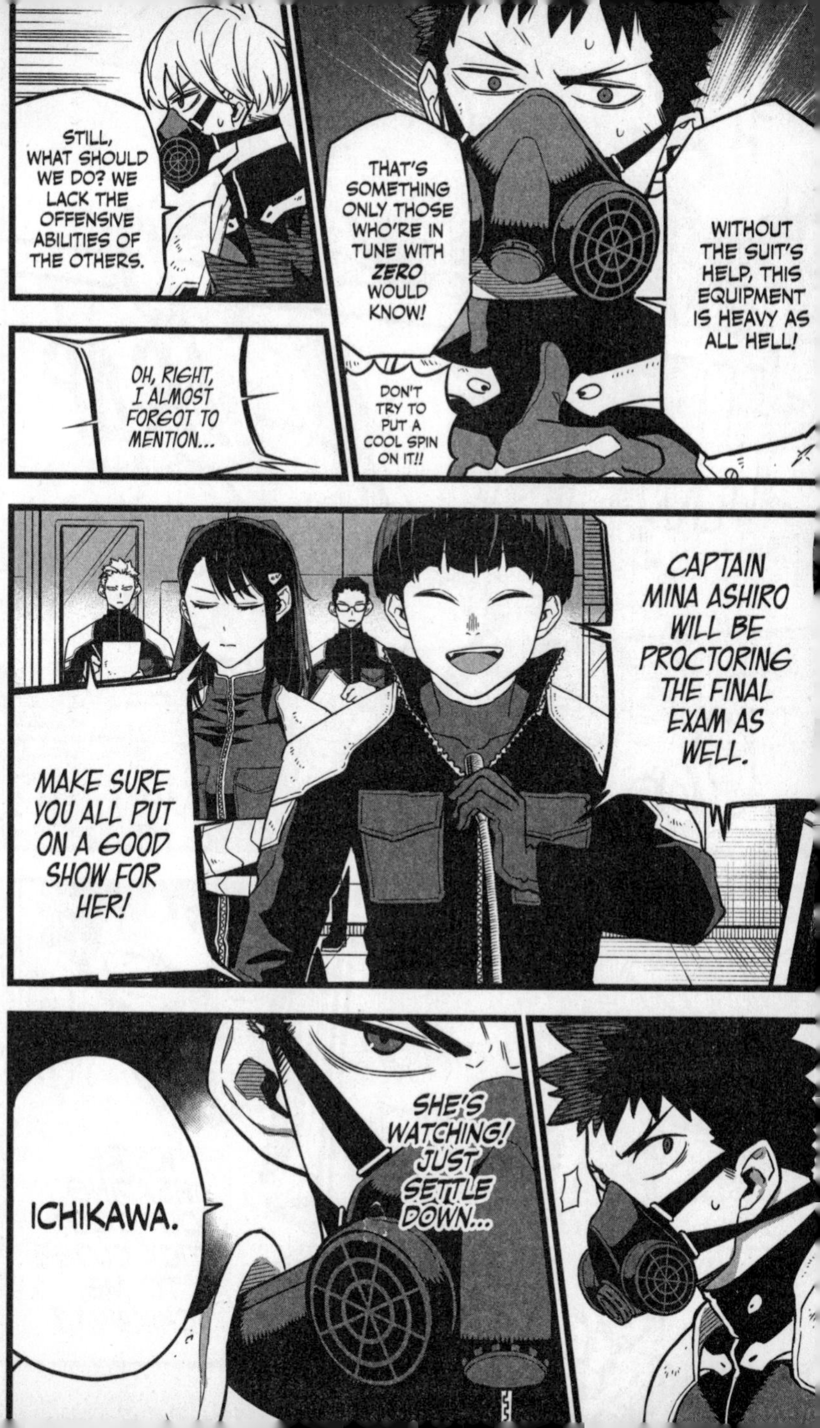
WITHOUT THE SUIT'S HELP, THIS EQUIPMENT IS HEAVY AS ALL HELL!
THAT'S SOMETHING ONLY THOSE WHO'RE IN TUNE WITH ZERO WOULD KNOW!
DON'T TRY TO PUT A COOL SPIN ON IT!!
STILL, WHAT SHOULD WE DO? WE LACK THE OFFENSIVE ABILITIES OF THE OTHERS.
OH, RIGHT, I ALMOST FORGOT TO MENTION...
CAPTAIN MINA ASHIRO WILL BE PROCTORING THE FINAL EXAM AS WELL.
MAKE SURE YOU ALL PUT ON A GOOD SHOW FOR HER!
SHE'S WATCHING! JUST SETTLE DOWN...
ICHIKAWA.

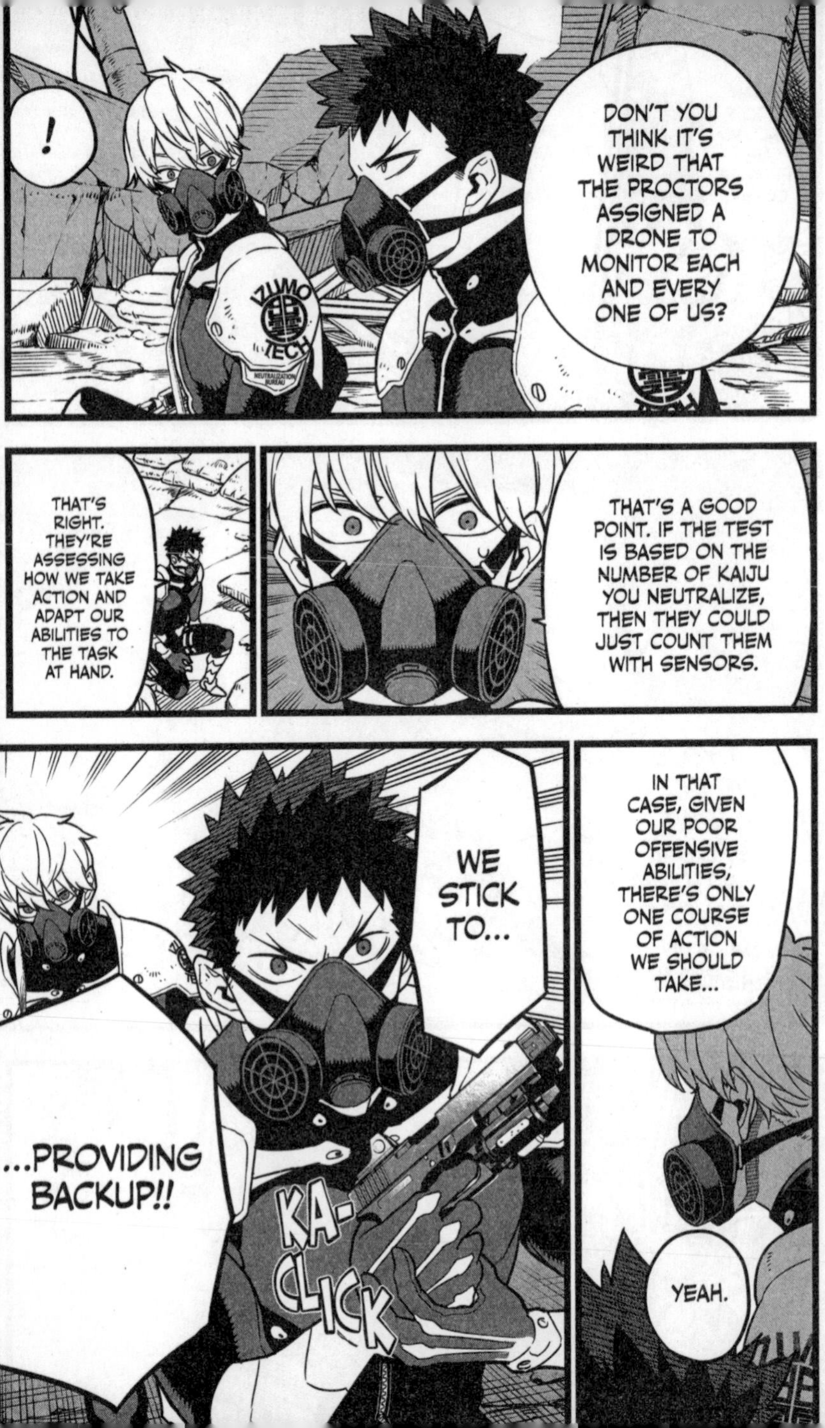
DON'T YOU THINK IT'S WEIRD THAT THE PROCTORS ASSIGNED A DRONE TO MONITOR EACH AND EVERY ONE OF US?
!
THAT'S A GOOD POINT. IF THE TEST IS BASED ON THE NUMBER OF KAIJU YOU NEUTRALIZE, THEN THEY COULD JUST COUNT THEM WITH SENSORS.
THAT'S RIGHT. THEY'RE ASSESSING HOW WE TAKE ACTION AND ADAPT OUR ABILITIES TO THE TASK AT HAND.
IN THAT CASE, GIVEN OUR POOR OFFENSIVE ABILITIES, THERE'S ONLY ONE COURSE OF ACTION WE SHOULD TAKE...
YEAH.
WE STICK TO...
...PROVIDING BACKUP!!
KA-CLICK

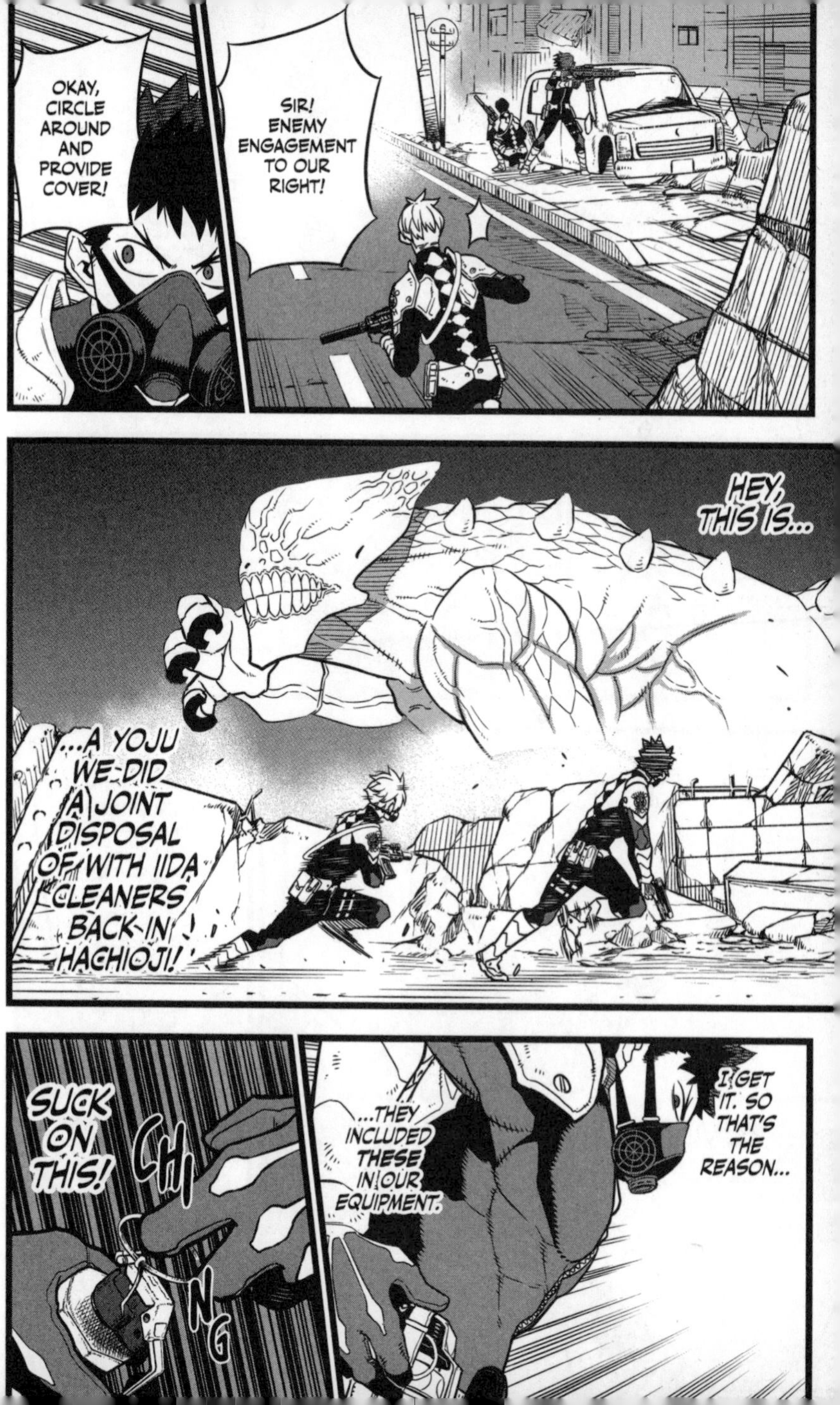
SIR! ENEMY ENGAGEMENT TO OUR RIGHT!
OKAY, CIRCLE AROUND AND PROVIDE COVER!
HEY, THIS IS...
...A YOJU WE DID A JOINT DISPOSAL OF WITH IIDA CLEANERS BACK IN HACHIOJI!
I GET IT. SO THAT'S THE REASON...
...THEY INCLUDED THESE IN OUR EQUIPMENT.
SUCK ON THIS!
CHING

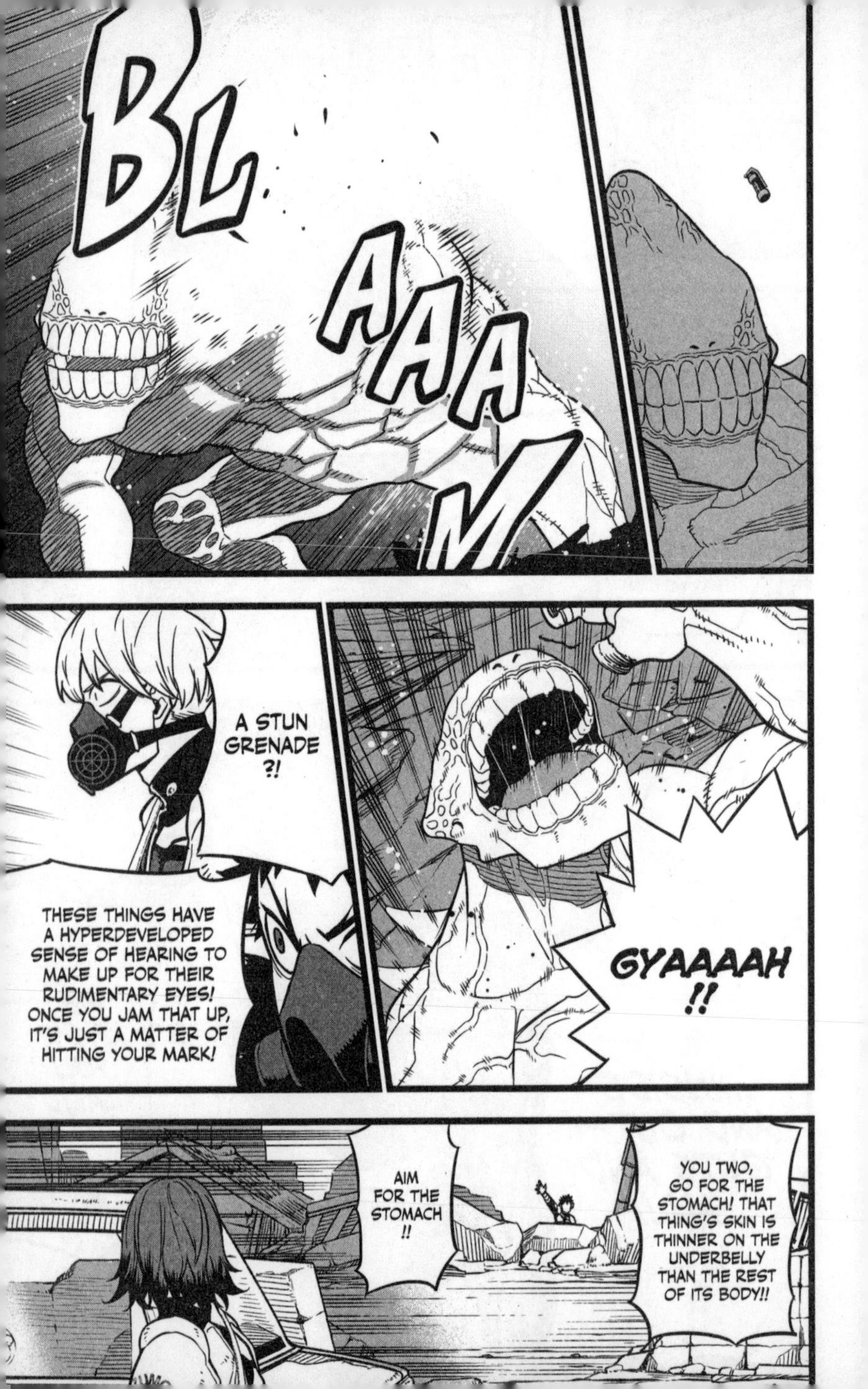
BLAAAAM
A STUN GRENADE ?!
GYAAAAH !!
THESE THINGS HAVE A HYPERDEVELOPED SENSE OF HEARING TO MAKE UP FOR THEIR RUDIMENTARY EYES! ONCE YOU JAM THAT UP, IT'S JUST A MATTER OF HITTING YOUR MARK!
YOU TWO, GO FOR THE STOMACH! THAT THING'S SKIN IS THINNER ON THE UNDERBELLY THAN THE REST OF ITS BODY!!
AIM FOR THE STOMACH !!

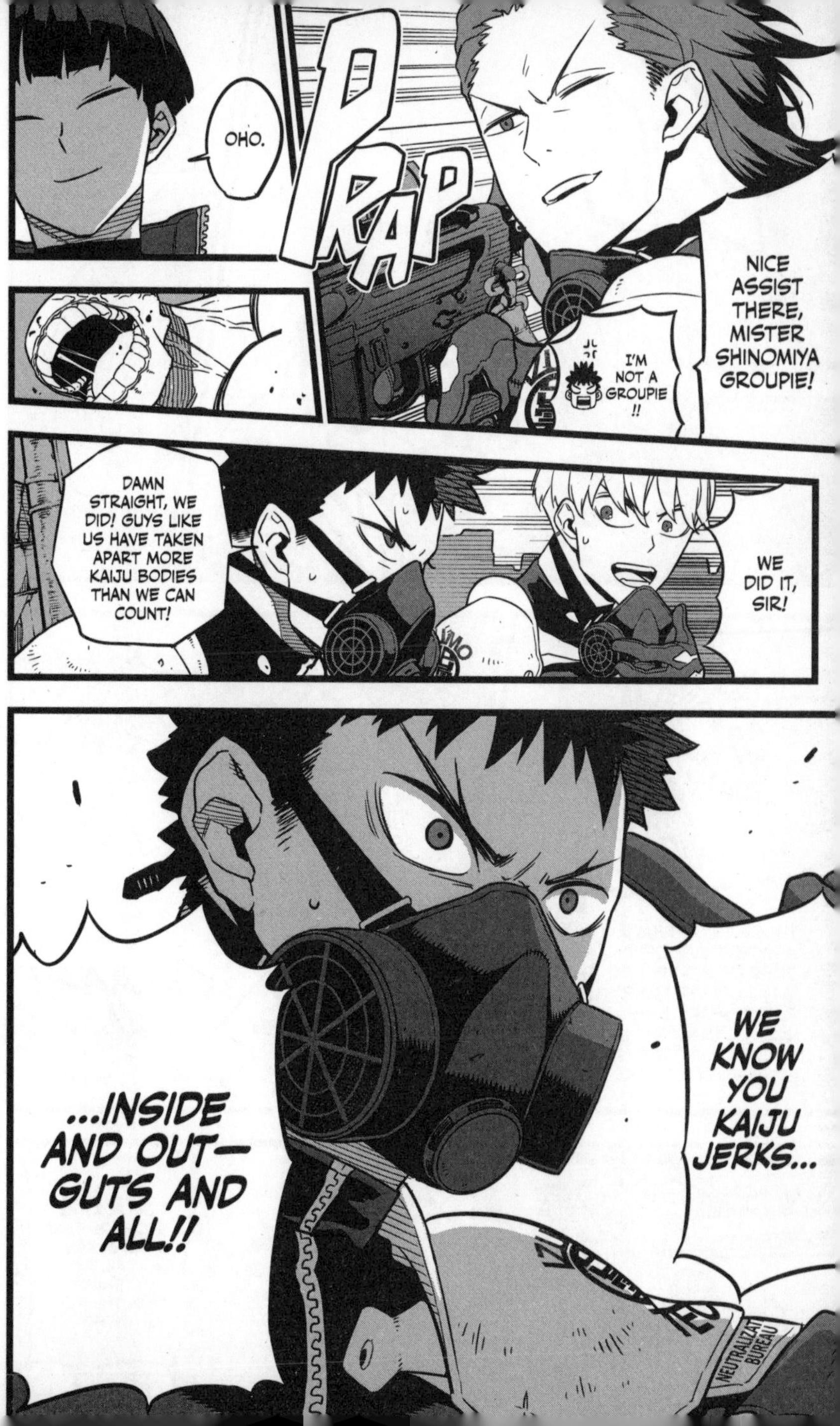
DRAP
NICE ASSIST THERE, MISTER SHINOMIYA GROUPIE!
I'M NOT A GROUPIE!!
OHO.
WE DID IT, SIR!
DAMN STRAIGHT, WE DID! GUYS LIKE US HAVE TAKEN APART MORE KAIJU BODIES THAN WE CAN COUNT!
WE KNOW YOU KAIJU JERKS...
...INSIDE AND OUT— GUTS AND ALL!!

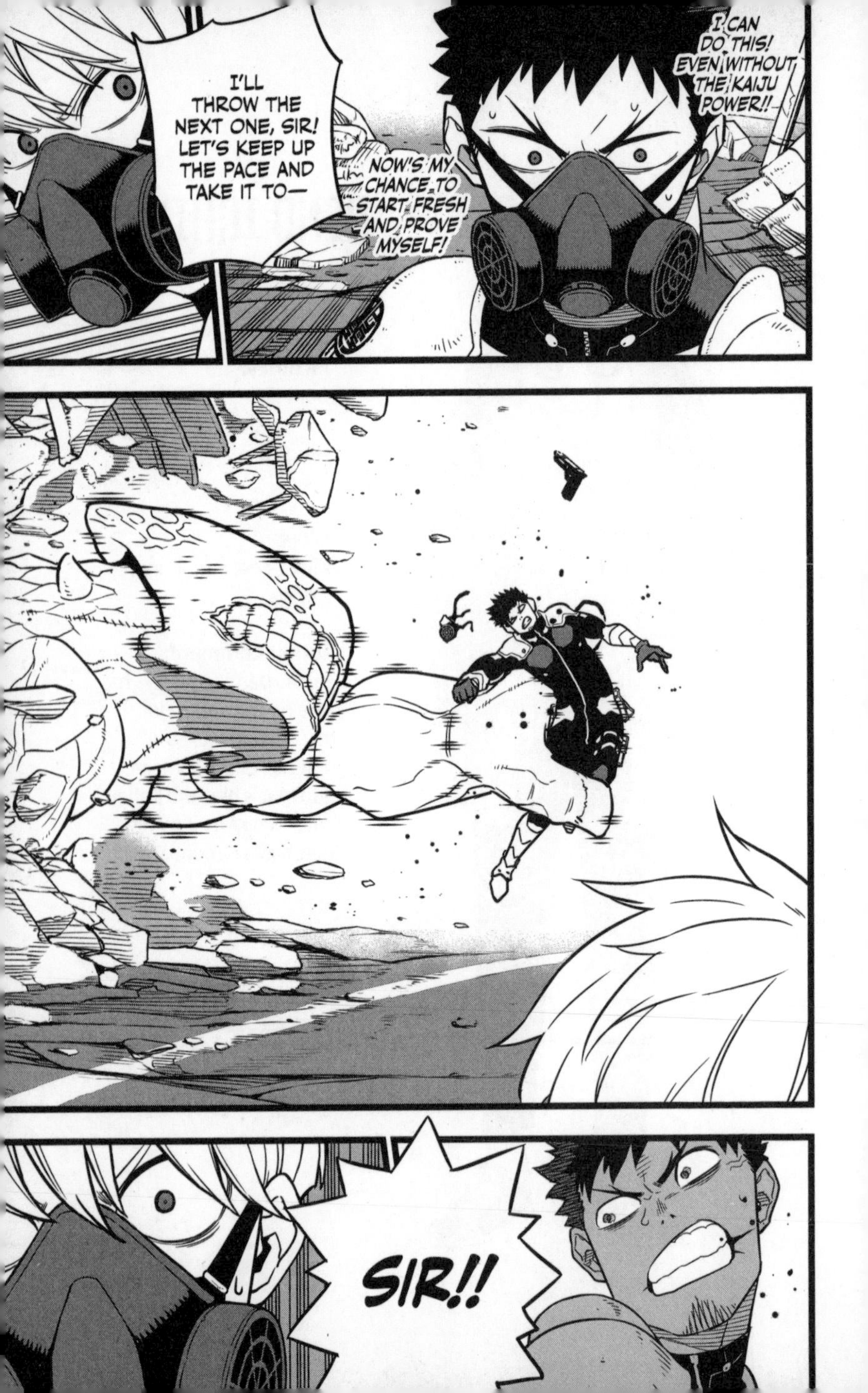
I CAN DO THIS! EVEN WITHOUT THE KAIJU POWER!!
NOW'S MY CHANCE TO START FRESH AND PROVE MYSELF!
I'LL THROW THE NEXT ONE, SIR! LET'S KEEP UP THE PACE AND TAKE IT TO—
SIR!!

# RENO ICHIKAWA

**Birthday:**
April 12

**Height:**
174 cm

**Likes:**
Music, cooking, shonen manga

**Author Comment:**
Kafka's partner. Always has a witty retort and a loud reaction. He makes up one-half of the comedic duo that is him and Kafka. When Ichikawa is by his side, Kafka is more at ease.

# CHAPTER 6

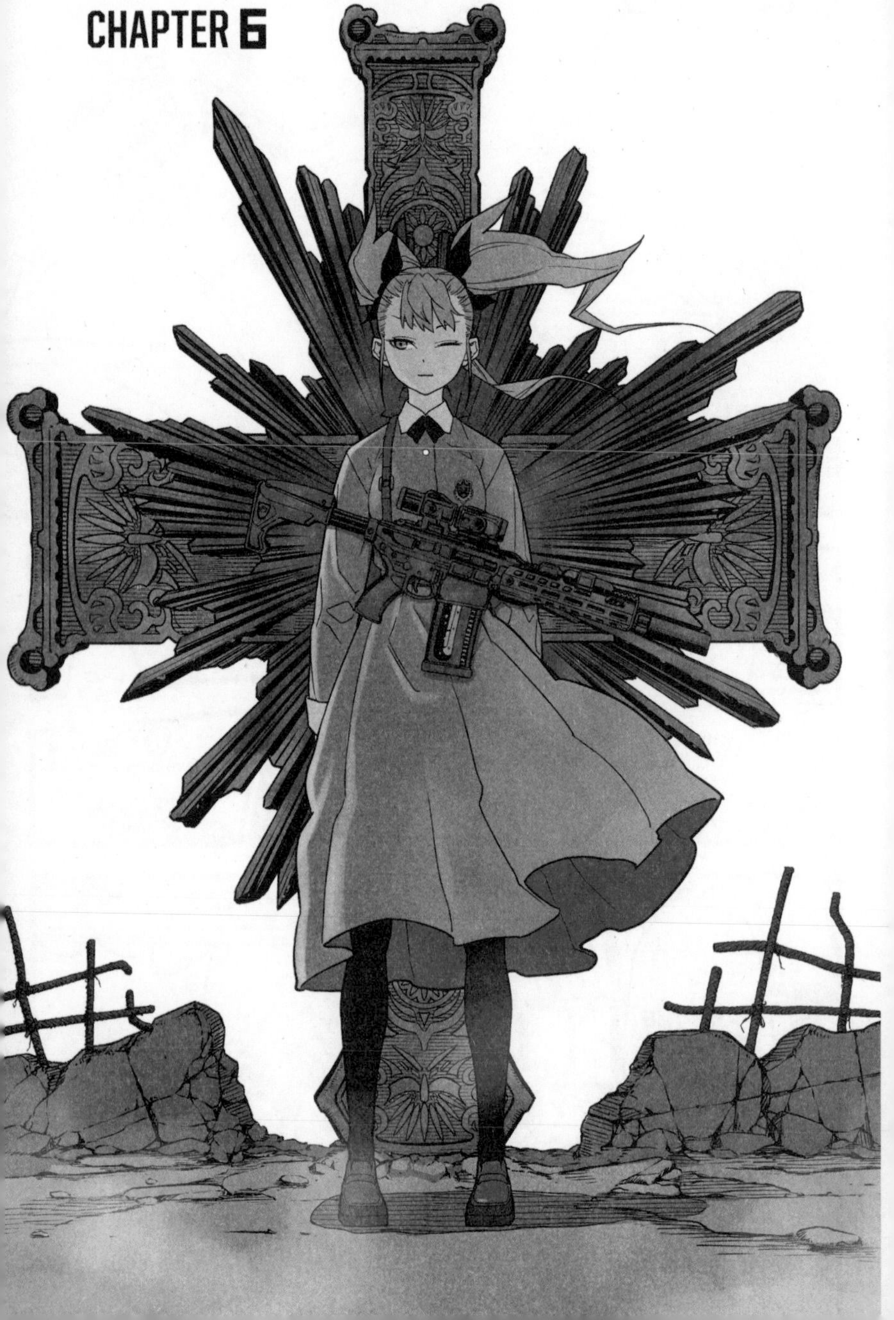

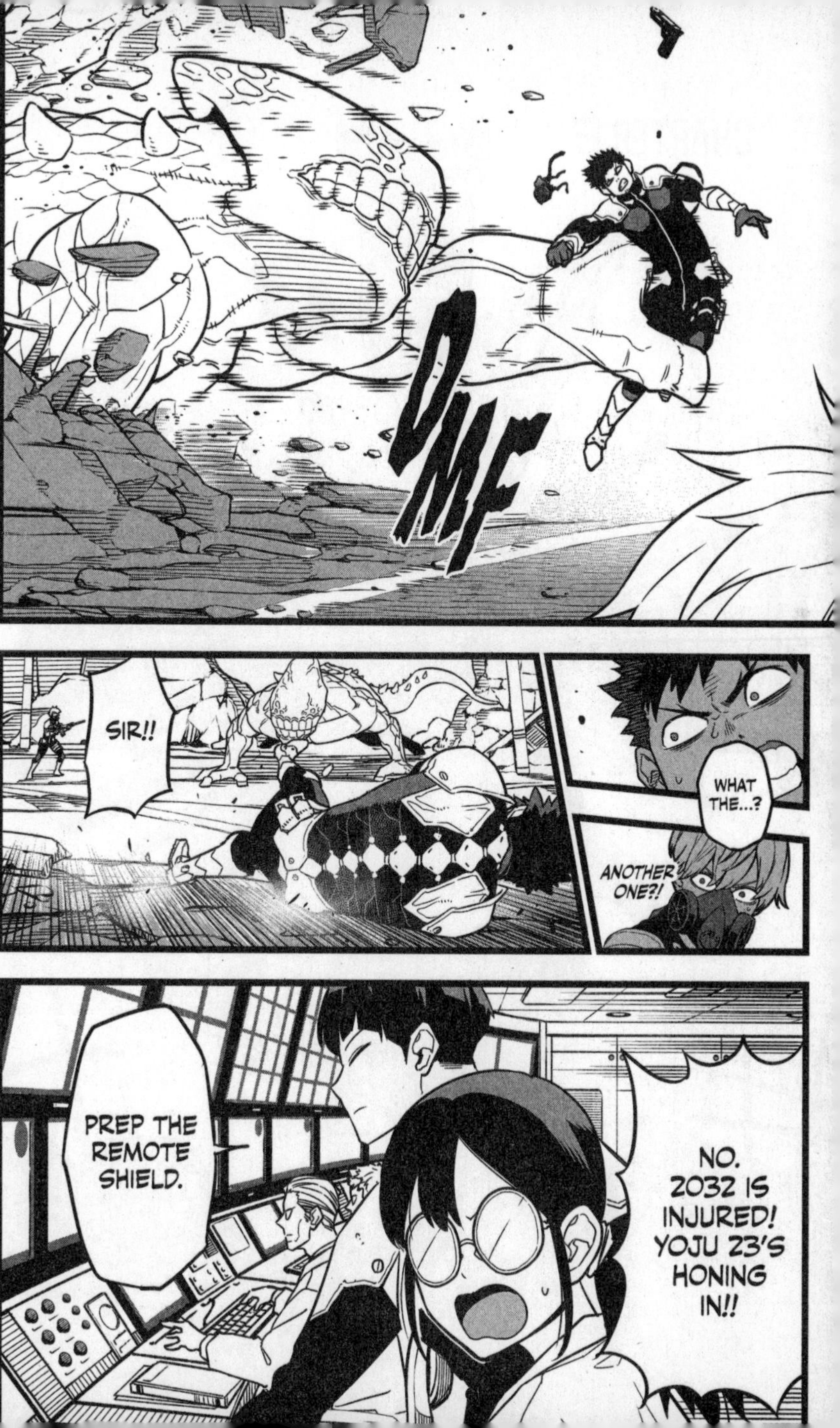
OMF
WHAT THE...?
ANOTHER ONE?!
SIR!!
NO. 2032 IS INJURED! YOJU 23'S HONING IN!!
PREP THE REMOTE SHIELD.

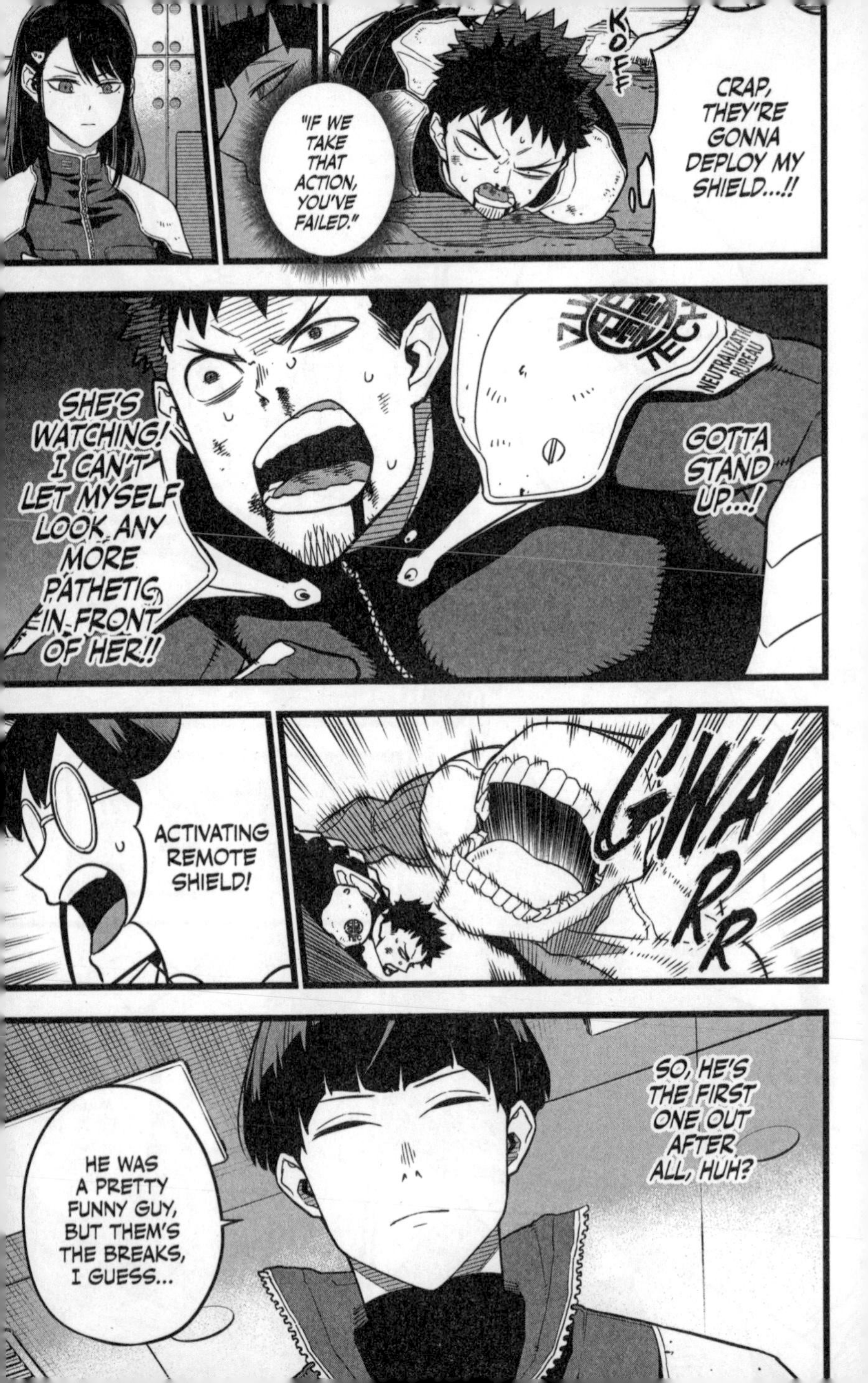
KOFF
CRAP, THEY'RE GONNA DEPLOY MY SHIELD...!!
"IF WE TAKE THAT ACTION, YOU'VE FAILED."
GOTTA STAND UP...!
SHE'S WATCHING! I CAN'T LET MYSELF LOOK ANY MORE PATHETIC IN FRONT OF HER!!
GWARRR
ACTIVATING REMOTE SHIELD!
SO, HE'S THE FIRST ONE OUT AFTER ALL, HUH?
HE WAS A PRETTY FUNNY GUY, BUT THEM'S THE BREAKS, I GUESS...

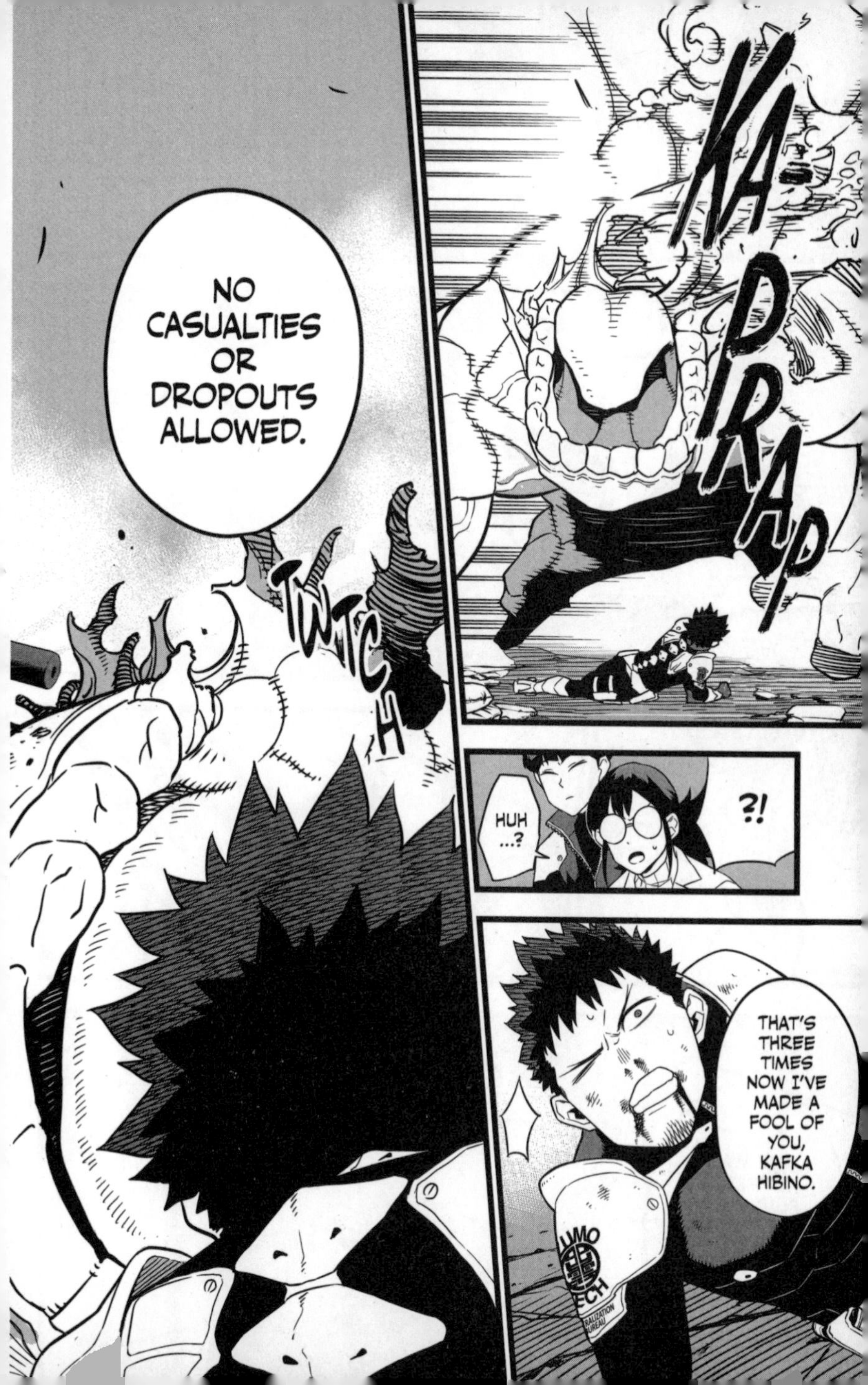
KADRAP
HUH ...?
?!
THAT'S THREE TIMES NOW I'VE MADE A FOOL OF YOU, KAFKA HIBINO.
NO CASUALTIES OR DROPOUTS ALLOWED.
TWITCH

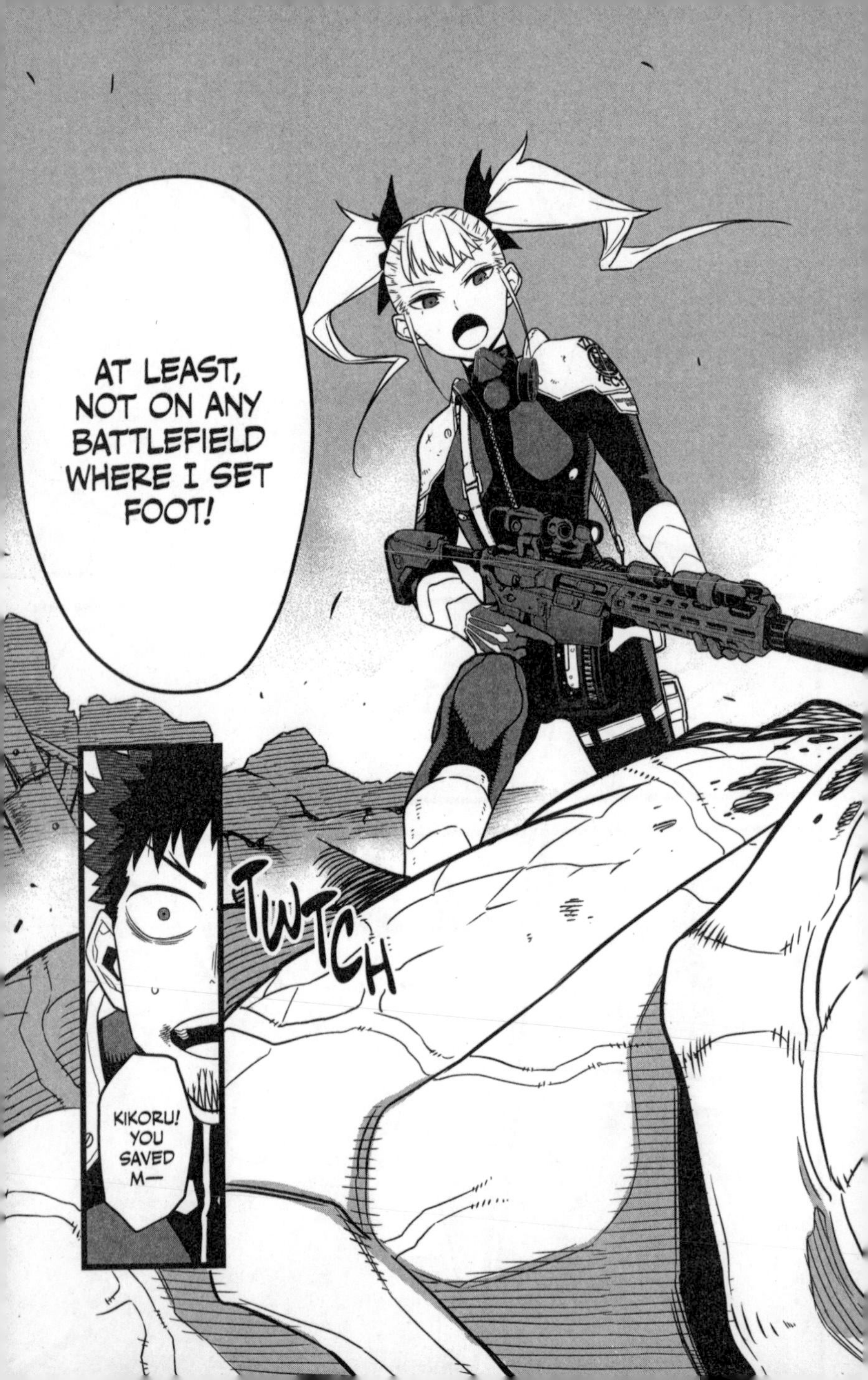
AT LEAST, NOT ON ANY BATTLEFIELD WHERE I SET FOOT!
TWITCH
KIKORU! YOU SAVED M—

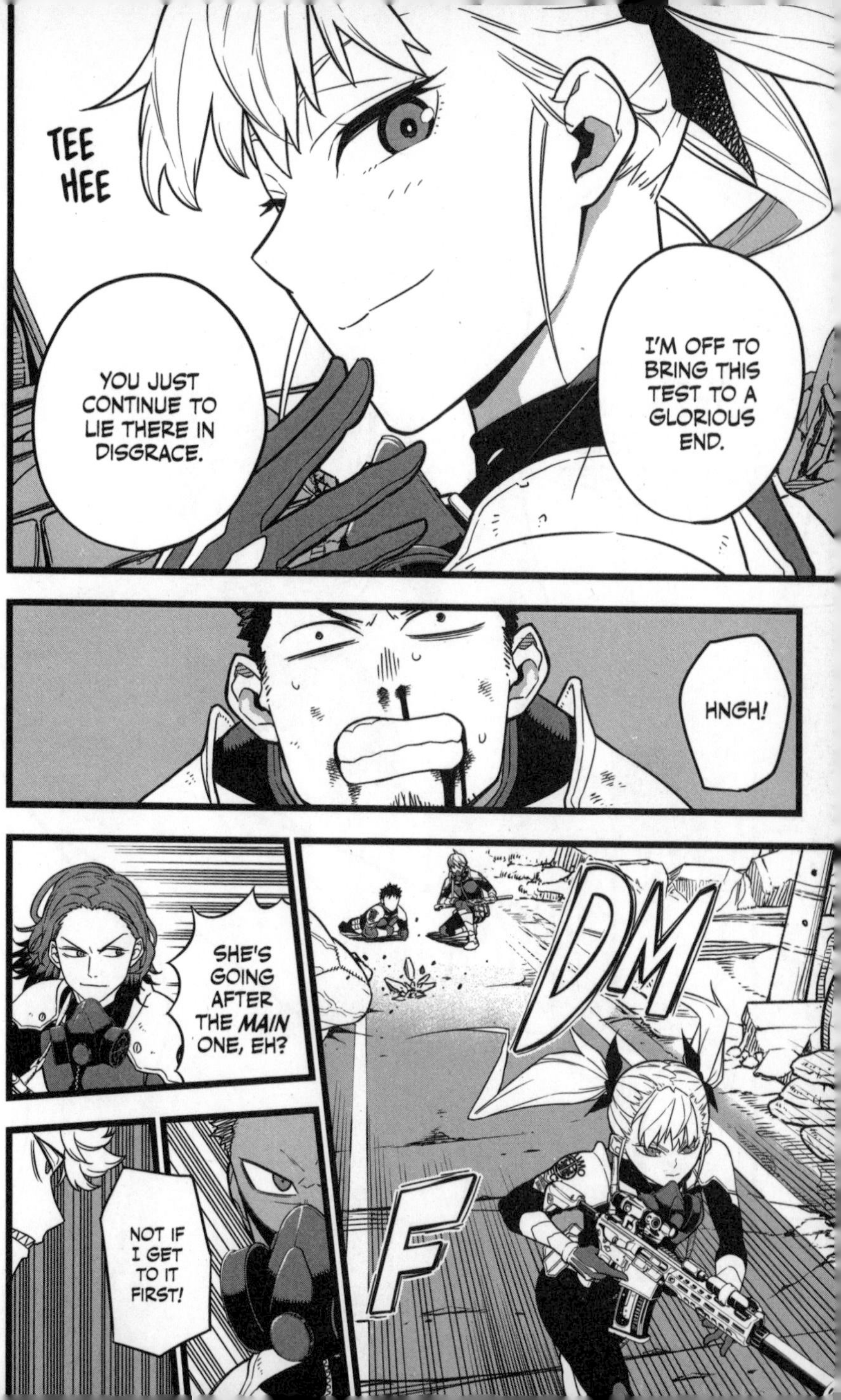
I'M OFF TO BRING THIS TEST TO A GLORIOUS END.
YOU JUST CONTINUE TO LIE THERE IN DISGRACE.
TEE HEE
HNGH!
DM
F
SHE'S GOING AFTER THE *MAIN* ONE, EH?
NOT IF I GET TO IT FIRST!

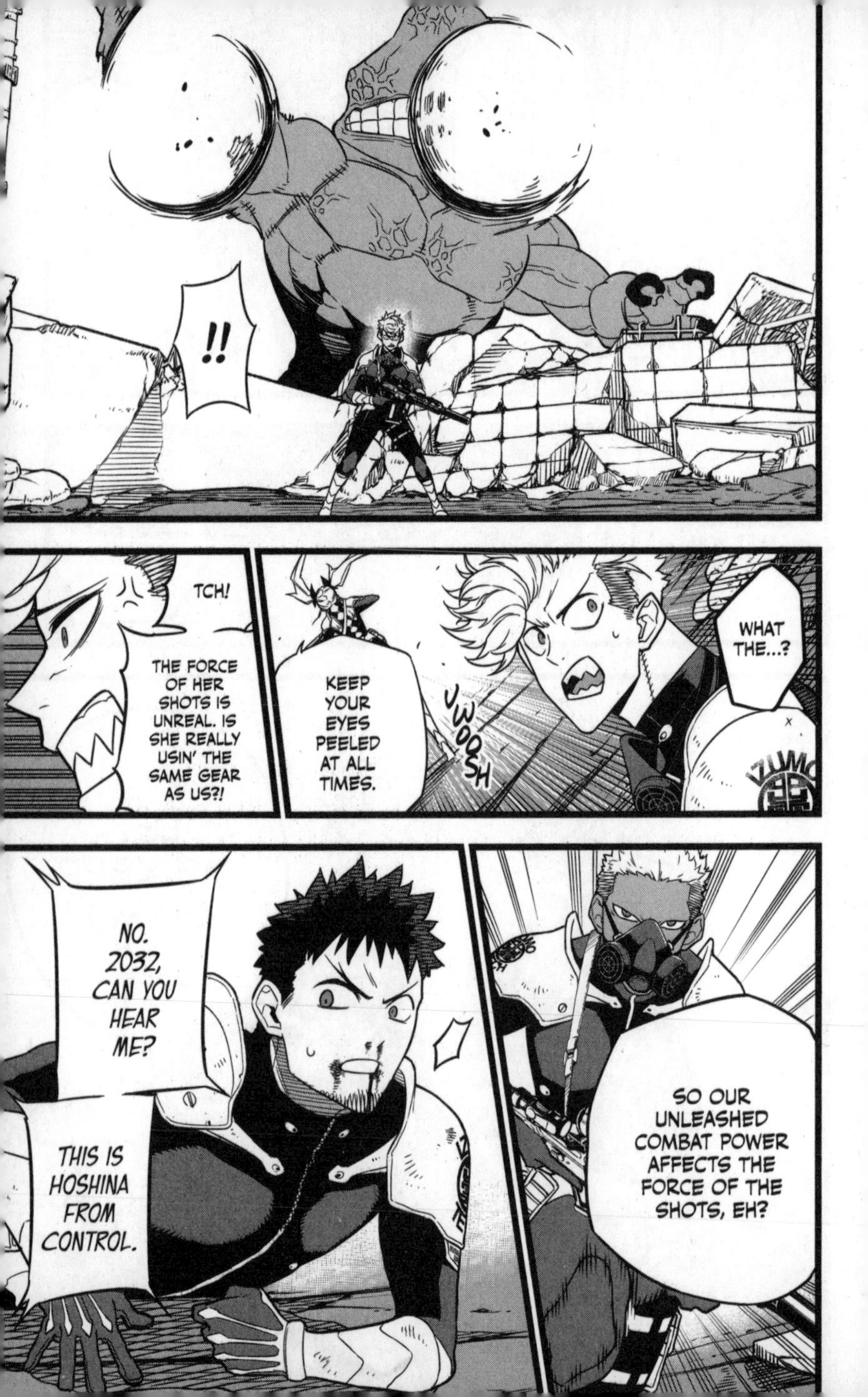
!!
WHAT THE...?
KEEP YOUR EYES PEELED AT ALL TIMES.
JWOOSH
TCH!
THE FORCE OF HER SHOTS IS UNREAL. IS SHE REALLY USIN' THE SAME GEAR AS US?!
SO OUR UNLEASHED COMBAT POWER AFFECTS THE FORCE OF THE SHOTS, EH?
NO. 2032, CAN YOU HEAR ME?
THIS IS HOSHINA FROM CONTROL.

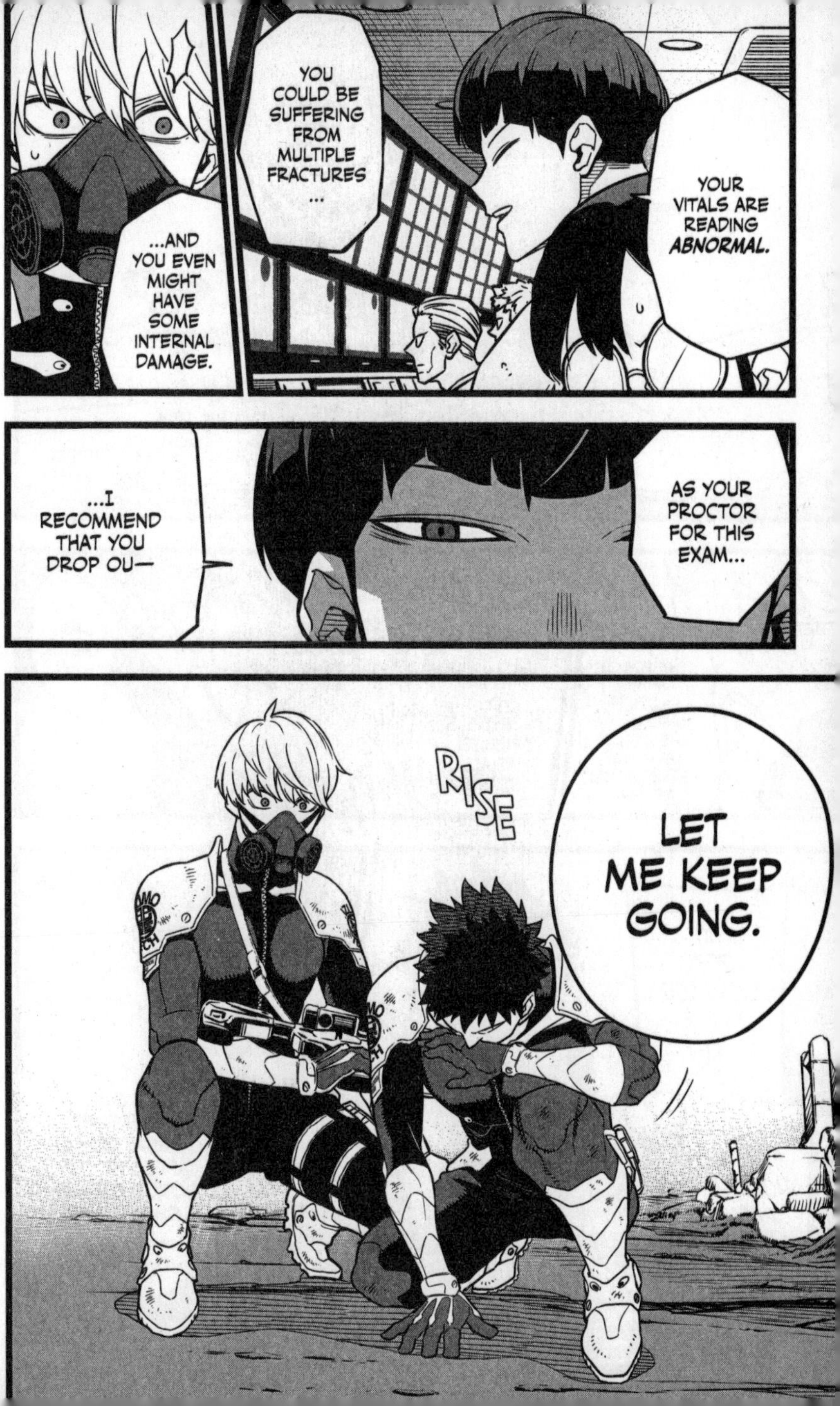
YOUR VITALS ARE READING ABNORMAL.
YOU COULD BE SUFFERING FROM MULTIPLE FRACTURES ...
...AND YOU EVEN MIGHT HAVE SOME INTERNAL DAMAGE.
AS YOUR PROCTOR FOR THIS EXAM...
...I RECOMMEND THAT YOU DROP OU—
RISE
LET ME KEEP GOING.

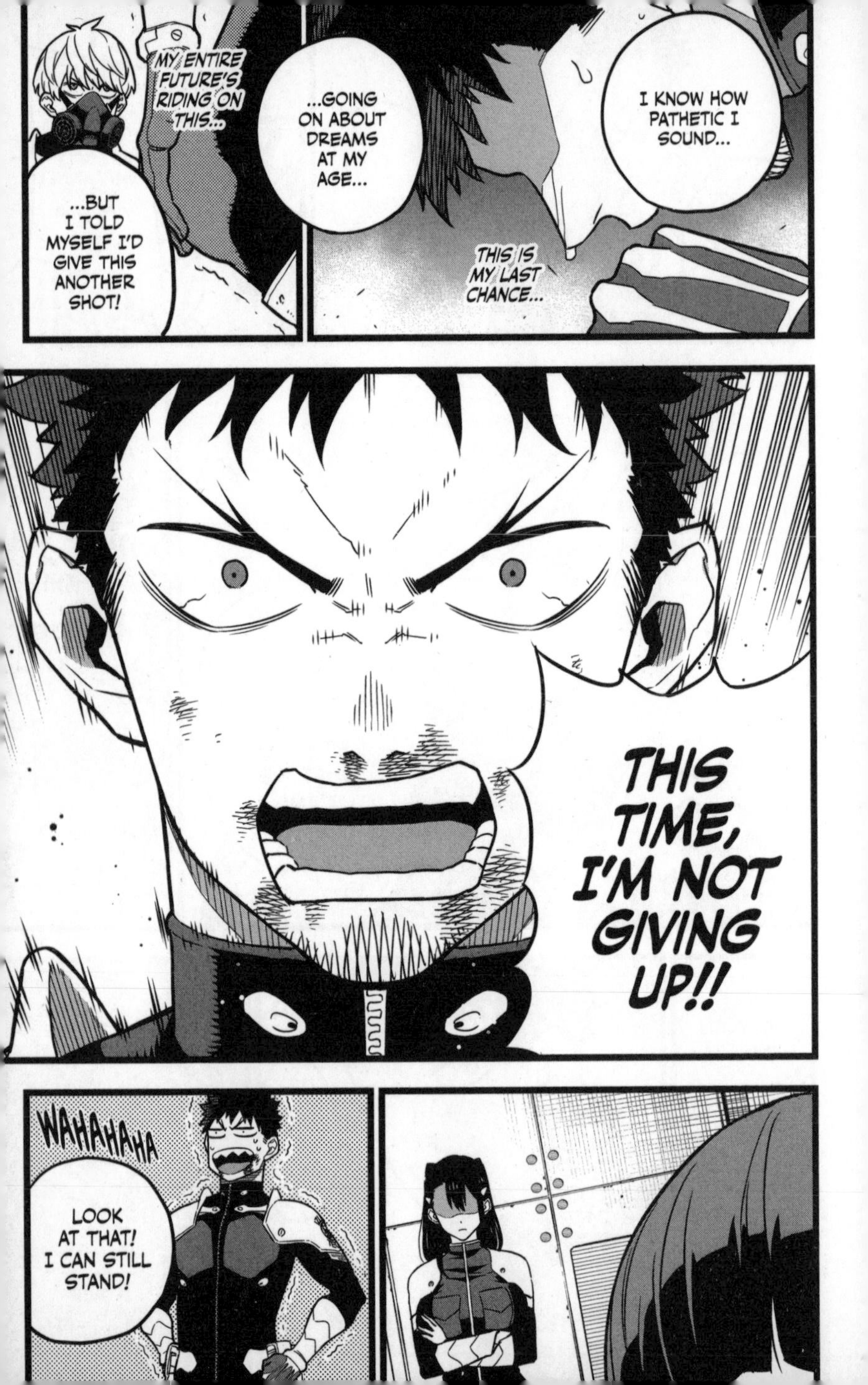
I KNOW HOW PATHETIC I SOUND...
...GOING ON ABOUT DREAMS AT MY AGE...
THIS IS MY LAST CHANCE...
MY ENTIRE FUTURE'S RIDING ON THIS...
...BUT I TOLD MYSELF I'D GIVE THIS ANOTHER SHOT!
THIS TIME, I'M NOT GIVING UP!!
WAHAHAHA
LOOK AT THAT! I CAN STILL STAND!

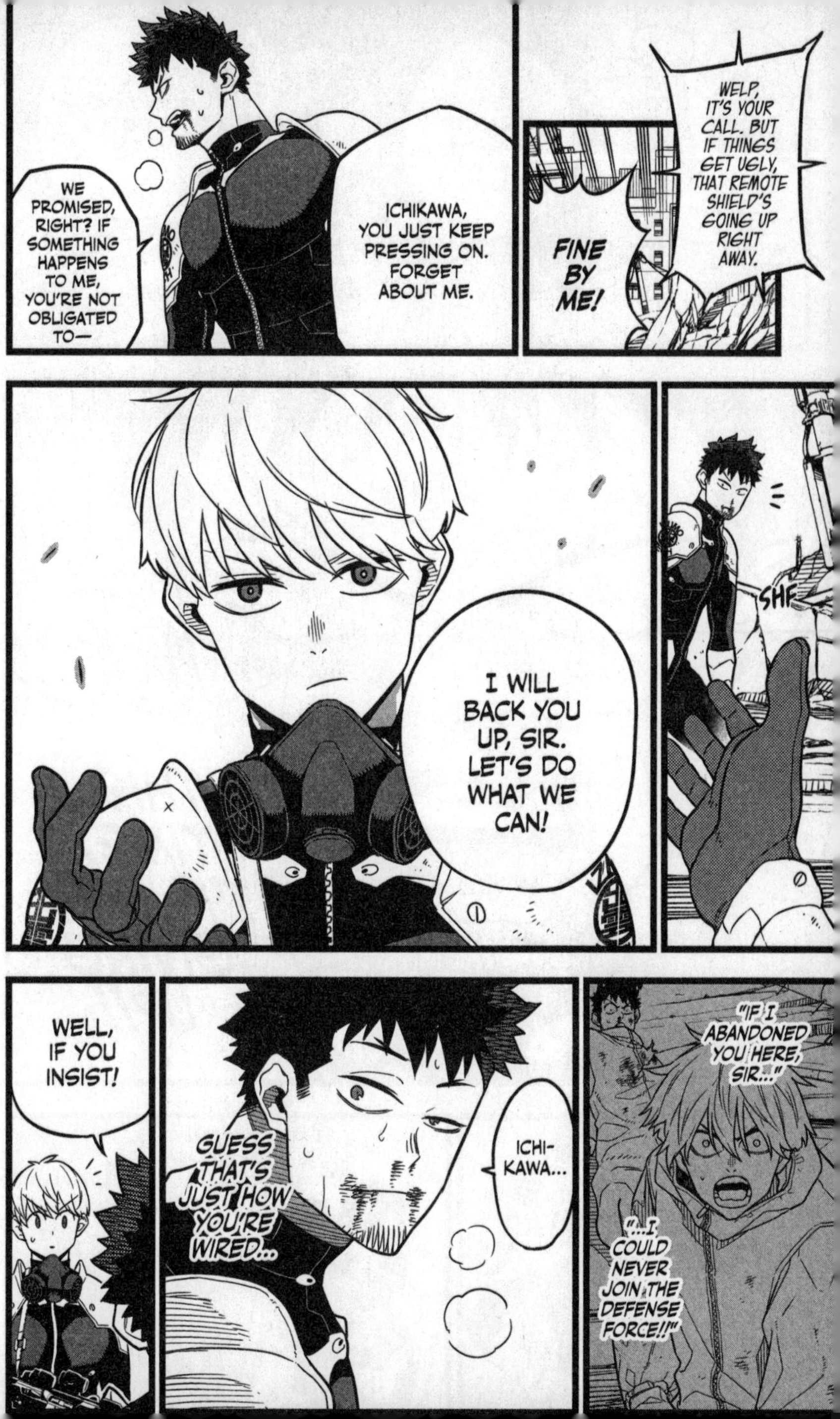
WELP, IT'S YOUR CALL. BUT IF THINGS GET UGLY, THAT REMOTE SHIELD'S GOING UP RIGHT AWAY.
FINE BY ME!
ICHIKAWA, YOU JUST KEEP PRESSING ON. FORGET ABOUT ME.
WE PROMISED, RIGHT? IF SOMETHING HAPPENS TO ME, YOU'RE NOT OBLIGATED TO—
SHF
I WILL BACK YOU UP, SIR. LET'S DO WHAT WE CAN!
"IF I ABANDONED YOU HERE, SIR..."
"...I COULD NEVER JOIN THE DEFENSE FORCE!!"
ICHI-KAWA...
GUESS THAT'S JUST HOW YOU'RE WIRED...
WELL, IF YOU INSIST!

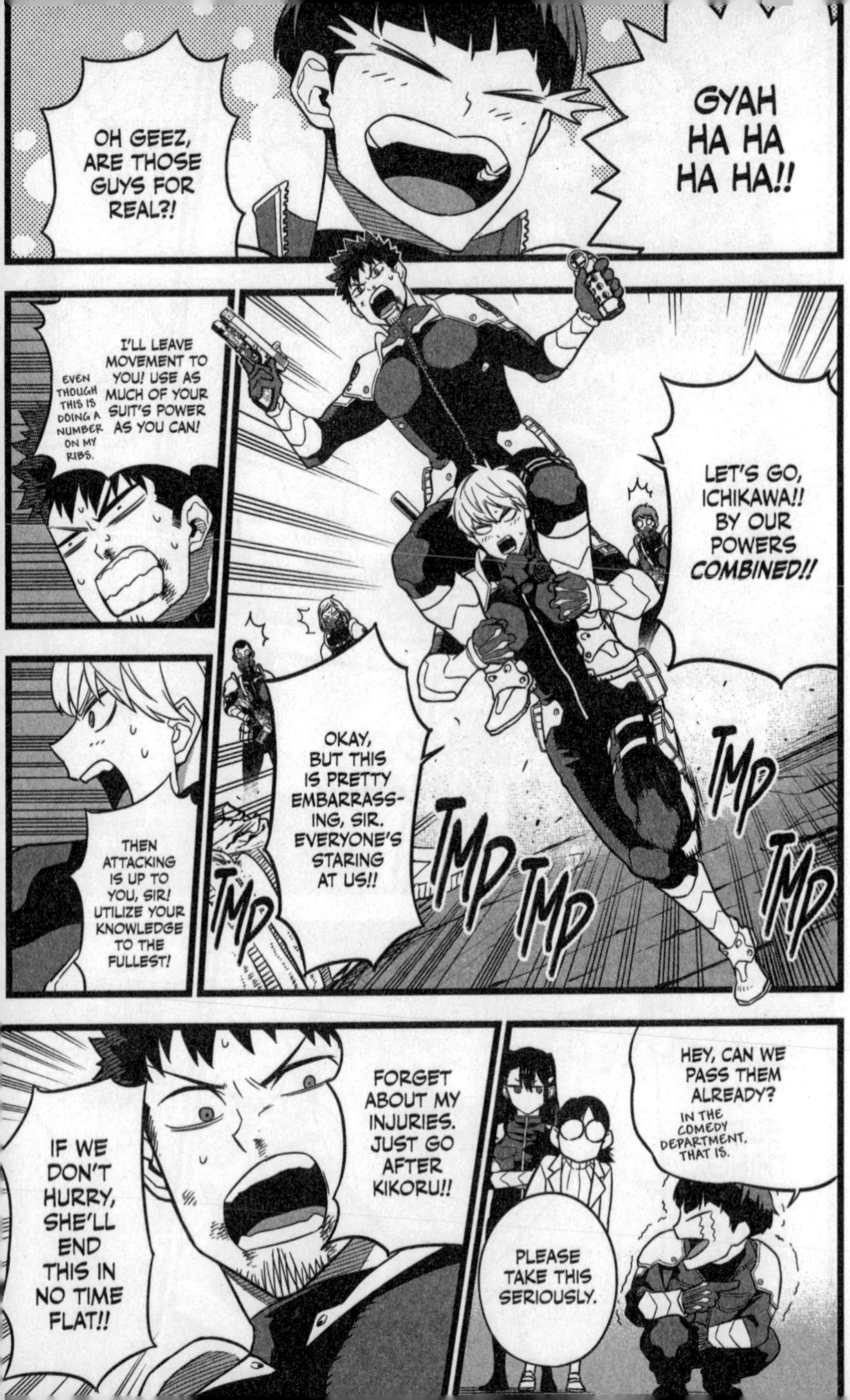
GYAH HA HA HA HA!!
OH GEEZ, ARE THOSE GUYS FOR REAL?!
LET'S GO, ICHIKAWA!! BY OUR POWERS COMBINED!!
TMP
TMP
OKAY, BUT THIS IS PRETTY EMBARRASS-ING, SIR. EVERYONE'S STARING AT US!!
TMP
TMP
TMP
I'LL LEAVE MOVEMENT TO YOU! USE AS MUCH OF YOUR SUIT'S POWER AS YOU CAN!
EVEN THOUGH THIS IS DOING A NUMBER ON MY RIBS.
THEN ATTACKING IS UP TO YOU, SIR! UTILIZE YOUR KNOWLEDGE TO THE FULLEST!
HEY, CAN WE PASS THEM ALREADY?
IN THE COMEDY DEPARTMENT, THAT IS.
PLEASE TAKE THIS SERIOUSLY.
FORGET ABOUT MY INJURIES. JUST GO AFTER KIKORU!!
IF WE DON'T HURRY, SHE'LL END THIS IN NO TIME FLAT!!

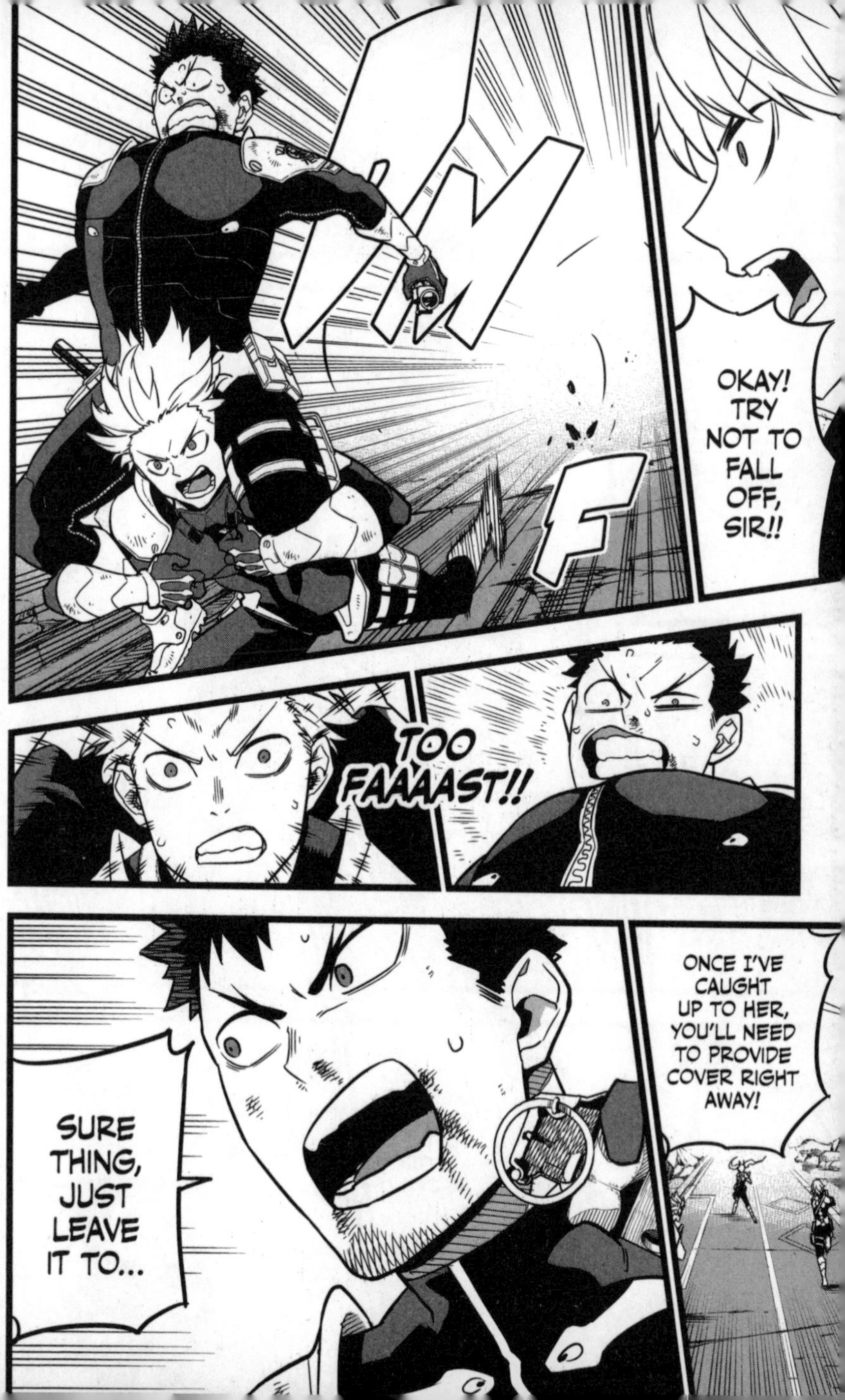
OKAY! TRY NOT TO FALL OFF, SIR!!
TOO FAAAAST!!
ONCE I'VE CAUGHT UP TO HER, YOU'LL NEED TO PROVIDE COVER RIGHT AWAY!
SURE THING, JUST LEAVE IT TO...

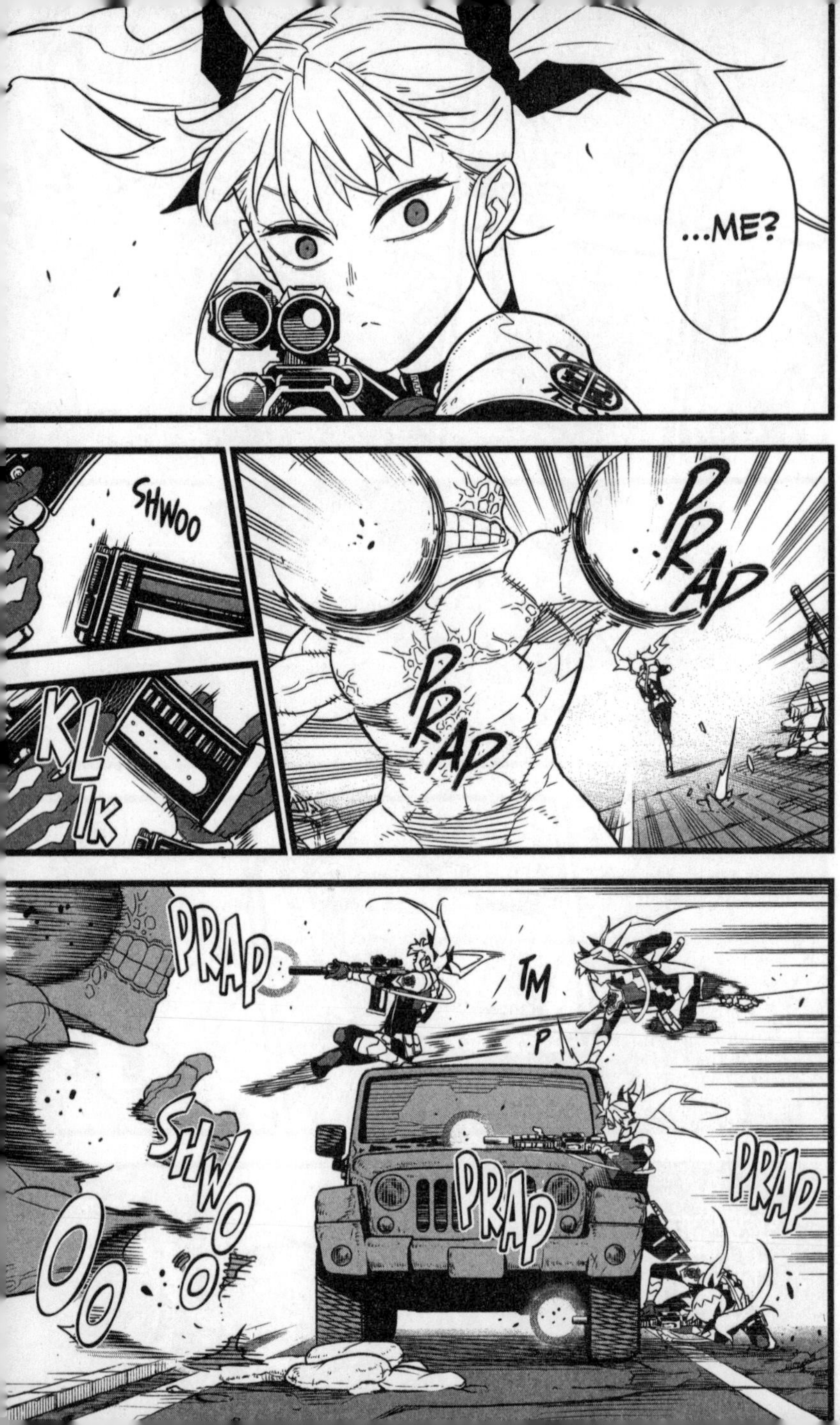
...ME?
PRAP
PRAP
SHWOO
KLIK
TM
P
PRAP
PRAP
PRAP
SHWOOOO

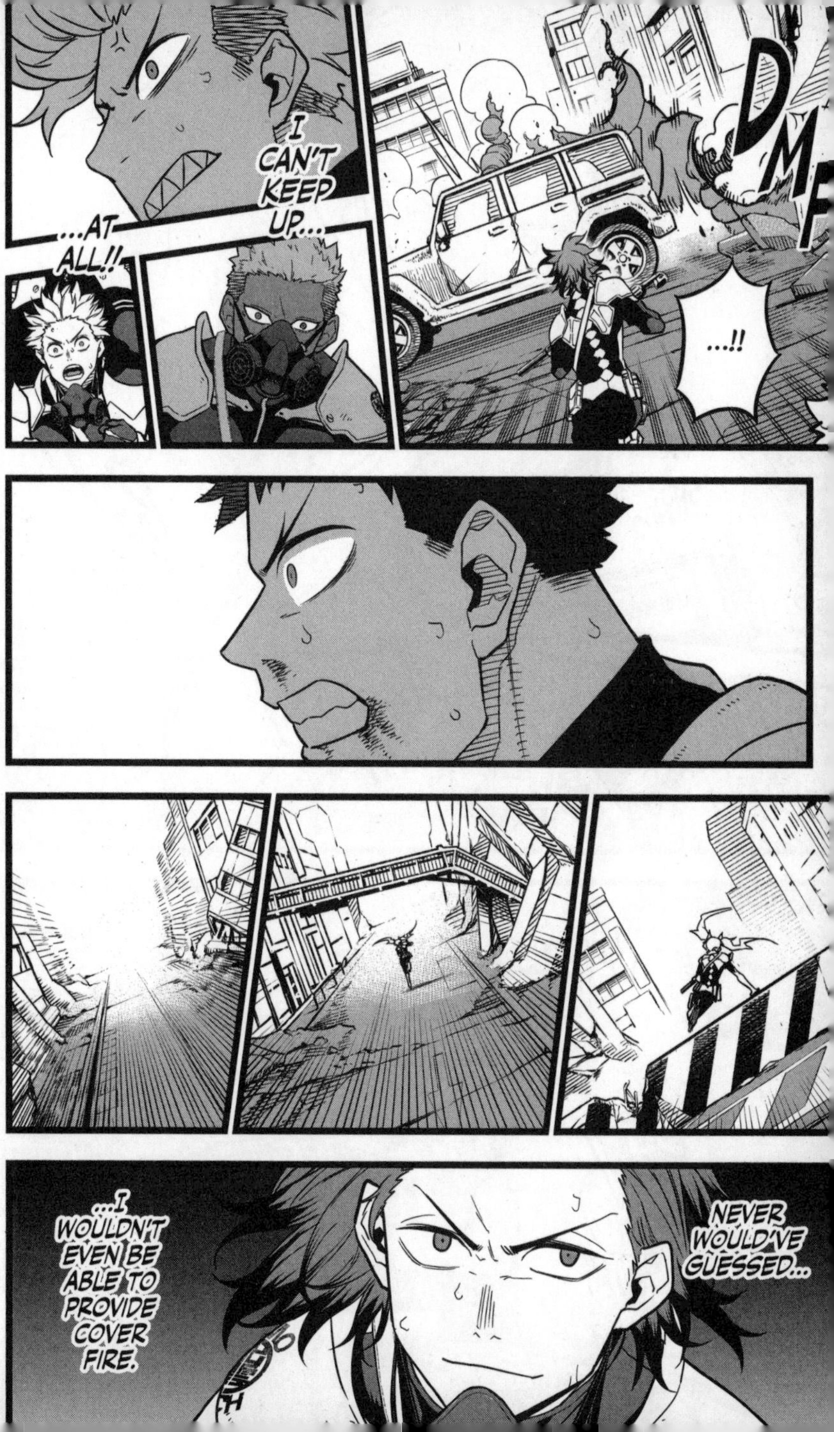
DMF
...!!
I CAN'T KEEP UP...
...AT ALL!!
NEVER WOULD'VE GUESSED...
...I WOULDN'T EVEN BE ABLE TO PROVIDE COVER FIRE.

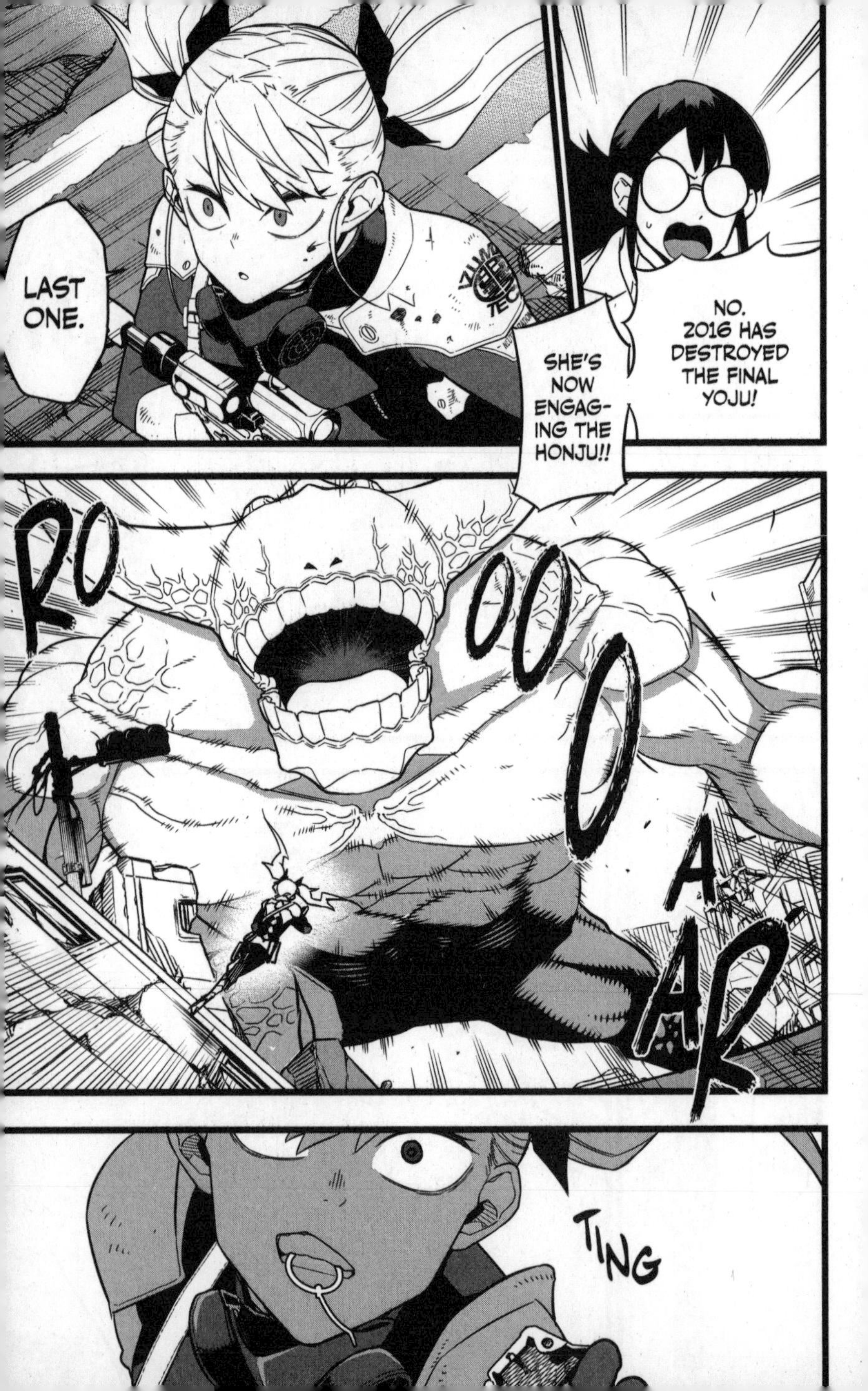
NO. 2016 HAS DESTROYED THE FINAL YOJU!
SHE'S NOW ENGAGING THE HONJU!!
LAST ONE.
ROOOOOAAR
TING

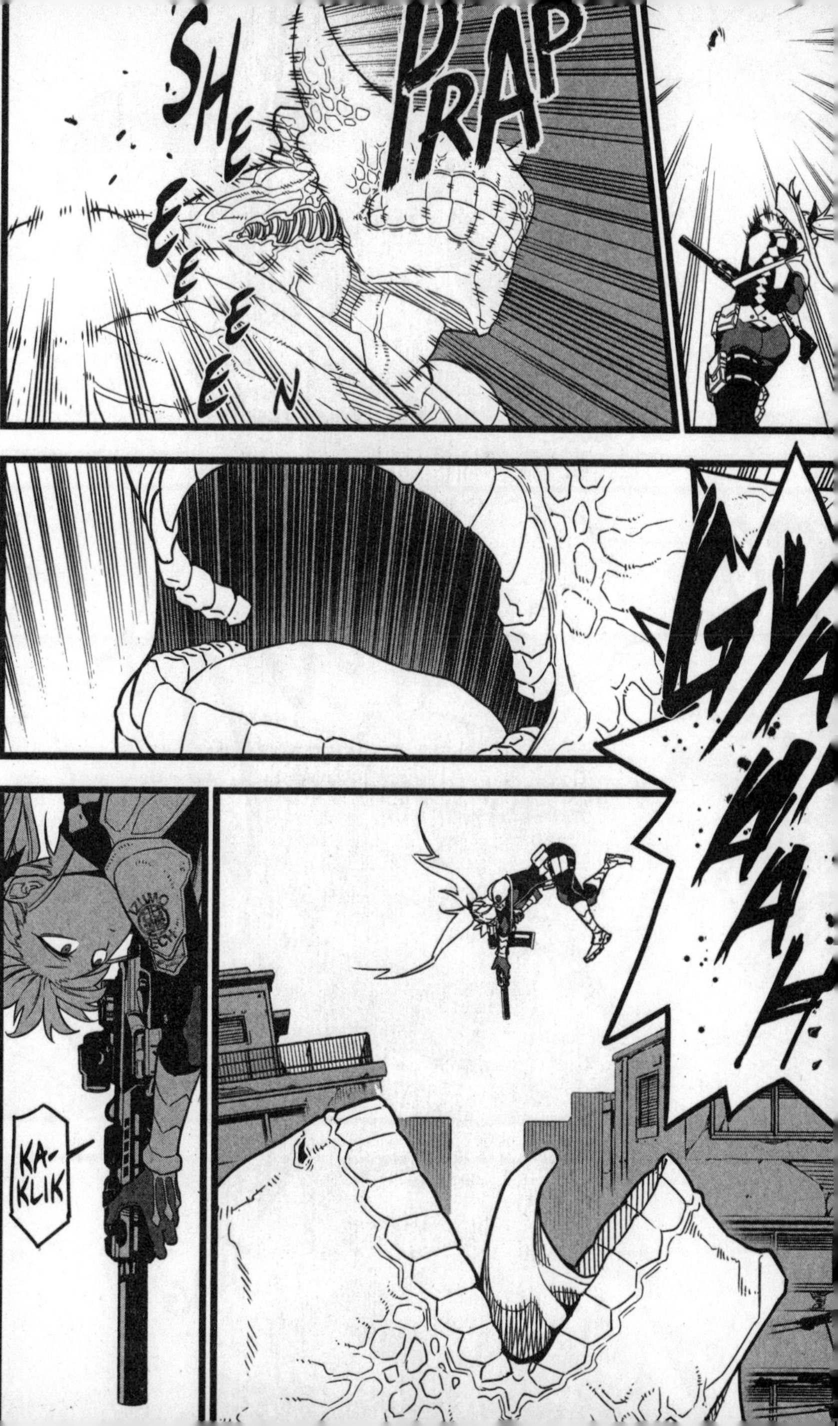
PRAP
SHEEEEEEN
GYAWAAH
KA-KLIK

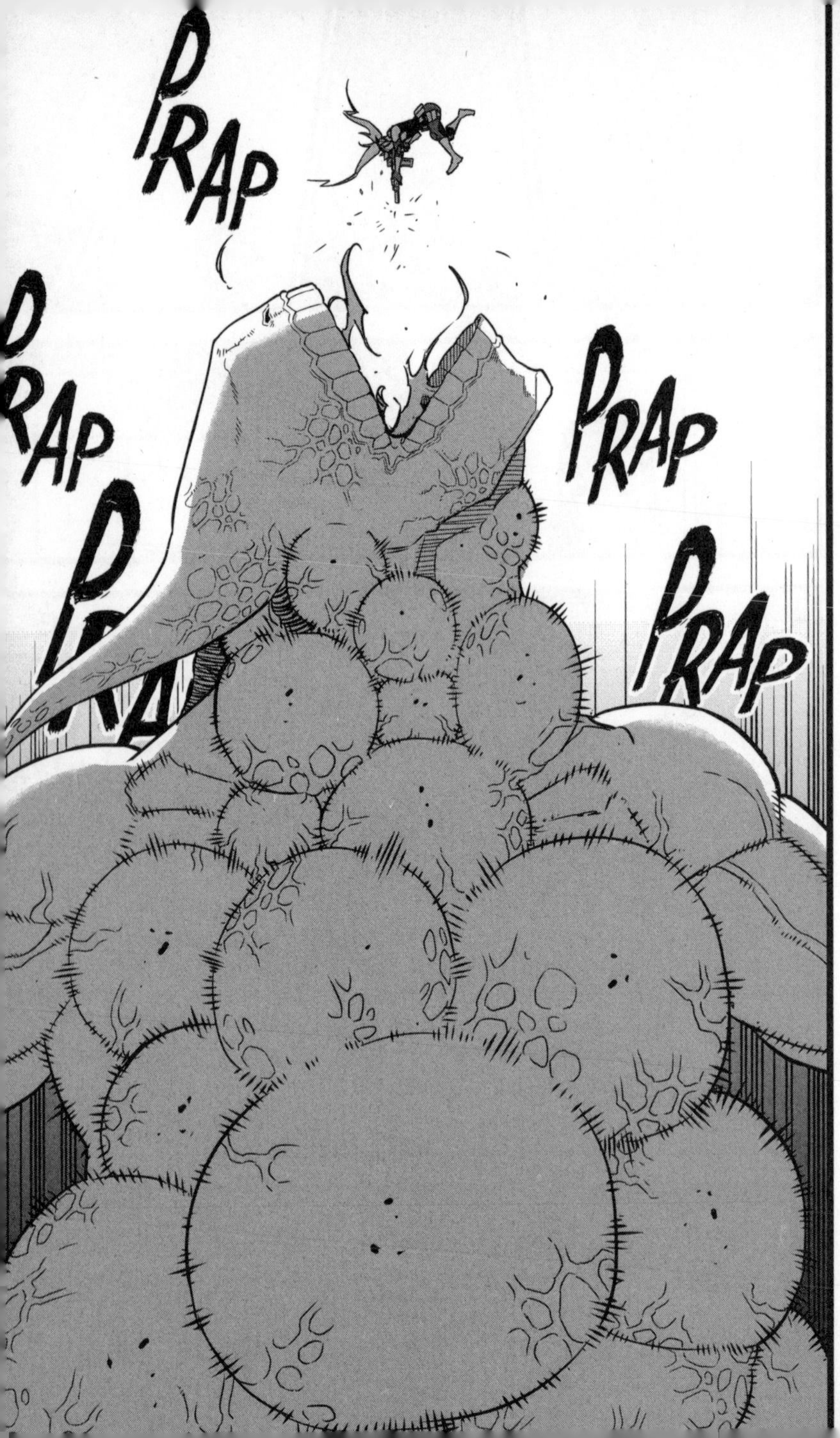
PRAP
PRAP
PRAP

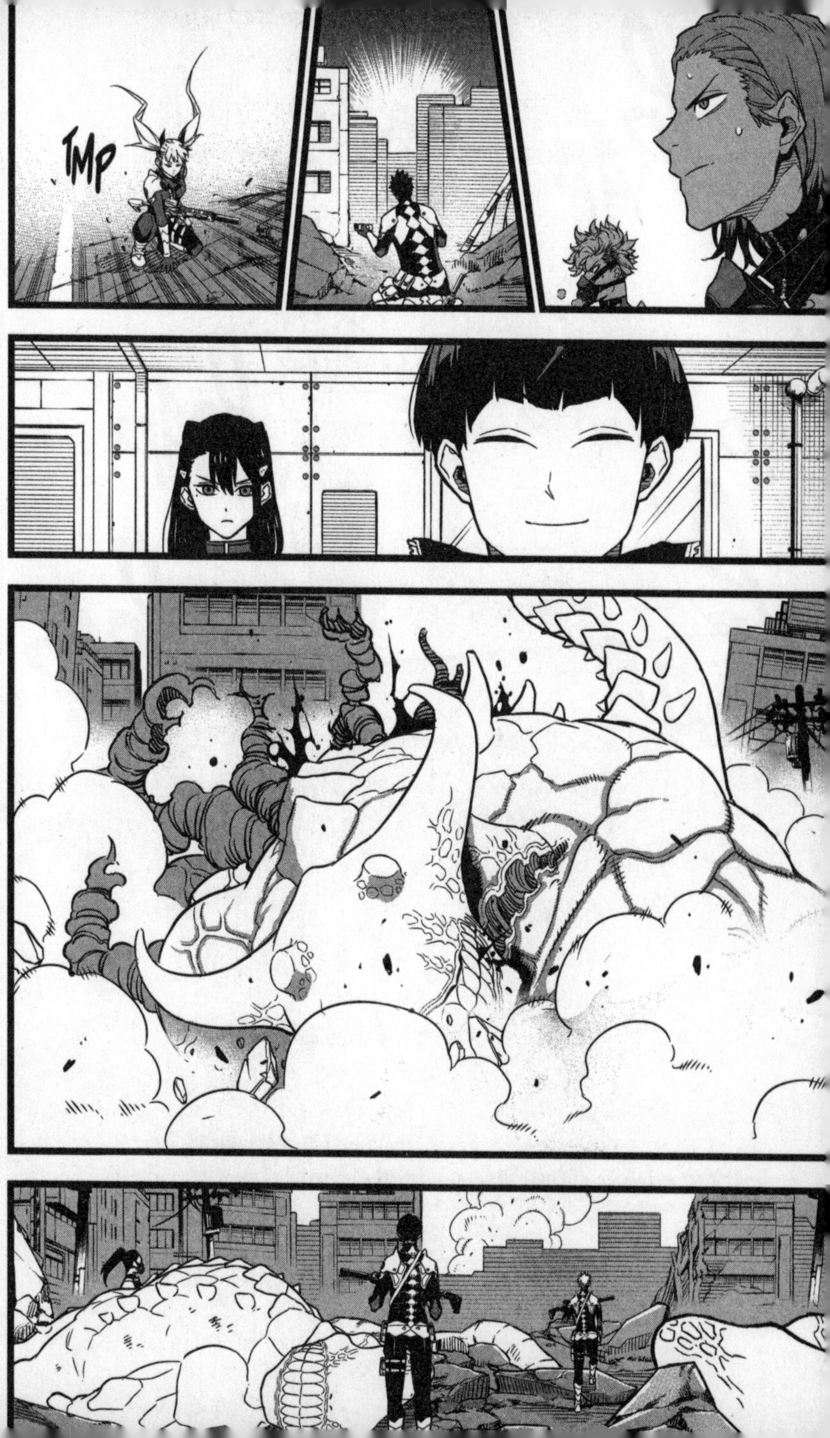
TMP

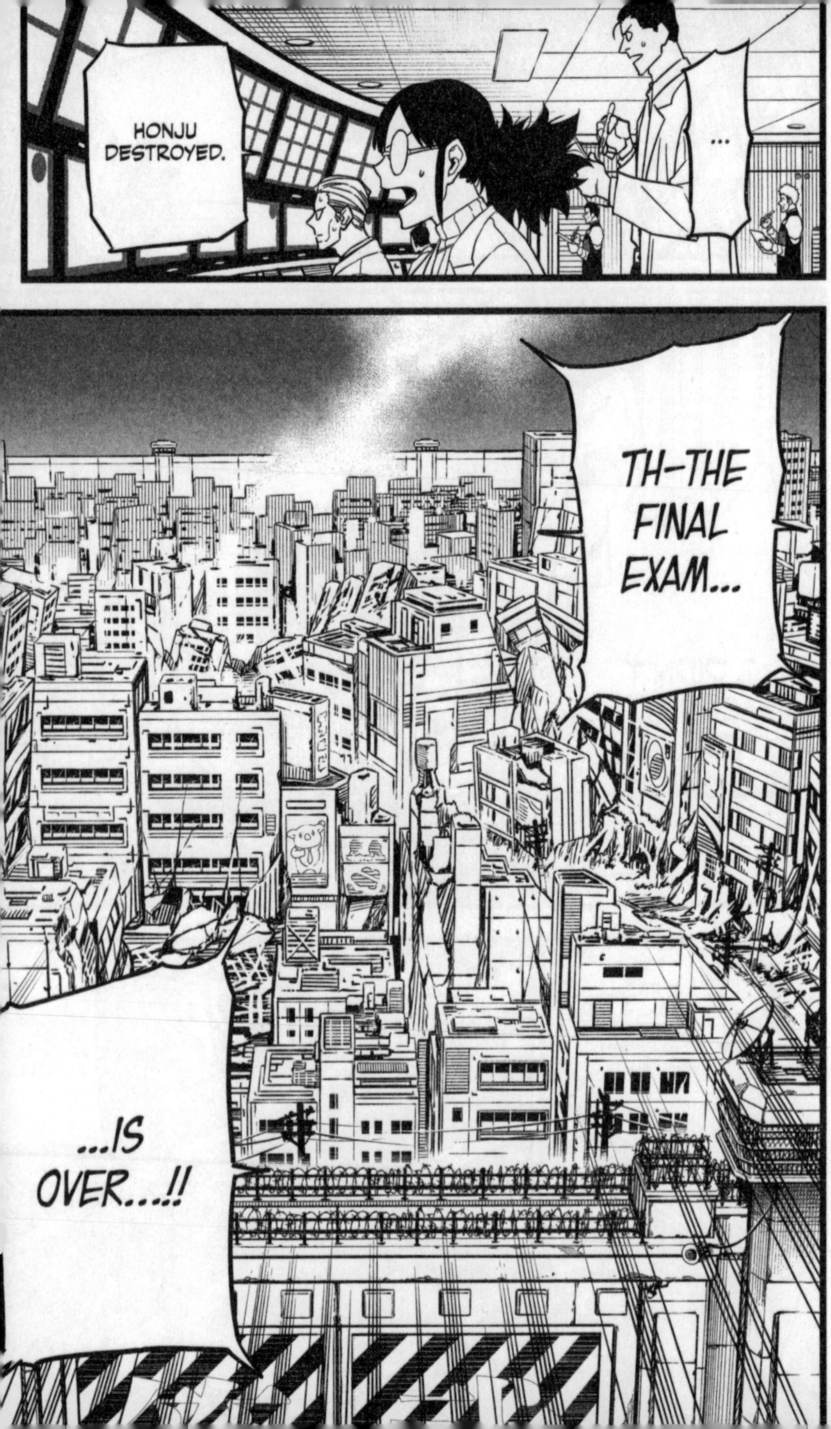
...
HONJU DESTROYED.
TH-THE FINAL EXAM...
...IS OVER...!!

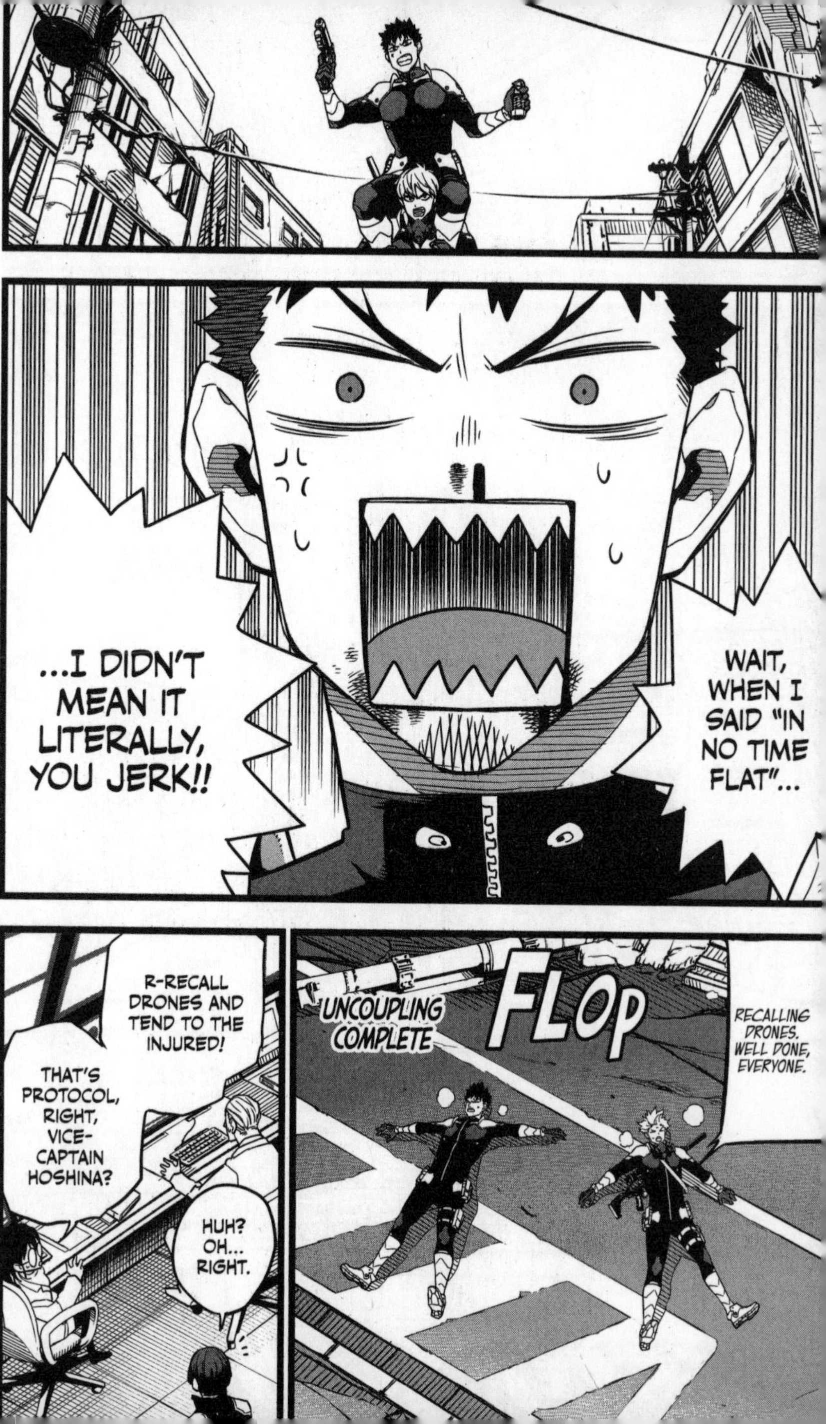
WAIT, WHEN I SAID "IN NO TIME FLAT"...
...I DIDN'T MEAN IT LITERALLY, YOU JERK!!
RECALLING DRONES. WELL DONE, EVERYONE.
FLOP
UNCOUPLING COMPLETE
R-RECALL DRONES AND TEND TO THE INJURED!
THAT'S PROTOCOL, RIGHT, VICE-CAPTAIN HOSHINA?
HUH? OH... RIGHT.

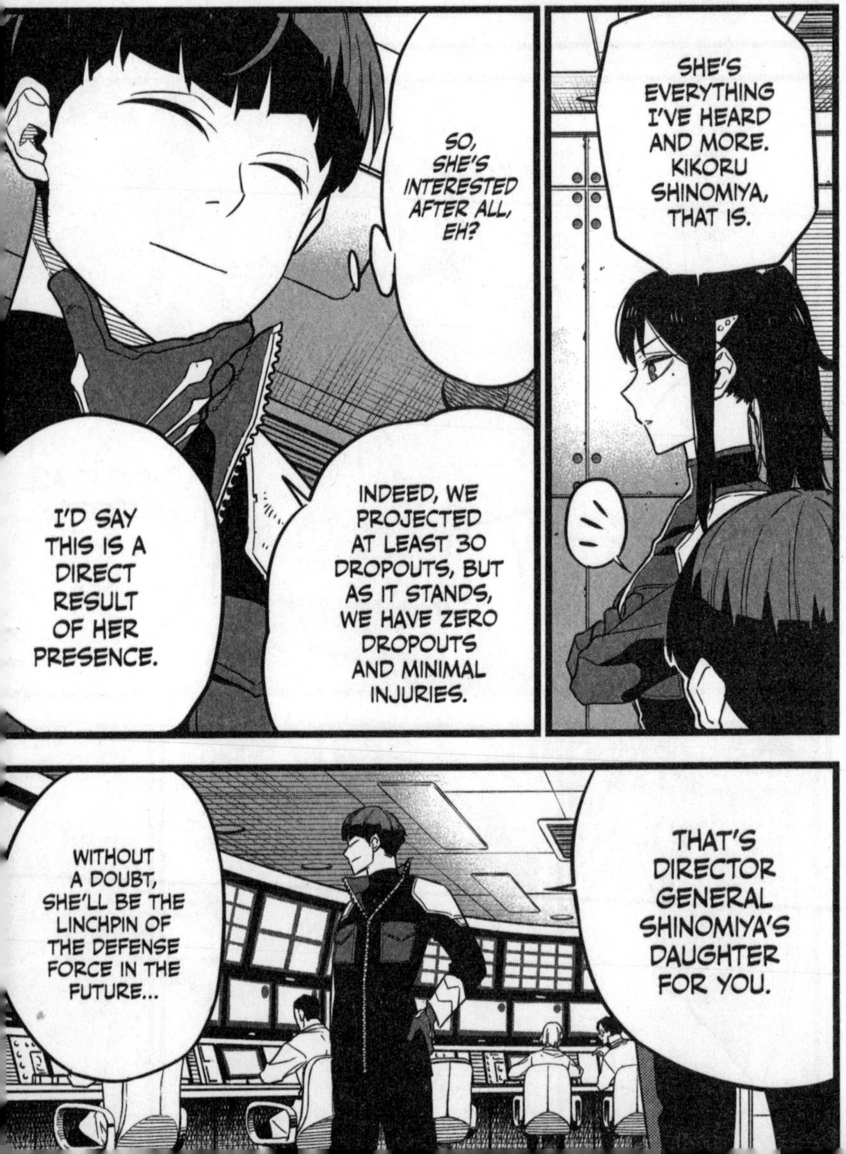
SHE'S EVERYTHING I'VE HEARD AND MORE. KIKORU SHINOMIYA, THAT IS.
SO, SHE'S INTERESTED AFTER ALL, EH?
INDEED, WE PROJECTED AT LEAST 30 DROPOUTS, BUT AS IT STANDS, WE HAVE ZERO DROPOUTS AND MINIMAL INJURIES.
I'D SAY THIS IS A DIRECT RESULT OF HER PRESENCE.
THAT'S DIRECTOR GENERAL SHINOMIYA'S DAUGHTER FOR YOU.
WITHOUT A DOUBT, SHE'LL BE THE LINCHPIN OF THE DEFENSE FORCE IN THE FUTURE...

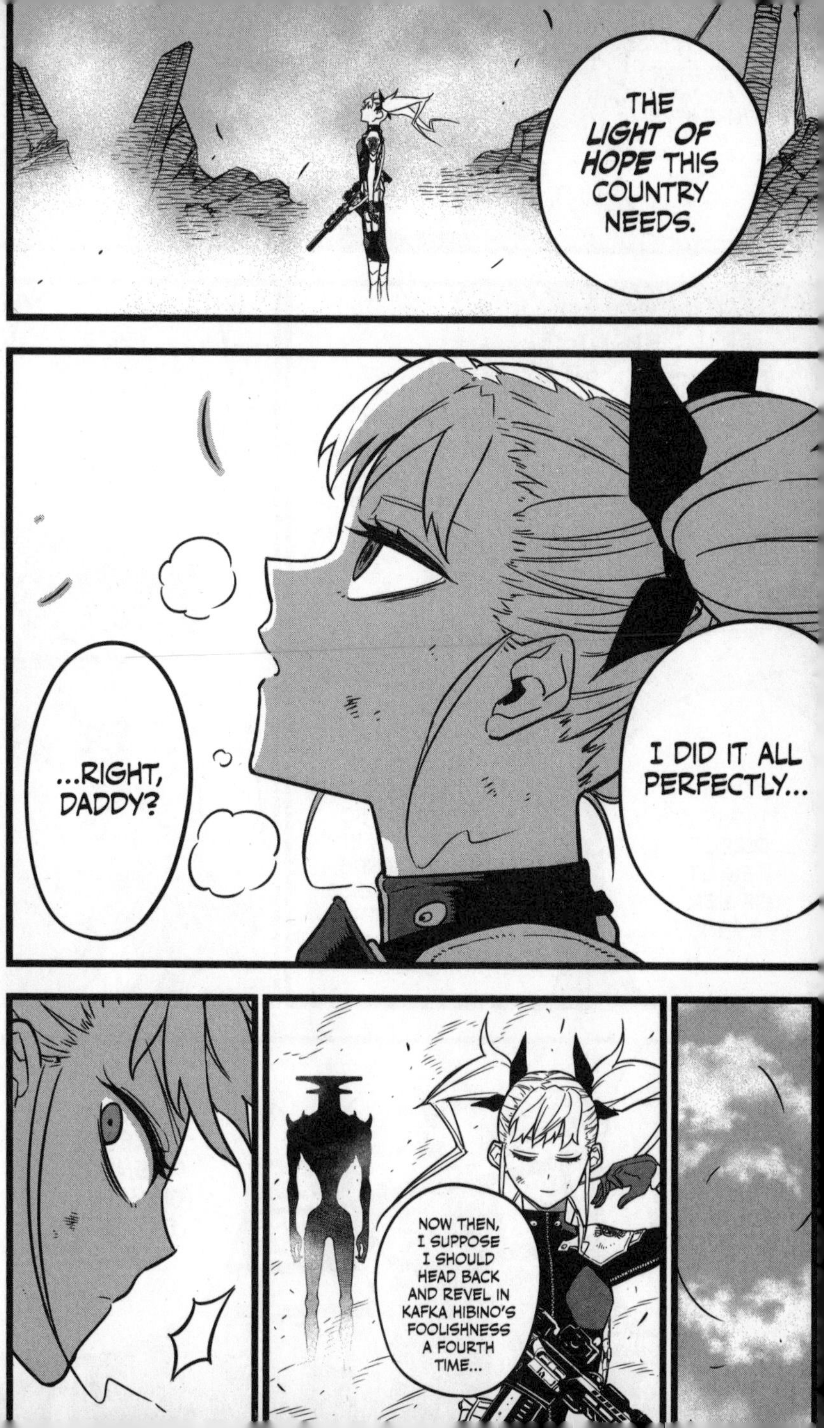
THE LIGHT OF HOPE THIS COUNTRY NEEDS.
I DID IT ALL PERFECTLY...
...RIGHT, DADDY?
NOW THEN, I SUPPOSE I SHOULD HEAD BACK AND REVEL IN KAFKA HIBINO'S FOOLISHNESS A FOURTH TIME...

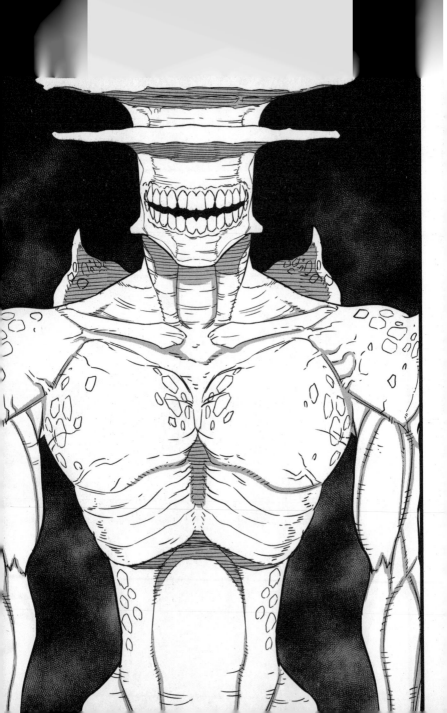

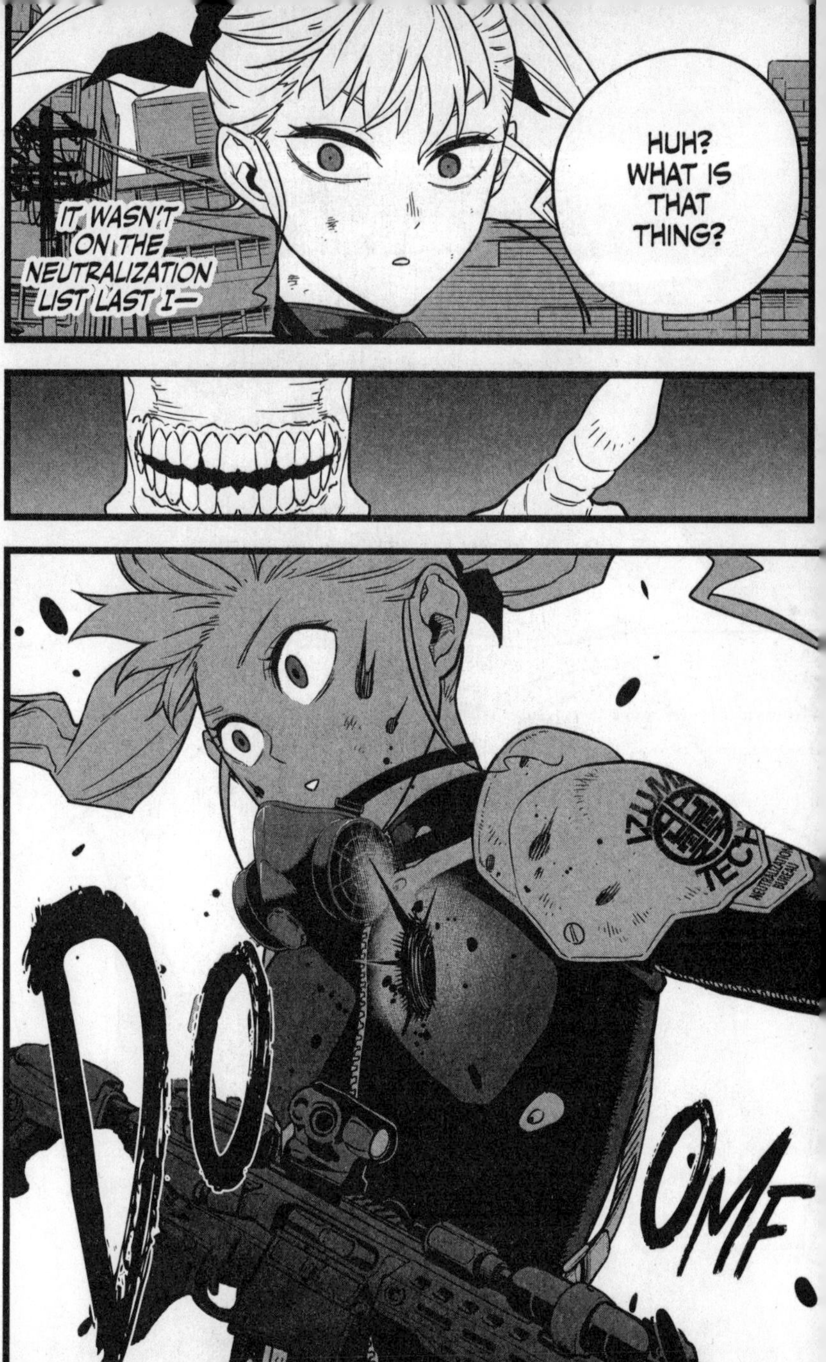
HUH? WHAT IS THAT THING?
IT WASN'T ON THE NEUTRALIZATION LIST LAST I—
DOOMF

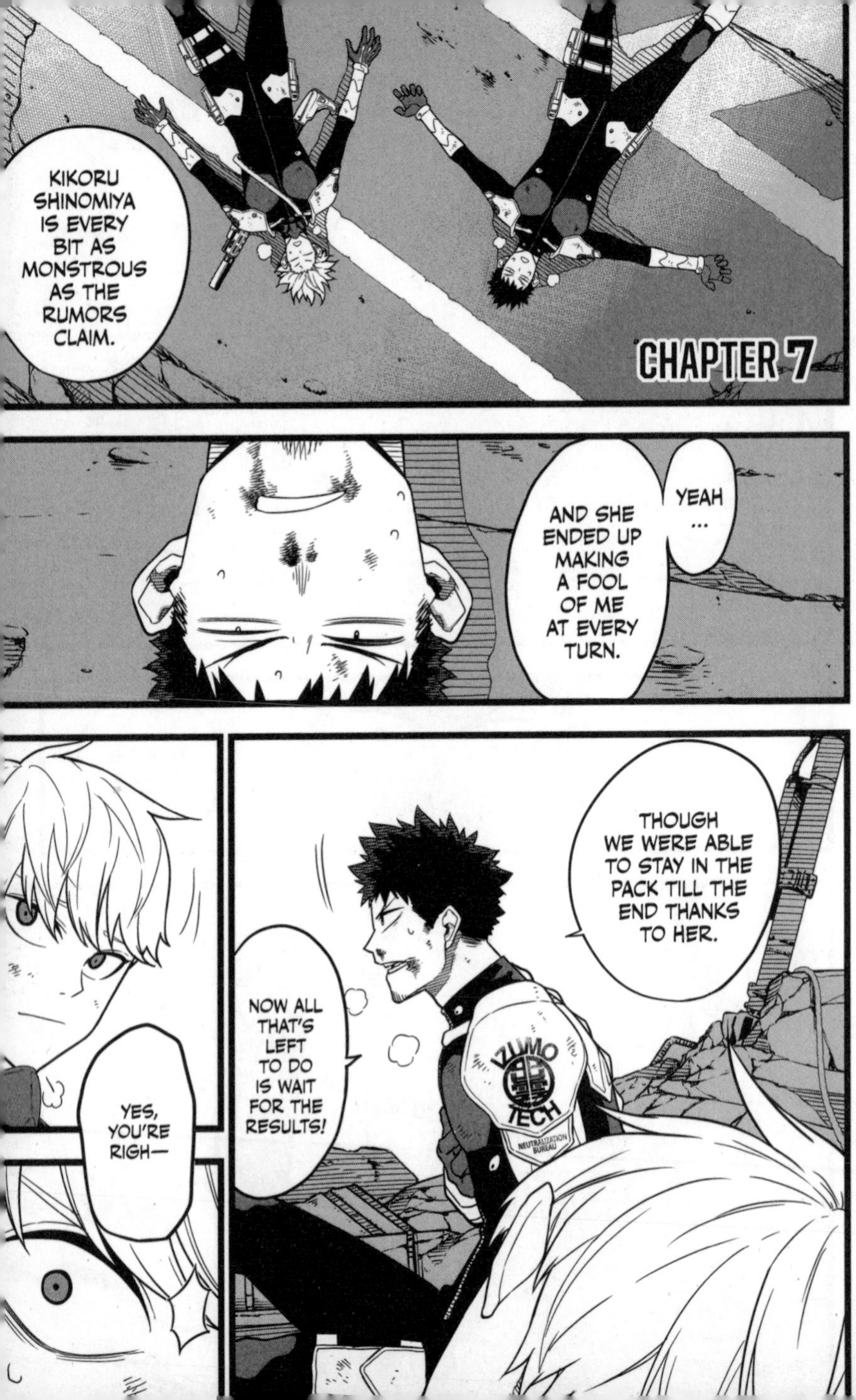
CHAPTER 7
KIKORU SHINOMIYA IS EVERY BIT AS MONSTROUS AS THE RUMORS CLAIM.
YEAH...
AND SHE ENDED UP MAKING A FOOL OF ME AT EVERY TURN.
THOUGH WE WERE ABLE TO STAY IN THE PACK TILL THE END THANKS TO HER.
NOW ALL THAT'S LEFT TO DO IS WAIT FOR THE RESULTS!
IZUMO TECH
NEUTRALIZATION BUREAU
YES, YOU'RE RIGH—

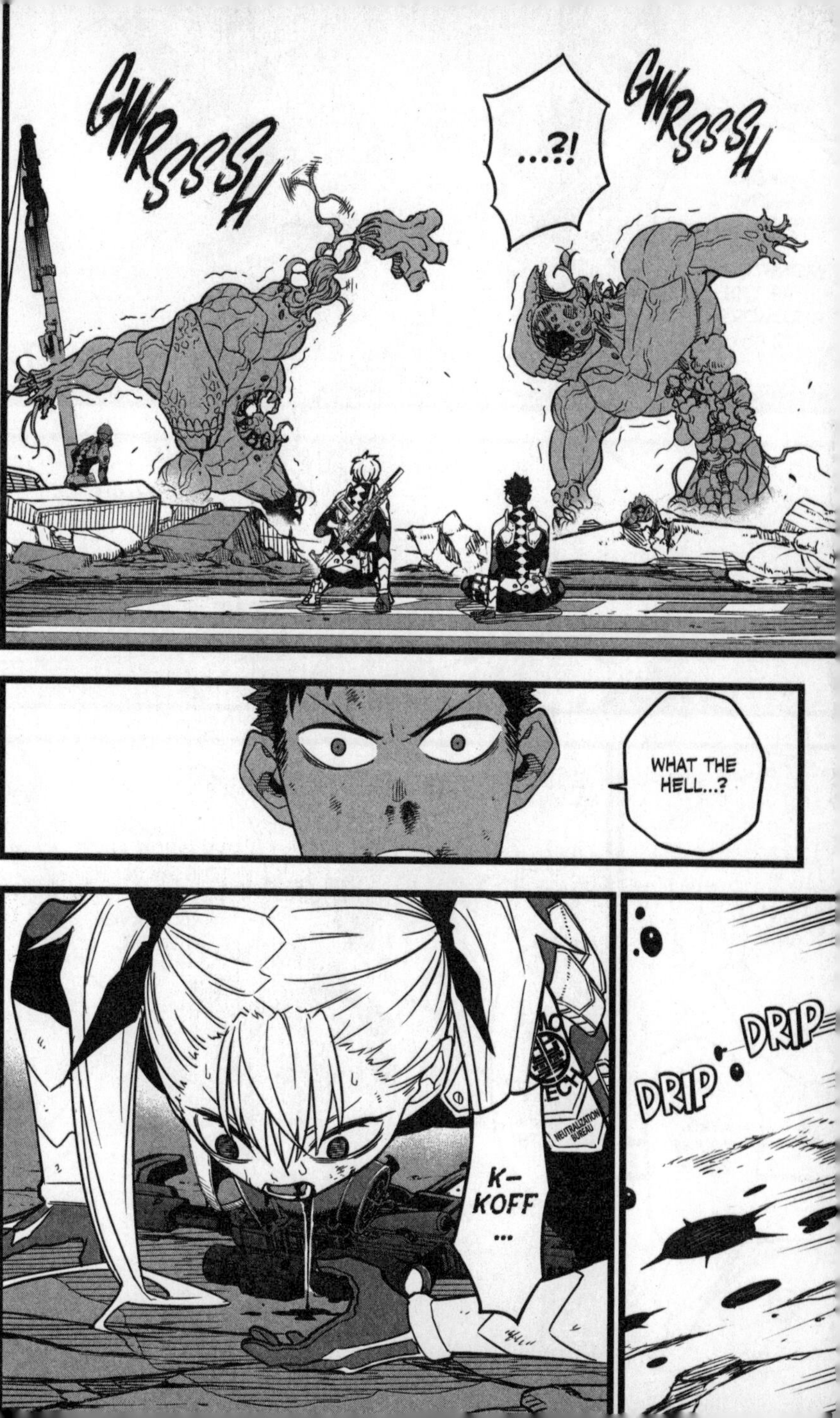
GWRSSSH
...?!
GWRSSSH
WHAT THE HELL...?
DRIP
DRIP
NEUTRALIZATION BUREAU
K-KOFF ...

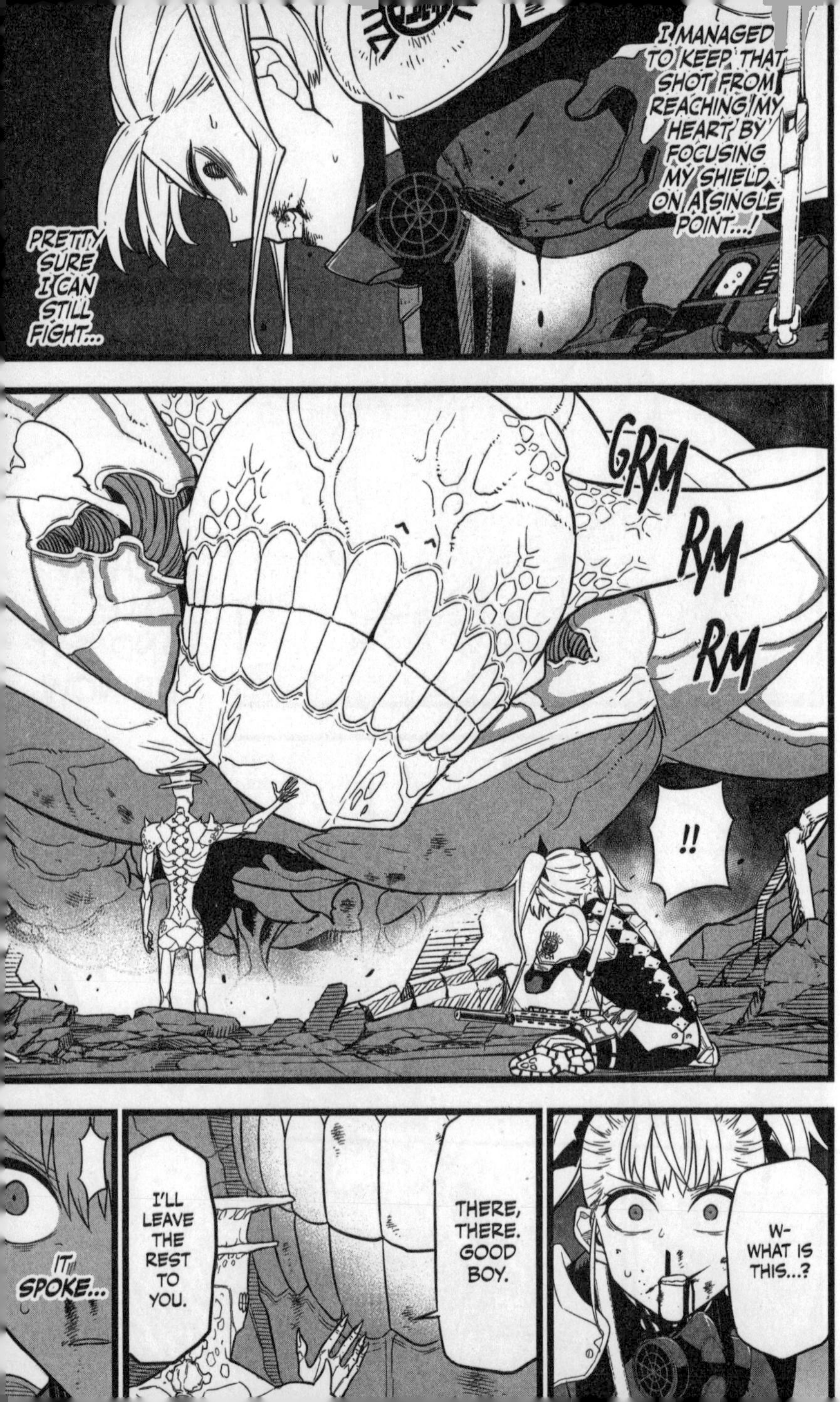
I MANAGED TO KEEP THAT SHOT FROM REACHING MY HEART BY FOCUSING MY SHIELD ON A SINGLE POINT...!
PRETTY SURE I CAN STILL FIGHT...
GRM
RM
RM
!!
W- WHAT IS THIS...?
THERE, THERE. GOOD BOY.
I'LL LEAVE THE REST TO YOU.
IT SPOKE...

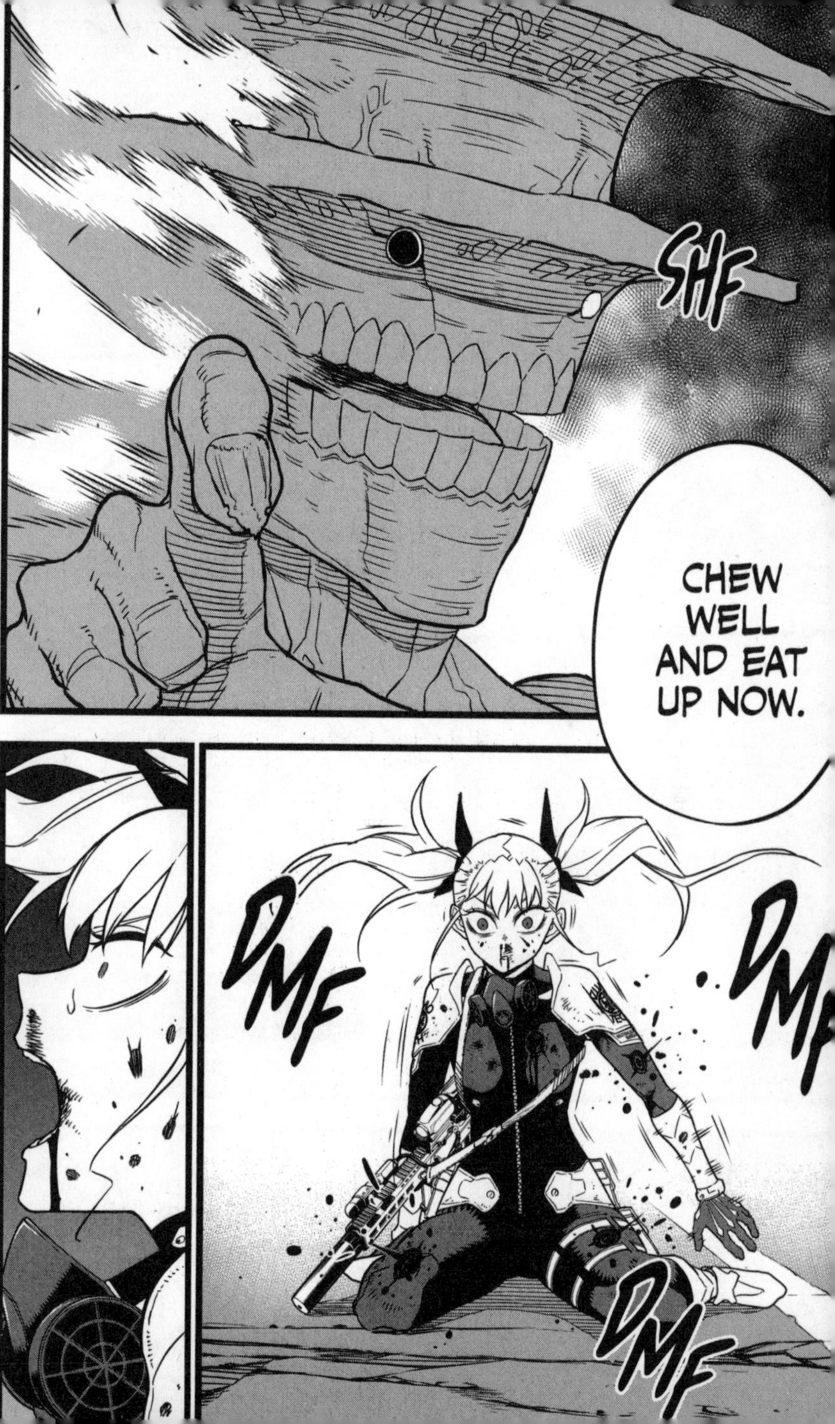
SHF
CHEW WELL AND EAT UP NOW.
DMF
DMF
DMF

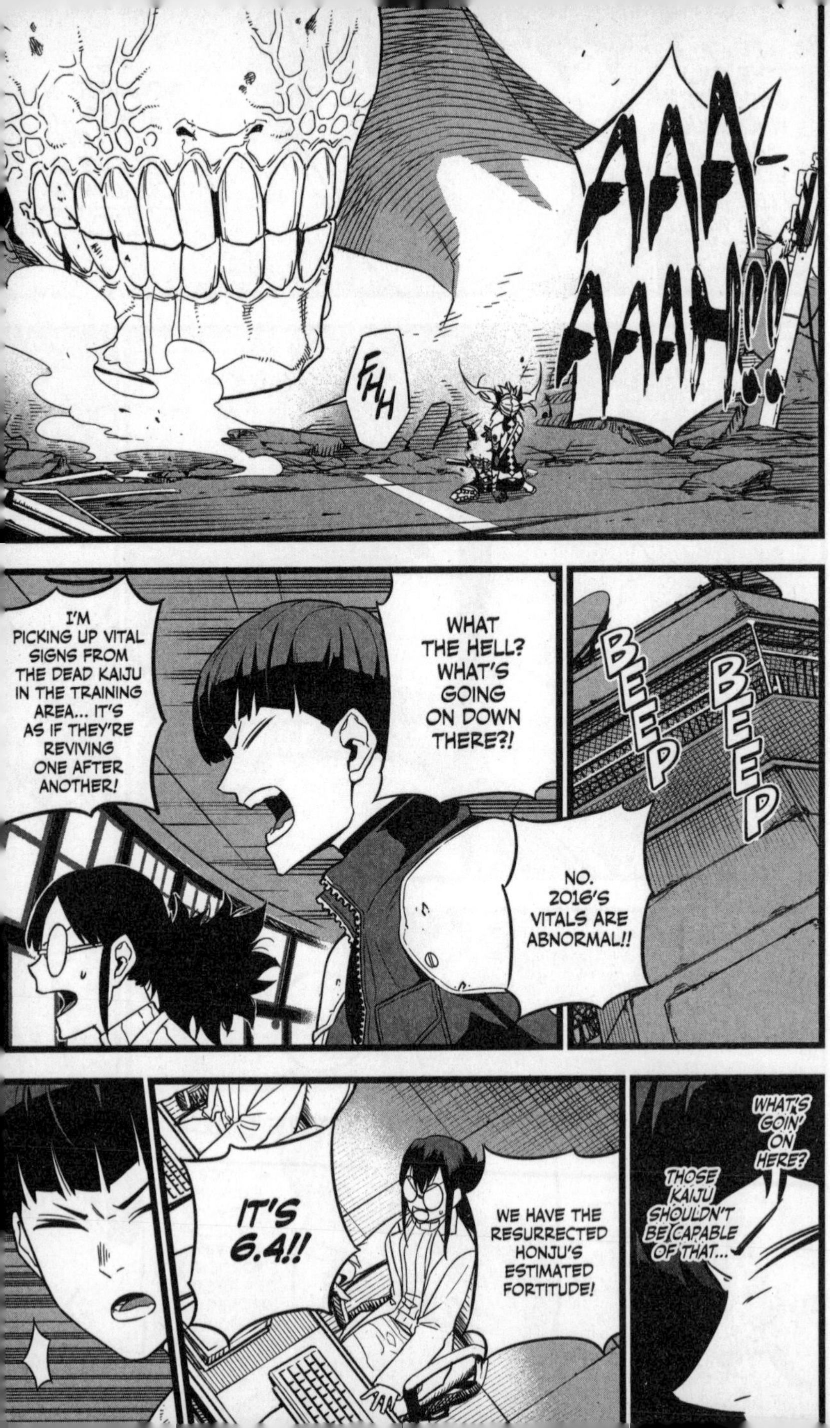
AAA-AAAH!!
FHH
BEEP BEEP
WHAT THE HELL? WHAT'S GOING ON DOWN THERE?!
I'M PICKING UP VITAL SIGNS FROM THE DEAD KAIJU IN THE TRAINING AREA... IT'S AS IF THEY'RE REVIVING ONE AFTER ANOTHER!
NO. 2016'S VITALS ARE ABNORMAL!!
WHAT'S GOIN' ON HERE?
THOSE KAIJU SHOULDN'T BE CAPABLE OF THAT...
WE HAVE THE RESURRECTED HONJU'S ESTIMATED FORTITUDE!
IT'S 6.4!!

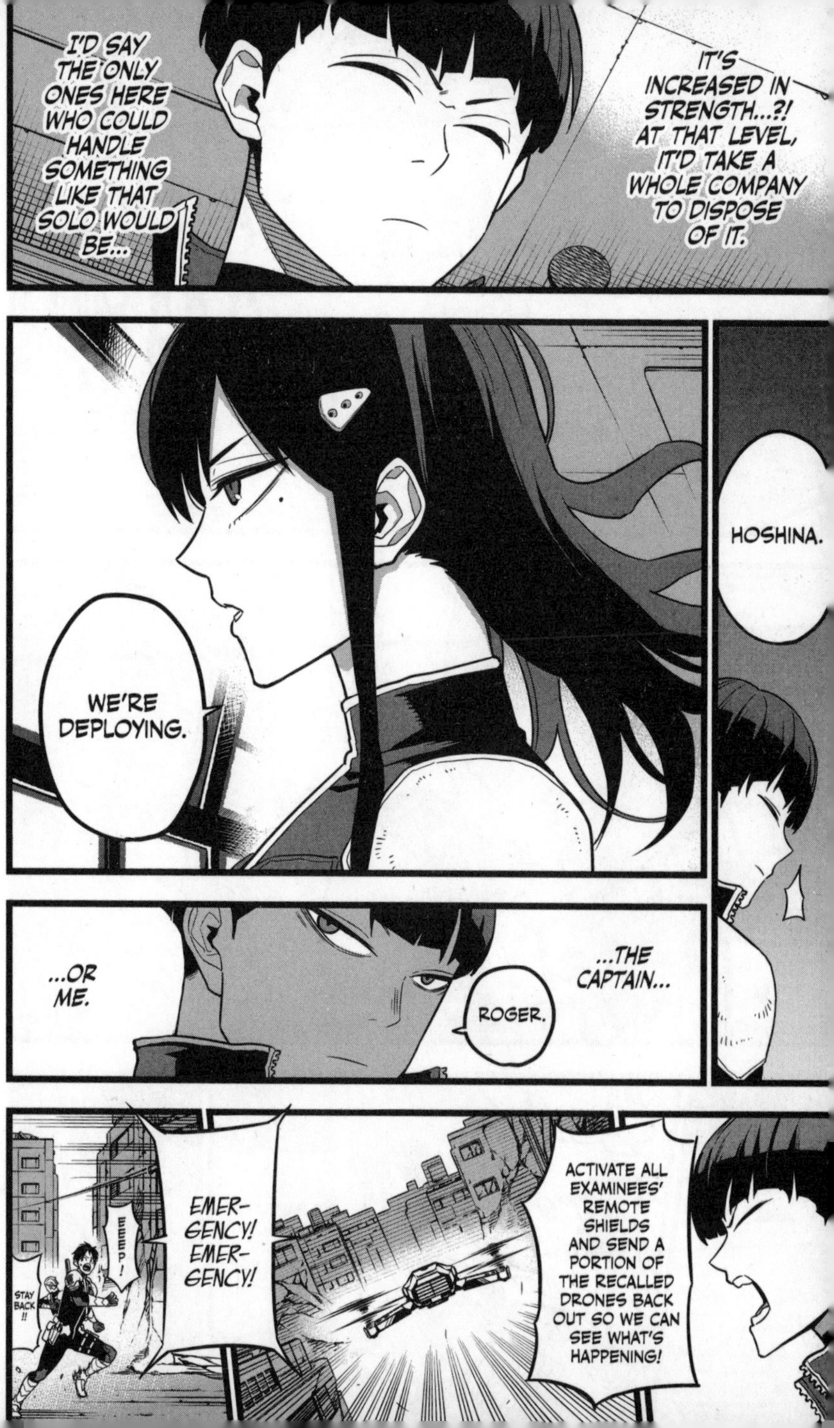
IT'S INCREASED IN STRENGTH...?! AT THAT LEVEL, IT'D TAKE A WHOLE COMPANY TO DISPOSE OF IT.
I'D SAY THE ONLY ONES HERE WHO COULD HANDLE SOMETHING LIKE THAT SOLO WOULD BE...
HOSHINA.
WE'RE DEPLOYING.
...THE CAPTAIN...
ROGER.
...OR ME.
ACTIVATE ALL EXAMINEES' REMOTE SHIELDS AND SEND A PORTION OF THE RECALLED DRONES BACK OUT SO WE CAN SEE WHAT'S HAPPENING!
EMER-GENCY! EMER-GENCY!
EEEP!
STAY BACK!!

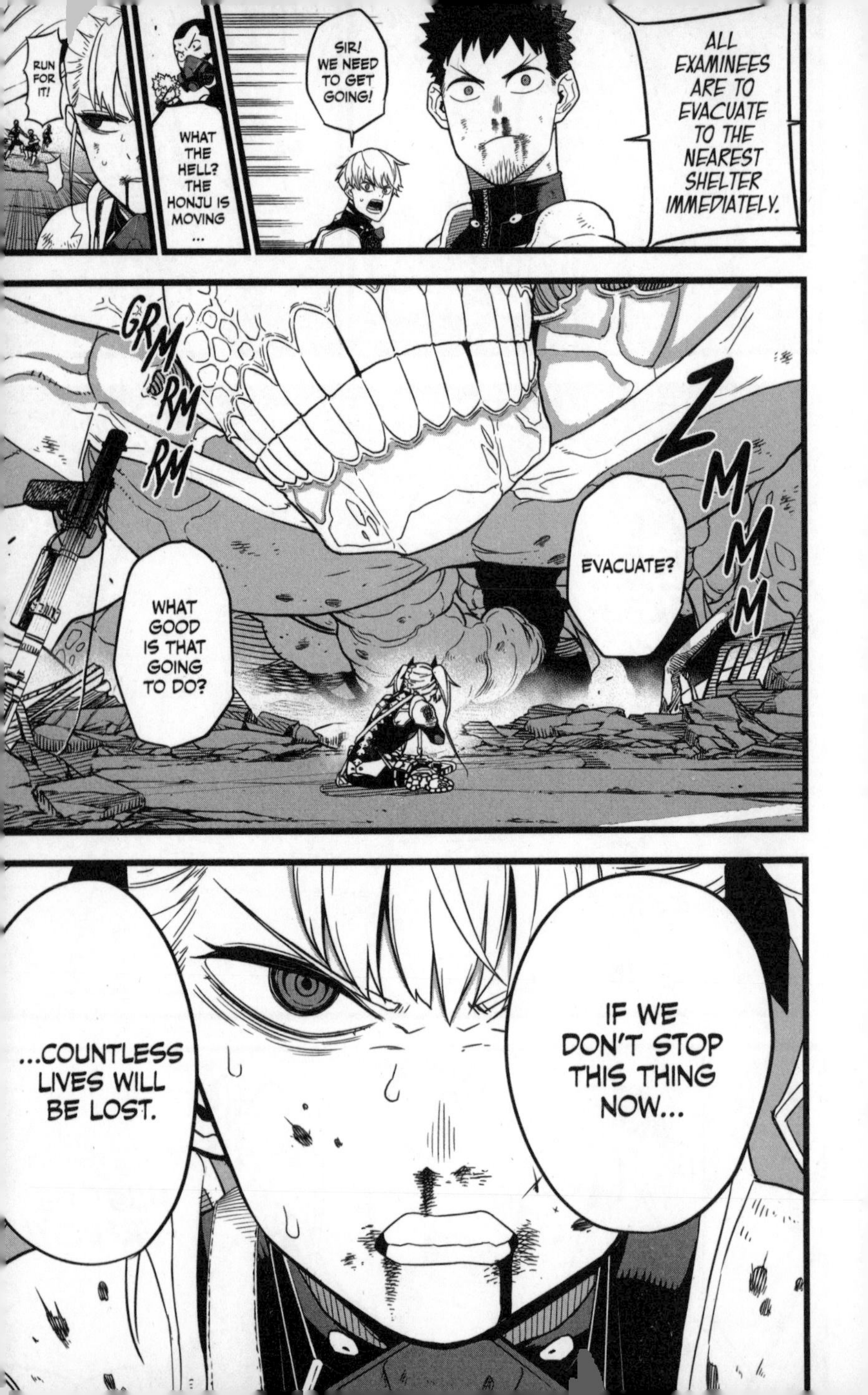
ALL EXAMINEES ARE TO EVACUATE TO THE NEAREST SHELTER IMMEDIATELY.
SIR! WE NEED TO GET GOING!
WHAT THE HELL? THE HONJU IS MOVING ...
RUN FOR IT!
ZMMMM
GRMRMRM
EVACUATE?
WHAT GOOD IS THAT GOING TO DO?
IF WE DON'T STOP THIS THING NOW...
...COUNTLESS LIVES WILL BE LOST.

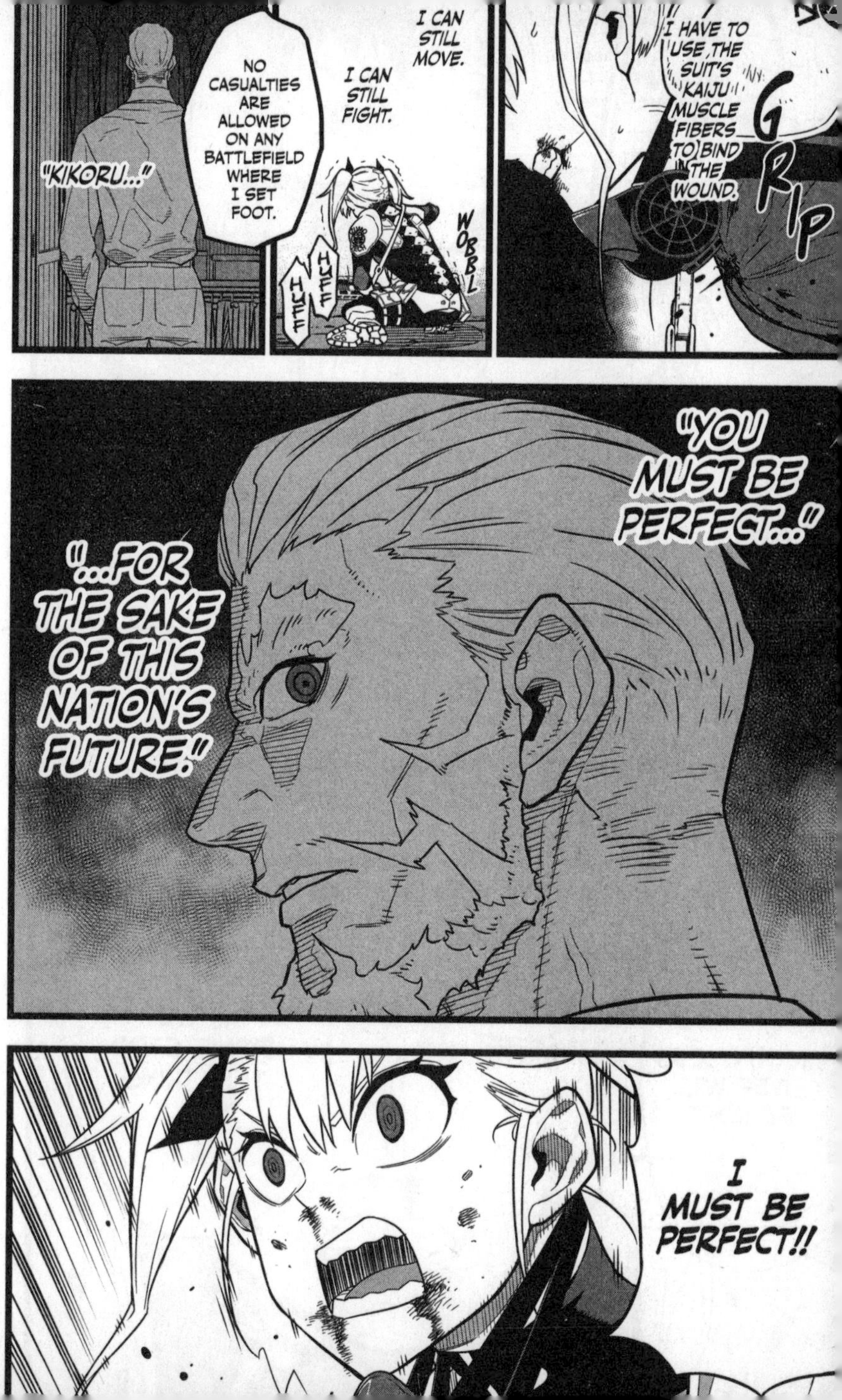
I HAVE TO USE THE SUIT'S KAIJU MUSCLE FIBERS TO BIND THE WOUND.
GRIP
I CAN STILL MOVE.
I CAN STILL FIGHT.
WOBBL
HUFF
HUFF
NO CASUALTIES ARE ALLOWED ON ANY BATTLEFIELD WHERE I SET FOOT.
"KIKORU..."
"YOU MUST BE PERFECT..."
"...FOR THE SAKE OF THIS NATION'S FUTURE."
I MUST BE PERFECT!!

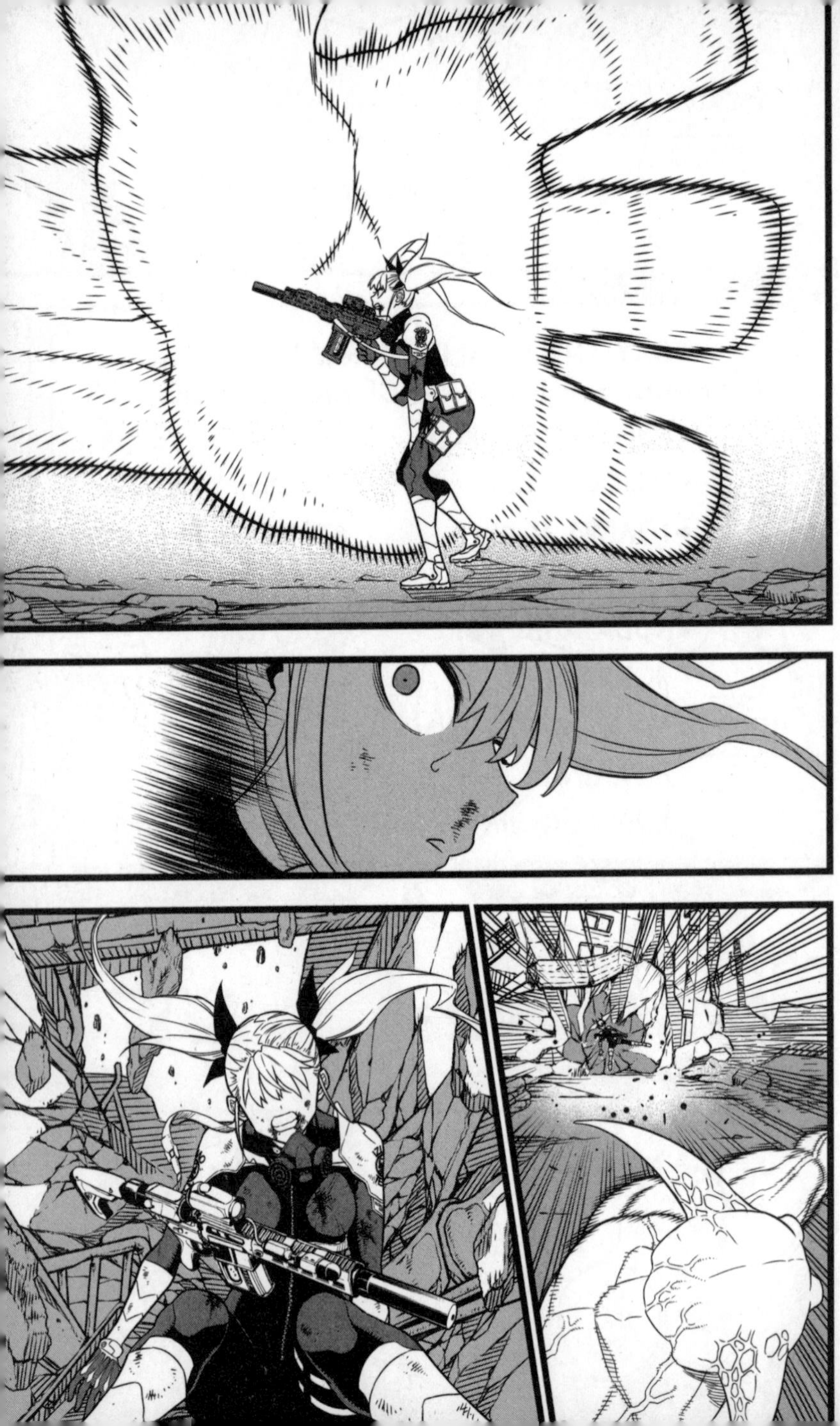

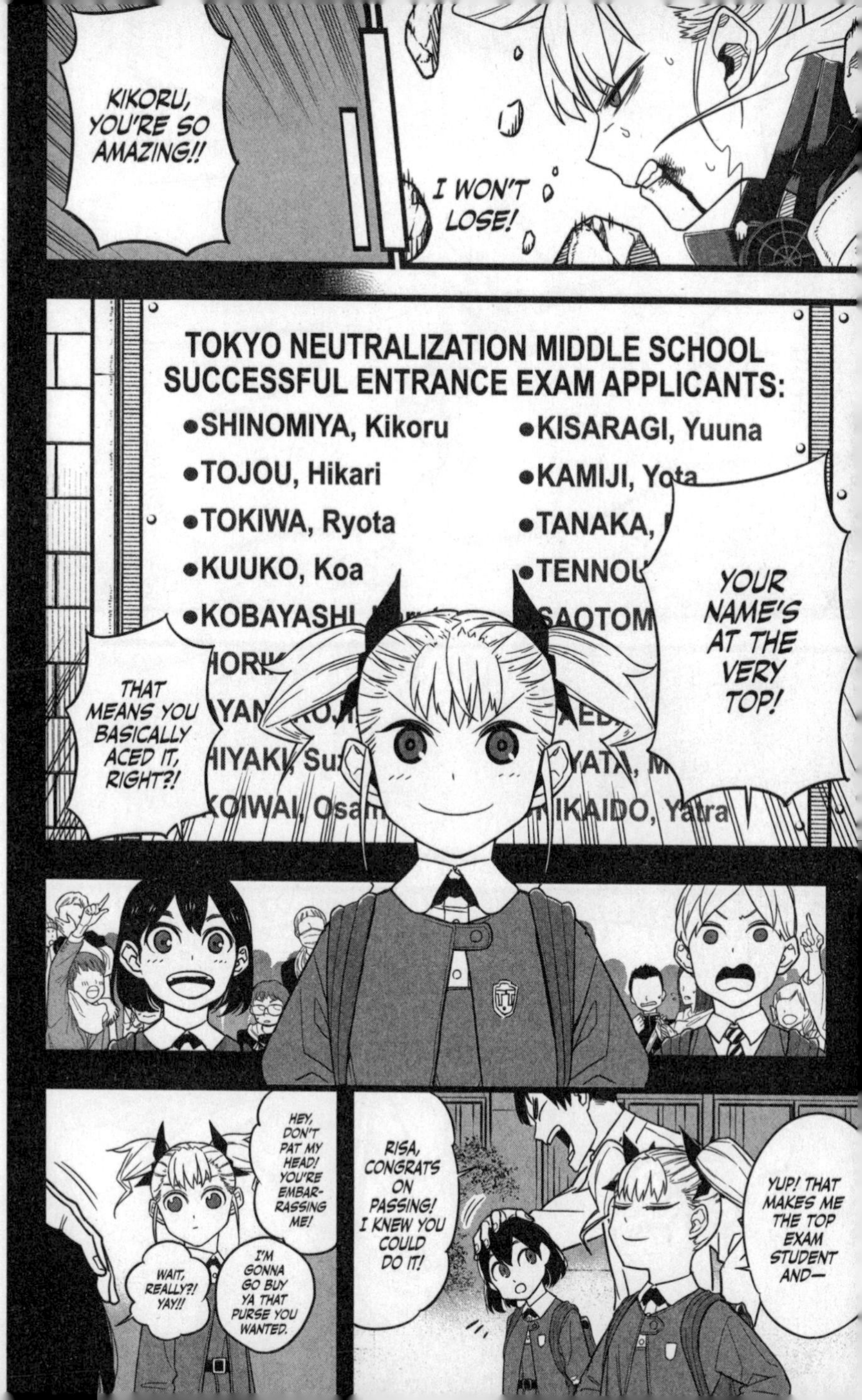

I WON'T LOSE!
KIKORU, YOU'RE SO AMAZING!!
TOKYO NEUTRALIZATION MIDDLE SCHOOL
SUCCESSFUL ENTRANCE EXAM APPLICANTS:
●SHINOMIYA, Kikoru
●TOJOU, Hikari
●TOKIWA, Ryota
●KUUKO, Koa
●KISARAGI, Yuuna
YOUR NAME'S AT THE VERY TOP!
THAT MEANS YOU BASICALLY ACED IT, RIGHT?!
YUP! THAT MAKES ME THE TOP EXAM STUDENT AND—
RISA, CONGRATS ON PASSING! I KNEW YOU COULD DO IT!
HEY, DON'T PAT MY HEAD! YOU'RE EMBAR-RASSING ME!
I'M GONNA GO BUY YA THAT PURSE YOU WANTED.
WAIT, REALLY?! YAY!!

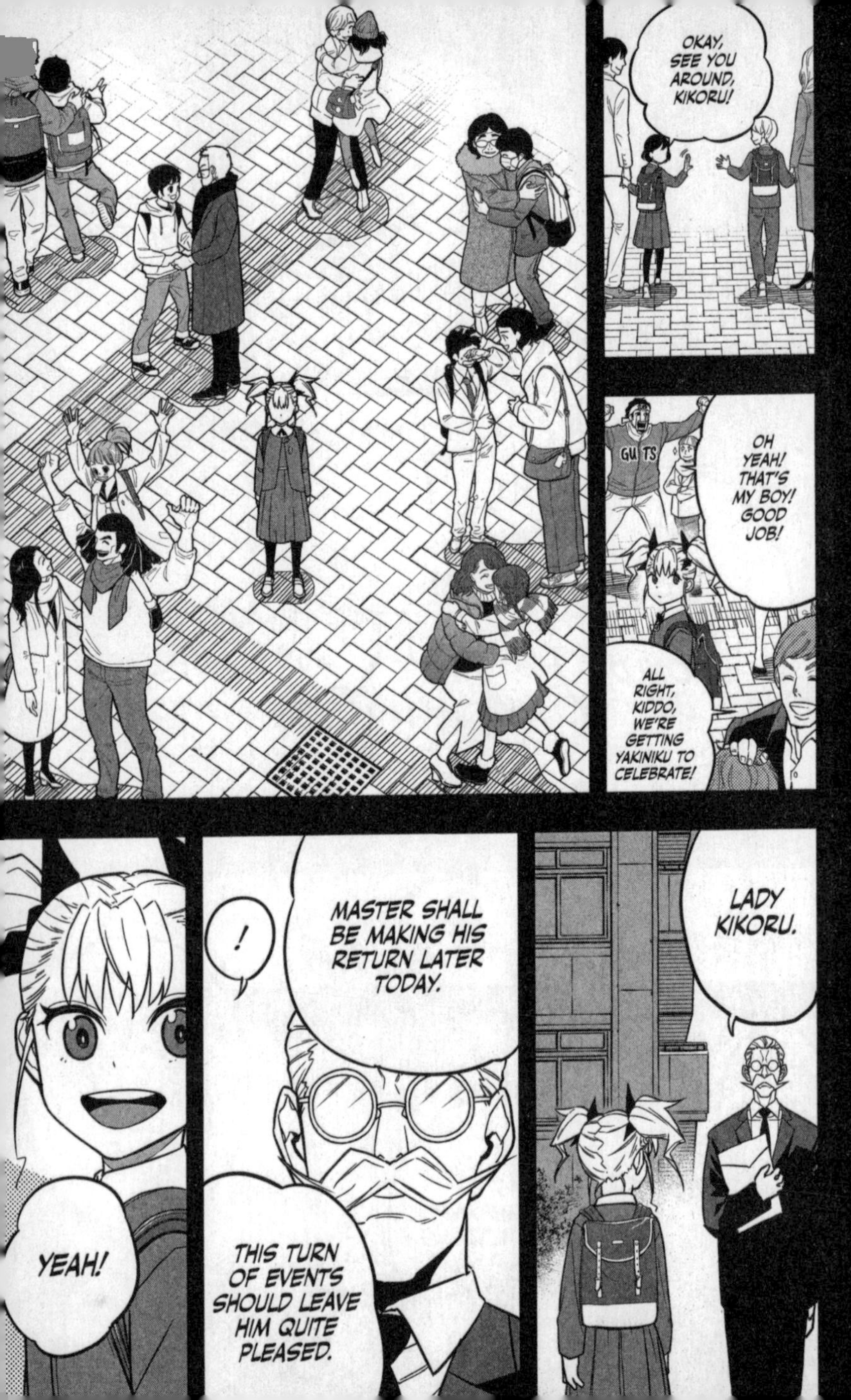
OKAY, SEE YOU AROUND, KIKORU!
OH YEAH! THAT'S MY BOY! GOOD JOB!
ALL RIGHT, KIDDO, WE'RE GETTING YAKINIKU TO CELEBRATE!
LADY KIKORU.
MASTER SHALL BE MAKING HIS RETURN LATER TODAY.
!
THIS TURN OF EVENTS SHOULD LEAVE HIM QUITE PLEASED.
YEAH!

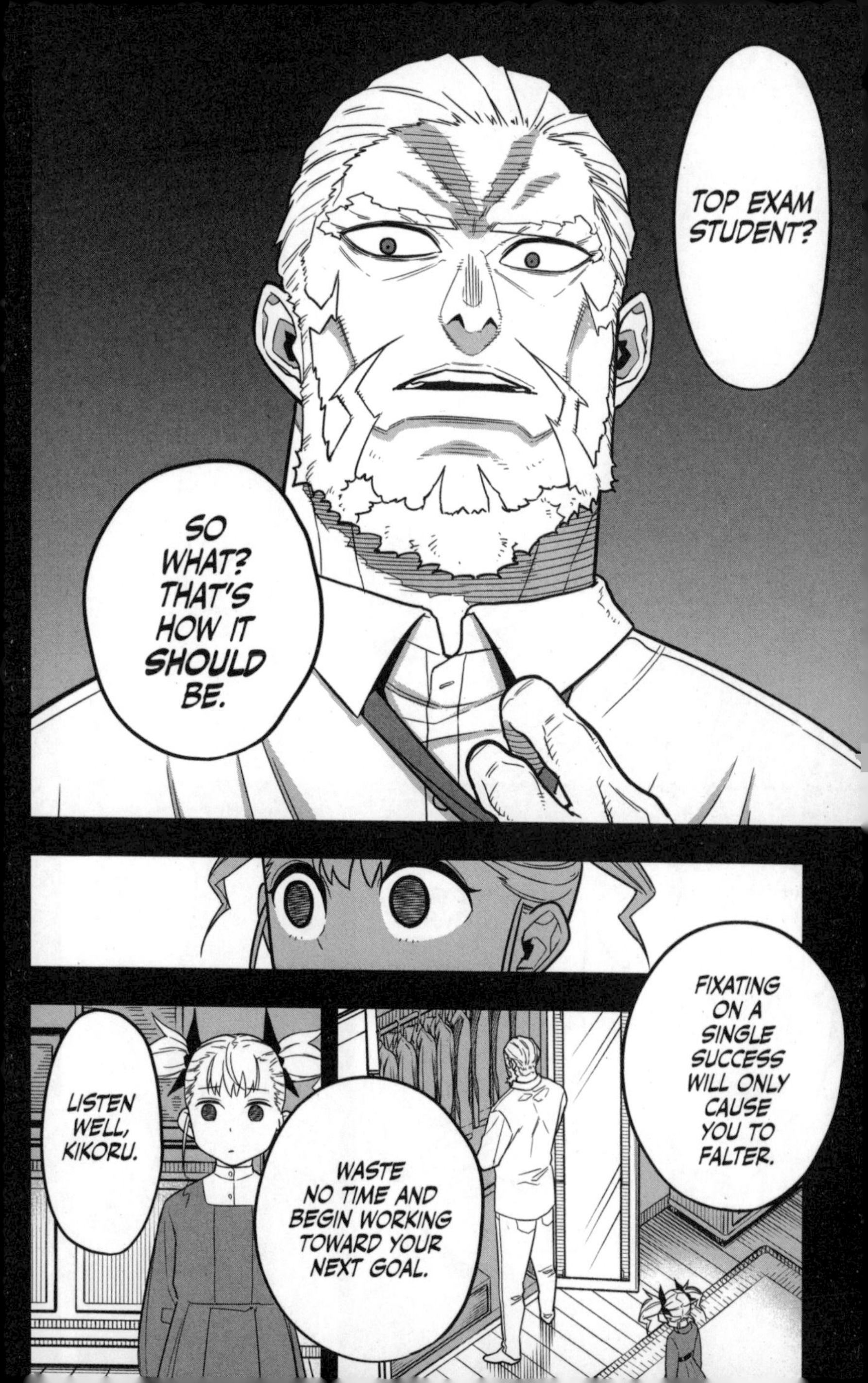
TOP EXAM STUDENT?
SO WHAT? THAT'S HOW IT SHOULD BE.
FIXATING ON A SINGLE SUCCESS WILL ONLY CAUSE YOU TO FALTER.
WASTE NO TIME AND BEGIN WORKING TOWARD YOUR NEXT GOAL.
LISTEN WELL, KIKORU.

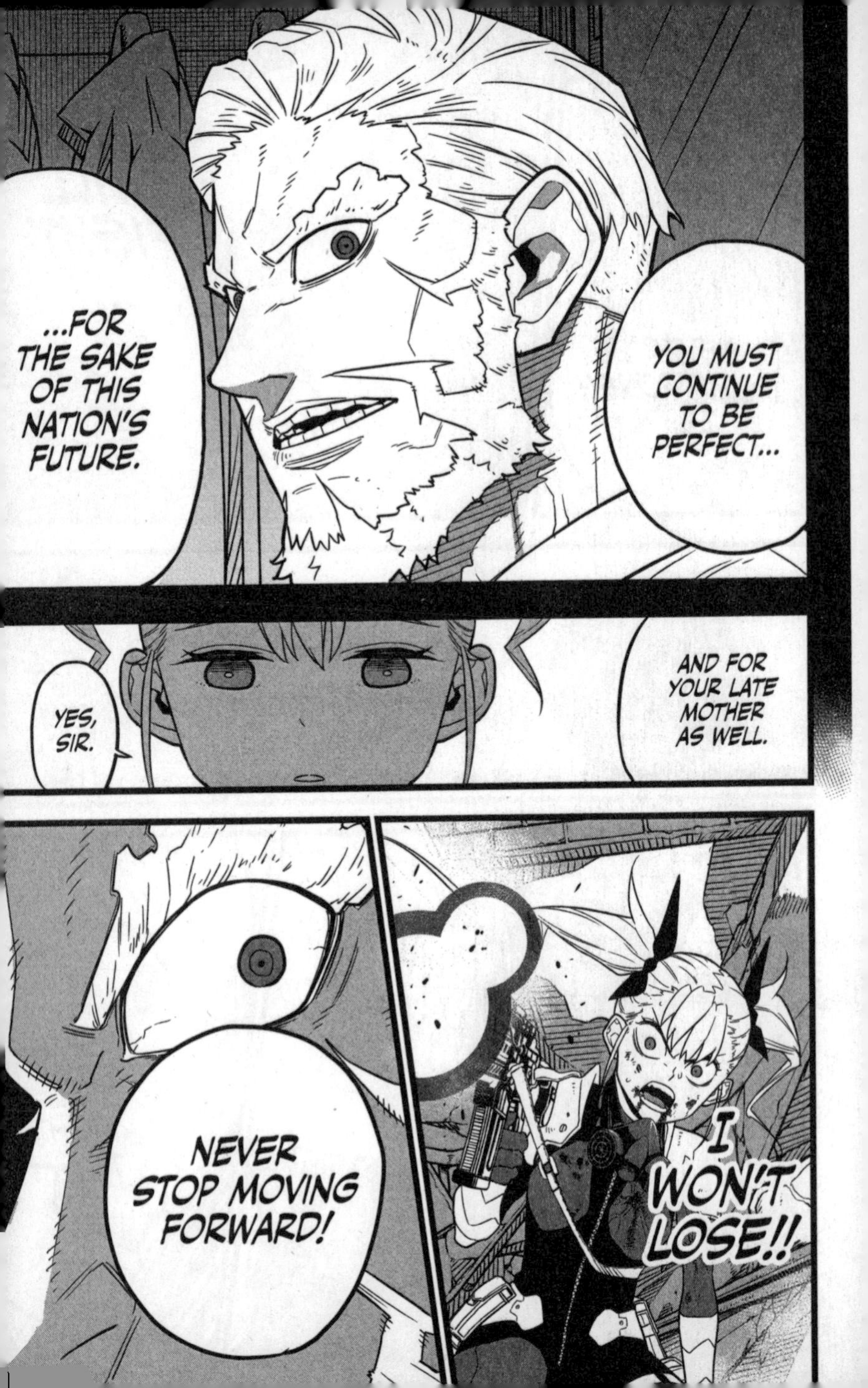
YOU MUST CONTINUE TO BE PERFECT...
...FOR THE SAKE OF THIS NATION'S FUTURE.
AND FOR YOUR LATE MOTHER AS WELL.
YES, SIR.
I WON'T LOSE!!
NEVER STOP MOVING FORWARD!

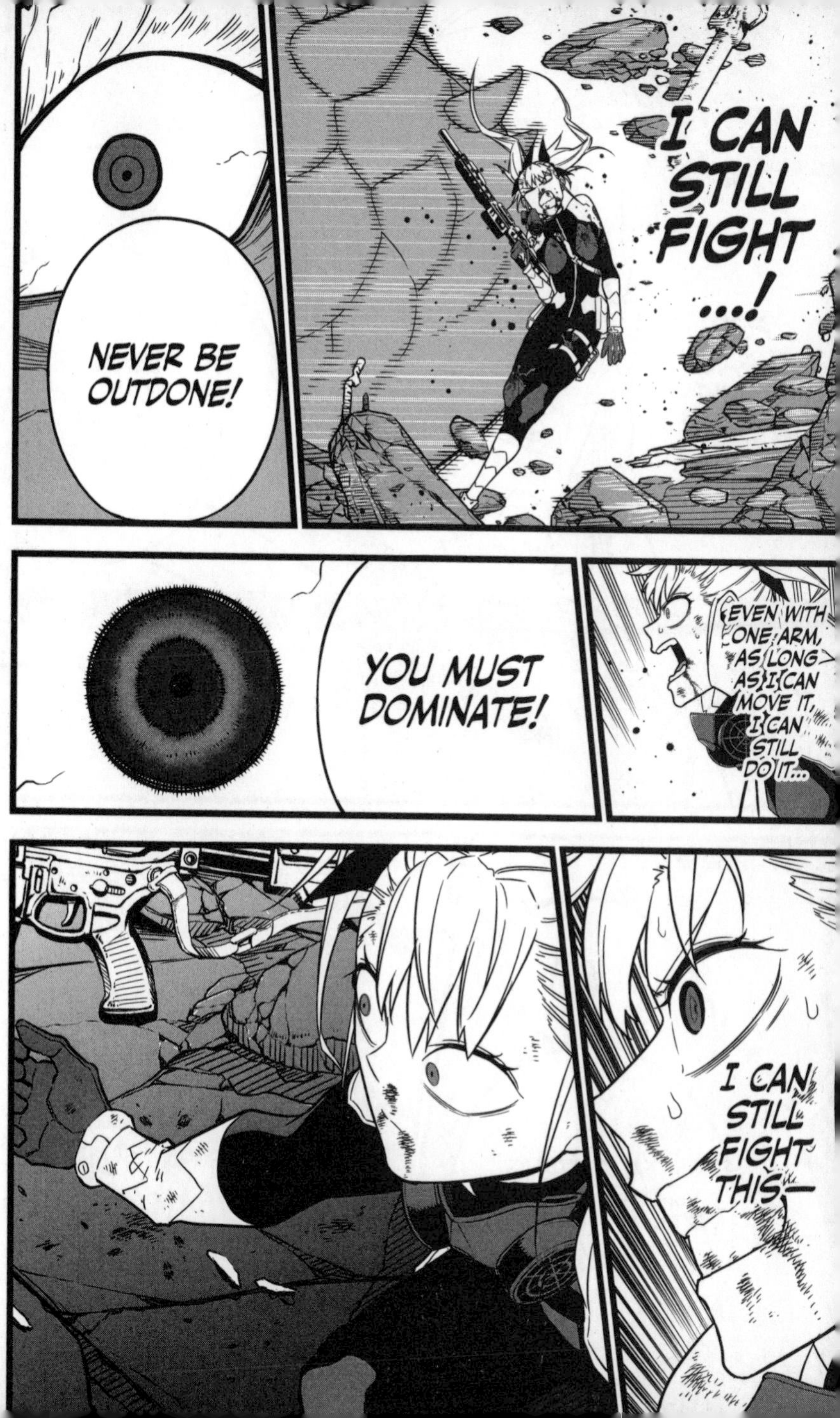
I CAN STILL FIGHT ...!
NEVER BE OUTDONE!
EVEN WITH ONE ARM, AS LONG AS I CAN MOVE IT, I CAN STILL DO IT...
YOU MUST DOMINATE!
I CAN STILL FIGHT THIS—

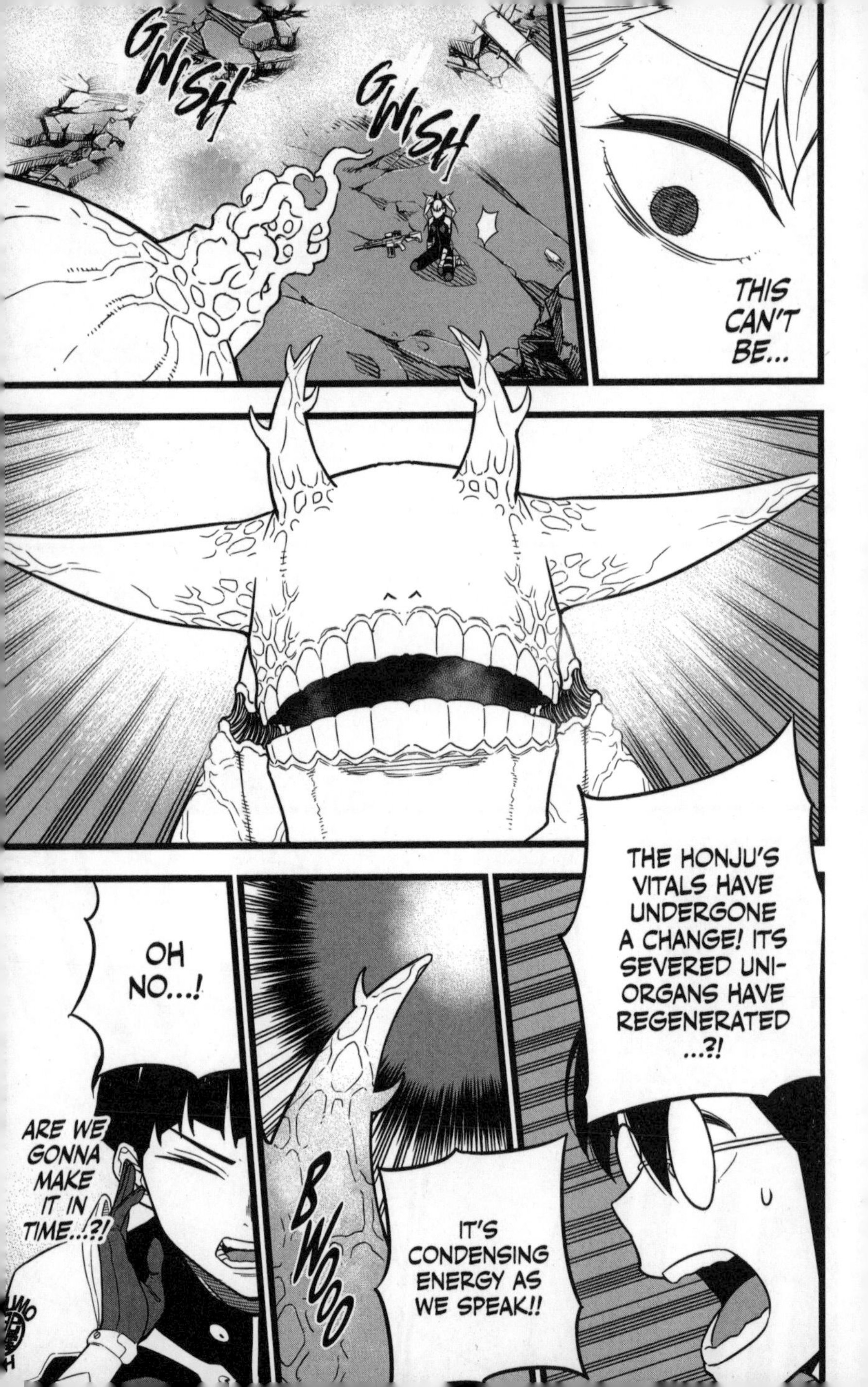
THIS CAN'T BE...
GWISH
GWISH
THE HONJU'S VITALS HAVE UNDERGONE A CHANGE! ITS SEVERED UNI-ORGANS HAVE REGENERATED ...?!
IT'S CONDENSING ENERGY AS WE SPEAK!!
BWOOO
OH NO...!
ARE WE GONNA MAKE IT IN TIME...?!

I'M SORRY, DADDY.

I WASN'T ABLE TO BE PERFECT AFTER ALL.

I'M SORRY...

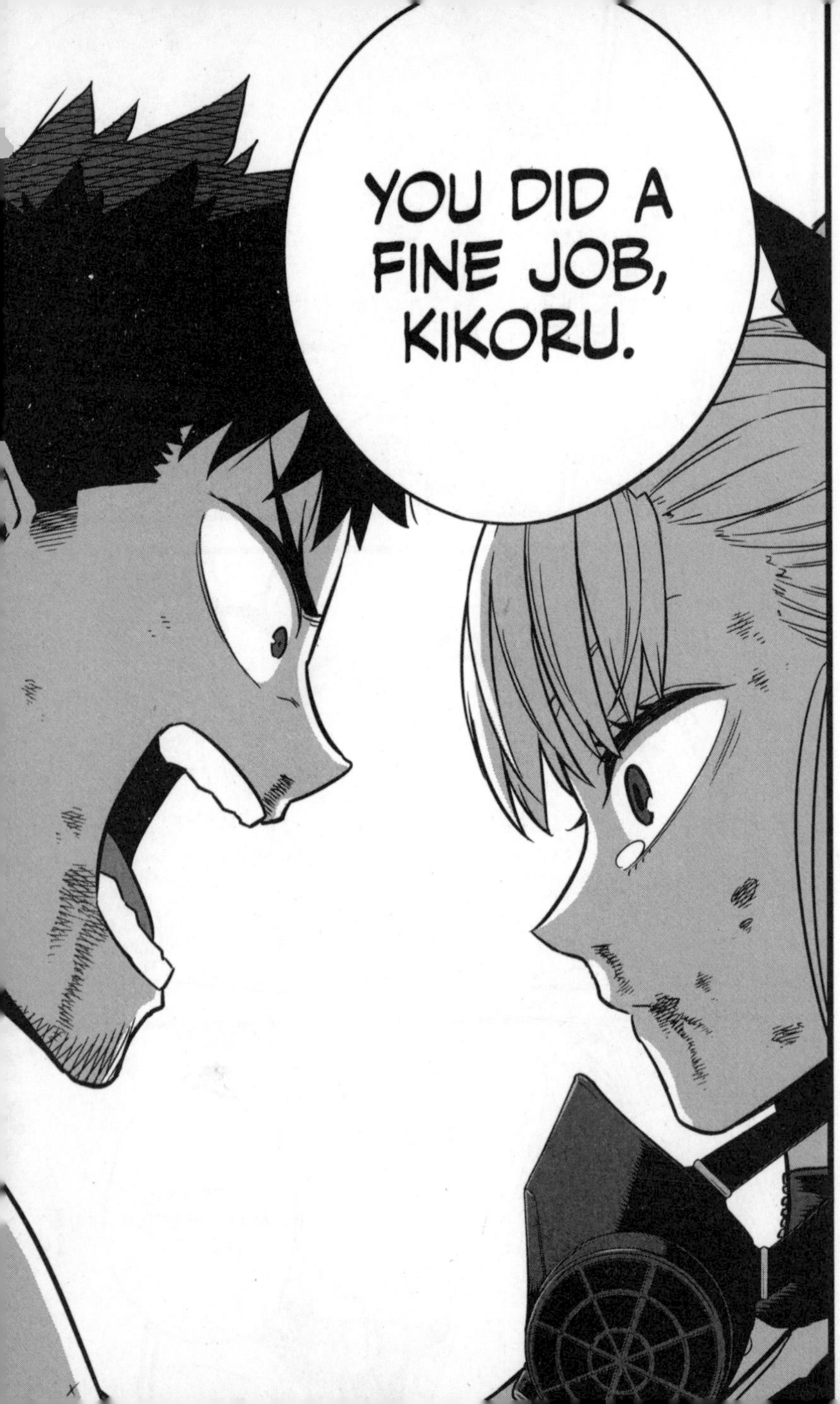
YOU DID A FINE JOB, KIKORU.

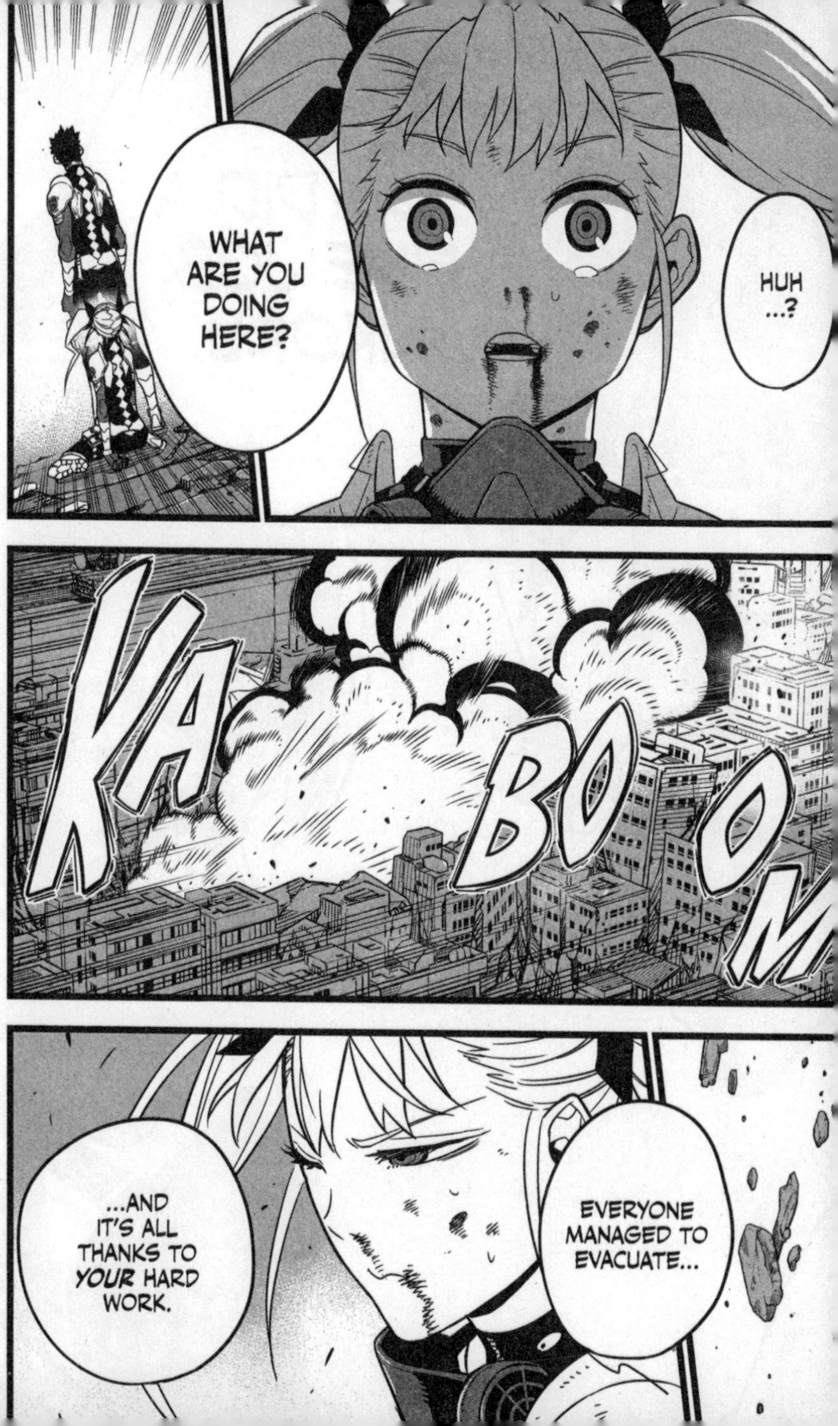
HUH ...?
WHAT ARE YOU DOING HERE?
KA-BOOM
EVERYONE MANAGED TO EVACUATE...
...AND IT'S ALL THANKS TO *YOUR* HARD WORK.

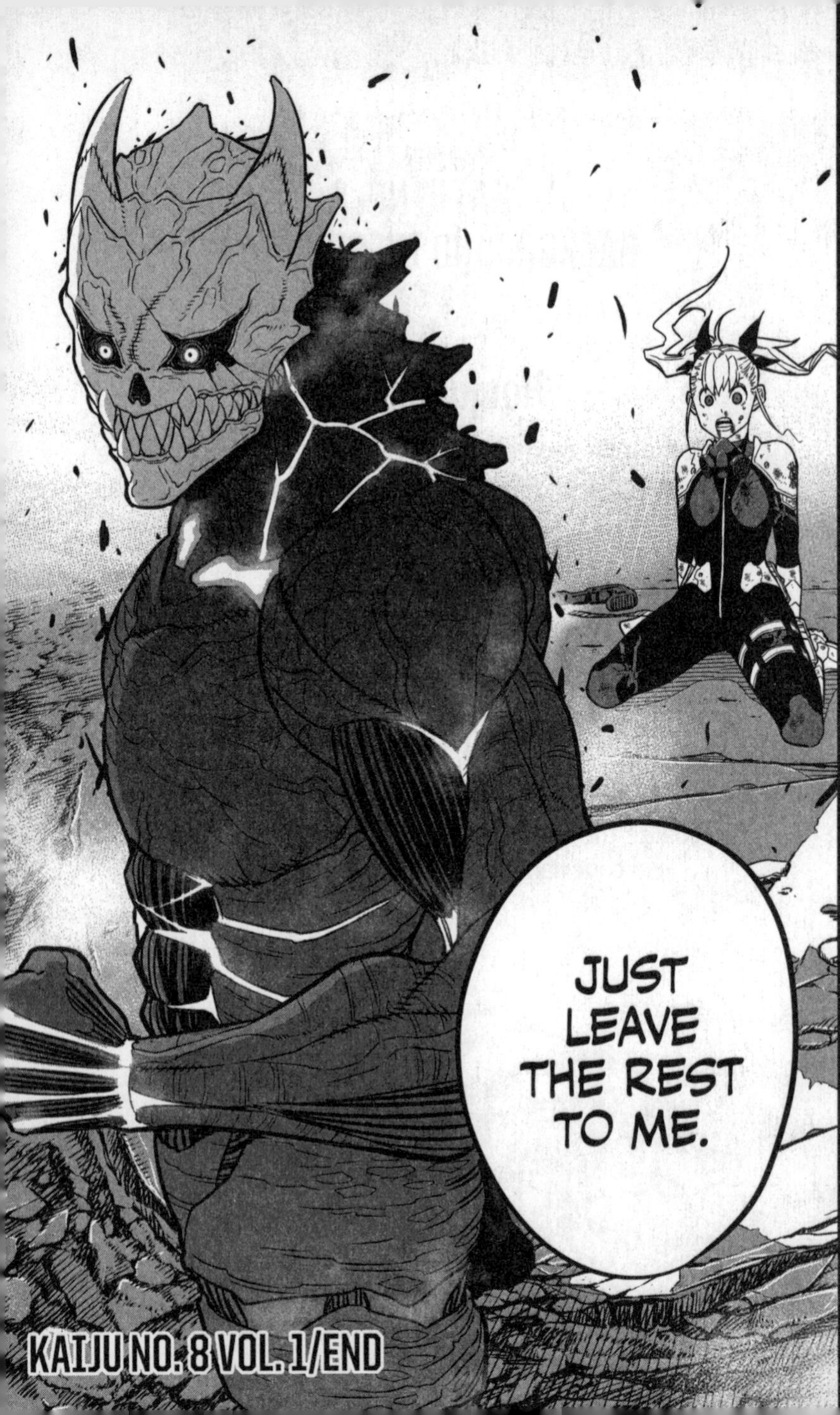
JUST LEAVE THE REST TO ME.
KAIJU NO. 8 VOL. 1/END

# KAIJU NO. 8
## BACKGROUND INFORMATION

## Honju and Yoju

While the more prominent and threatening kaiju that emerge are called *honju*, or "main beasts," the creatures that accompany them when they emerge are called *yoju*, or "residual beasts."

Yoju appear via many means—by traveling routes made by honju, leeching onto honju, being created by honju, and more. They come in a variety of types.

## Kaiju Numbering

When a kaiju proves to be extremely powerful or difficult to neutralize, the Neutralization Bureau assigns it a numbered code name for identification purposes.

# KAIJU NO. 8

## 1

STORY AND ART BY
NAOYA MATSUMOTO

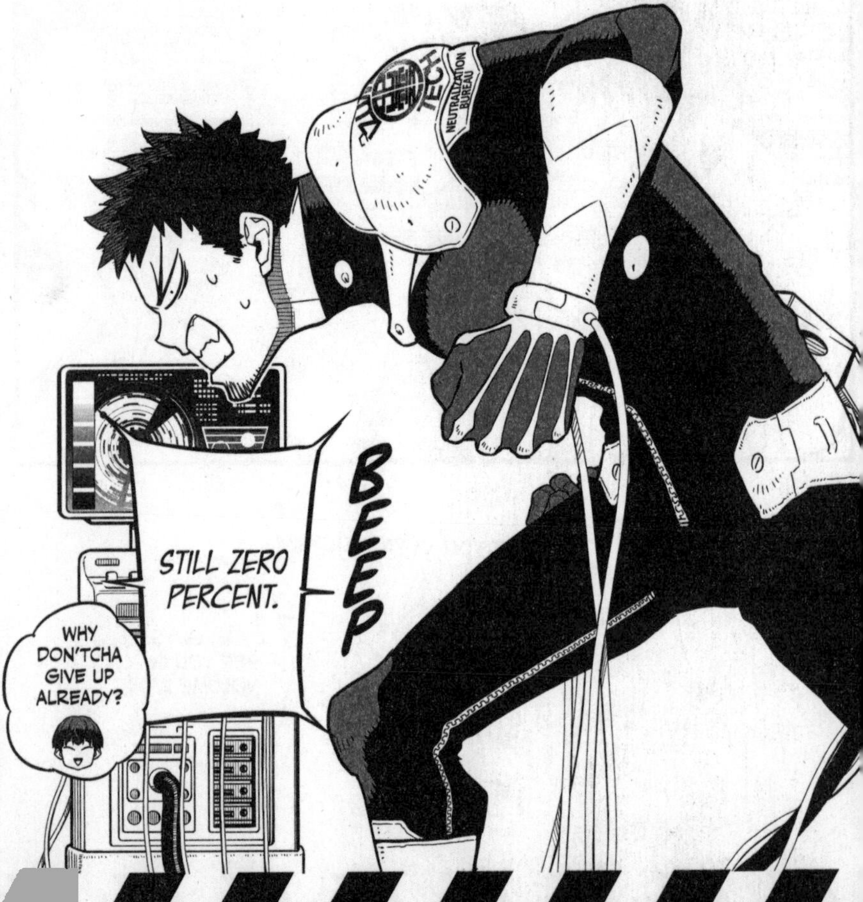
NEUTRALIZATION BUREAU
BEEP
STILL ZERO PERCENT.
WHY DON'TCHA GIVE UP ALREADY?

# THE OLD MAN VS. THE YOUNG TALENTS

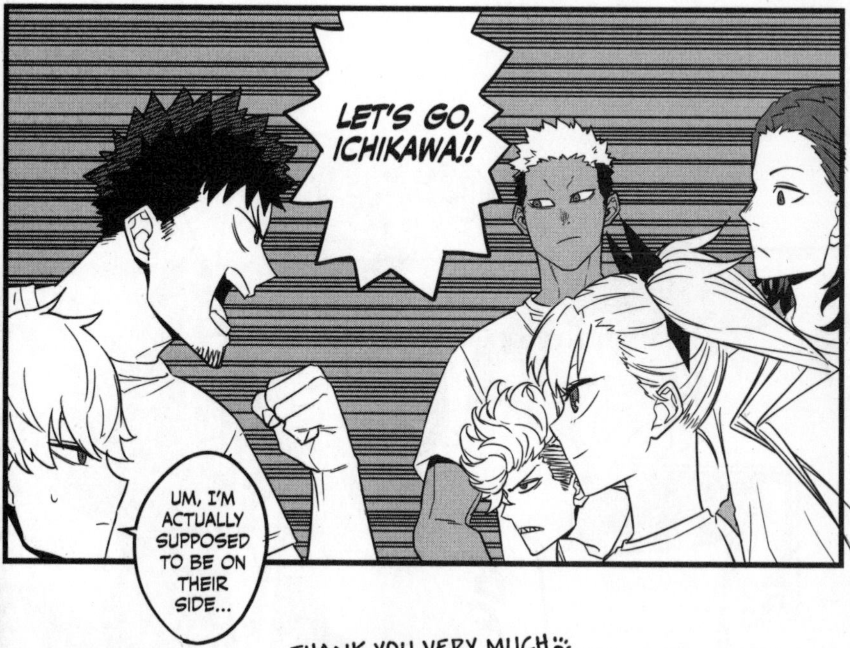
LET'S GO, ICHIKAWA!!
UM, I'M ACTUALLY SUPPOSED TO BE ON THEIR SIDE...

THANK YOU VERY MUCH

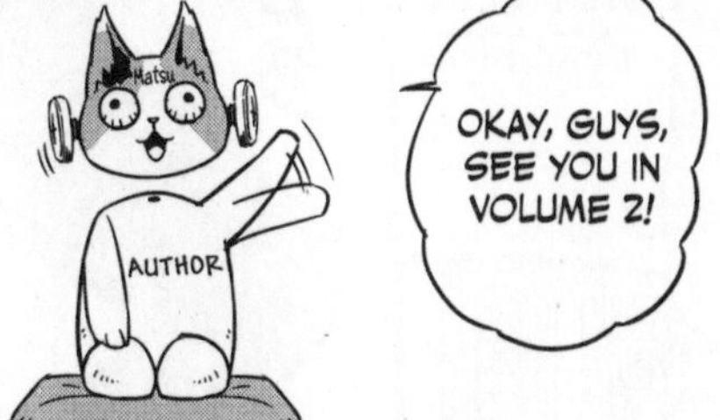
Matsu
AUTHOR
OKAY, GUYS, SEE YOU IN VOLUME 2!